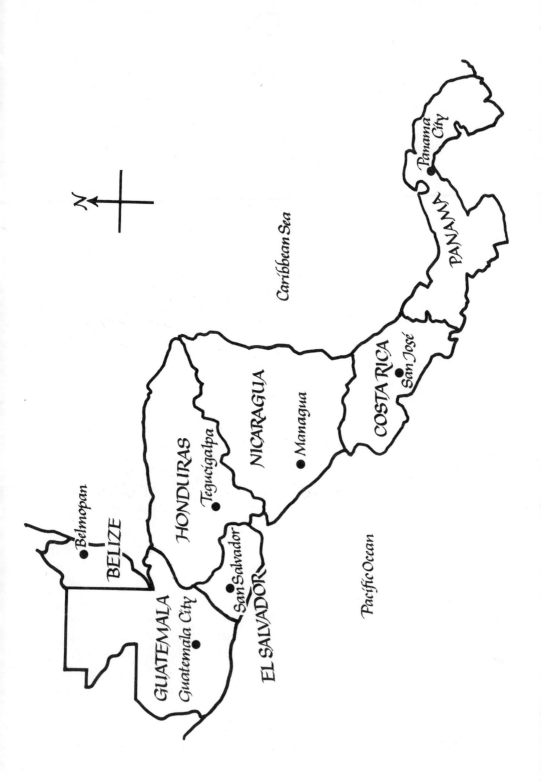

INSIDE CENTRAL AMERICA

Its People, Politics, and History

Clifford Krauss

SUMMIT BOOKS

NEW YORK · LONDON · TORONTO · SYDNEY · TOKYO · SINGAPORE

SUMMIT BOOKS
SIMON & SCHUSTER BUILDING
ROCKEFELLER CENTER
1230 AVENUE OF THE AMERICAS
NEW YORK, NEW YORK 10020

SUMMIT BOOKS AND COLOPHON ARE TRADEMARKS
OF SIMON & SCHUSTER INC.

DESIGNED BY EVE METZ
MANUFACTURED IN THE UNITED STATES OF AMERICA

1   3   5   7   9   10   8   6   4   2

LIBRARY OF CONGRESS CATALOGING IN PUBLICATION DATA
KRAUSS, CLIFFORD.
INSIDE CENTRAL AMERICA : ITS PEOPLE, POLITICS, AND HISTORY /
CLIFFORD KRAUSS
P.   CM.
INCLUDES BIBLIOGRAPHICAL REFERENCES AND INDEX.
1. CENTRAL AMERICA—POLITICS AND GOVERNMENT—1979–
2. GOVERNMENT, RESISTANCE TO—CENTRAL
AMERICA—HISTORY—20TH CENTURY.   3. CENTRAL
AMERICA—RELATIONS—UNITED STATES.   4. UNITED
STATES—RELATIONS—CENTRAL AMERICA.   I. TITLE.
F1439.5.K74   1991
972.805′3—DC20   90-25462
CIP
ISBN 0-671-66400-X

TO LINDA

ACKNOWLEDGMENTS

This book developed out of thirteen years of reporting and writing about Central America. During that time, I was fortunate to share ideas and companionship with many journalists, academics, and other researchers. I owe a special debt of gratitude to Paul Berman, Raymond Bonner, Dan Freedman, William Gentile, Robert Greenberger, Frederick Kempe, Charles Lane, James LeMoyne, Robert McCartney, Reed Miller, John Moody, Julia Preston, and Scott Wallace. I benefited from their advice, as well as that offered by Arthur Allen, Kenneth Anderson, Marc Edelman, Samuel Freedman, Lenny Glynn, Tim Golden, Al Kamen, John Lantigua, Tina Rosenberg, Philip Shepherd, and David Pitt, who were kind enough to read portions of my manuscript for style and content.

I was also graced with gifted and tolerant newspaper editors during the years I researched and wrote this book, including Eric Morgenthaler, and Karen Elliott House, and Lee Lescaze of the *Wall Street Journal* and Joseph Lelyveld, Howell Raines, Philip Taubman, and Bernard Weinraub of the *New York Times.*

I would have never gotten started had it not been for the Council on Foreign Relations, which granted me the Edward R. Murrow fellowship and, with the award, the time to think and write. Three people helped me make the most of that time. James Silberman, the editor-in-chief at Summit Books, first conceptualized the book. Summit's Dominick Anfuso was the kind of editor every writer wishes for; his blue pencil was sharp and sure. Gloria Loomis, my agent and friend, provided constant good advice and encouragement.

Thanks also to the archivists and researchers at the National Security Archives, Columbia University, The National Archives, The Library of Congress, the North American Congress on Latin America, and numerous libraries in Central America. Special cheers to Bernice Krauss, who proved to be a valuable library researcher. And to Judy Berke and Richard Meislin, who helped when my computer ignorance got the best of me.

And finally, Linda Ricci, to whom I owe my greatest thanks. As my constant companion, she never lost confidence in the book, even as she edited every draft. Her affection, encouragement, and good judgment were unflagging. Meeting her in El Salvador was one of the great gifts Central America gave to me.

CONTENTS

INTRODUCTION

On June 25, 1984, President Ronald Reagan assembled his top foreign policy advisers in the White House Situation Room for an emergency meeting. As the president scanned a black leather briefing folder, he said he wanted to review all aspects of his Central America policy. There was a sense of expectancy in the windowless, wood-paneled chamber because a senior administration official was meeting with a Nicaraguan delegation in Mexico City that very day to present a draft of a secret State Department peace plan.

Before the White House session got under way, the normally unflappable Secretary of State fidgeted, played with his tie, and gazed at the low ceiling and clacking wire machines. George Shultz knew this was going to be an ambush. Conservative White House aide Constantine Menges had advised National Security Adviser Robert C. McFarlane to convene a meeting of the National Security Council (NSC) after discovering that Shultz was working on a diplomatic solution to the administration's undeclared proxy war on Nicaragua without first consulting the Defense Department, the Central Intelligence Agency, or even the White House. Shultz had hoped to win the support of his colleagues once he had made progress at the bargaining table, but now his secret was out.

Shultz pleaded with Reagan and his fellow foreign policy advisers that a credible negotiation policy designed to demobilize much of the Sandinista army and expand political pluralism in Nicaragua could win congressional backing for the administration's ever-controversial Central America policy. "If Nicaragua is halfway reasonable, there could be a regional negotiated solution," he argued. But Shultz, who had angered many in the administration by flying to Managua for a brief visit only three weeks before, was totally outgunned.

As Central Intelligence Agency director William Casey and U.N. Ambassador Jeane Kirkpatrick nodded in agreement, Secretary of Defense Caspar Weinberger belittled Shultz's suggestion to hold negotiations in Washington and Managua as an effort "to dignify Nicaragua." McFarlane claimed that the Sandinistas were only interested in talks "as tactical exercises." Reagan agreed, according to Menges's notes from the meeting, saying it was "far-fetched to imagine that a Communist government like that would make any reasonable deal with us." Shultz was forced to dispatch an aide to telephone Mexico City and relay a coded message to special envoy Harry Schlaudeman to forget the peace plan. Negotiations with Managua were scotched before they got off the ground, and 15,000 more Nicaraguans died in a war that might well have been prevented by diplomacy.

What passed for Ronald Reagan's diplomacy in Central America was dominated by cold war anticommunism and grounded in the heavy-handed way Washington has dealt with Central America since President James Buchanan covertly aided a force of mercenaries to conquer Nicaragua in the 1850s. Obsessive, ideological fears clouded Reagan's vision, as was all too often reflected in his apocalyptic public speeches in support of his beloved "freedom fighters." A few weeks before the fateful June 1984 National Security Council meeting, Reagan told the American people: "If we do nothing or if we continue to provide too little help, our choice will be a Communist Central America with additional Communist military bases on the mainland of this hemisphere and Communist subversion spreading southward and northward. This Communist subversion poses the threat that 100 million people from Panama to the open border on our south could come under the control of pro-Soviet regimes."

Less prominent but no less guilty for simplifying and distorting the truth about Central America in the 1980s was the American left, whose analysis dominated college courses and much of the magazine and book literature on the subject. While on the right there was a remarkable capacity to miss opportunities for peace in Nicaragua, support reputed mass murderers and torturers such as Roberto D'Aubuisson in El Salvador and Gen. Efraín Ríos Montt in Guatemala, and even undermine true democrats like Oscar Arias in Costa Rica, there was an equal capacity on the left to romanticize such murderous guerrilla leaders as El Salvador's Joaquín Villalobos, and blame every problem in Central America on "American imperialism." In this peculiar moral universe, the left and right suffered a reflective political myopia.

Liberally inclined Americans found a passion and the resources to monitor every human rights abuse by the Contras in Nicaragua, even posting volunteers in many Nicaraguan villages. But they never saw fit to do the same in the Salvadoran countryside where the Marxist guerrillas they supported mined civilian agricultural fields, assassinated popularly elected officials, and forcibly recruited villagers, executing those who deserted. Profiles lionizing El Salvador's top guerrilla leader, Joaquín Villalobos, on public television and in liberal magazines never saw fit to acknowledge that it was Villalobos who was responsible for the death of El Salvador's leading poet, Roque Dalton, and reportedly authorized a campaign of car bombings that killed or injured dozens of people in front of a Pizza Hut, a teenage hamburger hangout, a shopping mall, and the parking lot of a movie theater.

"The [American] left looks at us as noble savages while the right looks at us as savage savages," complained Nicaraguan essayist Arturo Cruz, Jr., who defected from the Sandinista government to become a Contra. "The left thinks we are poor, violent, and corrupt because of the United States, as if we are incapable of making ourselves poor, violent, and corrupt. Meanwhile, the right thinks we have no capacity for redemption."

Having covered the region since 1977, I came to a different view from those who have dominated the United States discourse over Central America. This is a book that contains few heroes, liberators, or freedom fighters. Rather, this is a description of six distinct countries and their relationships with the United States, relationships that have almost always been mutually uneasy, exploitative, suspicious, reactive, violent, and driven by false assumptions. Even though the United States is responsible for a series of disastrous policies in Central America during the last hundred years, the United States is not responsible for everything bad that happens in Central America. Central America's chronic problems—poverty, social polarization, militarism, racism, and dependency on foreign powers—defy easy explanation or resolution. Their roots go back centuries, to the bloody Spanish conquest, the corrupt and autocratic colonial period, and a nineteenth-century agricultural revolution that tore the social fabric across the isthmus.

My interest in Central America began in a most unlikely setting: a gothic study in the Vassar College library, in the dead of a damp and chilly Hudson Valley winter in 1974. Bundled up in a wool sweater, I read Neill MacCaulay's biography of the Nicaraguan rebel Augusto César Sandino, an assignment for a modern Latin American history course I took as an afterthought during my junior year. I had never heard of Sandino. I was not even aware of the fact that U.S. Marines had occupied Nicaragua in the 1920s and 1930s. The discovery of lost history is what first engaged me. MacCaulay's *The Sandino Affair* would change my life in the most unexpected ways.

I immediately admired Sandino for his guts, his nationalism and anarchism, and his passion for the peasants and miners. To me, Sandino represented the values of dignity and social justice. My attraction to him was the kind of response that the Vietnam era produced in such abundance among my generation—a feeling that not only Vietnam but the entire history of American foreign policy was tainted. I wrote my senior thesis the next year on the Taft administration's military occupation of Nicaragua in 1909, thinking I had found a most relevant topic of study.

My intellectual dissidence then led me to graduate school, where I studied Latin American history, and finally to journalism school, where I dreamed of becoming a foreign correspondent. I was lucky that just as I graduated from Columbia Journalism School, the modern-day Sandinistas (who named their movement after Sandino) were organizing an insurrection. Central America was a backwater that more experienced reporters often snubbed, and UPI hired me in August 1977 to report on the region. Within three months I was on a flight from Mexico City to Managua to cover the first major Sandinista offensive leading to the overthrow of the Anastasio Somoza regime. I went to Nicaragua for the first time with Sandino on my mind. Not as yet an objective reporter, my intention was to cheer on the new Sandinistas and to help stop the next Vietnam—and if I couldn't do that, then to see the war, and feel it.

The next thirteen years encompassed the most violent period in the region's history since the Spanish conquest in the sixteenth century. I lived through this compelling era, seeing friends, colleagues, and sources die; hiking for weeks at a time with guerrillas and soldiers; even suffering a minor bullet wound myself in El Salvador. Through the personal and professional rigors, I moved from the worn ideas of the left to a deeper and more critical understanding of the region's political and cultural complexities. It was the people of Central America, and how they responded to the last decade's events—what the Marxists would view as the froth on the waves of history—that changed my perceptions of politics and the human condition. All too often I found that the leaders of the Central American radical left were out of touch with the workers and peasants they claimed to represent. Poor people wanted the schools and health clinics the left offered, but they frequently bristled when revolutionaries told them their traditional religious beliefs or desires to own their own plot of land were backward vestiges of capitalism and imperialism. But while I concluded that the Central American revolutionaries were flawed by their hard-line political philosophy and affinity to Cuba and the Soviet Union, I never stopped listening to their complaints and aspirations. Their cries against the way the United States treated their countries remain uncomfortably true.

In 1985, I spent an evening on the back patio of a Managua ranch house with Sofía Montenegro, an editorial writer for the Sandinista party newspaper *Barricada*. Sofía is in many ways a typical young middle-class Nicaraguan woman. She has a taste for New York fashions and socializing with Americans, but she also has a taste for radical politics. She spoke incessantly about the need to establish "a new relationship with the United States."

Sipping rum in our rocking chairs under palm trees that swayed in a damp breeze, we talked about President Reagan's efforts to push Congress into backing his Contra war. "We know everything about you and you know nothing about us. We play your baseball, we know your movie stars, your fashions. Our history is full of your people: Vanderbilt, Taft, Coolidge, now Reagan—they fill the pages of our history books. Yet our Sandino defeated your marines and you have the nerve not to include him in your history books. How can you kill us when you don't know who we are?"

Sofía was right. Despite the fact that the United States invaded Panama and played a vital role in civil wars in Nicaragua and El Salvador that took the lives of more than 90,000 Central Americans between 1977 and 1990, few Americans know who the Central Americans are. Numerous public opinion polls taken throughout the 1980s showed that the majority of the American people never grasped whether Washington backs the government or the rebels in El Salvador and Nicaragua. Fewer still know what the warfare in Guatemala is all about. It is especially difficult to explain this ignorance given that more than 2 million Guatemalans, Salvadorans, and Nicaraguans have streamed into our country during the last decade. It is time to begin to pay better attention, and reevaluate the United States' unfortunate role in this forlorn region with more objectivity, and more feeling.

1
Guatemala's
Heart of Darkness

The night mountain air was misty and cold as my colleague Dan
Freedman and I drove down the twisting two-lane road southeast of
Lake Atitlán in the middle of the Guatemalan highlands. By chance,
we found ourselves idling behind a Guatemalan police paddy wagon
carrying a cargo of human bodies.

Every fifty yards or so, the vehicle stopped just long enough for three
or four policemen to jump out and pick up drunken Indians lying
half-unconscious in ditches on either side of the road. It took two
policemen, one to grab the legs and the other the arms, to heave each
man like rubbery meat onto the pile in the back of the paddy wagon.
Feeling conspicuous behind our headlights, we tried to pass the vehicle
for at least twenty minutes. But the mountain road was fogged in, and
there was heavy oncoming traffic from Guatemala City destined for
the lakeside tourist town of Panajachel that Friday night.

Fortunately for us, the police didn't seem to mind our presence. They went about their business, as if they were garbage collectors doing an ordinary night's work. They drove off as soon as they filled the wagon with drunken bodies, leaving dozens more behind in the rain.

This was our first night in Guatemala, and Dan and I were stunned by this scene of cruelty and hopelessness. This crude police work was designed to spruce up the roads and promote tourism around Lake Atitlán, a priority for the military regime then led by Gen. Romeo Lucas García. But while tens of thousands of American and European tourists come annually to the Indian villages hugging the banks of Lake Atitlán to marvel at Guatemala's rich Mayan heritage, the inheritors of that heritage are treated by their fellow Guatemalans like some subhuman species.

There is a heart of darkness pounding in Guatemala. During the last thirty-five years, as many as 200,000 people have been killed here in Latin America's longest-running civil war, and most of them have been Mayan Indians. The Indians supply the foot soldiers for four small guerrilla armies fighting Central America's toughest army and most reactionary landed oligarchy, the Caucasian 2 percent of the population that owns 70 percent of the land. Human rights organizations monitoring Guatemala say that the country's many active volcanoes, which smoke and spew bright orange lava, are depositories for tortured bodies, many dropped alive into the craters by army troops and death squads in the pay of the wealthy. The otherwise exquisite rural valleys, sharply carved out of mountains terraced with cornfields, are spoiled by the sight of scores of Indian villages left abandoned following offensive sweeps by the army.

While foreign intervention and nationalism fueled the revolution in Nicaragua, and ideology, class tensions, and poverty did the same in El Salvador, a different variation of violence torments Guatemala: race war between the Mayan Indians and the Ladinos (the Guatemalan term for all non-Indians, including whites and mixed bloods [mestizos]). There have been more than thirty Indian rebellions against the ladino elite in the last three hundred years. The struggle for liberation and decency fired up with great intensity between 1978 and 1984. During those years, the Guatemalan army massacred 50,000 or more Indians while it forced 40,000 into militarized "model villages" and drafted more than 1 million into conscript civil patrons. A census taken in 1984 found that 120,000 Indian children were left orphans from the war. At the turn of this century, 80 percent of the 1.5 million inhabitants of Guatemala were pure Mayan; today, the figure is about 45 percent of the 8.6 million population. The genocide is gradual, but steady.*

Indian life in Guatemala is miserable. Illiteracy among the Indians reaches 80 percent; Indian infant mortality exceeds 100 per 1,000 live births; hunger and mental retardation are endemic. The soil in the overpopulated Indian highlands is usually poor because of deforestation, erosion, and exhaustion. Arable land is so scarce that many Indians must climb mountains to plant corn; farmers can be seen plowing mountainsides that are so steep they have to rope their bodies to trees to keep from falling. On the western and southern lowlands, Indian laborers as young as seven years old tend to the cotton fields of the oligarchs, spreading with their bare hands highly toxic pesticides banned in the United States.

The injustice can be seen everywhere. On Guatemala City's noisy and smoggy downtown Sexta Avenida, flashing neon lights advertise Wrangler jeans, Rolex watches, and Aca Joe beachware—transplanted First World consumerism. Whites drive Mercedes-Benzes; Indians push wooden carts. The customers and clerks in the stores are invariably either white or coffee-brown Ladinos attired in Western dress. Along the curb, under-class Ladinos and Indians compete for space to hawk their wares, but there is no question whose merchandise is more upscale. The Ladinos sell designer sunglasses, Stevie Wonder posters, blank cassette tapes, and hot watches. Some Indians sell underripe mangoes, peanuts, and lollipops; others beg.

There is little or no free expression for those who call for reform, whatever their race; such liberty only exists for those of wealth who protest whatever modest action the new civilian government takes to tax the privileged or otherwise modify the social structure. The University of San Carlos, the nation's seat of higher learning, is itself a killing field—from August 1989 through February 1990, eleven students and professors were assassinated or "disappeared." Newspaper offices that publish unacceptable articles are bombed. Guatemalan human rights activists, union leaders, and social democrats have the shortest life expectancies in Latin America.

From time to time, the United States government has rebuked

---

*There are twenty-three distinct Indian groups that speak roughly one hundred dialects in Guatemala. Scatterings of small Indian populations exist throughout Central America and Panama. The Miskitos of Nicaragua, the Nonualcos of El Salvador, and the Cunos of Panama are particularly noteworthy. Altogether, there are fewer than 250,000 Indians living in El Salvador, Honduras, Costa Rica, Nicaragua, and Panama.

Guatemala for its horrible human rights record, as in March 1990 when President George Bush recalled Ambassador Thomas A. Stroock to Washington for a week of consultations. The Bush administration's military aid program for Guatemala is microscopic—$3 million in fiscal 1990—by Central American standards. However, Washington's criticism has been mild and unsustained, in part for historical reasons. The United States has been partially complicit in the slaughter. At a crucial moment in Guatemalan history, President Dwight D. Eisenhower's Central Intelligence Agency overthrew a government that was working to modernize the society and enfranchise the Indian population. One reason for Eisenhower's hostility was the opposition of the United Fruit Company—at the time, Guatemala's largest landowner—to Guatemala City's attempt at land reform. Through the 1960s and 1970s, Washington financed the buildup of the Guatemalan army with more than $75 million in aid, helping to modernize what is today arguably the most repressive force in Latin America. During the worst years of the genocide, President Reagan voiced support for the military dictatorship and tried his best to resume military aid that was cut by the previous administration, but he was blocked by Congress.

When U.S. foreign policy and military strategists look at Guatemala, they see a land bridge, or buffer, between Central America's turmoil and presumably vulnerable Mexico. A Guatemalan revolution, at the very least, would mean that the country's considerable mineral wealth and sizable market could be tapped to aid the ailing economies of Cuba and, until 1990, Nicaragua. This view paralyzed Washington from ever taking meaningful action to stop the killing.

It was August 1980 when Dan and I arrived in Guatemala, just as the revolutionary war was heating up. One month earlier I had been an overnight editor for UPI on the New York metropolitan desk. Dan was a reporter for the Camden, New Jersey, *Courier Post.* We left our jobs to live in Guatemala because we believed that, with Nicaragua's revolutionary government already consolidated and El Salvador's rebellion well under way, Guatemala would be the next hot spot, and it would launch our free-lance careers. Our drive in Dan's green Volkswagen Rabbit, through Cleveland and Cincinnati, the prairies of east Texas, and the deserts and jungles of Mexico, gave us a geographical sense of connection between our country and Guatemala.

During our six months in Guatemala, we spent one month in Antigua, once the colonial capital for all Central America, to take Spanish lessons. Laid out on a plain under the shadow of the Agua volcano, Antigua is a city of ornately sculptured stone ruins, left crumbling by the earthquakes that have flattened Guatemalan civilization through the centuries. After completing our Spanish lessons, we moved to Guatemala City and lived in a grassy neighborhood named Jardines de la Asunción, or Gardens of the Assumption, an oasis of comfortable cinder-block houses surrounded by predominately working-class slums. In the morning, operating within blocks of our rented house, Dan and I saw plainclothes gunmen in unmarked blue Toyota jeeps, their automatic weapons ominously pointed out the windows. The death squads, paramilitary squads consisting of off-duty soldiers and police and covertly run out of the presidential palace, ruled the streets. I nervously checked through the curtains whenever a car idled in front of our house, and I consciously avoided routines, like using the same supermarket or post office, so as not to attract attention. We kept on the move and traveled the country.

Once we drove from Antigua to Guatemala City and crossed the dry plains of Chiquimula province on a highway laced with buttercups to the Caribbean port of Puerto Barrios. There we picked up a rusty steam ferry to sail to the town of Livingston. The town's inhabitants, as on much of the Caribbean coast of Central America, are English-speaking blacks, descendants of the black Caribs who migrated to Central America from the island of Saint Vincent in the seventeenth century. Built on wooden stilts, Livingston looks like shoreline towns in Belize, its English-speaking neighbor to the north.[*]

Teenagers leaning on long wooden fishing boats, smoking marijuana, and listening to a Belize radio station blaring Jamaican reggae on the beach at night, told me how they planned to join relatives in Brooklyn, where they would be able to find work. Unlike the Indians, these youths looked healthy and well fed. There was always plenty of fresh lobster, shrimp, and red snapper, which the Livingston folk cooked in banana leaves over a slow fire. It was a happy place, unlike most other Guatemalan towns. What primarily separated Livingston from the rest of Guatemala however, was not food or geography, but race. Livingston blacks told me they wanted nothing to do with the war between the Indians and Ladinos. Beyond this tiny refuge of

---

[*]The ministate of Belize (population: 150,000) is technically a part of Central America, but it is so marginal to the region's politics and culture that it is not included in this book.

Caribbean honky-tonk, Indian suffering was a blight throughout the land.

Dan and I routinely traveled into the central highlands to the traditional Indian highland market towns of Chichicastenango, Todos Santos, and Santiago Atitlán and haggled like other tourists with Indian merchants over exquisite handcrafted embroideries and wood carvings. There was nothing but bargains, because the Indians were desperate. The war brewing in the surrounding countryside was beginning to scare away the foreigners, and business was suffering. Indian merchants complained of traveling on foot in the bitter cold most of the night to sell a single $7 embroidered collar on an afternoon.

It was in Chichicastenango that I began to see firsthand that there was another side to the seemingly powerless Guatemalan Indian, one of militant cultural resistance. I attempted to take a photograph of an elderly Quiché woman burning pungent incense on an ancient Mayan altar laid into the steps of the colonial Santo Tomás Catholic Church. The Spanish conquistadores and accompanying churchmen had built Santo Tomás on the ancient altar to coax the Indians into worshiping at a church. The Quiché woman was a classic Guatemalan photo subject: she was an example of the survival of a merged Mayan-Catholic rite that the Quiché Indians invented as a response to the attempts by the Spanish conquistadores to convert them to Christianity. Before I could snap a frame, she flailed her arms at me, spat in disdain, then chirped something in the Quiché language like "Have you no respect?" I didn't know it at the time, but Indians believe a camera can take away their soul.

The contemporary Mayas have preserved much of their ancestors' cosmic mythology, which teaches the fatalistic but perhaps calming notion that history plays out in predictable cycles of grandeur and poverty. The highland Indians cherish the tale of Tecún Umán, the last king of the Quiché Mayan Indian empire, who lost his life in hand-to-hand combat with conquistador Pedro de Alvarado. According to legend, Tecún Umán will rise from the dead and once again reign over his people with a just hand.

Thousands of Indian women still make a living by weaving with the antiquated but functional backstrap loom, just as their pre-Columbian ancestors did. Land and corn are still revered throughout the highlands as they were in ancient times. In some villages, the world is perceived as a pyramid resting atop a shade tree; in others it is a beautiful, nurturing goddess. The Mayas have also preserved their 260-day calendar and even their pantheon of gods (earth, sun, moon, wind, heavens, and rain)—all mixed with the Roman Catholic saints. By speaking their languages and wearing tribal *traje,* the wonderfully colorful blouses, hats, pants, and sashes that differ in design and color from village to village, the modern Mayas not only follow tradition but make an explicit, potentially costly statement: "I am an Indian."

Their pride is mixed with anger. In late 1980, I visited Santa Catarina Palopó, a town squeezed between steep mountains and the banks of Lake Atitlán. Some 1,500 Cakchiquel Indians barely eke out a subsistence living ten months a year. "My family doesn't have enough land," said Manuel González, a twenty-eight-year-old Indian who still wore his traditional striped culottes. He said that as the rainy season ends in October, leaving only the smell of rotting corn behind, families begin to run out of food and money. In desperation, about four hundred Santa Catarina Palopó men and women migrated to cotton, coffee, and sugar plantations on the sweltering Pacific coast. "There is much pain in the lowlands and it is very hot," González told me. "Sometimes it makes me mad but I have no choice but to go." By the end of November, González had to take out loans of between $5 and $15 to feed his family in exchange for a month or two of work on the plantations. His advance was taken out of his daily salary, and in February he often returned to his farm penniless. This modern form of debt peonage gives Guatemalan coffee, sugar, and cotton oligarchs a competitive edge on world markets.

On yet another trip through the countryside, one in which Dan and I brought a nineteen-year-old guerrilla contact named Freddy as a guide, we traveled around the Ixil triangle, a remote highland Indian area where the rebel Guerrilla Army of the Poor (EGP) had made major inroads. Freddy carried false identification papers—he pretended to be an auto mechanic—for the inevitable army roadblocks. We drove west then north, past the Lake Atitlán area and up through Chichicastenango and the provincial capital of Santa Cruz del Quiché. From there, the roads into the mountainous pine forests and lush highland valleys become increasingly rugged but reveal spectacular beauty. We were heading into a guerrilla zone, a forest ranger told us, "It's like Vietnam in these mountains. The blue jays, even the leopards, have been scared away." Around a turn in the bend an army Bell helicopter hung in a tree, apparently shot down by a lucky bullet from a shotgun or rifle, as if to prove the ranger's point. On a rock by the side of the road was scrawled: "Long Live EGP."

Between the Ixil towns of Nebaj and San Juan Cotzal, a heavily armed, combat-ready army patrol stopped us and demanded identification. We showed our American passports, and Freddy showed his fake papers. "I can't guarantee your security," the officer warned. "The terrorists like to ambush around here." I was grateful that Freddy was accomplished at his subversive disguise. We continued on, vaguely hoping that we would meet some guerrillas.

By the time of our visit to San Juan Cotzal, that September day in 1980, most of the young men of the adobe and tile-roof town were already in the mountains as guerrillas or refugees. The town's nurses, teachers, and priest were long gone, refugees from death threats. Only the Evangelical ministers were thriving; their various congregations increasing rapidly in number.

Soldiers manning a machine-gun nest greeted us coolly at the entrance to town. The officer in charge was surprised the patrol had let us through, and he wasn't a gracious sort. In a long effort to convince him we meant no harm, we promised to stay for only an hour or so (we had no intention of staying the night anyway), and he finally allowed us to enter the quaint-looking cobblestone town, where some of the nation's best weavings are produced, festooned with primitive stick-figure designs.

I walked as quickly as I could in a vain attempt to escape army surveillance. Troops bearing Israeli Galil assault rifles were on every other street corner, their eyes alert and suspicious. San Juan Cotzal was an occupied town. Nevertheless, on my random walk through that mountain town I met a middle-aged Spanish-speaking Indian couple who eagerly brought me into their house for a cup of watery instant coffee. As a discussion of the violence unfolded, my two hosts began weeping, trembling and embittered. They took me to their living room to show me a confirmation photograph of their seventeen-year-old son Juan, who had been executed by the army less than two months before. The picture showed a handsome boy with big brown eyes and an eager grin.

"He wasn't involved in anything political," she said. "It was pure vengeance."

Juan's fate was sealed on July 28 when, under the cover of predawn darkness, an EGP commando squad raided the army outpost on the outskirts of San Juan Cotzal. Mustering all the firepower they could from their Belgian FAL and West German G-3 assault rifles, the integrated Ladino and Indian force surprised the soldiers and killed several before retreating. After town *orejas* (literally ears, or spies) told the shaken commander that certain civilians knew of the impending raid and didn't warn the soldiers, the troops forced open the doors of dozens of Indian homes, rounded up about sixty young males including Juan, executed them, and buried them in common graves.

THE MAYAS

The Guatemalan cycles of revolution and counterrevolution began centuries before the Spanish arrived in the Western Hemisphere. Small priestly elites ruled with an iron hand over the classical Mayan civilizations that flourished in the lowland rain forests of Guatemala's northeastern Petén panhandle between A.D. 300 and 800. Their city-states were noted for some of the greatest achievements in mathematics, astronomy, and architecture of the ancient world, but they were also characterized by a highly stratified class system, wars, and human sacrifice and mutilation to worship the gods. Entire Mayan cities were suddenly abandoned around the year 900, a social phenomenon that has long been the subject of debate among anthropologists. Disease, famine, and foreign invasion have been suggested as the agents of destruction. One theory holds that a social revolution—perhaps a massive insurrection by the peasantry—swallowed classical lowland Mayan society. In the Yucatán peninsula and the Guatemalan highlands southwest of the Petén less-developed Mayan societies survived for centuries by either co-opting or resisting waves of invasions by other Indian nations originating from central Mexico.

The harshest conquerors of all came in the sixteenth century. As Hernán Cortés put the final touches on his conquest of Mexico in 1523, he dispatched his deputy, Pedro de Alvarado, to expand the Spanish domain southward. Alvarado was typical of the freewheeling conquistadores who risked everything to honor the Spanish crown, promote the Catholic faith, and acquire gold and slaves. Born in 1485, seven years before Ferdinand and Isabella completed the conquest of the Iberian peninsula, Alvarado's generation was the first in six hundred years that would not grow up to fight the Muslim invaders. But they took their culture of religious war with them to the New World.

It took Alvarado—and his force of 120 cavalry, 300 infantry, and an auxiliary unit of hundreds of Mexican Indian fighters—two months to reach the Guatemalan highlands, arriving in February 1524. By the end of the decade, Alvarado had made alliances with competing Indian groups and conquered what is today Guatemala and El Salvador. Alvarado's best ally in putting down recurrent rebellions was European strains of smallpox, measles, and plague.

Alvarado made Guatemala the political and economic center of Central America, which it remained for the next three centuries. Colonial elites, consisting of the conquistadores and their families as well as churchmen, were granted what were known as *encomiendas*— royal awards enabling their holders, the *encomenderos,* to obligate entire Indian towns to do seasonal work, as a form of labor tax, called a tribute. Labor costs were kept to a minimum because the Indians subsisted by farming communal corn and bean fields on their own land.

Eager for souls, the Catholic Church took an active role in the effort to organize the depleted Indian labor force. Francisco Marroquín, Guatemala's first bishop, called for a "spiritual conquest" that would be accomplished by "congregating" Indians into church-controlled population centers called *congregaciones.* Spanish churchmen and civil authorities organized the Indian elders into *cofradías,* local governing committees that were supposed to convince the masses of the benefits of the *congregaciones* and the Catholic religion.

The ensuing Mayan resistance took many forms. There were repeated rebellions, which succeeded in minimizing colonial settlement of the highlands. But even when Indians were not fighting, they managed to preserve pieces of their culture by wrapping their own traditions into that of their oppressor. They made the Spanish-introduced chicken a sacrificial animal. They accepted the Catholic saints as new variations of their own gods, and the Spanish-instituted *cofradías* were transformed into promoters of a bizarre religious cult based on a pipe-smoking Indian named Maximón, a Mayan-Christian saint with a penchant for drinking the hardest moonshine.

Following uprisings in 1760 and 1764, King Charles III of Spain dispatched Archbishop Pedro Cortés y Larraz to the colony on a fact-finding mission. His report portrayed a racially divided, hate-filled society:

The Indians have an aversion and absolute hate for anything Spanish. . . . If these wretched people did not attend mass because they were inactive or lazy, or because they were playing or enjoying themselves, it would be one thing; but it is another to not attend because of a positive repugnance which is so strong that they hide in the woods and hide their children.

THE LIBERAL ERA

Central American independence from Spain, which came in the 1820s almost bloodlessly across the isthmus, made little difference in the lives of the Indians. The colonial Ladino elite cut the Spanish royal family out of local affairs, but it preserved the traditional position of the Indians at the bottom of the social order. The Central American provinces resisted an invasion by newly independent Mexico and formed a national confederation, called the United Provinces of Central America, with Guatemala City as the capital. It was the only time in history when all of Central America was united into one nation, and Indians were never considered citizens of the new republic.

Poor communications and competing local caudillo strongmen of the emerging rival Liberal and Conservative parties took power in different provinces, making unity fleeting. In general, the Liberals were members of the emerging commercial class who wished to integrate the confederation to unite the provincial economies among themselves and with the rest of the world; they adhered to the principle of free trade, public education, the separation of church and state, and social Darwinism. Conservatives wanted to preserve the power of the Church in secular society, protectionist trade regulations, and exceedingly limited suffrage.

The Liberals, under the leadership of Honduran caudillo Francisco Morazán, dominated the United Provinces in its early years. The Liberals got into political trouble when their free-trade policies led to the flooding of British goods on the Central American market, destroying much local business. Conservative caudillo Rafael Carrera and his mostly Guatemalan Conservative army rebelled, splitting the confederation in 1837. Guatemala, El Salvador, Honduras, Nicaragua, and Costa Rica then became separate nations.

The Indians of Guatemala and the rest of Central America generally took a dislike to the Liberals, who called for the confiscation of Church and indigenous communal lands in order to modernize Guatemala and the rest of Central America. Following the advice of their priests, the Indians joined Carrera's forces as guerrilla fighters to overturn the Liberals. In power for twenty-seven years, Carrera and the Conservatives treated the Indians with benign neglect; their defense of property rights benefited the Indian communities as much as it did the traditional oligarchy.

Guatemalan Liberals made a comeback in 1871 when, with financial support from Mexican President Benito Juárez, they militarily took Guatemala City. They dominated the country for the next sixty years, making the forced exploitation of cheap Indian labor a centerpiece of their modernizing schemes. Led by Gen. Justo Rufino Barrios, the restless son of a rancher who prided himself on his guitars, his library, and his fine collection of bulls, they organized Indians into work crews to build roads, bridges, and port facilities, including Puerto Barrios. Barrios blamed the Indians' poverty on their own sloth and cultural backwardness. His patronizing ideology rationalized a thorough overhaul of Guatemalan land ownership patterns—an expropriation of most Indian communal and Church lands, representing over 70 percent of Guatemala's cultivated lands, for the benefit of Ladinos and German immigrants to produce coffee for export. Once again the Indians resisted. Thousands fled into the mountains, and a guerrilla war broke out around the town of Momostenango. Barrios put down the revolt and in so doing invented modern Guatemalan counterinsurgency: his army burned crops to starve the rebels and forcibly resettled Indians who backed the rebellion. Liberal party dictators followed Barrios's policies for the next several decades.

Liberal Gen. Jorge Ubico, a motorcycle racer and authoritarian in the Barrios mold, ruled in the 1930s and 1940s, a period of rapid economic growth and the twilight of the Liberal era. He reinstituted colonial-style vagrancy laws that obliged landless Indians and Ladino peasants to work 150 days a year—either on a public or private project or farm. Ubico also drew his country far closer to the United States. He granted the United Fruit Company exemptions on import duties and real estate taxes, and encouraged the American banana company to invest in and expand the country's railroad system. With Ubico's help, United Fruit became the most important company in Guatemala. He also granted Washington military bases during World War II to help defend Caribbean supply lanes.

The new relationship, however, also exposed Guatemala's youth, professionals, workers, and military officers to Franklin Roosevelt's

New Deal ideals. Roosevelt's principle of the "Four Freedoms"—freedom of speech and religion, and freedom from want and fear—was repeatedly broadcast on Guatemalan radio and struck a popular chord. Opposition groups claimed the Roosevelt banner as their own, and compared Ubico's authoritarianism to that of Adolf Hitler. Their charge appeared all the more relevant when the Guatemalan dictator called on his cavalry to quash a series of labor strikes, killing hundreds in the process. Ubico's refusal to hold elections sparked massive student protests and, finally, a reformist army coup on October 20, 1944, which came to be known as the "October Revolution."

REVOLUTION AND CIA COUNTERREVOLUTION

The first president of the "October Revolution," the Argentine-educated philosopher Juan José Arévalo, called himself a "spiritual socialist" to distinguish himself from both the capitalists and the Communists. Arévalo discarded Ubico's secret police and repressive labor laws and began national literacy, cooperative farm programs, and voter registration drives. One lasting contribution was the establishment of the Indigenous Institute, a government agency designed to study, preserve, and protect Mayan culture and language.

The revolution made a significant, if not radical, impact on Mayan life. Inspired by government rhetoric, spontaneous peasant land invasions grew in number. Tens of thousands of Indians joined peasant leagues to demand higher wages from the coffee oligarchs; those leagues, in turn, informally aligned with the Ladino industrial unions to create a potentially revolutionary coalition. Local Indian leaders formed political parties and ran for office, and in many towns were elected to replace Ladinos in municipal government.

The revolution's turning point came with the 1950 election of Col. Jacobo Arbenz following the unresolved assassination of his chief military rival. The son of a Ladino mother and drug-addicted Swiss pharmacist who committed suicide, Arbenz was moody and frequently troubled, but he was also a nationalist and a brilliant military theorist. Influenced by his Marxist Salvadoran wife, María, Arbenz legalized the

Guatemalan Communist party, surrounded himself with Marxist advisers, and adopted much of the revolutionary lexicon. Arbenz proclaimed a national day of mourning following Stalin's death, and the pro-government press published columns supporting North Korea during the Korean War.

Arbenz set out to break the monopolistic control American companies wielded over the Guatemalan economy. Believing that the electricity provided by the American-owned Empresa Eléctrica de Guatemala was unfairly priced, Arbenz set up a hydroelectric power agency to undercut the U.S. company. The government constructed a port at Santo Tomás to compete with a United Fruit port facility at Puerto Barrios, and initiated a cross-country highway project to compete with a United Fruit railroad. Washington responded to such policies by cutting off economic aid to Guatemala in 1951. Arbenz spoke of overcoming underdevelopment by redistributing wealth and broadening the market within a capitalist framework not dominated by foreign interests. He initiated a land reform in 1952 that expropriated idle private farming property for redistribution to landless peasants. His reform strategy made United Fruit a prime target: only 15 percent of United Fruit's 550,000 acres of Guatemalan land was under cultivation at the time. Within two years, Arbenz expropriated 400,000 acres of United Fruit property and handed it over to tens of thousands of poor farmers. (In all, 100,000 mostly Indian families received plots of land that averaged ten acres in size.) Arbenz offered to compensate the company with $1.2 million, United Fruit's own valuation of the lost property's net worth as reported in its Guatemalan tax returns. Washington took exception and backed a United Fruit claim that it was owed $15.9 million.

According to a secret 1952 National Intelligence Estimate, the compiled assessment of the CIA and other intelligence branches, the Arbenz–United Fruit fight was a test of American will:

> If the Company should submit to Guatemalan demands the political position of the Arbenz Administration would be greatly strengthened. The result, even if it were a compromise agreement, would be presented as a national triumph over "colonialism" and would arouse popular enthusiasm. . . . The Government and the unions, under Communist influence and supported by national sentiment, would probably proceed to exert increasing pressure against other U.S. interests in Guatemala, notably the Railway.

United Fruit, which Guatemalans (as well as Costa Ricans and Hondurans) liked to call "The Octopus," had a long reach in the Republican party and the Eisenhower administration. Both John Foster Dulles, the Secretary of State, and his brother Allen, the director of Central Intelligence, had been lawyers for Sullivan and Cromwell, United Fruit's legal representative in Latin America. Assistant Secretary of State for Inter-American Affairs John Moors Cabot, whose brother had been a president of United Fruit and whose family included significant company shareholders, persistently pushed the company's case in the administration. United Nations Ambassador Henry Cabot Lodge, another strong anti-Arbenz antagonist, was also a major United Fruit shareholder. Meanwhile, the company took advantage of the McCarthyite political climate and tirelessly lobbied Congress.

With the discovery of a small Czech shipment of some dilapidated guns destined for pro-Arbenz forces, the Eisenhower administration found a pretext to turn the CIA loose on Guatemala with its "Project PB-Success." The CIA handpicked retired army Col. Carlos Castillo Armas, at the time a furniture salesman living in exile in Honduras, among competing Guatemalan exile caudillos to lead the so-called National Liberation Movement (MLN). Castillo Armas was totally dependent on the CIA for his supplies, funding, and Honduran base camps. His ragtag force of no more than five hundred men barely crossed the Honduran border when it was halted by the Guatemalan army after only a little fighting.

The anti-Arbenz cause did better from the air. A small CIA air force piloted by American contract pilots bombed Guatemala City and sparked a chain reaction that destabilized the government. In the meantime, CIA radio broadcasts whipped up rumors of Arbenz's impending doom with false reports that the Liberation armies were winning one imaginary battle after another on their way to the capital. Not even Arbenz, a once-reformed alcoholic who was drinking heavily again, knew for sure whether the Honduran-based broadcasts contained a kernel of truth. Arbenz, then only forty-one, simply lost his will in the face of the Liberation invasion and bombings. The Guatemalan air force, in what was effectively an act of rebellion against Arbenz, decided not to leave the ground to defend the city against the Americans.

Indian and Ladino peasant leaders eager to defend the land reform joined Communist party leaders in calling on Arbenz to arm popular militias, but the president waivered. He looked to his fellow army officers for support, and lost his self-confidence when he didn't find it. In the end, the Guatemalan leader wilted under the pressure and resigned on June 27, 1954, to live an unhappy exile first in Czechoslovakia and finally Cuba. John Peurifoy, the U.S. ambassador to Guatemala, flew to San Salvador to meet with Guatemalan military leaders to ensure that Castillo Armas came out on top in the post-Arbenz leadership. The CIA's top Guatemalan made his triumphant return to Guatemala City aboard the pistol-toting American ambassador's personal plane.

President Eisenhower reportedly turned to a contingent of CIA men visiting the White House following the coup and shook Allen Dulles's hand, saying, "Thanks to all of you. You've averted a Soviet beachhead in our hemisphere." In reality, the 1954 CIA coup in Guatemala was unnecessary even to achieve U.S. policy goals at the time, and unfortunate for all in the long term. A review of American intelligence reporting in the early 1950s reveals that U.S. analysts figured the Guatemalan army was a sure brake against Communism. They suggested that there could have been an army coup anyway, whatever U.S. policy. "The majority of the men in the armed forces share the opinion that the policy of the Arbenz government is contrary to the interests and well-being of the country," said a secret May 1953 CIA assessment of the "Attitude of Guatemalan Army toward Current Political Developments." It continued: "Army personnel [are] constantly being watched, [several words deleted] and the government is continually reporting the possibility of an armed revolt." In fact, several coup attempts nearly succeeded without direct U.S. involvement in 1953 and 1954; arguably, it was only a matter of time before one would have toppled Arbenz.

Without full support of the army, Arbenz would have needed overwhelming support of the masses to make a Communist revolution. But his moodiness, bad temper, and high-pitched voice robbed him of all charisma. Persistent rumors that he used hard drugs also hurt him. During an annual student political lampooning parade shortly before Arbenz was overthrown, a float included an Indian señorita being courted by Uncle Sam and a Russian bear. Poised behind the bear was Arbenz carrying an oversized hypodermic needle. As U.S. pressure in 1954 mounted, Arbenz attempted to assemble a gathering of his supporters in Guatemala City, but he couldn't even get that project off the ground.

Had the "October Revolution" survived, in one form or another, it might have advanced a process of integrating the Mayan majority into national life on more equitable terms. As for United Fruit, the company lost most of its banana lands and railroad interests in Guatemala anyway in antitrust suits pursued by the U.S. Justice Department during the decade following the coup.

Though the Eisenhower administration granted $80 million in economic aid to boost the Castillo Armas government over its three years in power, the abrupt reversal in official economic and social policy had a drastic impact on the daily lives of poor people. Thousands of peasants were thrown off their lands. Unemployment soared, wages dropped, and food was scarce in urban areas.

Beholden to a foreign power, and lacking a democratic mandate or full support of the army, Castillo Armas was forced to wield a cruel hand in attempting to suppress the social ferment active during the previous decade. The counterrevolutionary government disbanded industrial unions and peasant leagues, and rounded up 9,000 leftist suspects. As punishment to the insurgent Ixil Mayas for participating in the Arbenz land reform, Castillo Armas killed or imprisoned hundreds of their people.

Ubico's secret police apparatus was resurrected, and political prisoners were held and, in many cases, tortured for several years without ever standing trial. Castillo Armas's National Liberation Movement established a Committee Against Communism, which collected documents identifying 70,000 people who were active in unions or other organizations considered close to Arbenz or the Communists. Former CIA operative David Atlee Phillips, in his book *The Night Watch,* disclosed that he was one of several CIA counterintelligence experts to organize the files for use in Guatemalan intelligence operations. Over the next three decades, what became known as the Black List was the basic tool of the Guatemalan security forces in spying on the population. Tens of thousands on the list were eventually forced into exile, executed, or otherwise harassed.

By insisting that the obedient Castillo Armas take power after Arbenz resigned, the Eisenhower administration not only undercut democratic development but also divided the Guatemalan military. Castillo Armas's private MLN militia, which he refused to disband, was deeply resented by army officers. In August 1954, cadets of the Guatemalan military academy waged an attack on Castillo Armas's militia, killing about fifty rightists. The cadets were exiled as punishment and the dispute simmered.

Several veterans of the cadets' rebellion led a young officers' revolt in November 1960 against the corrupt rightist government of President Miguel Ydígoras Fuentes. The rebels, led by Capt. Marco Antonio Yon Sosa, argued that Ydígoras Fuentes had overstepped his constitutional boundaries by permitting the CIA to run military camps inside Guatemala to train anti-Castro irregulars. Yon Sosa launched his own Castro-style insurgency. Worried that Yon Sosa's rebels would get in the way of the Bay of Pigs invasion, Eisenhower again took extraordinary action in Guatemala.

The Eisenhower administration publicly dispatched an aircraft carrier to a position off Guatemalan shores as a show of muscle. In the meantime, the CIA, deploying exiled Cuban pilots, covertly flew B-26 bomber strikes (in six aircraft painted with the markings of the Guatemalan air force) to smother rebel army positions.

The rebels were defeated, but some escaped to Honduras to regroup. They returned to the Guatemalan highlands in 1963 having evolved into a Marxist guerrilla group they called the Rebel Armed Forces (FAR). Washington sent U.S. Green Beret advisers to revamp the Guatemalan army into an effective counterinsurgency force to fight the FAR. There were persistent reports that American Green Berets accompanied Guatemalan troops in the field, where they tested new counterinsurgency theories for use in Vietnam. At a cost of about 8,000 lives, the improved Guatemalan army defeated the FAR, though the group managed to regroup and survive in the jungles of the Petén to this day. The revolution and the counterrevolution unleashed other uncontrollable political forces.

Working sometimes in tandem with the official Guatemalan security forces and at other times alone, MLN gunmen went after urban intellectuals and unionists as well as rural activists. In the late 1960s and 1970s, under the leadership of Mario "Mico" Sandoval Alarcón, a Castillo Armas lieutenant, the MLN became an institutionalized political force that allied the landed oligarchy with the right-wing Ladino peasants of the eastern badlands. As president of the Guatemalan Congress in the early 1970s, Sandoval Alarcón, who called the MLN "the party of organized violence," funneled state funds into his paramilitary apparatus. His power had grown to such a degree that official party presidential candidate Gen. Kjell Laugerud García was forced to ask Mico to become his 1974 vice presidential running mate.

In that office, Sandoval Alarcón coordinated his paramilitary forces with those of the army. He has been quoted as saying, "I am a Fascist, and I have tried to model my party after the Spanish Falange."

In the wake of the counterrevolution, the conservative Roman Catholic church hierarchy set out to establish throughout the provinces Catholic Action, a project to build schools, clinics, and chapels as well as to combat the remnants of "radicalism" left behind from the Arbenz days. But in the hands of local and foreign clergy and Indians, the Catholic Action movement became an early vehicle for radical "liberation theology" and a seed for the next cycle of revolution, one that was to be more radical than the 1944–54 "October Revolution."

The Latin American church went through a revolution of its own in the 1960s and 1970s. Suffering from decreasing attendance and the increasing competition of the Evangelical Protestant churches, Roman Catholic leaders decided they needed to shed their traditional conservative image and speak up for the impoverished masses. At a Latin American bishops conference at Medellín, Colombia, in 1968, Church leaders borrowed much from Marxist thinking and spoke out against the "institutionalized violence" of the region's capitalist system. Following Medellín, priests and lay workers fanned out preaching the new liberation theology. Their words awakened the masses throughout Central America, particularly in Guatemala and El Salvador, and to a lesser extent Nicaragua.

In Guatemala, local priests encouraged landless Indian peasants from crowded highland villages to migrate north to the Ixcan jungles bordering Mexico to clear the land and homestead. This put them in direct competition with oligarchs and corrupt military officers who were accumulating lands in the same area at bargain prices. And it put them in contact with a tiny new guerrilla organization consisting of about fifty radical students called the Guerrilla Army of the Poor, (EGP). The leaders of the EGP intuitively saw the pioneer Indians of the Ixcan as a potential base of support, and their movement quickly spread.

Luis Arenas, a rich coffee and cardamom spice planter in the remote northern reaches of Quiché province, was known as the Tiger of Ixcan for his greed and ruthlessness. One night in 1975, he provided the cuxa (moonshine) and other party accoutrements for a grand fiesta in the Ixil Indian town of Chajul. Well into the night, with local leaders in a drunken stupor, Arenas offered to buy some of the town's prime corn land, and presented a deed approved by the Guatemalan government. Unable to read the terms of the contract, a few leaders thumbprinted their acceptance. Chajul later appealed to the National Institute of Agrarian Transformation to annul the document, but the government agency backed Arenas. A people long disdainful of Ladinos and migratory labor, the Ixils turned to the EGP. As in El Salvador and Nicaragua, local Catholic priests and lay workers encouraged the relationship.

The Guerrilla Army of the Poor ambushed and killed Arenas outside one of his plantations. News of his assassination traveled across the provinces and was celebrated by three-day-long marimba fiestas in nearby villages. The timber was dry; an act of nature supplied the spark.

A massive earthquake in 1976 left 22,000 dead and disrupted Guatemala's civic life. As hunger and disease spread, volunteers of Church and foreign aid organizations spread new political ideas throughout the highlands and helped organize peasants into rescue organizations that were easily converted into guerrilla support groups. In 1977, Indian miners went on strike, during which a few hundred set out on a march from western Huehuetenango province to the capital. By the time they reached Guatemala City, they numbered 100,000. From the earthquake relief work and the miners' march, local radical Christian organizations and a national Indian peasant union called the Committee for Peasant Unity (CUC) took root across the western highlands. CUC merged Socialist consciousness-raising with plantation and village organizing.

The growing popular movement alarmed the oligarchy and the regime of Gen. Romeo Lucas García. In the cities, death squads targeted students and union activists. In the countryside, they concentrated on the Church, killing nine priests and scores of lay religious workers. Finally, the military government began to apply increasing repression on the Indians themselves.

It was historically fitting that the massacres began in Alta Verapaz, an area of repeated Indian unrest since the conquest. On May 29, 1978, about 1,000 Kekchí Mayan Indians marched into the town of Panzós to see the mayor and confront him with a long list of grievances. Army officers, nickel strip miners, cattlemen, and coffee growers were grabbing their ancestral lands in the nearby Transversal region.

When the marchers reached Panzós, they were confronted by a contingent of 150 troops. Supported by right-wing vigilante gunmen posted on the rooftops, more than a hundred Indian men, women, and children were killed in a frenzy of gunfire. It was later revealed that, before the massacre, graves had been dug with earth-moving equipment donated by a local Ladino MLN political boss. Word of the premeditated murder spread, leading to a protest march by 60,000 people in Guatemala City nine days after the incident.

An emboldened Guerrilla Army of the Poor seized the opportunity to persuade Indians in many villages that their only protection lay in taking up arms and deepening their commitment. Meanwhile, a second guerrilla group, the Organization of the People in Arms (ORPA), quietly spread its influence in the southern highlands. The Indians joined ORPA and EGP in growing numbers through 1979, some as fighters but a much larger group as sympathizers willing to supply food and shelter.

To make matters worse for the regime, the Carter administration publicly criticized Guatemala's human rights record and cut off military aid in 1978 after Guatemala City refused to abide by administration human rights restrictions. Although Israel replaced most American supplies, the Carter administration helped isolate the regime. Guatemala became a pariah state, and foreign investment and tourism dropped.

In January 1980, twenty-seven Ixil Indians occupied the Spanish embassy, demanding an inquiry into human rights abuses in Quiché province and the withdrawal of the army from the province. Spanish Ambassador Máximo Cajal, sympathetic to the Indians, offered to mediate their disputes with the regime, and pleaded with President Gen. Romeo Lucas García to show restraint. Only three hours after the initial embassy occupation, shock troops from the National Police of Guatemala stormed the building. They threw grenades and firebombs into the embassy, setting it ablaze in broad daylight in front of hundreds of astonished onlookers. With police standing by, thirty-nine Indians and embassy office workers burned to death. As if the massacre weren't gruesome enough, the single Quiché peasant survivor was kidnapped out of his hospital room, tortured to death, and dumped on the campus of the National University. Rigoberta Menchú, a CUC activist whose father was killed in the embassy fire, later wrote: "The good thing was that Spain broke off relations with Guatemala immediately. Although if you think about it, Spain has a lot to do with our situation. They had a lot to do with the origins of the suffering of the people. . . ."

The Indian revolt reached throughout much of the isolated highlands. In the northern Ixcán jungles of Quiché province, entire Indian cooperatives were producing food for the guerrilla war struggle. Lakeside Santiago Atitlán, a large town in the middle of the tourist circuit, was in rebellion supporting ORPA. In July 1981, to mark the second anniversary of the Sandinista victory over Nicaraguan dictator Anastasio Somoza Debayle, coordinated Indian militia actions in Alta Verapaz, Chimaltenango, and southern Quiché caught the army by surprise and marked the opening of several new guerrilla fronts.

Although the top guerrilla leadership remained Ladino, Indians took command of battle units sharing a common indigenous language. According to one account, 80 percent of the rebel foot soldiers were Indians as guerrilla ranks swelled to almost 5,000 fighters (including militia). Perhaps the highpoint for the movement came in January 1982, when the four guerrilla groups formally united to form the Guatemalan National Revolutionary Unit (URNG). In its first proclamation, the URNG declared: "The Revolution will guarantee equality between Indians and Ladinos, and will end cultural oppression and discrimination."

The guerrillas had been so successful over the previous two years that they began to believe their own triumphal rhetoric. In reality, they had overextended themselves and left their masses vulnerable to the vengeful bloodletting that would follow.

In the months preceding the fraudulent March 1982 presidential election, the Guatemalan military turned the war around. First, the Lucas García regime extinguished the core of the guerrillas' urban cells with the advice and instruction of Israeli intelligence,* which trained police agencies to keep track of water and electricity bills. (Sudden rises in utility usage, the Guatemalans learned, frequently meant the existence of a guerrilla hideout.)

Then the army, led by the president's brother and chief of staff, Gen. Benedicto Lucas García, stamped out the guerrillas' rural civilian base. It was a vicious systematic strategy to "drain the water from the guerrillas' sea" that would come to include massacres, mass political

---

*Since Guatemala, Nicaragua, and El Salvador were among the first nations to recognize the State of Israel, Tel Aviv has played a role in Central America. Israel has supplied material and offered intelligence training to several of the region's armies.

reeducation, forced militia duty, and scores of "model villages" whose goals were to insulate the population from the guerrillas. Once heavily populated mountain valleys in the provinces of Quiché, Huehuetenango, and San Marcos were evacuated, with scores of villages and hamlets left as charred rubble. Those Indian villagers who were able to escape the massacres scavenged for months in the mountains and jungles before they reached safe haven in Mexico; others surrendered to army troops.

In designing his cruel but successful strategy, Benedicto Lucas García mixed some of the training and experience he had acquired at the French St. Cyr military academy and as a colonial military officer in Algeria for the French with the newest rural counterinsurgency doctrines the Taiwanese military were exporting to Central American corps. (The Taiwanese have active military training programs for Guatemalan and Salvadoran officers.) In essence, Benedicto Lucas García's strategy was the logical culmination of Guatemalan history. His model villages resembled the colonial *congregaciones;* his army's massacres were the same as those of the conquest; only the weaponry was more sophisticated.

The general said the United States was irrelevant to the war in Guatemala, saying it made little or no difference that Ronald Reagan had replaced Jimmy Carter as president. He laughed at suggestions made by reporters that his strategies originated in the Pentagon and were essentially the same tactics as those followed in Vietnam. "Why would we follow the lessons of a defeated army?" he snapped. "We Guatemalans know what works in our own country."

On the crest of military successes that still hadn't been reported in the international press, Gen. Benedicto Lucas García took me and a few other reporters on a helicopter tour of the Quiché front in March 1982. The swaggering barrel-chested general, who wore his army uniform so tight his biceps looked as if they'd rip through the cloth, was arrogantly self-confident when he put on his flying helmet and took control of the Bell 412 helicopter himself. "I'll show you how we're winning this war," he said with a toothy smile.

It sounded at the time like groundless bragging, but General Lucas García knew how to impress. Each of us gasped as he quickly dipped the helicopter down to show us the villages and surrounding cornfields that had been burned to the ground because residents supported the guerrillas. "You see," he said, "everything is under control."

He landed from time to time, and in one hamlet after another we found every healthy male had joined militias called "civil patrols." Lucas García assembled for our viewing scores of Indian peasants armed with only wooden sticks, machetes, and rusty carbines—a few of the rifles were hundred-year-old flint locks. The patrolmen stood in tight rows at attention and declared their allegiance to the flag and the army. Like robots the militiamen told us that communism is bad and the army is good. For their good behavior, the army was building them health clinics, housing, and schools and feeding the needy. "We've learned from this war," the general told me. "We're now on the side of the people."

We then flew to Chajul, in enemy Ixil country. The army had begun to permanently occupy the long-rebellious town, with checkpoints, hardened-rock street bunkers, and tight perimeter patrolling. A soldier directed me to the colonial church, where he said I would see how the locals had dressed one of the wooden saint statues in army fatigues as a sign of their affection. Indeed, it was true, and only months before that the same statue had been dressed in a guerrilla outfit. As always, the Indians were accommodating and disguising.

Across the country, in the eastern hills of Chiquimula province, the Gen. Romeo Lucas García regime reportedly handled the problem of how to control the small but independent-minded Chortí Indian population in a different fashion. The so-called Revolutionary party, a pro-government political machine, sent activists into Chortí villages in 1982 with pamphlets calling for revolutionary change. The radical rhetoric hit a chord, and many people registered as Revolutionary party members. Figuring that these same people would be potential guerrilla supporters, government-linked death squads targeted scores of them for execution. As brutal as such tactics were, they were also very effective in shredding the guerrillas' base of support.

Gen. Benedicto Lucas García never got credit for winning the war because he and his brother were kicked out of power by an anticorruption coup before his carefully designed army counteroffensive was completed. Encouraged to strike by MLN far-rightists who believed their leader, Sandoval Alarcón, had been robbed of the presidency in the March 1982 balloting designed to elect Gen. Luca García's hand-picked successor, the young officers turned to an Evangelical Christian Sunday school teacher, retired Gen. Efraín Ríos Montt, to clean up Guatemala. Claiming his government was inspired by God, Ríos Montt suspended the constitution, declared a state of siege, cashiered 324 elected mayors, and replaced civil courts with secret tribunals.

Ríos Montt put a virtual end to death-squad killing in and around Guatemala City, but he followed the basic counterinsurgency model pursued by the Lucas García brothers. He gave the strategy a name, "Beans and Bullets." Ríos Montt, in turn, financed and facilitated the work of Evangelical churches to spread the word to the Indians that rebellion was against the will of God and that Catholic liberation theology was the work of the devil. Tens of thousands of converts were made, splitting many Indian towns and villages into competitive and distrustful religious communities. Evangelical Christianity became a principal element of counterinsurgency—with the army helping to build churches for the survivors. (By the end of Ríos Montt's rule, about 20 percent of the Guatemalan population was Evangelical Christian.) Army sweeps herded tens of thousands of Indians into reeducation camps and model villages across the highlands, and literally took control of their bodies and minds. Concentrated in the model villages, the army could keep constant watch on the suspected rebel supporters and their families.

Acul, an Ixil village that had been bombed and burned to the ground, became one of about twenty model villages Ríos Montt's regime established. Civil liberties were (and still are) nonexistent; Indian residents were only allowed to leave the lands surrounding the village for their once-a-week twenty-four-hour civil patrol duty. Acul's Indians complained that civil patrol responsibilities and other restrictions prevented them from finding plantation work during the harvest season. The restrictions were a mixed blessing because they permitted the Indians to escape the brutal plantation labor. However, because the Indians didn't have enough land, they couldn't afford to live for a third of the year when they had no corn or beans to eat or sell.

The Indians' culture was particularly victimized in the model villages. At Acul, the Ixil Indian houses were constructed according to government specifications on tiny adjoining plots (along dirt streets named after the Guatemalan army and the Taiwanese government) in defiance of Indian cultural preference for a wide separation between houses for maximum land space and privacy. Many Indians could no longer afford to buy indigenous handwoven and embroidered *traje;* they were forced to buy and wear cheaper Ladino clothes instead.

Along with the Ixils, the Kekchís and Pokomchís of Alta Verapaz were particularly hit hard in the war, and then subjected to various forms of psychological warfare. In mid-1982, 1,500 Kekchís suspected of having guerrilla sympathies were forced to congregate on the outskirts of the city of Cobán in Camp Tzacol adjacent to the local army base. Army teachers taught the Indians Spanish and worked to break them psychologically. The teachers would repeatedly tell the Indians that they were stupid, dupes of communism, guilty of treason, and anti-Guatemala.

A 1983 report by the respected human rights group Americas Watch described how during a visit to Camp Tzacol military authorities openly admitted that "displaced persons" were subjected to indoctrination. It said: "They argued that it is necessary for the army to counter what they called the 'brainwashing' these people had experienced while allegedly under guerrilla control. Pointing randomly at groups of women and children, Colonel Ponce, the base commander, told us that they were all 'enemies' and 'Marxist subversives.' In fact, when asked by a member of the Americas Watch delegation, pointing to an Indian girl about three or four years old dragging a doll, whether she too was a 'subversive,' Colonel Ponce said, 'Yes, she also had a nom de guerre like many others.' "

Camp Tzacol was merely a way station in the gulag. After six months to a year there, Indian refugees were transferred to the Ideological Reeducation Center in Acamal, where the army issued them small houses and a bit of land. Entrance to the center was prohibited to all, even priests, but word got out that the Indians went through intense brainwashing emphasizing that the army was good and really wanted to help the Indians despite the recent massacres. After living in Acamal for a year or two, the Indians were transferred again, this time to Saraxoch, another model village. Here they were greeted by a sign that read: WELCOME TO THE NEW URBAN CENTER SARAXOCH, AN ANTISUBVERSIVE COMMUNITY, DISCIPLINE AND ORGANIZATION. The twice-brainwashed peasants were brainwashed a third time in Saraxoch; they were taught, for instance, to memorize and recite the following lesson: "We were fooled by the guerrillas and went to the hills and we committed crimes and sins and thank God the army came to save us."

The Reagan administration said virtually nothing as the Lucas García and Ríos Montt regimes slaughtered tens of thousands of Indians. Indeed, the White House repeatedly urged Congress in 1981 and 1982 to reverse the Carter arms embargo. Reagan managed to release $300,000 that had already been appropriated for military training, and authorized American companies to sell Guatemala trucks suitable for carrying troops. And after a meeting with Ríos Montt in Honduras in late 1982, Reagan said Ríos Montt had gotten a "bum rap" from American liberals. But in actual fact, Congress blocked military aid to Guatemala during the worst of the killings.

The Reagan administration began to reverse U.S. policy in January 1983 when it lifted the arms embargo, allowing the Defense Department to sell Guatemala $6.3 million worth of spare parts and other equipment for the Guatemalan air force's aging helicopter and A-37B jet fighter fleet. Claiming that Guatemala could go it alone, Ríos Montt refused to buy most of the equipment available. (Guatemala City reversed that decision in January 1984, following the removal of Ríos Montt.)

U.S. relations with Guatemala were tenser than with any other country in the region aside from Nicaragua. When the U.S. Agency for International Development (AID) issued a report in early 1983 suggesting that peasants be given the right to buy shares of plantation lands, Guatemala City called the finding "subversive." Washington removed its ambassador, Frederic L. Chapin, for a prolonged period in late 1983 when Guatemalan soldiers were found to be responsible for the killing of a Guatemalan linguist working for the U.S. embassy. When Chapin was transferred from his post the following year, the Guatemalan government refused to grant him the Order of the Quetzal, a traditional award given to departing friendly ambassadors. Army chief of staff Gen. Oscar Humberto Mejía Víctores explained the rebuff this way: "He did nothing for Guatemala."

Ironically, in neighboring El Salvador, U.S. military advisers pushed the Salvadoran army to copy many of the Guatemalan counterinsurgency techniques, such as instituting a civil defense militia. But the Salvadorans couldn't match the efficiency of the Guatemalans.

THE AFTERMATH

In late 1983, with the war virtually over, senior army officers overthrew Ríos Montt. The country was bankrupt and isolated, and officers led by the recently promoted Defense Minister Oscar Humberto Mejía Víctores realized they didn't need to occupy the presidential palace any longer to run the country. Guatemala would develop a limited democracy, beginning with a congressional election in 1984. The congress wrote a new, progressive constitution that formally guaranteed the civil liberties of all citizens. An independent human rights organization began to operate in the country after more than five years in which such groups had been banned. An independent weekly magazine named *Crónica* appeared. The Reagan administration was delighted, and American military aid once again began to flow to Guatemala City. For the Indians, however, democracy would mean more of the same.

In October 1985, on a presidential election campaign swing through the highlands of western Quezaltenango province, Christian Democratic candidate Vinicio Cerezo led a march of his followers through the Mayan town of Concepción Chiquirichapa. Cerezo, a cocky karate black belt who holstered a Browning 9mm pistol under the shoulder of his short-sleeved leisure suit, was on his way to give a speech in the central plaza, stepping briskly, hugging and shaking hands with anyone who looked friendly. "We're going to have a government that is for the people and by the people," Cerezo insisted.

A pretty Indian woman, speaking broken Spanish accented heavily by her native Mam tongue, grabbed Cerezo and tugged him aside. Cerezo followed the woman, understanding her desire to speak privately. Two older women, chirping among themselves in sputtering Mam dialect, followed behind the candidate.

"My husband," panted the young woman, "only three weeks ago, he was out in the cornfields, and he never returned. *They* got him, and for what? He was a good man."

Cerezo, who had survived three death-squad attempts himself, appeared sincerely moved. He nodded his head as if he had heard the same story many times before. "We're going to end all that," he said. "That's why I'm running."

One of the elderly women, garbed in a handwoven *huipil* blouse and wraparound striped skirt, hugged the candidate. "Many men in my family are dead. That's true for all our families," she cried with emotion. Cerezo stretched out his arms around her shoulders, held her, and said with moving deliberateness, *"They* won't get away with that anymore once I'm elected."

On the stump, though, speaking publicly, Cerezo was far more cautious. He wouldn't mention the model villages, civil patrols, or land reform. He vaguely promised to end the repression, but he didn't dare specify the national institution responsible for that violence. In private, the future president told me, "Frankly, the army is going to try to use me and I am going to try to use them. We'll see who succeeds."

I felt I already knew the answer after meeting that same month with Col. Byron Disrael Lima, one of the officers said to have the bloodiest hands in the Guatemalan army, who allowed me to spend a week with him at his command post in Santa Cruz del Quiché.

In the officers' mess under a painting depicting the Last Supper with the Apostles dressed as Indians, Colonel Lima and his staff were eating fatty steaks and tortillas and discussing warfare. A radio blared campaign jingles for the coming presidential election, which would end fifteen years of formal military rule.

A Vinicio Cerezo radio commercial promised a better life for peasants. "He's a demagogue," Colonel Lima snorted. "All politicians are liars."

A more conservative candidate, Jorge Carpio Nicolle, pledged during one of his commercials to spur economic growth and development. The stocky colonel burst out of his chair, strutted across the room, and turned down the radio. "There's a civilian wave in Latin America now," he exclaimed, his mustache twitching, "but that doesn't mean military men will lose their ultimate power." Then he added, "Latins take commands from men in uniform," Up and down the table, his junior officers nodded in agreement.

Privately, the forty-four-year-old colonel told me his heroes were Napoleon and Adolf Hitler, although he also said he wished Guatemalans, and particularly the Indians, would act with more confidence and ambition "like Israelis."

Colonel Lima governed the province of Quiché and its 380,000 people like a dictator. He personally supervised ten model villages and the building of roads, schools, and health clinics, and he continually jawboned gasoline stations to keep fuel prices down. Inflation seemed to be an obsession with him. Once, when he summarily slapped price controls on meat, butchers in Santa Cruz del Quiché screamed, so he cut their city taxes—without consulting the mayor. Another time he ordered farmers to stop shipping their beans out of Quiché, and he had his soldiers and police enforce the edict. The result: a rise in local supplies that brought bean prices in the province down by 33 percent while the national inflation rate was 60 percent. Colonel Lima was allowed such wide latitude by Guatemala City because Quiché was a priority combat zone, and because he had picked up considerable prestige as a ruthless commander for hitting the EGP there hard in 1982. The son of a Guatemalan colonel who was gunned down by guerrillas in 1970, Colonel Lima was obsessively anti-Communist. He believed they would get him if he didn't get them.

As part of his war strategy, he was always publicly glad-handing the Indians, as if to show that he could be a good friend as well as a bruising enemy. He embraced the village *cofradías,* the religious elders' societies first instituted by the Spanish, asking them to cooperate with him to keep the peace. After making a speech at an Indian beauty contest in the village of Chuguexa, Colonel Lima stood gamely as village elders took turns dancing in circles around him with a forty-pound statue of Santiago, a mythological hybrid of Christian saint and Mayan God, in tow. "General [Douglas] MacArthur understood," Colonel Lima said of such public relations efforts. "He always traveled with a film crew."

He treated the Indians of his region, the Quichés and Ixils, with a certain fearful respect, as an occupier of an always dangerous place. On the Sunday before the first round of the March 1985 presidential vote, he assembled 2,000 members of the civil patrol on a soccer field outside the market town of Chichicastenango to give them their election-day instructions. They were to respect voters, not tamper with the political process, and behave well before international reporters like myself.

"Let's let the past be the past," Colonel Lima told them. "I know many of you were fooled by the guerrillas a few years ago, but that doesn't matter anymore. You are magnificent Guatemalans now." The militiamen cheered, then marched past the colonel, who broke rank to shake their hands one by one. As the patrolmen went by, with many wielding nothing but long sticks, I said to the colonel, "I suppose you wish you had American aid to give them all rifles?" He turned to me, shook his head and replied furtively, "With rifles they could be dangerous."

Cerezo and his Christian Democratic party machine swept the presidential election with 70 percent of the vote. But only four days before his January 1986 inauguration, departing army dictator Gen. Oscar Humberto Mejía Víctores granted the Guatemalan army a blanket amnesty for its crimes. It was the first critical test for Cerezo, and he failed it completely; the new president agreed not to challenge the amnesty. Cerezo would later explain that Guatemala was not Argentina; while the Argentine army had been exposed to retribution by losing the Falklands War, the Guatemalan army had won its conflict.

Cerezo engaged in more symbolism than substance. Two weeks into his presidency, he purged the feared Department of Special Investigations (DIT), a police death squad. It would prove to be the boldest move of his 1985–90 presidency; even so, none of the agents were brought to trial or even charged with crimes. Of the six hundred agents dismissed, four hundred were reassigned to other National Police units. Meanwhile, the military's G-2 intelligence apparatus, the main death-squad organization, was left untouched. Cerezo turned out to be easier to handle in office than as an opposition politician—he didn't challenge the officer corps or seriously press the human rights issue. Colonel Lima and others continued to lead key regional commands which killed thousands of Indians. Before, Cerezo went before the U.S. Congress as a human rights advocate; now, as president, he had to ask for aid and bridle at liberal complaints he once would have made himself. He let the army run their model villages and civil patrols and govern the troublesome provinces like Quiché.

Cerezo did improve Guatemala's international image, open up foreign credit markets, slow inflation, and steady Guatemala's quetzal currency. Like the Sandinista government in Nicaragua, he sent health workers throughout the country in an antipolio campaign. With the support of the army, Cerezo attempted to increase Guatemalan business taxes with mixed success. Perhaps most importantly to the army, Cerezo's warm, long-cultivated relations with congressional Democrats began to open the spigot of U.S. military aid again. Even Harvard Law School granted its imprimatur to the Cerezo government by accepting a $500,000 grant from the U.S. government to send professors to Guatemala to train Guatemalan judges. With Harvard in tow, it became that much easier for liberals such as Senator Edward Kennedy to support a reinitiation of U.S. aid to Guatemala's police forces, which was cut off in the early 1970s when it was found that U.S. training was put to use by death-squad killers and police torturers.* Cerezo himself continued to carry his pistol and barely survived two serious coup attempts, one in May 1988 and another in May 1989, which was only stopped when the Bush administration's Assistant Secretary of State Bernard W. Aronson called top army chiefs. Aronson and U.S. Ambassador Thomas A. Stroock called on Guatemala City to improve its

*Harvard cut off the program in August 1990 in protest to the deteriorating human rights situation.

human rights record, but death-squad killings picked up again, targeting students and leaders of union and peasant groups.

The Cerezo years were full of raised hopes, most of which were dashed. Two aggressive weekly newspapers were founded but then forced to close, one after its offices were bombed. An antimilitary union theater group was founded and entertained workers at the Guatemala City Coca-Cola factory until two of the actors were shot by death squads, one fatally. Archbishop Próspero Penados del Barrio spoke out eloquently for land reform and Indian rights, but a series of death threats that went uninvestigated by the police made his life increasingly insecure. A new constitution seemed to make the participation in the mainly Indian civil patrols voluntary, but the military continued to force hundreds of thousands to join. Both Cerezo and the Guatemalan Congress set up human rights investigative units, but neither ever showed the slightist willingness to challenge the military.

Although the number of people dying in the highlands had substantially decreased, Guatemala seemed remarkably the same when I visited in April 1988 as it had eight years earlier, when I saw the police throwing around the drunken Indians. The daily newspapers still published articles about people disappearing for no apparent reason. The private sector was still ultra-right-wing and attempted to destabilize the Cerezo government at every opportunity. Rural massacres were down, but threats on urban intellectuals and labor leaders were up again.

There were all the same tensions. Quiché Indians in Totonicapán demonstrated aggressively for better public water service. In front of the government palace a Catholic priest was on a hunger strike, demanding land reform. Despite President Cerezo's stated goal to open a dialogue with the left, a group of dissidents, including Indian activist Rigoberta Menchú, attempting to return from exile were picked up by the Guatemalan security forces and thrown out of the country. The remnants of one of the guerrilla armies attempted but failed to blow up an oil pipeline in the Petén.

Popular organizations were also on the move, though at a much lower intensity than five years before. A new human rights group called the Council of Ethnic Communities, manned mostly by Indians, was organizing in the highlands and objecting to disappearances that the army wanted the country and the world to forget. A new confederation of workers and students, called the Unity of Labor and Popular Action, held rallies that attracted tens of thousands of people in Guatemala

City. Even an Indian peasant union informally aligned with the Guerrilla Army of the Poor was actively organizing again.

Was democracy changing Guatemala for the better? Maybe a little. But certainly the Indians were no better off. During a three-day trip I took into the jungles of Ixcán, I visited the thatched-roof settlement of Santa María Tzeja, where women carry their babies on their backs wrapped in shawls. Once a highly successful cardamom cooperative of Quiché Indians openly sympathetic to the Guerrilla Army of the Poor and Roman Catholic liberation theology, the community was destroyed by the army in February 1982 with an unaccounted number of people massacred. As I visited with refugees trickling back from Mexico, Santa María Tzeja was emerging again—but this time under the control of the army. The settlers were expected to work (for no pay) from time to time for the nearby command post, and in 1987 were even forced to go on a militia sweep through the surrounding jungles in search of guerrillas.

During the years when the Quichés were gone, the army and Evangelical churches brought in Kekchí Protestants to live on the abandoned fields. The competing Indian groups (each has about 250 people) could hardly communicate, but even if they did speak the same language, it might only have made a bad situation worse. The two groups wanted the same land, and with refugees coming back to reclaim their lost fields, tensions will only quicken. The Evangelicals control the ever-present civil patrol, which spies on the Quiché Catholics, who the army still considers subversive. When the Quichés attempted to restart the farm cooperative, the Kekchís refused to cooperate.

It is too soon to say how the Indian and religious mix will affect indigenous culture in Santa María Tzeja. "We have no experience in this," said Beatrice Manz, an American anthropologist who researches the Ixcán region. "At least the Spanish were nice enough to keep the Indian groups apart." Felipe Cante, fifty-five, one of five Quiché men attempting to rebuild the cooperative, expressed little hope in the future. "Because of the army, we have lost everything," he said. "We had cattle, and it's lost. We've asked for a road, and nothing happens. I can't tell you what difference Cerezo makes."

The army continued to punish Santiago Atitlán, the lakeside Tzutujil Indian town of 36,000 people that openly sympathized with the ORPA guerrilla group. Army death squads had disappeared a few hundred people and also sacked local radio station Voz de Atitlán

(Voice of Atitlán) for broadcasting news and literacy lessons in native Tzutujil. Charitable organizations and other radio stations replaced the lost equipment with donations over the next few years, but the station, even to this day, doesn't dare broadcast literacy programs, except in Spanish.

"What is our sin?" one of the Tzutujil Indian station employees, who lost two cousins and two brothers-in-law in the violence, asked me during a 1988 visit to Santiago Atitlán. "Trying to improve our community! The repression never stops! Police shot their guns in the air during the last Holy Week procession, another harassment. Our children threw stones at them." He paused. "Then in November [1987] an army sergeant came to see me. He wagged his finger and threatened me: 'Tenga cuidado. Be careful. The guerrillas have you on their death list.' Naturally, it's not the guerrillas who I fear." (Ten people on a death-squad list of about a hundred Santiago Atitlán area residents were abducted and killed in late 1987 and early 1988.) As I got up out of my chair to leave his office, the radioman told me, "Try to understand, there's no change in our feelings for our culture, there's just a constant fear. And if you publish my name, the army will take me away." The condition of the Indians was no different in large part because the great powers in Guatemala—the oligarchy and the army—remained the same.

To see if democracy was having any influence on the attitudes of the landed oligarchy, I visited coffee baron Mario Falla González at one of his several plantations outside of Antigua. Born into old wealth and only in his thirties, Falla was the leader of the influential National Farmers Union and a key right-wing political opponent of the Cerezo government. Soft, plump, and ingratiating, Falla was a racist through and through, even though he decorated his office with Mayan block prints and primitive paintings depicting indigenous themes. He spent the better part of an afternoon trying to convince me Indians were poor because that's the way they liked it. He said even if he could afford to pay his Indian seasonal migrant labor more than $1.80 a day—and he claimed he couldn't—they wouldn't spend their extra money on anything anyway.

"We were taught they are lesser humans," he admitted. "They don't have the same needs that we do. They need less. Poverty exists in Guatemala, but the problem is the lack of desire on the part of Mayas to improve themselves."

As we entered his plantation cottage, he noticed his gardener, Nasario, a crusty old man, standing there with a running hose in his hand, barefoot. "Nasario, tell me the truth, why aren't you wearing shoes?" The gardener answered, "It's too hot."

As if he had proved something profound, Falla turned to me and said, "He just doesn't want to wear shoes. It's not Indian custom."

When his Indian housekeeper, Beta, entered the dining room to serve rolls and butter, Falla pointed at her as if she were a museum piece. "Do you know where Beta went when she was sick? To a witchdoctor. The bad health of *our* people bothers me, but in part it's *their* own fault." Beta stood there shyly, reacting with a mild smile and a nod.

After lunch we took a drive to his shady coffee fields, deep in the pine and cypress forest, to see some of the best beans grown anywhere in Latin America. Walking through the bushes, I saw about a dozen Indian women, all migrant workers, pruning and handling plastic bottles of smelly chemicals (to kill crop plague) with their bare hands and without face masks.

Falla told me the "Indian women are good at this kind of work because it's not hard, it's delicate work."

We approached a picker named Francisca Ortiz, a Quiché woman from the village of Joyabaj. "Doesn't she look better than your typical sad old lady sitting on the porch of a cheap hotel in Miami Beach?" asked Falla. At age fifty, Francisca looked broken. I asked her privately what she thought of her work. She responded, "I have no husband. What can I do? The life of the Indian is always the same."

And what of the attitudes of Colonel Lima? Had democracy mellowed him? I visited him again in March 1988, at which time he was army commander in the eastern ranching province of Chiquimula, a mostly Ladino, ultraconservative area where the National Liberation Movement still dominates and guerrillas rarely dare to venture. It was just the place where an officer couldn't get into trouble over human rights; there was no one around suspicious enough to kill or torture. We spent most of our time swimming in a nearby semiprivate swimming pool, eating Chinese food, playing Ping-Pong in the officers' bar, and, of course, talking about Guatemala, politics, and war. Colonel Lima was unreconstructed by democracy.

Soon after his inauguration, Cerezo wanted to send him to Caracas as a military attaché. But the high command resisted. After a newspaper column named Colonel Lima as a coup plotter in 1987, Cerezo once again tried to transfer him out of the country. And again, the high command said no. During my 1988 visit, he told me, *"Poder militar,* military power, still exists here, in Argentina, all over Latin America. Military power is power." He showed absolute disdain for civilian government anywhere in Central America: "Cerezo is a soft socialist, like [Costa Rica's] Arias and [El Salvador's] Duarte. Arias and Cerezo are both dreamers and lovers." (In the months after I left him, Colonel Lima participated in the two coup attempts, and he was finally transferred to the Guatemalan embassy in Peru.)

On a Friday night, over a bottle of Johnnie Walker Black and a bucket of ice, we watched an old Walter Brennan western on television at his house. It was the standard stuff about the American dream: a pioneer family clears a field and fights off a drought and every other calamity to make a life for themselves. Colonel Lima loved it. "You see," he said. "That's how we have to build our country." He figured Guatemala today was just about what the United States was like a century ago. "The cowboys killed a lot of Indians, too, and kicked them off their lands. It was necessary because the Indians have never developed anything on their own." It was the closest he ever came to admitting that his army was even capable of harming a Mayan Indian. "Ever since the conquest," Colonel Lima told me, "it's been a process of modernization, extinguishing the backward ways of the Indians. That will go on another hundred years."

The resiliency of military rule and the sorry future facing Guatemala's Indians was apparent as early as 1990 when retired Gen. Efraín Ríos Montt reappeared on the political scene as a leading candidate for the presidential election. The constitution technically prohibited candidates who had participated in past coups, but Ríos Montt picked up impressive support among Ladinos, who dominate the voting population. His past record of genocide appeared to help him more than hurt him.

2
The Salvadoran Quagmire

"Watch how we are winning over the people," Salvadoran army Capt. Francisco Villacorta told me over the rumble of his truck convoy as we entered the town of San Francisco Morazán, a traditional guerrilla hideout. "Don't worry about a thing," he continued, as he fixed his hair and the heavy gold chain hanging around his neck. "If they dared to leave any snipers behind, we'll blow them away."

On this July afternoon in 1986, the Fourth Brigade swaggered into San Francisco Morazán without firing a shot. As his seventy-five troops searched the mud huts for guerrillas, Captain Villacorta climbed the bell tower of the muted aqua and yellow colonial church with an electronic bullhorn in his hand. "Together the people and the armed forces are for peace," he bellowed. His speech was mechanical, as if he were reading from a script. "We call on you to denounce those who collaborate with the terrorists. They are Communist mercenaries ordered from Cuba and Nicaragua. They say they want social justice, but all they want is to make us a nation of slaves. We invite you to join us for festivities!"

For the rest of the afternoon, a ten-piece mariachi band, a clown, a magician, and a couple of skimpily clad dancers performed between speeches by Salvadoran army officers and social workers calling on peasants to reject the guerrillas. Meanwhile, army barbers cut hair as soldiers passed out rice, clothing, and medicine. Scores of peasants stood in line for the various services, and they appeared to be truly pleased. Hundreds more chose to remain in their homes.

Monsignor Napoleón Magaña, the local priest, explained to me that some of the residents were timid because they feared they would be spotted by guerrilla spies. "Others haven't forgiven the army for killing so many of their neighbors in the past." Only three months before, government soldiers had killed two unarmed children—one twelve years of age; the other thirteen—and cut their ears off.

That night, after the soldiers and I ate a few cans of beans and fruit cocktail, we slept peacefully on the ground in the central plaza.

The next morning, the town secure, two helicopters landed on the edge of town, one with two U.S. military advisers and the other with two CIA agents. As the advisers inspected this "psychological operation" that they engineered back in the capital, the CIA men, clean-cut, wearing black army boots and camouflage pants and bearing rifles, walked around the town asking peasants questions. As the CIA men made notes on their clipboards, the peasants joked behind their backs about how poorly they spoke Spanish, and how profusely they sweat in the heat.

The agents were surprised to see me. One wouldn't talk to me at all. The other, who would identify himself only as "George," bragged, "You wouldn't have seen this in 1981 and 1982, or see the army winning hearts and minds. This is low-intensity conflict doctrine in action."

Low-intensity conflict, or LIC, is Pentagon and CIA jargon—a strategy designed to beat back messy Third World revolutions without deploying American ground forces. By sponsoring humanitarian and political activities such as land reform, military civic action, and free elections, LIC attempts to convince civilians that their government offers hope for a better life. The doctrine is the heart of the American policy in El Salvador; since the Carter administration sent twenty Green Beret advisers here in 1979, the U.S. project has been nothing less than to remake the country. Over the next ten years, the United States poured more than $5 billion into this tiny nation of 5.3 million people to quintuple the size of the armed forces, sponsor six elections, redistribute land to hundreds of thousands of peasants, construct a working judicial system, and otherwise finance a wide array of social, military, and poltical projects.

There are few nations in the world that need more help. Poverty and polarization are extreme, going back to the vicious exploitation of the peasantry by the oligarchy during the colonial era. A civil war has raged here for more than a decade, taking the lives of 75,000 people. Most of those killed weren't combatants, but poor people or middle-class activists taken out of their beds and murdered in the middle of the night by death squads. There is no end to the war in sight.

On one side of this conflict is the Farabundo Martí National Liberation Front (FMLN), a fractious coalition of five Marxist rebel armies that dates its origins to a peasant uprising in 1932. Its 5,000 to 10,000 combatants make up a highly disciplined and motivated force. Each rebel army controls its own territory and runs a network of peasant, student, and union organizations that demonstrate in the streets, collect weapons, and clandestinely provide cover for guerrilla operations from cells around the country. The FMLN fights its war in the name of the poor.

On the other side is the armed forces, backed by an assortment of right-wing political parties and the remnants of the old landed oligarchy. The armed forces include 47,000 men in the army, navy, and air force, and a total of 10,000 more in the security forces: the National Guard, the National Police, and the Treasury Police. The security forces oversee murderous vigilante groups in the countryside and, in coordination with civilian ultraright groups, other death squads that fight the dirty war in the cities. Fed on war and American aid, the armed forces' political and financial power have grown to the point where it is a law unto itself.

Tiny El Salvador seared the American consciousness in the early 1980s as no other foreign policy issue had since Vietnam. Opinion polls showed Americans worried when they saw the Green Berets back in a godforsaken jungle, participating in a war those same polls showed Americans could not differentiate from the one next door in Nicaragua. The television images were anything but reassuring. Americans watched a massacre of twenty-three Salvadorans on the steps of a cathedral and the bodies of four American churchwomen dug up after they were raped and murdered by soldiers outfitted by the United States. As American students marched on Washington to protest U.S. policy, El Salvador became a rallying cry for the American Conservative movement as well. Senator Jesse Helms of North Carolina defiantly ushered Roberto D'Aubuisson through Washington, even when the State Department labeled the right-wing Salvadoran as a terrorist death-squad leader.

Just as the Salvadoran revolution has deep roots, so does U.S. policy here. At the height of the cold war, Washington latched on to Salvadoran army Fascists to construct an intelligence apparatus to combat communism. Past American policies came to haunt the Carter administration when that same military network evolved into the death squads. President Jimmy Carter attempted to beat the revolution by building a political center with social reforms, but the death squads struck back by murdering the moderate Salvadorans in whom Carter placed his hopes for peaceful change. As Ronald Reagan came to office, a raging civil war overwhelmed any chance for conciliation.

By the time I stumbled across the CIA agents in San Francisco Morazán that summer of 1986, the El Salvador issue had lost its heat. Following three relatively free elections, a friend of the United States, moderate Christian Democrat José Napoleón Duarte, was president. Death-squad killings were reduced from eight hundred a month to less than twenty. More importantly, to American officials, such as the two CIA men I found in San Francisco Morazán, the Marxist rebels had been reduced from a mass popular movement to a sectarian militia prone to desperate terrorist acts.

But that was 1986, and the fragile military and political balance jerry-rigged by Washington would hold only for a short time. Over the next four years, El Salvador deteriorated steadily like a man-made artificial beach is inevitably eroded day by day by an ocean's tides.

For a time, U.S. policy had contained the poisons of El Salvador's sick society, but in the end all the effort was overwhelmed. The army high command and the courts refused to prosecute death-squad leaders or break down their apparatus. Massive Christian Democratic corruption wasted Duarte's political support. Heightened popular expectations for a more equitable El Salvador were replaced among the civilian population by frustration and bitter disappointment. The political center self-destructed, and the extreme right wing returned to power in 1989. Death-squad activities escalated again, and the tentative negotiating process between the government and the rebels collapsed.

U.S. policy was repeatedly rendered irrelevant by extremists of both sides, who, as if joined in some profane conspiracy, undermined peace negotiations, social reforms, and the cause of human rights at every key juncture. Salvadorans call themselves patriots, but loyalty rarely goes beyond one's family, political party, guerrilla group, or military academy graduating class. For all Washington's efforts, El Salvador is today what it has always been: a nation of betrayal and terror, where military strongmen, wealthy oligarchs, and village thugs seek final solutions of one political extreme or another.

"Why doesn't God make a miracle and civilize our country?" pleaded María Beltrán during an interview in 1987. A scrawny peasant woman who looked twenty-five years older than her fifty-two years, she had lost three children, two in bombing attacks on her village of El Barillo and a third in the cross fire between the army and rebels. "All that poor people like me can do," she said, "is fly our white flags over our little houses, tend to our chickens and pigs, and pray."

El Salvador would be a hopeless place even without war. It is a crowded, deforested, eroding land that has lost most of its fertility and wildlife. Salvadoran peasants only twenty years ago ate white-tailed deer, armadillo, spider monkey, and cottontail rabbit as inexpensive daily fare; today, most wild animals except crop-eating rodents are extinct, and corn tortillas and beans make up the average daily diet.

Exiled Salvadoran novelist Manlio Argueta, in his 1980 novel *One Day in Life*, gave voice to one typical peasant teenage girl this way:

> My parents could send me only to the first grade. Not because they didn't want to but because we were so many at home and I was the only girl, in charge of grinding corn and cooking it and then taking tortillas to my brothers in the cornfields. My brothers used to kill themselves chopping and hoeing. My father, too.
>
> My mother and I would take care of the house. All together there were fourteen of us—I and my folks and eleven brothers—even after three children had died. They died of dehydration. I remember how my father held the last one by his feet so that blood would run to his head, but nothing happened. He died with his head caved in. All their heads sunk in after serious bouts of diarrhea; once diarrhea begins there's no salvation. They all died before their first birthday.

Nowhere are Central America's class divisions, poverty, and violence more on display than in the capital of San Salvador, which like the country itself is inappropriately named after "The Holy Savior." While the rich live on the high ground at the base of the San Salvador volcano on the west side of town, the poor have the misfortune to live in the depths of the city's volcanic folds, or barrancas. These shantytowns of tin shacks, called *tugurios,* are inhabited by peasant families that have mostly arrived from the provinces over the last fifteen years to escape war and hunger in the countryside. *Tugurio* people lack running water and electricity. They carry pots of water on their heads over streets and footpaths of pitted dirt, and go from one odd job to the next to feed their many children. Some *tugurio* people hawk newspapers, roses, pet iguanas, and turtle eggs at major intersections, but most are hidden from the rest of the population.

San Salvador's rich hide their Japanese gardens and European paintings behind high brick walls topped by broken bottles, gun ports, watchtowers, and closed-circuit television cameras. For years they helped finance death squads to defend their privilege, with only mixed success. Enforcing a sweeping land reform in 1979, the Salvadoran army confiscated much of their land. Some of the rich were even targeted by those they considered allies—renegade army death squads who kidnapped for ransom. "El Salvador will never be the same for us," Orlando de Sola, one of the country's richest men, told me over dinner in 1985. "This democracy you Americans want for us means nothing more than chaos."

Large billboards around the city portray grim-faced children crippled by the rebels below the message: MORE INNOCENT VICTIMS OF FMLN LAND MINES. Blackouts caused by regular guerrilla sabotage of the nation's electrical grid are punctuated by the sounds of screeching brakes and honking horns at intersections after traffic lights go out. At the city's supermarkets, security guards wielding shotguns and pistols click their safeties as they patrol the aisles. At night there is the sputter of gunshots and return fire in one barrio or another.

"You have to be macho, foolish, or innocent to live here without being afraid most of the time," my regular taxi driver, Gregorio Aguilar, told me one day. Gregorio, who was quick to take chances and boast about them, had all three of those characteristics in abundance. He was an excellent companion who loved to drive his rattletrap taxi into the countryside in search of a guerrilla camp, or a waterhole to swim in. He told me that El Salvador needed an *"hombre fuerte con huevos,"* a "strongman with balls." It was not surprising that his favorite politician was Roberto D'Aubuisson, the reputed death-squad leader. "D'Aubuisson," Gregorio argued, "says he can end the war in six months. Why not give him a chance? The people here drop like flies no matter who is president."

In 1987, Gregorio was tortured and shot once in the face by an unknown assailant in the nearby town of Santa Tecla. One would normally chalk up such a murder as a death-squad incident, but that didn't make sense to me: Gregorio openly defended the far-right, and it is highly doubtful the left would have bothered to kill him. His fellow drivers could only guess why he was murdered. One said such killings usually occur in El Salvador over a woman, while another suggested that Gregorio was marked because he had been too helpful to American reporters like me.

EL SALVADOR'S TORTURED HISTORY

A mounting political crisis had brought U.S. Army Maj. A. R. Harris, the U.S. military attaché to Central America, to El Salvador, in December 1931. He filed the following report:

> About the first thing one observes when he goes to San Salvador is the number of expensive automobiles on the streets. There seems to be nothing but Packards and Pierce Arrows about. There appears to be nothing between these high-priced cars and the ox cart with its barefooted attendant. There is practically no middle class between the very rich and the very poor. . . . A socialistic or communistic revolution in El Salvador may be delayed for several years, ten or even twenty, but when it comes it will be a bloody one.

There has been an inevitability to revolutionary violence in El Salvador for four centuries. El Salvador's Pipil Indians were some of the toughest opponents faced by the Spanish conquistadores in the sixteenth century, but the Spanish made a concerted effort to conquer the land because of its large Indian population and its rich volcanic soil. Their appetite for land grew when European textile production and trade boomed in the seventeenth and eighteenth centuries. Wealthy

Salvadoran colonialists stole lands from the Indians to cultivate indigo from which to extract rich blue dye. As the Spanish made fortunes, rotting indigo frequently attracted vermin and disease in the over-crowded mills. Reports by Catholic priests indicate that the pestilence that accompanied indigo production wiped out entire Indian villages; planters used up one population, then moved on to the next. Not surprisingly, indigo production spurred four major insurrections during the first third of the nineteenth century.

The most serious Indian revolt erupted in 1832 when a wealthy planter put one of his Nonualco Indian workers in the stocks. Anastasio Aquino, the imprisoned man's brother, responded by leading a peasant mutiny. His slogan was "Land for those who work it!" Thousands of Indian and mestizo peasants joined Aquino's cause. His forces occu-pied the city of San Vicente and could have taken San Salvador itself, but Aquino lacked national vision. He simply wanted to consolidate a territory where Indians and other peasants were granted some form of autonomous control. By holding back, Aquino gave the Salvadoran authorities time to organize a pan–Central American force against him. Armed with heavy cannons, it easily defeated the Indians. Aquino was captured, tried, and executed; the authorities displayed his decapi-tated head in a cage.

Indigo prices soon fell precipitously, and El Salvador needed a new export crop. The colonialists pushed coffee cultivation with a decree that assured anyone title over Indian communal land simply by plant-ing coffee on it. The Indians rebelled at least five more times between 1872 and 1898.

Such drastic social change, and the turmoil that inevitably followed, demanded a large, modern army. President Gerardo Barrios hired a Colombian general to establish military discipline and codes of con-duct, four French officers to instruct in cavalry and artillery tactics, and a Spanish general to open the first Salvadoran military academy. Such was the beginning of a long tradition by which the Salvadoran armed forces relied on foreign advisers for military doctrine. But the social doctrine they reinforced was pure Salvadoran.

As coffee brought suffering to the poor, it enriched the elite. The wealthy built graceful mansions and sent their children to school in France and Spain. Between 1880 and 1930, there were a series of coffee growers who ruled the country as its president: Francisco Dueñas, Tomás Regalado, Pedro José Escalón, Fernando Figueroa, Jorge Meléndez, Juan Enrique Araujo, and Alfonso Quiñonez

Molina—the forefathers of the modern-day oligarchy. By the early 1930s, only 10 percent of the people owned land. At the same time, coffee prices plummeted as a function of the world depression, living conditions worsened, and a spirit of rebellion inspired by the Russian and Mexican revolutions spread.

Agustín Farabundo Martí was the kinetic son of a middle-class landowning family who discovered Marxism at the National University in San Salvador. He was a youth of dogmatic conviction who reflexively rejected authority figures. In one classroom debate, he challenged a professor to a duel to the death over an arcane point of sociological theory. In the late 1920s, Martí journeyed to the mountain camps of Nicaraguan rebel leader Augusto César Sandino, whom he hoped to convert to communism. But Sandino's mission was limited to expelling the U.S. Marines occupying his country. Spurned by the Nicaraguan nationalist, Martí returned to El Salvador in 1930 to unify students, workers, and Indian peasants into a single movement. Farabundo Martí became first secretary of the Communist party of El Salvador.

Farabundo Martí's call to arms provoked a schism among Salvadoran leaders, pitting a new class of liberal coffeemen like Arturo Araujo against far-right growers and their henchmen in the military. Elected as president in 1931, Araujo hoped to mollify the fledgling rebels with higher wages, free public education, clean water, and land.

Araujo's election sparked a rise in expectations. Within forty-eight hours of his March inauguration, thousands of workers and peasants assembled outside the presidential palace for a three-day demonstration demanding radical land reform. Police arrested Farabundo Martí at a massive march on Araujo's home. The new liberal president fell into an impossible situation, one that would become all too common for Salvadoran centrists: he tried to placate the far-right and far-left. Araujo stopped short of implementing the sweeping reforms he had promised, but he sealed his fate anyway by attempting to cut the defense budget and army salaries. On December 2, 1931, army officers moved against Araujo, opening the presidency to hardline Vice President and War Minister Gen. Maximiliano Hernández Martínez.

Martínez was a small, rumpled, easily underestimated man. He was a mystic who sponsored séances and trained himself to look into the sun for hours without blinking. Martínez was called "El Brujo," the warlock, and he attempted to put his nation under a trance on national radio. "It is a greater crime to kill an ant than a man," he told his people, "because a man who dies is reincarnated while an ant dies forever."

Martínez was as clever as he was eccentric. One of his first acts as president was to put off municipal elections long enough to allow the Communist party to register candidates and reveal its supporters. His real aim became apparent when he suspended the vote a second time: he wanted the security forces to know every Communist in the land. The election suspension sparked a number of labor strikes and demonstrations, and led the Communist party leadership to decide that working within the democratic system was useless. The central committee, in a supposedly secret vote that leaked, decided it was time to rebel.

The insurrection could not have gone worse. Government intelligence was so good, and Communist plotting so bad, that a San Salvador newspaper published the January 22 date of the planned rebellion days before it happened. Communist party leaders decided to go ahead with the insurrection anyway, perhaps because communications with rebel Indian village leaders was so poor they had no choice. Three days before the revolt, police arrested the party's three top leaders, Farabundo Martí, Alfonso Luna, and Mario Zapata, and later executed them by firing squad.

On the morning of the revolt it appeared as if the ancient Indian gods had woken from their long deep sleep. Izalco volcano erupted in fury, along with more than a half dozen other volcanoes in northern Central America. Clouds of ash blackened the skies as the Indians of Sonsonate and Ahuachapán provinces marched to kill or be killed. For forty-eight hours, the rebels avenged the indignities of almost half a millennium, murdering about one hundred Ladino landowners and merchants, dragging many out of their beds. Their carnage, however, could not compare to the massacres that would follow. This was a battle of machetes against machine guns.

Martínez unleashed the National Guard and vigilante groups, which slaughtered some 20,000 people, or 1.4 percent of the population, within two months.

Miguel Mármol, a Salvadoran Communist party activist, described the repression in the Sonsonate town of Armenia years later in his memoirs (as told to poet Roque Dalton):

> . . . a general named Pinto personally killed 700 peasants after his soldiers forced them to dig their own graves, one by one. General

Ochoa, who was the governor of San Miguel, forced the arrested men to crawl on their knees up to where he was sitting in a chair, in the courtyard of the barracks, and he'd tell them: "Come here, smell my pistol." The prisoners begged him in the name of God and their children, crying and pleading with him, since before entering the courtyard they had heard intermittent gunshots. But the barbarian general insisted and convinced them: "If you don't sniff the pistol it's because you're a Communist and afraid. The one has nothing to hide, fears nothing." The peasant sniffed the barrel and right there the general put a bullet in his face. Then he'd say, "Send in the next one."

The massacre, known as La Matanza, marked a turning point in Salvadoran history. Most Indians renounced their native language, costumes, and customs to protect themselves. The left, cut to pieces, went underground for more than a decade, and only made a tentative comeback in the 1940s and 1950s in the labor movement and at the National University. The army destroyed all records relating to the massacre, then replaced the oligarchy as the most powerful sector of society. Generals, not landowners, have ruled El Salvador ever since.

EARLY U.S. POLICY

By the 1930s, the United States was the most important power in the Caribbean, having conducted regular military interventions in Haiti, the Dominican Republic, Cuba, and Nicaragua. But El Salvador had no Caribbean coast, and it had so far escaped American attention. The Salvadorans liked it that way. When the 1932 insurrection broke out, an American naval commander sailing off the port of Acajutla radioed to the Salvadoran authorities, offering to land the marines. Martínez said no thank you.

Martínez had other foreign friends; he looked to Fascist Italy and Germany for inspiration and advice. El Salvador was one of the first countries to recognize Franco's Fascist regime in Spain and the Japanese puppet government in Manchuria. Martínez founded his own Fascist National Pro-Homeland party as the only legal party in the country, and fielded black-shirted militia members organized along the lines of the European Nazi parties. Fascist Rome supplied the Salvadoran air force with a modern fleet of Caproni fighter planes and bombers. Most significant of all the Fascist infiltration of El Salvador was the appointment in 1938 of an active German army colonel, Eberhard Bohnstadt, as director of El Salvador's military academy and adviser to the high command. Bohnstadt trained an entire generation of Salvadoran officers in everything from goose-stepping to intelligence.

The Fascist tendencies lingered in El Salvador, even as the Allied armies swept through Germany. U.S. Ambassador John F. Simmons cabled Washington that the newest dictator in 1944, Col. Osmin Aguirre y Salinas, was "an enthusiastic apologist for the Nazi ideology." Mexico, Guatemala, and Costa Rica broke relations with Aguirre y Salinas to isolate him, but the Roosevelt administration's Assistant Secretary of State for Inter-American Affairs, Nelson Rockefeller, decided to recognize his government. Rockefeller and the American military believed the Salvadoran army was needed to guarantee American security interests, and they rationalized that a generous military aid program could modernize the thinking of the Salvadoran army.

In fact, a faction of American-trained, reform-minded Salvadoran officers, who called themselves the Young Military, began to rise through the ranks in the 1950s. They were first of three generations of officers who would seek to loosen the traditional ties of the army and the oligarchs. The Eisenhower administration, suspicious that their politics might lean too far to the left, withheld support. Their October 1960 coup succeeded anyway. The reformist officers brought into their government social democratic intellectuals and technocrats pledged to support land reform, unions, Indian rights, and an expansion of social security, education, and health care. Their line sounded too much like Fidel Castro's; Eisenhower withheld recognition.

The election of John F. Kennedy in November worried Salvadoran hard-liners. Fearful that the Democrat would embrace the reformist junta, the army right struck on January 25, 1961. The toppling of the junta wiped out hopes for democratic change in El Salvador for more than a decade.

"Those who make peaceful revolution impossible," President Kennedy lectured the oligarchs and dictators of Latin America, "will make violent revolution inevitable." However, when it came to making policy, particularly covert policy, Kennedy failed to follow his own advice. Fascinated by counterinsurgency, the Kennedy administration chose El Salvador as a laboratory. Without the knowledge of the American ambassador, the CIA launched a secret Salvadoran intelligence agency operating from the presidential house. It became known as the Salvadoran National Security Agency, or Ansesal.

The CIA supplied Ansesal with electronic and photographic equipment as well as an archival system to collect and cross-index files on thousands of Salvadoran leftists. The Americans turned to National Guard Col. José Alberto "Chele" Medrano to take charge of the agency and, according to retired Salvadoran police sources, also hired and paid him to coordinate intelligence gathering for all of Central America. According to a secret 1967 report on public safety programs in Central America, Americans helped direct the organization of a "fingerprint file of more than 300,000 individuals."*

Medrano was an unlikely choice—he had been on the outs with the Salvadoran military establishment since the mid-1950s when he was linked to a scandalous extrajudicial execution of dozens of common street criminals in a San Salvador prison. President Julio A. Rivera had only recently rehabilitated Medrano to shore up his position with the military right and the oligarchy. Colonel Medrano was known to protect the security of properties of favored oligarchs from labor unrest, and was probably paid for his protection. There was a personal connection between Rivera and Medrano as well. Only one class apart at the military academy, the two colonels had studied together under Colonel Bohnstadt. Indeed, Medrano was Bohnstadt's favorite pupil because of his tough-mindedness, independence, and love for the goose step.

According to a lieutenant who served under him at the time, Colonel Medrano was an unreconstructed Fascist in the 1960s who also had the political acuity to embrace the Americans. The colonel was known to leave his car parked in a prohibited zone in front of the U.S. embassy, and then pass building security without having to remove the .44 Magnum he wore openly over his shoulder. "It was like he owned the place," said the former lieutenant. "Medrano taught the officer corps how to use the Americans. He played them like a fiddle. While he accepted their technical assistance and money, he had his own agenda."

---

*Though the public safety program report didn't mention Ansesal by name, it stated that an American agency identified as "CAS," a code word for the CIA, "is lending aid to an intelligence unit of 15 persons headed by Col. Medrano [and] directly responsible to the presidential palace. Col. Medrano claims to have a 30,000-man military reservist informant network."

Colonel Medrano frequently flew to Washington, visiting CIA headquarters often and even the White House on at least one occasion to be personally decorated by President Lyndon Johnson. U.S. military advisers in El Salvador singled out Medrano for a three-month counterinsurgency training tour in South Vietnam.

Medrano told American journalist Allan Nairn in 1984 that "Orden [Medrano's name for his informant network] and Ansesal grew out of the State Department, the CIA, and the Green Berets during the time of Kennedy." Orden (Spanish for "order"), Medrano told Nairn, was designed in large part by Green Beret Col. Arthur Simons and ten American advisers "to indoctrinate the peasants." Under Medrano's leadership and U.S. advice, Ansesal functioned as the intelligence command center for the National Police, National Guard, Treasury Police, air force, army, and navy.

By 1970, Ansesal employed informants all over El Salvador; one in every fifty people in the country was an *oreja*, or "ear," for the agency. To be a member of Orden was one of the few ways a peasant could gain respect inside and outside his community. It usually also gave him access to a gun—no small thing in this macho society. Medrano organized Orden as his personal political, military, and intelligence outfit. At campaign time, Orden became an appendage for candidates whom Medrano* personally favored. By the late 1970s, Orden had 80,000 members. It would provide the far right with a political base in the countryside for the next twenty years.

As Orden became increasingly important in the countryside, so did leftist groups, as priests, lay workers, and activists of the new Christian Democratic party spread liberation theology, the religious doctrine that reinterpreted the New Testament with Socialist eyes. They organized peasants into communal Christian-based communities, self-help groups designed to form cooperatives and pressure local politicans for social programs. Catholic activists brought the small peasant groups together into a national organization called the Christian Peasant Federation (FECCAS), which led strikes and other work actions. FECCAS and Orden went head to head for the hearts of the peasantry.

---

*Medrano went on to become a general, the hero of a brief 1969 war against Honduras, and an unsuccessful presidential candidate. The war was fought over Honduras's refusal to accept hundreds of thousands of landless Salvadoran peasants on their lands. The war was a military standoff but effectively sealed El Salvador's population safety valve. Medrano was assassinated in 1986.

. . .

In San Salvador, a group of young professionals, many educated in the United States, most the sons of an emerging middle class, held a series of study groups to consider local politics in light of Pope John XXIII's call to improve the lot of the poor. The study groups led to a political party modeled on the Christian Democratic parties of Venezuela and Chile. Among their leaders was José Napoleón Duarte, the country's most prominent civil engineer.

Duarte ran for mayor of San Salvador in 1964. His campaign immediately picked up support from the small middle class, but he needed the votes of the poor. Traveling the barrios on the back of a truck, Duarte challenged the primacy of the military. The poor were too fearful to leave their homes to hear him, so he aimed his loudspeaker at their houses: "You don't have to come out. Just listen to us."

Duarte had a sense of his own destiny as well as that potent political force: good luck. The son of a humble tailor, Duarte built his self-confidence winning badges as a Boy Scout and then starring on his high school basketball team. His father won enough money in the national lottery to send his ambitious son to Notre Dame University, where he studied economics and engineering. Duarte came to believe anything was possible. To everyone's surprise but his own, the poor people who listened to his speeches from inside their shacks came out to vote, and elected him.

As mayor, Duarte improved public transportation and lighting. Most significantly, he organized poor barrios into self-help committees that picked up the garbage, paved local streets, and provided ambulance services for the sick. He gave the poor a sense of empowerment, and won reelection by a landslide in 1966 and 1968.

Duarte sensed an historic opportunity to run for president in 1972 on a unity ticket with Communist and Social Democratic parties. Duarte and his leftist allies swept to victory over two right-wing candidates (including General Medrano), but the election board declared Col. Arturo Molina, the official army candidate, the victor. Salvadorans knew the election was fixed, but the Nixon White House remained silent. Washington was unhappy with Duarte's Marxist allies and unwilling to endanger relations with the Salvadoran armed forces.

The fixed election was unpopular even among some officers in the armed forces. Army mavericks rebelled in protest but met the resistance of the conservative air force and army troops in the western provinces. Duarte took to the radio waves in support of the insurgents, calling on supporters to build barricades to keep the progovernment soldiers from the capital. But the air force broke the back of the resistance by bombing the insurgent barracks. Army troops captured Duarte and broke his cheekbones with rifle butts. Washington intervened to save Duarte from possible death only after Father Theodore Hesburgh, the president of Notre Dame and an old friend of the Salvadoran politician, cabled Secretary of State Henry Kissinger requesting his help. At Washington's urging, the military allowed Duarte to leave the country for a seven-year exile in Venezuela.

With the democratic option closed, revolution became inevitable. Denied a role in the system, the Communist party split, with its most dynamic members joining the first underground cells of the Popular Liberation Forces (FPL) under the command of former party secretary Salvador Cayetano Carpio, alias "Marcial." Other Communist activists joined dissident Christian Democrats and radicalized Church activists, forming a second guerrilla organization, the People's Revolutionary Army (ERP). (The FPL and the ERP remain today the two largest guerrilla armies in the FMLN coalition.)

One of the primary tactics of the guerrilla left in the mid- and late 1970s was the kidnapping of foreign businessmen and Salvadoran oligarchs. They amassed a war chest of $70 million, donating an estimated $10 million to Nicaragua's Sandinista National Liberation Front (FSLN) guerrillas—thus solidifying their relationship with their Nicaraguan comrades.

After the failed coup, President Arturo Molina sensed that the urge for reform had not been quieted. He proposed a modest land reform in 1976, but his efforts ran into a violent reaction from the oligarchy. Landowners charged that the government was turning Socialist, and Orden and death squads going by the names of the Falange and the White Warriors Union began murdering peasants. With only lukewarm support from the Ford administration, Molina couldn't stand up to the pressure, and he backtracked.

It was not the killing of Salvadorans but the murder of a twenty-four-year-old backpacking American tourist named Ronald J. Richardson that caught the attention of the Ford administration. U.S. Ambassador Ignacio Lozano was convinced that the Salvadoran armed forces were responsible for killing Richardson. Outraged that the Salvadorans would kill an American and fail to prosecute those responsible, Lozano recommended that Washington deny the Salvadorans a loan to build the San Lorenzo dam until the suspected cover-up was resolved.

As the scandal unfolded, Jimmy Carter won the presidency, promising to make human rights a cornerstone of his foreign policy. But Carter's interest did not lie in a country or a case that few Americans had heard of. Carter fired Lozano, and replaced him with Frank Devine, an ambassador who was more prepared to accommodate the regime. The Salvadoran military read Lozano's departure as a green light to steal another presidential election in 1977 and further repress the population.

On my first trip to the country, in May 1979, I attended a press briefing in Ambassador Devine's office. Activists linked to the FPL guerrilla group were occupying three foreign embassies demanding freedom for political prisoners. "I know things look bad," Devine said, "but this government should be given credit for the land reform and efforts at controlling population growth." An aide suddenly appeared and interrupted the briefing with bad news. Only minutes before government forces had opened fire on a demonstration taking place in front of the Metropolitan Cathedral, killing twenty-three people. A CBS videotape of the massacre clearly showed that the slayings were unprovoked. In the minutes prior to the slayings, the video showed, police looked fidgety, uncomfortable with the task at hand. They took their positions in a single line and began shooting their assault rifles in the air as they marched toward the cathedral. In unison, they gradually lowered their barrels, until their guns were trained on their victims.

The Sunday after the massacre, I went to mass to hear Archbishop Oscar Arnulfo Romero. Speaking before 1,000 poor people at a San Salvador church, Romero, trembling in anger, endorsed a resolution proposed in the U.S. Senate by Senator Ted Kennedy to respond to the massacre by cutting American aid. Romero's flock cheered.

In his two years as archbishop, this son of a telegraph operator from the provinces had become a major threat to the regime. A small, soft-spoken, bespectacled man, he traveled the country preaching the right of workers and peasants to organize for higher wages and land. He excoriated the government for perpetrating "institutionalized violence," implicitly encouraging local priests to support the emerging rebel movement. "The poor are the body of Christ today," he said. "Through them he lives on in history." Military officers called Romero a guerrilla, even though he came to his position as a more traditional, apolitical member of the clergy. His conversion to liberation theology came in response to the systematic killing of his priests by death squads, two in his first eight weeks as archbishop, five by the time the massacre occurred on the steps of his cathedral. Leaflets dropped around San Salvador by rightists read: "Be a Patriot: Kill a Priest." With each murder, Romero moved farther to the left, and the people appeared ready to follow him.

After the mass, I followed the archbishop to a small office on the side of the chapel. As he slipped off his vestments to travel to a provincial parish for another mass, we spoke for a few moments. He looked tired, but he had the most serene manner about him. In mocking solemnity, he probed, "So how do you like our country?" It was an uncomfortable question and I could only shrug my shoulders. He responded with an attempt to comfort. "Perhaps you can come back in a more peaceful time," he said. I asked about the rumors of death threats. "I get phone calls now and then in the middle of the night," he said. "Not everyone loves the archbishop."

THE WAR BEGINS

The modern Salvadoran revolutionary war began in earnest with yet another reformist military coup, this one staged on October 15, 1979, against President Romero. Led by young officers, the new junta pledged both an end to repression and sweeping reforms, including a nationalization of the banks and a land redistribution designed to break the back of the oligarchy. The goal of the young officers was self-preservation. They acted to save their military institution from the fate of the Nicaraguan National Guard, which had been annihilated by the FSLN only three months before. The Young Turks were bold, bringing Christian Democrats, liberal businessmen, Socialists, and even a Communist into the ruling five-man junta and cabinet. It was El Salvador's last hope—a compromise coalition government.

Within days of the coup, José Napoleón Duarte returned from his seven-year Venezuelan exile to lead his Christian Democratic party and prepare for the free elections promised by the junta. He was welcomed as a national hero by a throng of 30,000 people. As Duarte's motorcade drove through the streets of San Salvador, leftist students and workers, some armed, stoned his car. A gunman pointed a pistol at Duarte, but a bodyguard slapped the weapon out of his hand before he could do any harm.

The junta got off to a shaky start because neither the guerrillas nor the far-right in the army would let it succeed. Two days after the coup, ERP guerrillas took over a San Salvador barrio and called for a popular insurrection. The army moved in with tanks and helicopters and slaughtered twenty-four people. More than a hundred demonstrators, strikers and peasants demanding land reform, were shot down in the streets by the military during the first week of the new regime.

In the chaos, the coup's most progressive military leader lost his standing to several more senior and conservative officers whose covert goal was to subvert the junta. A troika of hard-liners—Defense Minister Col. José Guillermo García, Deputy Defense Minister Col. Nicolás Carranza, and Col. Carlos Eugenio Vides Casanova, the National Guard commander—blocked many of the junta's goals, including investigations into corrupt and violent military activities.

Through late 1979 and 1980, there were actually two governments. One was the junta, which was led by army moderates Col. Jaime Abdul Gutiérrez and Col. Adolfo Majano, along with a revolving-door assortment of civilians including Jesuit University rector Román Mayorga, social democrat Guillermo Ungo, and finally Duarte. The second government consisted of a clandestine network that worked out of the intelligence branches of the security forces and the army. While the junta called for dialogue with the left and army restraint in dealing with a plethora of pro-guerrilla union strikes, demonstrations, and land occupations, the shadow government was at work massacring protesters and leaders of the democratic left. Uncomfortable with the leftists included in the government, Ambassador Devine stood aside.

This was the most crucial moment in modern Salvadoran history, as the moderates who survived in the junta struggled openly against both the far-right and the far-left. The only actor who might have been powerful enough to propel events toward a centrist outcome was the Carter administration. But unable to reconcile his human rights policy with a commitment to anticommunism, Carter waivered. The administration rushed six Green Berets and $300,000 in fresh military aid as a sign of support to the junta, but by the time it moved to bolster the moderates four months later, most of the best people in the government had already resigned.

· · ·

In its early days, the junta moved to abolish Orden and Ansesal and to cashier dozens of right-wing officers, including National Guard intelligence chief Maj. Roberto D'Aubuisson. The hard-liners, however, made sure such acts were mere formalities. Junta member Colonel Gutiérrez reportedly allowed D'Aubuisson, a burning anti-Communist with a tense jaw and shifting eyes, to filch Ansesal's files on the country's leftists from the presidential house. Those files, which the CIA had designed more than a decade before, would now be used to kill thousands of people and destabilize a junta that the Carter administration officially supported.

Born to a father who was a door-to-door salesman and a mother who was a civil servant, D'Aubuisson began his military training at age fifteen. He graduated from the San Salvador military academy near the bottom of his class; but what D'Aubuisson lacked in academic ability, he made up for with determination, raw energy, and guile. While superior students entered the more prestigious army, D'Aubuisson was assigned to the National Guard, the rural security force detailed to controlling peasant discontent. While other officers demonstrated a fascination for weaponry and battlefield tactics, D'Aubuisson, with his photographic memory, excelled in interrogating prisoners and assembling files on suspects. His superiors sent him to New York and Virginia for police intelligence courses, and then to Taiwan to study counterintelligence and Communist subversion. National Guard Commander General Medrano took a shine to D'Aubuisson. He assigned the young lieutenant to the kind of sensitive missions that earned D'Aubuisson a fearsome reputation and a fond nickname from the general as one of "my little assassins."

On Medrano's recommendation, the Salvadoran military high command assigned D'Aubuisson in the mid-1970s to the International Police Academy in Washington and the School of the Americas in the Panama Canal Zone, leading to his ascent to the rank of major and to the position of intelligence chief of the National Guard, and finally to deputy director of Ansesal. In that position, operating out of General Romero's presidential palace, he was a coordinator of a half dozen intelligence agencies attached to the armed forces. Years later, D'Aubuisson's superior, Col. Roberto Eulalio Santíbañez, the head of Ansesal until 1979, said that D'Aubuisson was the principal officer assigned to targeting victims for death squads.

D'Aubuisson was one of the leaders of a cabal of about fifty businessmen, landowners, and military officers who expanded the country's major death squads, which called themselves the Squadron of Death, the Secret Anti-Communist Army, and the Maximiliano Hernández Martínez Brigade—the last in honor of the dictator responsible for the 1932 massacre. A powerful coalition was emerging. According to published reports, a few oligarchs, particularly coffee and cotton multimillionaires Roberto Sol Meza and Orlando de Sola, provided the financing for weapons and logistics. Led by Deputy Defense Minister Carranza, army right-wing ideologues provided the military resources. (Sol Meza, de Sola and Carranza have denied any involvement with the death squads.) Tens of thousands of peasant families who had been associated with Orden provided the movement with a social base and volunteers.

While the right-wing militarists set up death squads, paramilitary militias, and safe houses around the country, like-minded wealthy landowners and industrialists formed a public political support group called the Broad National Front (FAN)—the first step toward the founding of a political party, the Nationalist Republican Alliance (Arena). The cabal usually coordinated its activities with the G-2 intelligence sections of the National Police, the Treasury Police, and the National Guard, with the support and coordination of Deputy Defense Minister Carranza.

It is not certain that D'Aubuisson was the most important leader of the death-squad network, but he certainly was the most public. He appeared on national television almost weekly to read names from the Ansesal files, and within days the people named would die. D'Aubuisson identified Mario Zamora, the Christian Democratic attorney general, as a clandestine guerrilla during one broadcast in February 1980. A couple of days later, gunmen burst into Zamora's home as he was giving a party. To protect his guests, Zamora identified himself to the death-squad assailants; they then forced him into a bathroom and shot him in the head. Zamora's killing nearly destroyed the government. The Christian Democratic party pledged to quit the junta unless those responsible for the assassination were brought to justice. But no one was arrested, and D'Aubuisson was subject to no official questioning about the matter.

The left-wing group in the government was outraged. As much as a third of the Christian Democratic leadership, including Mario's brother Rubén, the junta's chief of staff, resigned from the government and the party. What was left of the Christian Democratic party threatened to leave the government unless the army finally fulfilled its pledge to promulgate sweeping reforms. On March 6, 1980, the army complied; they occupied more than two hundred large estates and handed them over to peasant committees representing more than 150,000 farmhands. It was a decision that cost the country's forty top families several hundred million dollars. The junta nationalized banking and receipts on foreign trade to ease credit for the new cooperatives and to finance an array of new social projects. The junta leaders, Colonels Majano and Gutiérrez and newly appointed Christian Democratic member José Napoleón Duarte, declared the beginning of a democratic social revolution.

Robert White, the new American ambassador, applauded the Salvadoran program "as the most revolutionary land reform in Latin American history." The outspoken Boston Irishman came to El Salvador with firm instructions from the Carter administration and Congress to clean up the Salvadoran regime and open the way for elections and social change. At a Senate confirmation hearing, Senator Jacob Javits of New York, a Republican, told White: "You are a proconsul, so far as we are concerned. . . . You really have to be an activist and take a chance with your career. If not, this just isn't going to go." Not in the country a month, White discovered how powerless a proconsul can feel in El Salvador.

On the morning of March 24, 1980, Archbishop Oscar Arnulfo Romero spent a lengthy session with his confessor. Friends say he knew his days were numbered. The threats against his life came daily now. Romero knew that his homily the day before may have sealed his death warrant. He had urged soldiers to disobey orders to kill: "I beseech you, I beg you, I order you in the name of God. Stop the repression!"

That evening, Romero was to say mass in the chapel of a Church-run cancer hospital. Associates had urged Romero to cancel his appearance after local newspapers publicized his scheduled visit. But Romero wanted to keep his appointment; the mass was in honor of the late mother of a friend, Jorge Pinto, a radical journalist whose newspaper, *El Independiente,* had been bombed and closed by the military. At the end of Romero's homily, a single assassin stepped into the central aisle, trained his high-powered rifle at the archbishop, and pumped a single bullet through Romero's heart. The assassin was never caught, though he was reputedly later murdered by right-wing colleagues to keep him quiet.

Colonel Majano, the most liberal member of the junta, suspected D'Aubuisson immediately. Majano was a brilliant chess player, but as a leader on the five-man junta, he rarely showed boldness or imagination. The Romero assassination convinced him his reform movement was fading. When loyal officers discovered plans for a meeting by right-wing officers at a farm outside San Salvador to plot a coup, Majano telephoned Panamanian dictator Gen. Omar Torrijos, who urged Majano to move against D'Aubuisson.

Majano dispatched a force of soldiers to surround the farmhouse and seize anyone found inside. They arrested D'Aubuisson and more than a dozen officers, including several who have since been identified as leaders of death squads and a kidnapping ring. Majano loyalists also captured a detailed notebook, kept by air force Capt. Alvaro Rafael Saravia, one of the officers arrested. The notebook noted arms purchases, connections to financiers in the oligarchy, and the links between intelligence sections of the security forces and army. There was an entry for Operation Pineapple—which Ambassador White and other analysts identified as the plot to assassinate Archbishop Romero—listing the purchases of a night-vision scope, automatic pistols and rifles, and four security guards.*

The arrests shook the army. Some reformist officers called on Majano to take over the government and open a dialogue with the left. But most militarymen were shocked that Majano would arrest fellow officers without first consulting the high command. As coup rumors intensified, White and Duarte toured army barracks across El Salvador together to urge calm. Majano waivered, as a military judge dropped the charges against all the officers, and the high command transferred all his allies from key command positions.

"This is a baloney coup," joked U.S. embassy spokesman Howard Lane. "The right cuts the junta one slice at a time. And we're left trying to hold the slices together."

Dan Freedman and I began traveling regularly by bus from Guatemala City to San Salvador in October 1980. What we saw in El Salvador was beyond Washington's ability to comprehend—it had little to do with any civilized society, capitalist or Communist.

---

*Seven years later, Antonio Amado Garay, Captain Saravia's driver, testified in a Salvadoran court that it was he who drove the assassin to the chapel where the archbishop was killed, and that he had later overheard Saravia report to D'Aubuisson that the mission had been completed. To this day, no one has been prosecuted for the crime.

Part of our daily routine was to hitch along with network television crews on morning drives around San Salvador, checking roads and leftist barrios for tortured bodies. The victims included a pregnant woman with her belly slit open and a man with his castrated penis sticking out of his mouth. Most bodies were simply shot up, with notes tied around their necks identifying the death squad responsible for the crime. We would find a few every day—and our searches were incomplete and unsystematic. More than two hundred people were dying like this every week around the country.

One night I went to the city morgue following the police raid of a rebel safe house. More than twenty bodies were heaped together behind the morgue; a handful of women in the pile had their panties and stockings rolled down to their knees. I didn't understand it at the time, but the death squads were accomplishing their task: destroying the rebel urban and (to a lesser extent) rural popular base, and terrorizing everyone else. The guerrillas would never recover from the 1980–83 repression, which devastated their urban cadres.

Another night, on a bus between San Salvador and Santa Tecla, I struck up a conversation with a skinny eleven-year-old boy wearing tattered pants who collected fares from passengers. His name was Reynaldo Fuentes, and he earned the equivalent of $1.50 a day and permission to sleep in the rusty vehicle for his labor. Reynaldo was a war orphan from Jocoaitique, a village in the eastern province of Morazán, and he told me his story. One night a gang of men broke into his house and killed his parents, two brothers, and two sisters while they were still sleeping in bed. Reynaldo jumped out the window, badly cutting his arm, and he hitchhiked hundreds of miles to San Salvador. "I can never go back there again," Reynaldo told me. His smudged face, tearless, even passionless, looked too serious to be that of a child. "They would kill me, too." I asked who "they" could be. Reynaldo shrugged. "Who knows?"

One day we interviewed Leonel Gómez, the number-two man in the government land reform institute. Gómez talked about the army's corruption and violence, and how he himself had once narrowly escaped the wrath of the death squads by hiding in a pile of garbage. "The people don't have faith in the government; I'm a government employee and I don't have any."

We asked him how it was possible that a government could give land to the peasants with one hand and take their lives away with the other. Dan asked him point-blank, "If the government is so bad, how come you work for it?" Gómez lost his patience, "You Americans, you'll never understand El Salvador!"

"Señor Gómez," I pleaded, "that's why we're here—to learn about your country."

"You really want to know El Salvador?" he asked. When we assured him that we truly did, Gómez offered to send us out into the country-side with his top team of technicians, the team he sent to the toughest parts of the country. We assured him that we were ready. The four Salvadorans Gómez recommended agreed to take us with them on their rounds for a few days on the condition that we buy the beer. We gladly agreed, and the next day we were off.

The first morning, six of us drove west in a government jeep to the sprawling La Carrera cotton hacienda, the prize farm of Juan Wright, one of the wealthiest oligarchs in the land. Only seven months before, the junta had rewarded more than four hundred peasants membership in a new cooperative, as it did at a total of 263 nationalized estates. The peasants at La Carrera elected a governing board, sustained production, and built new housing with their profits. The jaguar cages and swimming pool in Wright's backyard were empty, but the closets of his ranch-style mansion were still well stocked with alligator shoes and European suits. "This will be a museum one day," said a peasant farmer at La Carrera. "We try not to touch Señor Wright's house."

The next day we saw a different side of the land reform, at the El Peñón cattle ranch. As at La Carrera, a peasant board of directors was in charge, but while production appeared to be going well, a sense of gloom prevailed. Five truckloads of army troops had broken the hopes of the cooperative membership only four months before. On June 12, 1980, National Guard troops rounded up seven peasants, five of them co-op directors, lined them up on a clay bank along a path on the ranch, and executed them. (Some two hundred peasants had been similarly killed by soldiers and paramilitary death squads seeking to reverse the land reform.)

For days, the corpses at El Peñón rotted in the mud. Their fellow workers were afraid to move them until local authorities gave them permission to bury the bodies. Seven crosses marked the victims' graves on a small patch of land in clear view. "Our lives are improving," said one rancher who asked not to be quoted by name, "but there is always this feeling of insecurity."

We traveled with Leonel's team north to Chalatenango province in search of the guerrillas. We failed to find more than two or three, but we managed to make it to Las Vueltas, where we found a makeshift refugee camp full of Orden families guarded by National Guard troops. The men had a nasty look about them, unkempt and hard. The women and children looked disoriented under disheveled lean-tos. Like the ranchers of El Peñón, they had terrible stories to tell. They said they were victims caught in the middle; the junta didn't support or respect them while the guerrillas wanted to clear them out of the countryside. "The Communists," said one large mustachioed man who called himself Juan, "are oppressing us. They forced us out of our houses. They hanged one of my friends and his entire family—all five of them." I knew about Orden, and I resisted feeling sympathy for people I thought of as thugs; but Juan's story gnawed at me nevertheless. There seemed to be little decency in any quarter.

We wanted to reach the El Pichiche land reform cooperative before dark the next day, but even for our four-wheel-drive vehicle the going was slow, along the rutted unpaved roads near the Pacific shoreline. El Pichiche had been organized by the Popular Revolutionary Bloc, a leftist group tied to the guerrillas. The people who lived there could go either way; the land reform might sway them to the side of the junta, or perhaps they would join the rebels in the hills.

As we curved around a bend, a motley group of about ten gunmen, armed with a variety of weapons, climbed out of two patches of bushes and blocked our vehicle. At first glance I gleefully thought we had finally found the guerrillas. Our Salvadoran guides knew better. A beefy uniformed National Guard sergeant led the band. This was probably a reconstituted Orden unit attacking the land reform.

"On the ground," one of the gunmen ordered us. I figured my American passport would do some good in this situation, but the gunman shepherding me out of the jeep looked at it upside down, probably because he couldn't read and didn't know what this document meant anyway. Dan, our four Salvadoran friends, and I stretched out on the ground, in the middle of the road, with our arms and legs stretched out. I felt my heart hammer at my ribs. Why, I thought, didn't the Salvadorans say something, anything to get us out of this? Our friends were as frozen by the same terror as we were.

Finally, one of them exclaimed, with all the authority he could muster, "We're from the government." Without hesitation, the gunmen changed their attitude. They helped us off the ground and dusted us off with their bare hands. "Why didn't you say so before," laughed the National Guardsman.

Their friendliness had limits. They ordered us to turn back, which we did. Then they attacked El Pichiche. We heard the firing in the distance as we drove away as fast as we could to the nearest bar where for hours we celebrated being alive. We later heard that the peasants at El Pichiche successfully defended their cooperative and forced the gunmen into a hasty retreat.

Bill Hallman, then chief of the political section at the U.S. embassy, called me into his office to hear about our experience. Hallman was clearly shaken, and he let down his diplomatic guard. "You know, Cliff," he said with a sigh, "I served in Argentina during the worst days of the dirty war, and it was never as bad as this. I think we have to try to stop the guerrillas here, but I wake up at night wondering, How much worse could they possibly make this place?" The moral ambiguities seemed to trouble and demoralize much of the U.S. embassy.

Just as we were completing our talk, there was an explosion, and the embassy lights went out. The guerrillas had attacked the embassy compound with a single shot from an RPG-2 rocket-launcher. There was scattered gunfire. Bill and I fell to the ground. It took more than a half hour for government forces to arrive at the compound, suggesting they didn't consider the U.S. embassy a building particularly worthy of defense. Hallman was worried. "It makes you wonder, Who are our friends here?"

Ambassador White was still a faithful friend to the junta's main liberal, Colonel Majano, in hopes of reforming the military and negotiating with the left. The ambassador branded D'Aubuisson a terrorist and refused him a visa to the United States. But such gestures were mostly symbolic, given that the far-right was winning on most issues. Conservative officers blocked the nationalization of middle-size coffee farms, a crucial phase of the land reform. Investigation of army human rights abuses and corruption was a dead issue. Death-squad killings rose to one hundred a week.

The Carter administration thought its policy of increasing military aid as a carrot for more progressive government behavior would move El Salvador in a moderate direction. But in its desire to break the oligarchy and redistribute wealth, it helped reinforce a far more repressive force, the armed forces. That policy would carry through the Reagan administration.

· · ·

The night of Ronald Reagan's election victory, embassy spokesman Howard Lane handed out Reagan-Bush buttons to embassy personnel and guests at a cocktail party at the El Presidente Hotel. Lane's gesture was an obvious joke; a close associate of White's, he was a known Jimmy Carter booster. The diplomats felt obliged to appear satisfied with the Reagan landslide, but to each other they whispered their dismay. Outside the El Presidente, reaction to the Reagan victory was less cautious: the guerrillas blew up a downtown San Salvador McDonald's. San Salvador's wealthy neighborhoods of Escalón and San Francisco were joyous. Their residents discharged their shotguns into the sky, dragged their marimbas into the streets, and danced with glee.

Salvadoran right-wingers blamed their troubles on Jimmy Carter's human rights policy and the "Communist" Ambassador White. Now things would change. The Republican platform called for a strong U.S. policy against Russian and Cuban subversion in Central America, without bothering to mention the problem of death-squad violence. Candidate Reagan had told his audiences that a human rights policy, however noble in intent, should not destroy old allies as it had the Shah of Iran and Anastasio Somoza of Nicaragua. He believed Carter's Latin America policies were counterproductive and had to be reversed; toleration of right-wing murderers was unfortunate but necessary in the untidy world of geopolitics.

In the days following the November 4 election, John Carbaugh, an aide to Senator Jesse Helms and a member of the Reagan transition team, flew to Guatemala City to meet with D'Aubuisson and Guatemalan ultraright politician Mario Sandoval Alarcón. On the same tour, he flew to Argentina to meet with members of the military junta. The very fact that these meetings took place was interpreted throughout Central America as a sign that the new administration would tolerate the activities of the far-right, however violent. Helms personally did D'Aubuisson the greatest favor during the transition by convincing incoming White House special counselor Edwin Meese to get the visa restrictions against D'Aubuisson lifted. The right saw only a green light from Washington, and returned to its strategy of high-profile assassinations.

On November 27, one hundred policemen surrounded a San Salvador Catholic high school while gunmen seized six leaders of the Democratic Revolutionary Front, an influential social democratic group. The gunmen piled the activists into a van, tortured them, and dropped their bodies on the shores of Lake Ilopango. D'Aubuisson publicly applauded the action and traveled around to the country's army barracks urging officers to join him in a coup. Outraged, White rushed to the scene of the crime, but his censure was undercut from Washington. Jeane Kirkpatrick, incoming ambassador to the United Nations, commented, "People who choose to live by the sword can expect to die by it."

Next, the Salvadoran right turned their guns on Americans. On December 2, four National Guardsmen stopped three American nuns and an American lay volunteer at a roadblock, then raped and killed them. Two days later, as Ambassador White watched the churchwomen's bodies being unearthed beside a country road, he swore, "This time they won't get away with it." Again White was undercut by Kirkpatrick, who told the *Tampa Tribune*, "The nuns were not just nuns. They were political activists." The only officer to suffer for the nuns' killing had nothing to do with the crime; hard-liners forced Colonel Majano, the hapless liberal, to resign. On January 3, 1981, the right struck again. Gunmen, taking orders from two military intelligence officers, marched into the dining room of San Salvador's Sheraton Hotel, pulled their machine pistols, and at point-blank range shot two American land reform advisers and a top Salvadoran peasant leader.

Frustrated by his lack of influence on the far-right in El Salvador and the incoming Reagan administration, Ambassador White resorted to a broadside in the American press. He complained to reporters from the *New York Times* and *Washington Post* that the transition team was undermining him by leaking papers criticizing the El Salvador land reform and suggesting that he be fired. He groused that Cleto DiGiovanni, Jr., a former CIA station chief in Guatemala and candidate for a National Security Council (NSC) post, skirted the embassy when he came to El Salvador to build ties with far-rightists. The activities of the Reagan transition team, he said, rendered irrelevant his efforts and those by Duarte and moderate Salvadoran officers toward building the center. "When civil war breaks out in this country," he said bitterly, "I hope they get their chance to serve."

For their part, the guerrillas quickly realized that the incoming administration was ready to do whatever was necessary to stop them from winning the war. On January 10, 1981, with Cuban and Nicaraguan military aid, they staged a massive multipronged attack, which they called the Final Offensive, on San Salvador and several other cities. An army barracks in Santa Ana deserted, but everywhere else military units held. After three days, the offensive dissolved. The expected popular insurrection never materialized. It was the first sign that the government's repression had effectively decapitated much of the opposition and traumatized the civilian population.

The new Reagan administration made El Salvador the first battle cry on its foreign policy agenda. The handwringing Carter years were over. Secretary of State Alexander Haig said the administration "would draw the line" on Soviet expansion in El Salvador, even if that meant taking military action against Cuba—"going to the source," as he put it, of the arms shipments to the FMLN guerrillas. El Salvador, Haig assured Reagan at one White House meeting, "is one we can win."

The administration outlined its view of the El Salvador crisis on February 23, 1981, with the release of its White Paper entitled "Communist Interference in El Salvador." Based on more than ten pounds of captured rebel documents, the White Paper charged that Salvadoran Communist party leader Shafik Hándal had traveled to Vietnam, Ethiopia, and four Eastern European countries seeking weapons for the guerrilla cause. There also was evidence that weapons shipped from Cuba were transferred through Sandinista Nicaragua on their way to El Salvador. The White Paper concluded that El Salvador represented a "textbook case of indirect armed aggression by Communist powers." In response to the findings, the NSC developed an aid program for El Salvador that included $91 million in fresh military and economic aid and the deployment of fifty-six Green Beret advisers (an increase from the twenty Carter had sent). Thomas Enders, the Assistant Secretary of State for Inter-American Affairs, described the administration's vision of El Salvador this way: "If, after Nicaragua, El Salvador is captured by a violent minority, what state in Central America will be able to resist, how long would it be before the major strategic U.S. interests—the [Panama] canal, sea lanes, oil supplies—were at risk?"

The initial Reagan administration disregard for human rights unleashed a backlash that the administration ultimately had to accommodate. Fueled by the killings of Romero and the American churchwomen, churches across the United States mobilized against the war. Six nuns occupied the offices of Charles Percy, the senator from Illinois and the chairman of the Foreign Relations Committee, until they were forcibly removed by police. Senators and congressmen received thousands of letters and telegrams—most written from church congregations—urging them to vote against aid to El Salvador. There were signs that the antiwar student movement was also resuscitating. Some 30,000 students marched on Washington against the war, and demonstrations were becoming a regular feature of campus life. Bumper stickers began appearing around the United States that read: "El Salvador Means Vietnam in Spanish."

Forty-one House Democrats and four Democratic senators introduced bills in March to cut all military aid to El Salvador. Lacking the votes, two Democratics—Senator Christopher Dodd of Connecticut and Congressman Stephen Solarz of New York—came up with a compromise that would force the administration's hand on human rights. Their legislation required the president to "certify" every six months that San Salvador was: investigating the killings of the American land reform workers and American churchwomen, improving human rights, pushing ahead with land reform and elections, and attempting to find a negotiated settlement to the war. Otherwise, Congress would force the administration to halt aid and withdraw the advisers.

White House aides Edwin Meese and James Baker were aware of the depth of feeling in Congress, and they were concerned that such resistance could hurt the administration's conservative domestic agenda. They urged Reagan to compromise, and their approach was strongly supported by the State Department and U.S. embassy in El Salvador. The new American ambassador to El Salvador, Deane Hinton, shared his predecessor's conviction that a military victory could only be based on social reform and democratic rule.

Embassy "Grim-Grams," the weekly reports on human rights abuses, documented the systematic repression of unions and peasant organizations. The land reform had stalled. Joblessness was growing. And the war was going poorly. The Salvadoran army was slow to learn and slower to fight. Despite the Pentagon's prodding, the Salvadoran armed forces remained a "nine-to-five army," one that maneuvered only in large units—and never at night. Salvadoran officers infuriated the advisers by insisting on spending their weekends in San Salvador, comfortably away from the war. By 1982, the guerrillas loosely controlled more than half the countryside. With the support of his superiors in the State Department, Ambassador Hinton pushed the Reagan administration to reverse its initial policy and back the various social and political reforms first pushed by the Carter administration.

The ambassador and his chief military aide, Special Forces Col. John Waghelstein, were two cigar-chomping, poker-playing men who married Salvadoran women and grew to appreciate the harsh realities of El Salvador. Hinton and Waghelstein discovered a disproportionate number of guerrilla attacks were targeted at the land reform around the country and specifically in Usulután and San Vicente provinces, where the lion's share of El Salvador's agricultural exports are produced. "We went back to the counterinsurgency, low-intensity conflict book that had been unfashionable since Vietnam and dusted it off—land reform, military force restructuring, psychological operations, human rights," said Waghelstein, himself a Vietnam veteran. "If we were going to win this war, we had to win it economically and politically. We concluded that the most important piece of turf was the six inches between the ears of every peasant."

Out of the embassy sessions chaired by Hinton and Waghelstein came the National Plan, designed to sweep Usulután and San Vicente provinces clean of guerrillas, and then implement a massive public works program employing thousands of refugees to rebuild schools, housing, bridges, and roads. The plan harvested mixed results. Successful in San Vicente at flushing out the guerrillas for a time, it was a disaster in Usulután. First, the guerrillas managed to thwart the army as it tried to drive them from this southeastern province of lowland swamps and rugged mountains. The embassy's strategy also ran into trouble when local Salvadoran officials stole lumber, medicine, and food for use by their own families or sale on the black market. The rebels also stole supplies, but they at least used them the way the embassy had intended. The guerrillas built schools, offered classes, and set up health clinics with the stolen supplies, thereby making their pitch for popular support more credible.

The embassy made a priority of pushing the legislative elections in March 1982. Hinton and Waghelstein counted on the election of centrists to the Constituent Assembly, which would write a constitution, appoint a Supreme Court, and select a provisional president to replace the junta. Although the Christian Democrats won a comfortable plurality, D'Aubuisson and his Arena party showed surprising strength and were able to fashion a right-wing coalition with smaller conservative parties to take control of the new legislature.

Suddenly it looked as if the assembly would choose Roberto

D'Aubuisson as the next president of El Salvador, and that, in turn, the U.S. Congress would cut off all aid. Reagan dispatched trouble-shooter Vernon Walters to El Salvador to deliver a message to top army officers: block D'Aubuisson's election. The high command duti-fully agreed, and the legislators selected Alvaro Magaña, a mild-man-nered banker known for giving officers easy loans. D'Aubuisson rose to the presidency of the assembly instead, where he played a leading role in paralyzing much of the land reform and selecting a far-right-wing Supreme Court. According to published sources, he also established a new group of death-squad killers, enlisting the assembly's security guards, whose ammunition was kept in an assembly storage room. The new democracy and the old-fashioned fascism made an uneasy mix.

The Reagan administration began talking tough about human rights in the fall of 1983 as death-squad activity surged again and Salvadoran courts blocked progress on the cases of the American churchwomen and labor advisers. Concerned that the deterioration in the human rights situation could lead to an eventual congressional aid cutoff, U.S. embassy personnel took matters into their own hands. They began leaking to the press U.S. intelligence information on the death-squad network. Vice President George Bush rushed down to San Salvador that December to read the riot act. At a dinner hosted by President Magaña, Bush spoke in no uncertain terms: "Every murderous act [the death squads] commit poisons the well of friendship between our two countries and advances the cause of those who would impose an alien dictatorship on the people of El Salvador. These cowardly death-squad terrorists are just as repugnant to me, to President Reagan, to the U.S. Congress, and to the American people as the terrorists of the left." Then Bush privately handed the high command a list of a dozen officers to be thrown out of the armed forces. As usual, the Salvadorans complied with the pressure in part, firing or transferring a number of officers to diplomatic posts out of the country. But not a single officer was prosecuted. When push came to shove, the Salvadoran army never believed the United States would abandon them to a guerrilla victory.

THE GUERRILLAS

I made contact with the Popular Liberation Forces (FPL), one of the five Salvadoran guerrilla groups in the FMLN coalition, through their representatives in Mexico City. I paid the rebels an advance of $100 for food and other expenses.

It was December 1981 when I set off with two left-wing solidarity journalists, one West German and the other Argentine. We received our final instructions in Managua, Nicaragua, and drove a borrowed rickety van 240 miles to Tegucigalpa, Honduras. We needed to sneak across the Honduran border into the deepest rebel territory in El Salvador. Posing as relief workers, we rented a plane to fly to a refugee camp on the Honduran-Salvadoran border, where we would begin our hike into the northern Salvadoran province of Chalatenango. After a few days of waiting, we were off—with a caravan of refugees and guerrillas carrying bags of corn and rice and other supplies to the rebels. For three days and nights we walked, passing small guerrilla outposts and hamlets of rebel supporters along the way. Several villages were empty, having been torched to the ground by the army. One destroyed church carried the graffiti inscription: "The Atlacatl Battalion was here" with a skull and bones for the "o" in battalion.

This was a different El Salvador than the country I knew. Despite the presence of deep trenches and bomb shelters in every village, and talk of the coming "enemy" offensive, this rearguard "controlled zone" had a happy, liberated feel about it. Peasants happily offered us tortillas and oranges along the way, and they wanted to talk politics. That came as a surprise; I had taken it for granted that Salvadoran peasants always kept their thoughts to themselves out of fear. Here, residents bragged that they were part of a social experiment that would someday replace the "sick, capitalist society." People felt responsibility to one another, and responsibility to their nation.

One night a peasant family offered me shelter in their mud shack. I slept on the sandy floor beside the husband and wife and their two children. They insisted that I take their only blanket to protect myself from the night's chill mountain air. In gratitude, I offered to lend them my short-band radio—they turned the dial to Radio Havana without hesitation. We dozed off, huddling together to share body heat. When I apologized for my odor from the days of hiking, they told me not to worry; and early the next morning, the woman of the house, Irma, fetched water from a nearby river before I awakened so I could bathe. "This is socialism," she explained. "If we are to make a new El Salvador, people have to look out for each other."

I needed all the help I could get. After days of tough hiking with little to eat, I could barely stand up anymore. My legs were terribly sore, and I had an unquenchable thirst. Fleas attacked my ankles and stomach, leaving annoying allergic rashes over much of my body. The rebels saddled up a horse for me, and we continued on to our destination—the village of Portillo del Norte—to celebrate New Year's Eve.

As I rode up the small mountain leading to the village, I saw peasant women chattering in happy clusters, slapping uncooked meat pies into neat triangles for roasting. Peasant men slaughtered five steers, then tied the carcasses from tree limbs and shred them with crude stubby machetes. Normally, rebel villages barbecued skewers of salted beef about once a week; fresh meat was a treat behind the lines, one reserved for religious holidays and military victories.

Portillo del Norte celebrated New Year's Eve with verve. The revolution was still young enough to believe the rhetoric about "inevitable victory," even though the general population hadn't obeyed a rebel call for insurrection the previous January. Two dozen "revolutionary youth" provided the entertainment for hundreds of guerrillas and villagers who gathered, forming a theater in the round, by the light of a gas lantern.

In one skit, a child lottery vender attempted several sales pitches to the other actors without success, because none had any money to buy a chance. The vender tried his luck at begging, but that didn't work any better. Left without choices, the vender joined the guerrillas. His vision clarified, he shouted, "If Nicaragua won, El Salvador will win!"

The skits over, a grizzled, straw-hatted peasant leader stood up and gave a lecture about the national legislative elections coming in March, the first vote since the coup of 1979. "The enemy wants to gain prestige," the peasant explained. "But we know that elections will never bring popular revolution. We are fighting for a society in which we are all brothers. A society where there is no egotism. A society of love. We have to change man!"

Over my three weeks of hiking and living behind the lines I found that the guerrillas and their "masses" had tremendous morale and discipline fed by two basic motivations. One was a mixture of political and religious faith in the possibility of creating a better future. The other was pure and simple vengeance. Almost everyone I met had lost at least one relative to Orden or the military.

In the village of La Laguna, I met a petite, pretty, and confident fifteen-year-old militiawoman named Irena. Her bright red plastic earrings belied a tough ideological line that ran off her lips as an endless complaint: "The oligarchy owns everything. We don't have to live under this domination. . . . In the capitalist system, women are instruments of men. That doesn't have to be."

I asked Irena what convinced her to go to war. Stiffening her back and face, she told me how Salvadoran and Honduran army troops cut down her parents and five sisters nineteen months before in a frenzy of gunfire and mortar shelling aimed at hundreds of refugees escaping across the Sumpul River into the Honduran hills. Irena climbed ashore soaked in her family's blood. "When I saw my entire family dead in the river," she said of her political baptism, "I decided I had to fight the enemy with a rifle in my hand." She spoke to me as she greased her Korean War–era M-2 carbine.

Despite constant battle preparations, what passed for everyday life went on. Peasant women spent their days pressing tortillas with stones, sewing uniforms, and washing clothes. Peasant men, pistols at their sides, worked the fields as always. When they weren't in school, children carried wooden logs on their shoulders and filled sandbags. There were makeshift barber shops and primitive health clinics. Small churches around the region had been torched and otherwise desecrated by the army, but that didn't stop villagers from praying together in the charred ruins at least twice a week. Even romance thrived behind the lines.

"The revolution makes love more passionate because we are comrades," remarked Marlin, a twenty-two-year-old guerrilla saboteur, as he squeezed his girlfriend, Roxana, a nurse, around the waist. Roxana, who was seventeen, said the two had met three weeks before when she was transferred to the rebel health clinic at La Laguna. "We will get married whether an enemy offensive comes or not. The war can only delay the wedding day, not stop it. . . . It is difficult to have a baby now, but I will be able to take care of it. After the revolution, children will have a chance to live better. That is why we are fighting."

The rebels were already building an alternative society in Chalatenango. La Laguna, a typical rebel village, was governed by a "people's power" government that collectivized farming in 1981 after expropriating land left behind by fleeing Orden families and others who didn't want to live with the guerrillas. A five-man civilian directorate, popularly elected but ultimately managed by the FPL party, took responsibility for such decisions and supervised a Women's Committee, a Production Committee, and the Organization of Children. The directorate proudly pointed to the improvement of the peasant diet by diversifying crop cultivation to include tomatoes, cabbage, and garlic. The directorate initiated surveys to determine the needs of every family and specify how much working time each farmer ought to devote to his individual plot and how much to collectivized land. Periodically, a representative of La Laguna's directorate would meet with representatives of other villages in the so-called Council of People's Power Secretariats, where they regulated regional trade of oranges, coffee, and salted freshwater fish.

"Part of our strategy is to control more and more territory and organize more and more people," Comandante Salvador Guerra, a member of the FPL high command, told me. "This is as much to win the war as it is to organize a revolutionary government that represents the interests of the people. Our people administer their own people— economic production, agriculture, housing reconstruction, health, and education—with whatever resources are available."

I witnessed guerrilla education in the nearby village of El Jicaro. Mireira, the nineteen-year-old teacher, wore a lime chiffon dress over her black army boots. She began the first-grade class, the first of the term, with two questions:

"Are you all going to be the militiamen and guerrillas of the future?"

"Yes," cried the forty students, who ranged in age from five to twelve.

"And are you going to fight the enemy?"

"Yes!" the children screamed.

Following a spirited cacophonous rendition of the FPL hymn, Mireira wrote on the blackboard: "My mother takes part in the war" and "Father, mother, and I work in the home as a collective." The older children dutifully read aloud, many smiling with pride at their accomplishment. Many of their parents could not read their own names. After ninety minutes of rigorous reading and writing drills, the students filed off the porch of the abandoned ranch house that served as a school for what amounted to recess: frolicking ambush drills through the forests. After class, the kids dug trenches around the village perimeter.

The woman in charge of education in that sector of Chalatenango was a gritty nun named Sister Rosa. It took me and my armed escort three days to backpack through guerrilla territory, from La Laguna to Patamera, in order to meet her. I found Sister Rosa sewing and chatting with peasant women on the porch of her one-room adobe house, a short run from the nearest trenches. She showed me a book containing the photographs of thirteen nuns and priests who had been killed by death squads in El Salvador since 1977. "He who defends the poor can be crucified at any time," she said.

Sister Rosa was eager to talk about the rebel cooperative farms flourishing in Chalatenango. "The early Christians lived in communities like ours. One helped the other. Like in socialism. It is clear from [the Gospel of] Saint Paul what kind of community they had. Our base communities put into practice mutual help, like in the days of the early Christians. If I love God, I have to love my brother." Sister Rosa interrupted the interview to speak to a sobbing teenage mother who requested an emergency final-hour baptism for her dying infant daughter. "In this country such a child could live if it had a rich family that could afford the necessary hospital care," Sister Rosa told me later, "but here such a poor child dies."

The guerrillas and their supporters won my admiration for their attempts at building a more humane society. But the mind control I witnessed at the school troubled me. Salvador Cayetano Carpio (alias "Marcial"), the FPL commander-in-chief, demanded such total obedience from his followers that his movement took on the look of a messianic religious cult.

At least three times a day, in every village behind the lines, guerrillas, militiamen, and supporters lined up in neat rows to dutifully recite the incantation: "Comandante, Solo Hay Uno, Marcial! Comandante, There Only Is One, Marcial! Comandante, Solo Hay Uno, Marcial! . . ." They would go on for a minute or so, never breaking the repetitious monotone.

The rebels treated Marcial as a prophet, not as a human being. At sixty-two, he had more experience and international contacts than anyone in the entire rebel movement. A seminarian as a youth, Marcial went on to be leader of the bakers' union and secretary general of the

Communist party until he quit in 1970 to found the FPL. Under his leadership, the FPL grew from a small underground cell in San Salvador into a popular movement that operated through much of the country.

I never got to meet Marcial, but I was repeatedly told he was "scientific," "correct," and "visionary." Rebel fighters spent their days memorizing Marcial's mimeographed pamphlet entitled "El Salvador: The Prolonged Popular War." To rise up the ranks, from militiaman, to local guerrilla, to regular guerrilla, and finally to vanguard unit, the guerrilla fighter was tested on his or her knowledge of Marcial's dogma, or "mystique."

Marcial's dream went something like this: the FPL army and party would meticulously educate and organize the workers and peasants, even if it took years before they would rise up to crush the army. Then the Salvadorans would join forces with other Central American rebels and spread the revolution beyond El Salvador's borders. Marcial anticipated that the United States would intervene, and the Central Americans would duplicate the heroism of the Vietnamese and bury the Yankees once and for all. Marcial liked to be called the Ho Chi Minh of Central America, and he purposely groomed his wispy beard so he might look like the Vietnamese leader.

I was struck by the FPL's fanaticism and orthodoxy. I raised my concern to a couple of guerrilla commanders in a late-night talk over syrupy coffee and cigarettes. In a moment of animation, I told them of my skepticism. "If you follow the path of Vietnam, North Korea, or the Soviet Union," I said, "you are making a big mistake!" I knew I had stepped over the line. "I mean," trying to recover, "you don't have to be Stalinists." One of the guerrillas snapped back at me, "Make your own revolution." We changed the subject.

But what I said was true, we would find out. Marcial's cultism was indeed eating away at the movement. Comandantes of the other rebel groups resented him, and they gradually persuaded other FPL leaders that he had to go in order to unify the FMLN's military and political effort. Ten months after I left guerrilla territory, the FPL's second-in-command, Melida Anaya Montes (alias "Ana María"), formerly the teachers' union leader, challenged Marcial. In March 1983, Comandante Ana María requested a vote of the FPL political bureau on a number of issues, including unity with other rebel groups and negotiations. The leaders supported Ana María over Marcial, effectively marginalizing his power.

But Marcial and his closest followers weren't ready to give up control of the FPL. While Marcial sought support in Libya from Muammar Qaddafi the following month, six of his associates pounced on Ana María in a safe house in Managua, slit her throat, and stabbed her with an ice pick eighty-two times. The initial FMLN communiqué blamed the CIA for the assassination, but the Sandinistas found the charge that the CIA could run amok in their capital too uncomfortable to accept. Sandinista police conducted an independent investigation after Ana María's funeral and discovered that Salvadoran leftists under Marcial's instructions were responsible. Days later, an FMLN communiqué claimed Marcial had admitted responsibility and committed suicide. Few doubted he was executed.

Following the deaths of Ana María and Marcial, another leader with a fratricidal past arose as the dominant figure in the FMLN—Joaquín Villalobos, who has remained in that position ever since. Villalobos's ERP, based in Morazán province, is the largest and most militarily aggressive of the five guerrilla groups, but it has never acquired the political base of the FPL under Marcial. Villalobos is aloof but forceful, a baby-faced man who got involved in revolutionary politics while studying economics at the National University. He joined the emerging radical Christian student movement, dropped out of school, found his way into the ERP in the mid-1970s, and quickly rose to the leadership. Villalobos was challenged, however, by Roque Dalton, the foremost intellectual in the ERP and arguably the finest poet of his generation. Villalobos charged that Dalton was a double-agent of the CIA and the Soviet Union, and reportedly had him executed following a 1975 show-trial. Dalton's comrades subsequently formed their own guerrilla movement, the National Resistance (RN). The wounds from those executions, the two most famous in a series of family bloodlettings, continued to throb throughout the war.

The FMLN's brutal history was not lost on the vast majority of Salvadorans. The guerrillas controlled their rural zones and they enjoyed significant support in the urban barrios, but there was increasing evidence that the people did not support them sufficiently to win. When the guerrillas called for an insurrection in January 1981 to overthrow the junta, few civilians rose up, and the offensive fizzled in a week. The massive voter participation in the 1982 Constituent Assembly elections was another blow to the guerrillas.

THE DUARTE YEARS

Theoretically, defeating the guerrillas was simple. El Salvador needed an effective government to demonstrate that it deserved the support of its people. It needed a president that looked more attractive than Marcial or Villalobos. The Reagan administration and Congress desperately hoped José Napoleón Duarte, the Christian Democratic candidate for president in 1984, could fill the bill.

But Roberto D'Aubuisson and his Arena party stood in the way. D'Aubuisson's presidential campaign attracted large crowds in the countryside with his promises to end the war in six months. He pledged "total war" as opposed to the U.S.-sponsored "limited" war with its human rights restrictions. Many Salvadorans found his strategy appealing. Referring to the green and white colors of Duarte's political party, D'Aubuisson punctuated his message on the campaign stump by plunging a machete through a watermelon: "Just like the Christian Democrats: green on the outside, red on the inside!" To the Fascist D'Aubuisson, moderates and Communists were the same.

The White House directed the CIA to back Duarte's candidacy with a $2 million contribution for public relations work through a Venezuelan public relations firm called IVEPO. "We are officially neutral," a U.S. embassy official told me, "but the whole world knows we need Duarte to push needed reforms and keep Congress on our side." He added, "Duarte has a messianic image of himself, and you know, he just may be El Salvador's only hope."

I followed the Duarte campaign to the eastern city of San Miguel that March. A local colonel blocked traffic to hold down attendance, but tens of thousands of workers and peasants filled San Miguel's central plaza for Duarte. The candidate gave a rousing speech, promising to negotiate an end to the war, redistribute the nation's wealth, and end human rights abuses. He specifically pledged to prosecute five famous human rights cases involving the army and the death squads. His strongest response from the crowd came when he pledged to bring to justice the murderers of Archbishop Romero. "We will change this society! My friends, the days of the death squads will end when we are in power!"

But that same night, at dinner, Duarte's closest adviser, Julio Rey Prendes, suggested differently. Asked how far his party would go on human rights, Rey Prendes took a sip of scotch, drew on his Marlboro, and smiled as if to be naughty. "Look, we're not going to be Alfonsíns," he conceded, referring to the civilian president of Argentina, who was pressing hard for military reform. "The past is the past. We must concentrate on the present and guard against future violations." The Christian Democrats were all too ready to raise public expectations and then cheat on them.

When Duarte squeaked past D'Aubuisson in the second round of the elections, the debate over El Salvador policy in the U.S. Congress was quelled once and for all. House Majority Leader Jim Wright, an election observer, proclaimed, "I have seen this country of El Salvador go through the travail and the birth pangs of a democracy. Let us not let that democracy be stillborn; nor die in its infancy." Congress opened the aid spigot full throttle. Shortly after Duarte's inauguration, Congress approved $70 million in supplemental military aid, raising the 1984 total to $196 million, roughly equivalent to the amount approved by American legislators during the last three years combined.

Washington's confidence in Duarte's ability to reform El Salvador was misplaced. The new president couldn't deliver on his campaign promises. The ultraright continued to control the courts, handcuffing Duarte's otherwise feeble efforts to prosecute human rights violators. The army ran the war and, with increasing amounts of U.S. aid, cut an ever more omnipotent presence in the provinces—eventually overshadowing local government with U.S.-financed civic action projects like bridge and road building. And finally, the FMLN became ever more hardened, sectarian, and brutal. Yet El Salvador dropped from Washington's attention for three years, except for the occasional crisis, like the assassination of four U.S. Marines in a San Salvador café by the guerrillas in June 1985.

Ambassadors Thomas Pickering and, later, Edwin Corr could have been pressing harder for human rights, military reform, and democratic development—the three publicly stated goals of U.S. policy. But time after time, those laudable objectives, as well as safeguards against military and civilian corruption, took a backseat to short-term efforts at keeping the Duarte government stable and flush with congressional funding.

Washington set a pattern of soft-peddling on such issues almost immediately following Duarte's inauguration. The Salvadoran army swept through a guerrilla zone in northern Cabañas province in July and slaughtered nearly seventy peasants around the village of Los Llanitos. The Catholic church's Tutela Legal human rights organization and several foreign journalists documented the incident with lists of victims. Duarte said he would investigate while Washington made no comment. A month later, army troops surrounded hundreds of rebel supporters in Chalatenango province, forcing them to attempt an escape through the highwaters of the Gualsinga River. About fifty people were killed, from drowning and army bullets. Again, Washington said nothing as Duarte looked on, powerless.

To make matters worse, Assistant Secretary of State for Inter-American Affairs Elliott Abrams, in a remarkable interchange between himself and human rights activist Aryeh Neier some months later on ABC's "Nightline" program, denied that either massacre had ever taken place:

TED KOPPEL: Secretary Abrams, why was neither of those incidents reported [in the State Department's El Salvador country report]?

ABRAMS: Because neither of them happened. Because it is a tactic of the guerrillas every time there is a battle and a significant number of people are killed to say that they're all victims of human rights abuses.

NEIER: That's why the *New York Times*—

ABRAMS: Ted, there's one very important point here.

NEIER: —and the *Boston Globe* and the *Miami Herald* and the *Christian Science Monitor* and Reuters and all the other reporters who went to the scene and looked at what took place, they were simply being propagandists for the guerrillas? Is that right?

ABRAMS: I'm telling you that there were no significant . . . there were no massacres in El Salvador in 1984.

One of President Duarte's few worthy moments came in October of his first year in office when he surprised the world by offering, before the U.N. General Assembly, to meet with the guerrillas face-to-face in El Salvador. The Reagan administration was cautiously supportive. The Salvadoran officer corps was highly skeptical but somewhat assuaged by the fact that Defense Minister Gen. Carlos Eugenio Vides Casanova would join Duarte in the talks. The FMLN, overjoyed to receive such recognition and legitimacy from the government, agreed to the meeting. The two sides quickly set the time and place for the peace session: October 15 in the cool highland resort of La Palma, a town in war-torn Chalatenango province.

It was a magic, momentary interruption to the war, for me as well as millions of Salvadorans. The night before the peace talks rebel guitarists came down to La Palma from the surrounding mountainous pine forests to entertain visitors and the foreign press. The leading guerrilla representative, Comandante Fermán Cienfuegos, marched a hundred miles with an armed guard of three hundred guerrillas, to join Duarte. The Salvadoran president entered the town accompanied by no security, only the Salvadoran Boy Scouts. By the time the participants arrived that morning, thousands of guerrilla and government supporters had gathered and mixed not as enemies but as fellow countrymen, hoping against hope that the war would finally end.

As we all waited expectantly, the negotiators met inside a church with Archbishop Arturo Rivera y Damas serving as mediator. For six hours the two sides discussed their respective interpretations of Salvadoran history over soggy fried chicken and french fries. According to the guerrillas, nothing had changed since the war began in 1979: the 1982 and 1984 elections and the land reform hadn't meant a thing. San Salvador was still run by the death squads, the rebels claimed. Duarte gently disagreed but said he was glad to hear their views. All went amicably, except for one detail: Gen. Vides Casanova was miffed that guerrilla negotiator Facundo Guardado wore a uniform he had taken off the body of a Salvadoran army lieutenant.

The two negotiating teams agreed they would not leave the church without offering the Salvadoran people something hopeful. Rey Prendes and Rubén Zamora, a leftist representative, drew up a communiqué calling on the two sides to set up a commission to "humanize the conflict" (meaning to work out an end to army bombing and guerrilla mining), include all parties in the peace process, and eventually negotiate a cease-fire. A nationwide television audience heard Comandante Cienfuegos endorse "pluralistic democracy" at the end of the session.

The prospects for peace appeared to have improved substantially. That night, at a reception at the presidential residence, Duarte was entertaining leading Christian Democrats. Rum and scotch were flowing freely. The good feelings were contagious.

Was there a chance for peace in El Salvador after all? Adviser Rey Prendes told me more had been accomplished that afternoon than he had thought possible. "They never asked for anything impossible," he said. "They were very nice. They shook hands with us three times before they left." Duarte, visibly tired with bags under his eyes, was more pensive. "There is hate in the hearts of people on all sides," he told me. "The structure of the society has been based on the culture of terror. The extreme right will try to stop my efforts." As if prophesying his own assassination, he concluded, "One terrorist can do a lot of damage."

I took Duarte's final words to be a reference to one of D'Aubuisson's men. But he might just as well have been speaking of guerrilla Comandante Joaquín Villalobos, the rebels' best military strategist.

From his stronghold in far-off Morazán province, Villalobos had hoped to participate in the La Palma talks. But Duarte would not meet his condition, that an army helicopter ferry him to the site of the talks. Duarte said he was reluctant to assume responsibility for Villalobos's safety. So Villalobos tried to undo whatever was accomplished in his absence.

Within twenty-four hours of the talks, Radio Venceremos, which is run by forces commanded by Villalobos, played the role of the spoiler by raising a shopping list of demands, including the lowering of army officers' salaries and immediate withdrawal of American advisers. A week later, guerrilla forces in Villalobos's region of command placed a bomb aboard a helicopter carrying several ranking officers, killing the army's most popular and effective leader, Col. Domingo Monterrosa.

The two sides returned to the bargaining table for one more peace conference in November. The rebels made new, more recalcitrant demands that amounted to a government surrender and integration of the two armies. Duarte was forced to cut off the talks, otherwise risking a military coup.

The limits of Duarte's powers became painfully evident in his handling of past human rights abuses. A string of embarrassments began in May 1985. A lawyer who defended the five National Guardsmen imprisoned for murdering the American churchwomen in 1980 went public with an astonishing confession: he had been tortured—his ribs were broken—by the National Guard until he agreed to enter into a "conspiracy" to cover up the involvement of senior officers in the case. The lawyer, Salvador Antonio Ibarra, speaking from exile in Texas, indicated he would have used evidence of a cover-up by National

Guard commanders as a defense had he not feared for his life. The revelation put Duarte in a delicate position. Despite his campaign promises, Duarte's priority was his dependence on his Defense Minister, Gen. Carlos Eugenio Vides Casanova, who had been commander of the National Guard when the nuns were killed. Duarte played it safe and insisted he was sure higher officers hadn't been involved in the killings.

A few weeks later there was a break in the Sheraton Hotel case involving the 1981 killings of the two American land reform advisers and a Salvadoran peasant leader. Three witnesses implicated army Capt. Eduardo Avila in the killings with vivid testimony. But a judge ruled there was insufficient evidence to indict Avila. In the meantime, bullets found at the site of the murder, which allegedly matched a machine pistol owned by Avila, disappeared while in the possession of judicial authorities. Duarte could do nothing.

The Duarte retreat on human rights appeared complete by the end of the year. In November, Duarte disbanded his much-publicized presidential investigative unit designed to investigate the most sensitive human rights cases of the early 1980s. Then, for Christmas, the army promoted two of the worst reputed human rights violators in the armed forces, Lt. Col. Denis Morán and Maj. Ricardo Pozo of the Treasury Police, both of whom had been close associates of D'Aubuisson's and were reportedly included on the Bush death-squad list in 1983.

And the war raged on. Reinforced with the tripling of military aid, the expanded armed forces—now 57,000 strong—went on the offensive. In the 1986 Operation Phoenix, the military succeeded in sweeping the rebels off Guazapa volcano, a key guerrilla strongpoint less than twenty miles north of the capital. Repeated government offensives in Chalatenango and Morazán forced the guerrillas to remove most of their civilian supporters from their zones of control. San Salvador's enlarged fleet of supersonic jet bombers and helicopters was used to devastating effect. The FMLN asked its allies in the Soviet bloc to grant them SAM antiaircraft missiles, but Moscow, Havana, and Managua, apparently fearing how the Reagan administration might respond, wouldn't go along.

As the army and air force pressed the FMLN, the rebels—in particular Villalobos's ERP—resorted to forced recruitment of hundreds of peasants into their armies, including children as young as twelve years of age. They also began a selective campaign of executions of villagers suspected of collaborating with the army. Such practices frightened many peasants living in or near guerrilla zones. Many packed their belongings and moved to the cities or refugee camps, clearly diminishing the rebels' support in the countryside.

But by late 1985, the guerrillas came up with new, effective countermeasures that would eventually stem their downward drift. To counteract the government's superior air power, the rebels broke up their battalion-sized units into tiny forces of twelve to twenty-five men, which could more easily escape detection. They steered clear of direct confrontations with the military, relying increasingly on booby traps and mines to inflict casualties on their enemy. Sensing there was more political tolerance under Duarte, the rebels infiltrated the cities and replenished their cells in the labor movement and National University. At the same time, they kidnapped and assassinated scores of local elected officials so as to break down provincial authority. The rebels could not turn the clock back to 1980, but they proved adept at prying for openings. In their words, they wanted to "sharpen the contradictions" between the Duarte moderates and the right-wingers in the private sector and military. The strategy depended on creating tensions that would force the uneasy allies to divide.

With that in mind, the guerrillas kidnapped Duarte's favorite child, his firstborn daughter, Inés, in September 1985. In his 1986 autobiography, Duarte recalled his thoughts when he learned the news: "I could not let my feelings take over. . . . All my children took for granted that, as president of the country, I could not make bargains for their release." But that's exactly what he did. The army high command wanted Duarte to refuse to bargain with terrorists, but the president's fatherly instincts proved stronger than his political will. After more than a month of personal suffering, Duarte broke down: he agreed to guerrilla demands that he free twenty-two political prisoners and transfer ninety-six wounded rebels out of the country for medical treatment. In return, the guerrillas handed over Inés and thirty-three small-town mayors they had kidnapped over the previous months. The army was furious, and Duarte's space to operate narrowed even more.

What finally ruined Duarte's government was the age-old scourge of corruption. Although Duarte was himself honest, he was far too loyal to top Christian Democrats who often valued money over their country. Cabinet ministers with yearly salaries below $30,000 built mansions worth in excess of $500,000—sometimes using government labor in the process. Several Christian Democratic officials steered government contracts toward corporations that they controlled through a phantom holding company called Corporación H, according to a classified memo prepared in 1985 by a private American consultant for the U.S. embassy. Among the directors of Corporación H were the president's son Alejandro and party treasurer Rafael Pleites. The Salvadoran people began to take notice of the rampant corruption following an October 1986 earthquake that devastated San Salvador; local officials skimmed off so much international assistance, U.S. embassy officials later admitted, that the residents of entire barrios were needlessly left homeless for more than a year.

Fedeccrédito, a sprawling public credit agency charged with providing public service jobs for war refugees, illustrated the corruption problems. The agency distributed its largesse much like a Chicago political machine for the benefit of the Christian Democratic party. A classified 1986 State Department report revealed that 70 percent of the participants in at least one large town, Ilobasco, "were hired on the basis of Christian Democratic party membership." Membership in the party was a prerequisite for any Fedeccrédito job. The abuses were so widespread, according to the report, that "mismanagement and politicization of the program, and the corruption which is a natural consequence, have passed tolerable levels. . . ." Road and bridge projects typically were left unfinished while local officials pocketed the money.

Fedeccrédito poisoned the Christian Democratic party for many Salvadorans, including Norma Gómez, a twenty-one-year-old snack bar attendant in Chalatenango city. When I met her in June 1987, Norma sweated over a greasy blackened pan making chicharrones, fried pork skins, and pupusas, tortillas stuffed with pork, cabbage, and cheese. Her cinnamon-colored skin and jet black hair would have made Norma exceedingly attractive had it not been for the unsightly welts from some sort of skin disease up and down both her arms.

Only three years before I had met her, Norma tried to find a custodial job at a local public hospital. She went to the local Christian Democratic party headquarters for help. Party activists advised Norma to join the party and work in Duarte's presidential campaign. She traveled around Chalatenango pasting up campaign posters for a couple of hot meals a day and some expense money.

Duarte won the election, but Norma didn't land a hospital job. Instead, the local branch of Fedeccrédito offered her a temporary job carrying earth and debris at a road construction site for the equivalent of $25 a week. After a week working on the U.S.-financed project, a Fedeccrédito foreman named Toño made a pass at Norma, suggesting she couldn't take rest breaks from work unless she slept with him. Norma said she was forced to tear away from his grabbing arms, and she quit. (Sexual harassment against refugee women employed by Fedeccrédito became so prevalent that the agency got the reputation in the region for fostering immoral behavior—no small thing in an area known for its conservative moral values.)

"I don't need to get treated that way," Norma told me. "The Christian Democrats in Chalatenango are pigs."

For years, even as State Department officers in Washington were losing patience, U.S. Ambassador Edwin Corr paid little attention to the corruption. Embassy officials grumbled that Corr's attitude seemed to be that corruption was normal for Latin America, so why should Washington expect El Salvador to be different? A Panglossian attitude ruled the U.S. embassy. But in March 1988, the Salvadoran people were angry enough with Christian Democratic corruption to return control of the National Assembly to the far-right Arena party.

Duarte made one last attempt to save his presidency by actively boosting a peace proposal by President Oscar Arias of Costa Rica. The Arias Plan called for peace negotiations, democratization, complete press freedom, and reintegration of refugees throughout Central America. Duarte promised to comply faster and more completely than Sandinista Nicaragua. He guaranteed the security of political exiles who were willing to return to El Salvador. Scores of activists responded, including Guillermo Ungo and Rubén Zamora, who helped found a new social democratic political party named the Democratic Convergence. Suddenly, Ungo and Zamora were organizing openly and appearing on television. Duarte also encouraged tens of thousands of refugees, guerrilla supporters from the early 1980s who lived mostly in Honduras, to return to their country in peace.

Duarte furthermore decreed a general amnesty, under which five hundred leftist political prisoners were released. But the army exacted a price for Duarte's act of reconciliation, one that will probably cripple the human rights cause for a generation. Under the demand of the army high command, Duarte was forced to exempt death-squad members and military men from future prosecution.

The Roman Catholic church pressured the assembly to exempt one crime from the amnesty: the 1980 assassination of Archbishop Romero. Duarte sought to use the shift on the Romero case to his political advantage, publicly announcing new evidence that linked the murder to D'Aubuisson. The Arena-controlled Supreme Court threw out the evidence, and after Arena won the 1988 legislative election, the National Assembly fired the attorney general.

The Reagan White House and Congress hoped the Duarte presidency would usher in an age of democracy. Instead, it was the armed forces, the very institution that had traditionally repressed the Salvadoran people, that benefited most from the increased American aid that came during the Duarte years. With U.S. congressional pressure off, the army was given a free hand to expand its influence—and in turn enrich its officers.

Washington expanded the Salvadoran navy to intercept arms shipments coming across the Gulf of Fonseca from Nicaragua, but naval officers were more interested in collecting "taxes" from shrimpers. Meanwhile, top army personnel invested massively in real estate and construction projects with money skimmed off U.S. aid programs. During the Duarte years, the army PX—known as the Cooperativa de la Fuerza Armada—grew from a modest shop into a massive three-story duty-free contraband dispensary. By the end of 1986, provincial commanders making modest salaries drove BMWs.

The army proved to be better at stealing than at fighting. Severe flaws in the Salvadoran army were exposed in early 1987 during one spectacular rebel attack in which the entire El Paraíso army base was destroyed. Seventy soldiers and an American adviser were killed. The post's officers showed their lack of spirit by ducking into a basement bomb shelter rather than lead their men in combat (and they were not disciplined afterward). The U.S. military mission later discovered that the rebel attack was an inside job; leftist infiltrators sent radio signals to their comrades in the mountains who were guiding the attack.

I personally witnessed the checkered progress of the army in January 1988 while on a trip through guerrilla territory in Chalatenango province. Following a four-hour hike, *Washington Post* reporter Douglas Farah and I arrived at San José de Las Flores, a town resettled by guerrilla supporters the year before. After guzzling some warm Coca-Colas, we walked to the church to speak to the nuns. On the way, we saw four teenage guerrillas sitting under a burning sun in the central plaza playing with a yo-yo. There was time to talk to them later—or so we thought.

Suddenly, incoming rifle and machine-gun fire careened through the town. An army unit of forty soldiers had snuck through rebel lines. Where the guerrillas had been playing with their yo-yo only moments before, soldiers took their positions, indiscriminately firing everything they had, including a grenade launcher.

Three of the rebels managed to escape into the hills, but a fourth one, only fourteen years old, was hit in the side and trapped on a side street. "I surrender! I surrender!" he cried out as he dropped his rifle. A soldier demanded to know how many guerrillas were in town, and he responded that there had been only the four of them. "He is lying. Kill him!" ordered another soldier. A third soldier trained his M-16 on the prostrate guerrilla, pulled the trigger three times, and blew the rebel's forehead off, splattering brain tissue along the cobblestone street and on the branches of an overhanging tree.

This murder broke all the rules taught to Salvadoran soldiers by their U.S. advisers. It is not only morally correct to take prisoners but militarily effective. Prisoners can be valuable sources of information. And their capture sends a signal to others that it pays to surrender rather than fight to the last bullet. And in this case, where the boy was killed in front of civilian witnesses, this abuse also offended people the army should have been trying to win over.

"The soldiers show no respect," grumbled one elderly man who witnessed the execution. Meanwhile, the children, particularly the little boys, were fascinated by this display of war and death. A nun came over to the body, which neighbors quickly covered in a pink and green blanket, to say a prayer and give a political talk. "He died," she said, "defending the defenseless."

THE COLLAPSE OF U.S. POLICY

U.S. policy collapsed on March 19, 1989, when the Salvadoran people elected Alfredo Cristiani, a coffee oligarch and presidential standard-bearer of the neo-Fascist Arena party, in a landslide victory. Salvadorans refused to listen to outgoing President Duarte, now dying from liver cancer, who sternly warned his people days before that an Arena victory would bring a repressive "totalitarian" state controlled behind the scenes by party founder and reputed death-squad leader Roberto D'Aubuisson. Making the best of the defeat for the centrist forces, U.S. Ambassador William Walker borrowed a phrase from tranquilly democratic Costa Rica, and called the election day "a civic fiesta."

Walker's remarks were more glib than illuminating. This was no fiesta. Minutes before the polls opened, the FMLN sabotaged the country's telephone and electrical grids, shut off the water to most homes, and attacked twenty-three towns across twelve of El Salvador's fourteen provinces. The offensive penetrated a few working-class barrios in San Salvador, and even secure neighborhoods reverberated from bombing and shelling twenty miles to the north, on rebel positions on Guazapa volcano. Scores of soldiers, guerrillas, and civilians (including three journalists—two specifically targeted by government troops) died in the combat.

Guerrilla Comandante Ana Guadalupe Martínez, speaking on Radio Venceremos, called on voters to stay home, explaining, "The weaker the voting the more it guarantees the prospects for peace in the future." Martínez defied logic. Guerrilla actions discouraged tens of thousands of less committed voters, leaving the polls to Arena's more highly motivated electorate. That is what the FMLN wanted—a clear, polarized choice between it and the far right, and a Salvadoran government less likely to attract the billions of dollars of U.S. congressional support that the Duarte Christian Democratic government drew in over the previous five years.

Arena's Cristiani won 53 percent, and second-place Christian Democratic candidate Fidel Chávez Mena won 36 percent, while voter turnout was considerably lower than in previous years. Democratic Convergence candidate Guillermo Ungo, a social democrat identified with the guerrillas, won only 3.4 percent of the vote. (About 6 percent of the voters either defaced or left their ballots blank, while minor parties split the rest of the vote.)

It is not an easy task to understand how hundreds of thousands of Salvadorans could vote for the party founded by a man linked to the murder of their popular archbishop (not to mention thousands of other citizens) only nine years before. But in a society where the law has never been respected, peasants identify with the man with the *pantalones* (pants) or *huevos* (balls), the strongman who can resolve the country's war. As former U.S. Ambassador to El Salvador Robert White put it, "The average Salvadoran is looking for someone to protect him and his family. After nine years of war, there is a nostalgia for the better, more secure, life under the *patrón*. There is another matter: in the hamlets, there is the widely held suspicion that authorities know who you voted for."

More than anything else, the vote for Arena's Cristiani was a rejection of policies pursued over the previous years by Christian Democrats and the army. In the end, the attraction of the far-right was similar to the attraction of the far-left: the popular desire for radical change. The incoming Bush administration believed it had no choice but to accept the will of the Salvadoran people and to try to mollify the far-right, including D'Aubuisson.

Only months before, D'Aubuisson was persona non grata to U.S. diplomats; after the presidential election, he was called "a player" by Ambassador Walker, invited to embassy functions, and granted an audience with Vice President Dan Quayle in San Salvador. Quayle pleaded with D'Aubuisson not to "embarrass" Cristiani. Death-squad killings slowly mounted, and within months it became clear that Cristiani was not fully in control.

Cristiani appeared to desire peace, and he agreed to restart peace talks with the FMLN in October, almost exactly five years after Duarte's ill-fated meeting with the rebels in La Palma. This time the far-right derailed the peace process by placing a bomb in the headquarters of a leftist labor federation, killing ten people on October 31. In quick retaliation, the FMLN dropped out of the talks and launched the fiercist offensive of the war.

Some 1,500 FMLN guerrillas ducked army patrols and infiltrated San Salvador on November 11, 1989, through the volcanic folds on the capital's north and east sides. Declaring this on Radio Venceremos to be "the final counteroffensive" and "the final chapter of fifty years of war," the rebels took positions in the grimy slums of Mejicanos, Soyapango, Zacamil, and Ciudad Delgado, forcing residents in many cases out of their homes to build fortifications. The FMLN simultaneously attacked several provincial towns, including Zacatecoluca, where they took control and destroyed part of a hospital to get the strategic high ground. In the city of San Miguel, the rebels reinstituted their old practice of forced recruitment when the local population refused to join their attack.

The aim of the offensive was to overthrow the government and ignite a popular insurrection. Guerrillas attacked the homes of Cristiani, his vice president, and other top civilian and military officials in an effort to decapitate the government. All the leaders escaped harm (the president of the National Assembly survived by hiding atop the limb of a mango tree in his courtyard). Then the FMLN-aligned labor movement declared a national strike. The people neither joined the strike nor the insurrection, demonstrating again that the base of popular support for the revolutionary struggle was as narrow as it was deep.

I interviewed dozens of refugees escaping barrios subjected to rebel attacks. Most were disgusted with the rebels for having brought the war into their homes and exposing their families to army counterattacks. In the barrio of Cuscatancingo, the guerrillas forced civilians to dig trenches for them, then refused them permission to leave the area of combat. "I can't figure their motives at all," said Angel Rodríguez, a twenty-two-year-old student who managed to escape the fighting. "They used us for shields." A twenty-three-year-old electrician from the shantytown of Enmanuel, who would only identify himself as Pedro, said of the guerrillas, "They kidnapped people. They said we'll blow up your doors if you don't let us in."

No matter the guerrilla failures, the offensive revealed the persistent, deep weaknesses of the country's U.S.-financed structures and institutions. The army proved too incompetent to defend even its own capital. The high command, afraid units might crack under the pressure, relied on the air force to strafe and rocket the barrios of San Salvador—a tactic that killed or wounded innocent civilians and spurred a human rights outcry around the world.

The army's performance deteriorated so badly that the United States almost intervened militarily. President Bush dispatched the top secret Delta Force counterterrorism unit to San Salvador after guerrillas stormed a luxury hotel where twelve Green Beret advisers were staying. For twenty-seven hours, the Green Berets and more than twenty heavily armed rebels had stood their ground on separate floors. Neither side wanted to engage in battle. The American commando unit prepared to go into action but were saved the trouble when Church and Red Cross officials negotiated with the Salvadoran government the safe evacuation of the guerrillas, the American advisers, and other guests from the hotel.

The rebel offensive shrank what little political tolerance had developed in the past eight years. Leftist Democratic Convergence leaders Guillermo Ungo and Rubén Zamora were forced to flee to friendly foreign embassies for refuge while army troops and police raided churches, union halls, and human rights organizations. Arena responded to the offensive by pushing their agenda through the National Assembly: a set of "antiterrorist laws" that outlawed most labor strikes and the distribution of subversive literature and imposed prison terms of twenty years for most public protests. Government officials put increasing pressure on the local news media to tailor their reporting to suit the Arena political position. Channel 12's "Al Día" news show, which for the previous four years had served as a forum for a wide range of views, shut itself down in protest.

Worse still, sectors of the government appeared to be encouraging a vigilante spirit among the population. Cadena Nacional, the government radio network, invited citizens to pick up arms to fight the guerrillas, saying, "You are the first line against communism." The air force dropped leaflets inviting "the Salvadoran patriot" to fulfill the "legitimate right to defend your life and property. If in order to do that you must kill FMLN terrorists as well as their internationalist allies, do it!"

The only person in El Salvador who appeared to see any hope in the situation was Ambassador Walker, the man people back in Washington came to call "Ambassador Sunshine" for his reddish hair and rosier vision of Salvadoran affairs. From his underground briefing room, Walker told reporters that the guerrillas "had blown their wad" with this offensive. Three days into the offensive, Walker claimed that the whole ordeal "leaves those of us who make U.S. policy very satisfied. I have every confidence that the democratic left will have the same space they had before after this offensive is over." I had heard Ambassadors White, Hinton, Pickering, and Corr use almost the exact words during past crises.

Only two days after Walker's briefing, I was reminded of those hateful days of 1980 and 1981 as I walked with *Newsweek* correspondent Charles Lane in the parking lot of the Camino Real Hotel. Two visibly distressed reporters rushed up to us with the news that the rector of Catholic University, Ignacio Ellacuría, and five other Jesuit priests were found dead that morning. On the way to the university's campus, Chuck and I remembered the death of Archbishop Romero. Unlike Romero, who had grown increasingly critical of the junta as death-squad killings mounted in 1980, Ellacuría had voiced unexpected support for Cristiani's efforts to restart the peace process, which was probably why far-right elements killed him.

On the lawn outside a dormitory lay three of the priests and a cook, their corpses covered by bed sheets. Shaken, I walked behind Chuck into the cinder-block dorm, plainly furnished and full of religious and philosophy books. Once the intellectual center of the country, this refuge of reason was now pockmarked with bullet holes and littered with raw brain matter.

"Don't look," Chuck urged me as he withdrew his head from one of the dormitory rooms. There lay Father Amado López sprawled out, his head split open by a bullet. My immediate thought was that right-wing Salvadorans were laughing at Washington; they could do whatever they liked as long as they fought communism. What had eight years of American policy accomplished?

Moments later, a special U.S.-trained National Police investigative unit arrived on the scene. An officer immediately closed off the area around the dormitory and told a priest, "We are all committed to getting to the bottom of this crime." We had heard it all before.

Ambassador Walker said publicly that the guerrillas might have perpetrated the crime. But a congressional panel, in an investigative report released four months later, documented the reluctance of the high command to prosecute the killers. Its study found that after an American military adviser reported information linking Col. Alfredo Benavides, director of the military academy, to the crime, it took the Salvadoran government five days before it would admit that its own army was culpable. The Salvadoran government arrested Col. Benavides, three lieutenants, and four privates in connection with the murders but the Salvadoran army refused to question any top commanders, even though there was evidence that a radio call made from a meeting of the High Command may have set the murders in motion. Investigators found the commanders, the majority of whom graduated in the military academy class of 1966, were more interested in protecting their brethren officers then getting to the bottom of the crime as they were ordered to do by President Cristiani. Perhaps most disturbing of all was the fact that the commando unit alleged to have killed the priests had strong ties to the United States. The two commanders of the unit were both graduates of special courses given at Fort Benning, Georgia. Worse still, the unit had been undergoing a training course conducted by Green Berets only two days before the assassinations. There was no suggestion that the Green Berets had previous knowledge of the plot, but the case only underscored the limitations of American military training and American attempts to extract the hatred that permeates Salvadoran society.

At the Jesuits' funeral, politicians of divergent ideological stripes, including Cristiani and Zamora, attended in a rare demonstration of unity. There were tears in most people's eyes for the dead priests but perhaps also for the country. The pessimism of the moment was symbolized in the ritual itself when a young girl threw a gray pigeon into the sky as a sign of her hopes for peace. The bird refused to fly.

3
Nicaragua:
Foreign Intervention
and Revolution

Just two months after their heady 1979 victory over the dictatorship of Anastasio Somoza, Comandante Daniel Ortega Saavedra and two junior members of the new Nicaraguan junta visited the White House to call on President Jimmy Carter. Ortega had cut his shaggy hair as an explicit gesture of respect. But once he entered the Cabinet Room with the American president, the young Nicaraguan leader suddenly turned surly.

Breaking diplomatic decorum, Ortega bitterly reminded Carter that this was the very room where so much of Nicaragua's tragic history had been made. He then launched into a lecture on American interventions in Nicaragua, beginning with an American mercenary army's invasions in the 1850s, a series of U.S. Marine occupations between 1909 and 1933, and the founding of the Somoza dictatorship and Somoza's National Guard, a praetorian army that repressed the Nicaraguan people for forty years. The Monroe Doctrine, the big stick, and Dollar Diplomacy, Ortega concluded, were nothing but different forms of "Yankee imperialism." Ortega promised that his movement, the Sandinista National Liberation Front (FSLN), would break the imperialist hold on his country.

While Hondurans, Costa Ricans, and Panamanians tend to be polite to foreigners, and Guatemalans and Salvadorans tend to be inscrutable, Nicaraguans are by nature cocky, rebellious, and blunt about it. Ortega was no different. The comandante's nationalist and antigringo feelings ran deep. His parents had both been active against the U.S. Marine occupation in the 1920s and 1930s, and he had lost his younger brother Camilo just a few years earlier in the war against Somoza, the last dynast of a U.S.-supported dictatorship.

Carter, who had studied up on Nicaraguan history and understood that he was faced with the unintended results of decades of misbegotten policies, listened to Ortega patiently. He nodded his head, let a moment go by, and then responded sternly, "You know, we really have to get beyond that."

The American and Nicaraguan officials then strolled over to the Rose Garden for a photo session. Apparently, Ortega had no interest in flowers or posing. He walked over to Carter, and quietly let loose with one final outburst: "You Americans built the National Guard and supported Somoza for years!"

Carter looked the angry young Nicaraguan in the eye and tried to humor him: "Let's make a deal," said the American president. "You don't criticize my predecessors and I won't criticize yours." Ortega managed to break into a smile, and Carter skillfully seized on the opening: "You know, we can have a relationship if we both try."

That was easier for Carter to say than for Ortega to accept. To Americans, Nicaragua was a tiny, insignificant country, one not easily found on a map. But for Nicaraguans like Ortega, the United States was the colossus of the north, an overbearing imperialist power that constantly intervened in their society. Ortega's anger blinded him to his nation's self-interest in getting along with the United States; indeed, the Sandinista psyche was enmeshed in its relationship with the United States. The Sandinistas, like Nicaragua's political culture in its entirety, were the product of imperialist intervention. The result was often antagonism as the Sandinistas struggled to define an autonomous identity—and with it, for the first time in their history, a sense of national purpose and a modern state.

Four days after his meeting with Carter, Ortega addressed the U.N. General Assembly. To the consternation of the White House, then embroiled with a skeptical Congress to grant economic aid to the Sandinista government, Ortega praised Cuba and the Palestine Liberation Organization (PLO) and charged that "imperialist forces" were attempting to destabilize his revolution.

Carter was out of office a year or so later, and the U.S. effort at peaceful engagement with Sandinista Managua ended. Had Ortega somehow been invited back to the new president's Cabinet Room, he would have seen that Ronald Reagan had hung a portrait of Calvin Coolidge on the wall. It was Coolidge, much admired by Reagan for his free-market principles, who had sponsored Nicaragua's National Guard in the 1920s. While Reagan admired Coolidge, Ortega admired Augusto César Sandino, the Nicaraguan guerrilla leader who had fiercely resisted the marines Coolidge sent to occupy his country. Few Americans remember, but Coolidge's Nicaragua policy led to a heated battle with Congress; likewise, Reagan's Nicaragua policy led to a similar confrontation on Capitol Hill and a scandal that nearly destroyed his administration.

Each generation of American leaders, from William Howard Taft to Coolidge to Reagan, forgot or failed to comprehend the bitter fruits of their predecessors' Nicaragua policies: that from the humiliation of one Nicaraguan generation came the rebellion against the Yankees in the next. But Ortega, and the FSLN's hard core of party and army cadres, never forgot.

Even before the deeply conservative Reagan administration took office in 1981, confrontation between Washington and the Sandinistas appeared inevitable. While class and ideological conflict had driven the repeated civil wars in next-door El Salvador, foreign intervention— British, then American, and finally Soviet bloc (especially Cuban)— has been at the root of Nicaragua's long history of dictatorship and rebellion. A succession of foreign interventions left Nicaragua to this day without a workable political culture, one in which a government generates strong feelings of national identity and manages the nation's diversity without employing military force.

If it weren't for foreigners, this nation of 3 million people would probably have had a peaceful history. It is not a country of class conflict like El Salvador. Indeed, the upper classes have often been generous and liberal, and wages have traditionally been high because of the historic shortage of labor and abundance of land. Through all its wars, there have been few massacres of civilians, and death-squad killings have been infrequent (by regional standards), whether under the Somoza dynasty or under the Sandinista regime.

The heroes of Nicaraguan political folklore have always been those who fought against foreigners, beginning with Diriangen, the sixteenth-century Indian chief who resisted the Spanish conquistadores; Cleto Ordóñez, a lowly sergeant who fought the Mexicans in the 1820s; José Dolores Estrada, a colonel who fought against American invader William Walker in the 1850s; and finally Benjamín Zeledón and Augusto César Sandino, rebel leaders who resisted U.S. military occupation forces over the first three decades of the twentieth century. More often than not, those heroes were also forced to fight other Nicaraguans, those like the Somozas, who were quick to ally themselves with powerful foreigners.

Ironically, the Sandinista revolution—intended to unleash Nicaragua from the grip of American imperialists—made the country dependent on competing imperialist powers. Events in Washington and Moscow, whether related to the Iran-Contra scandal or the accession to Mikhail Gorbachev, were played out as key determinants of Nicaraguan politics. All too often, the warring Nicaraguans have been betrayed or poorly served by their foreign allies. But the Nicaraguans never seem to learn.

Indeed, all the modern players on the Nicaraguan scene frequently appear more concerned with foreign policy than with what is happening in their own country. While the Sandinistas looked to the Cubans and Soviets, the various Contra groups that arose in the early 1980s launched their counterrevolution against the Sandinistas dependent on the guidance and assistance of the United States, Honduras, and Argentina. During the heated 1989–90 Nicaraguan presidential campaign, Daniel Ortega ran against the United States while his opponent Violeta Chamorro ran against the crumbling Soviet bloc.

Nicaraguan history, marked by recurrent invasion and occupation, gave the people strong, albeit ambivalent, feelings about foreigners. This can be seen through Nicaragua's rich cultural history, particularly in its literature. In El Güegüense, a seventeenth-century operetta (Latin America's first), a Nicaraguan merchant, attempting to defend his son in court, cleverly confuses a Spanish judge by employing puns in the local Indian dialect, and then mockingly dances around the court to show his disrespect for colonial authority. (This colonial theatrical protest is still performed today during festivals in the towns of

Masaya and Diriamba, with the special richness of Nicaragua's colloquial Spanish.) More than two hundred years later, the classic Nicaraguan poet Rubén Darío wrote "Ode to Roosevelt," in which he described the character of Theodore Roosevelt and the American people
in bitter fashion:

> You think that life is a fire,
> that progress is an eruption,
> that the future is wherever
> your bullet strikes.
> > No.
>
> . . .
>
> Long live Spanish America!
> A thousand cubs of the Spanish lion are roaming free.
> Roosevelt, you must become, by God's own will,
> the deadly Rifleman and the dreadful Hunter
> before you can clutch us in your iron claws.
> And though you have everything, you are lacking one thing:
> > God!

Roman Catholic priest and Sandinista activist Ernesto Cardenal
tied the history of Nicaragua to that of the United States in a series
of critically acclaimed "documentary poems." In his 1972 free-form
epic Nicaraguan canto called "Zero Hour," Cardenal came to a
thoughtful analysis that described the country's dialectical, mutually
reinforcing historical strands of domestic division and foreign manipu-
lation:

> Internal disorganization and corruption fostered foreign
> intervention consequently intervention fostered the
> disorganization and corruption and developed them
> (that stares you in the face).
> Whence, therefore:
> imperialism as a disturbing and disrupting element etc.
> fostering backwardness corruption etc. in Nicaragua: violating
> treaties constitutions judicial decisions
> provoking civil war manipulating elections bribing
> it has protected thieves prostituted politics impoverished
> > the people

impeded union kept its agents in power against the people's
     will:
thereby raised the cost of living defended
oppression and brought death.
Thus Nicaragua (when Sandino appeared) found herself with
part of her territory alienated, the external debt
sky high, financial life entirely subject to
the group of New York bankers, and no progress.

A NATION AT THE CROSSROADS

Spain's King Philip II, France's Napoleon III, Thomas Jefferson, and
Cornelius Vanderbilt all saw a great future for Nicaragua. For them,
it would be the site where man would accomplish his dream of linking
the Pacific and Atlantic oceans. But foreign intruders and their Nicaraguan allies always conspired to make Nicaragua's future anything but
splendid.

Aztec scouts from Mexico first made contact with the peoples of
South America on Nicaragua's Rivas peninsula, and for two centuries
the thin piece of land between the Pacific Ocean and Lake Nicaragua
served as a center of cultural interchange. Fearing that Rivas could be
seized by a competing power to interrupt their trade for Colombian
emeralds, the Aztecs sent military expeditions to occupy the peninsula.
But as the Aztecs consolidated their grip on Rivas, a much stronger
foreign power descended on America—the Spanish.

Like the Aztecs, the Spanish viewed Nicaragua as a prime trading
site. Competing Spanish conquistadores fought each other for control
of the region, which they coveted more than any other spot in Central
America. The Spanish were not alone in appreciating the potential of
Nicaragua's network of lakes and rivers between the two oceans.
Dutch, French, and English buccaneers preyed on Spanish shipping
and took effective control of Nicaragua's Atlantic coast. The English
made the Miskito Indians loyal allies for more than two centuries by
trading them trinkets, beads, rum, and tortoiseshell in exchange for
firearms and Sumo Indian slaves. Joint English-Miskito military expeditions went on pillaging rampages through the Nicaraguan countryside, ransacking the cities of Matagalpa and Granada during the mid–

sixteenth century. The English formalized the relationship, and political control over the Atlantic coast, in 1687 when the colonial governor of Jamaica crowned a Miskito King Jeremy, the first king the Miskitos ever had. The Miskitos came to see the Union Jack, whose colors and design inspired mystical appeal, as their flag.

Independence from Spain only brought more chaos. The merchant elite of Granada wanted to join a united Central American confederation and founded the Conservative party to press its interests, while the cattlemen and farmer elite of León declared its loyalty to Mexico and formed their own Liberal party. The rivalry of two major cities embroiled the new nation in civil war through much of the century. London took advantage of the turmoil by landing naval forces in San Juan del Norte in 1841, renaming the port Greytown. The English cruised up the San Juan River and captured a fortified settlement at San Carlos on Lake Nicaragua and claimed the so-called Mosquito Reserve—essentially a third of Nicaragua—as their own protectorate six years later.

Transportation tycoon Cornelius Vanderbilt followed the British exploits in Nicaragua in the newspapers and pored over colorful maps of Central America at his desk in New York City. At age forty-four, the "Commodore" founded the Accessory Transit Company to fulfill the dream of linking the seas at the isthmus. Vanderbilt set up a network by which he took California Gold Rush travelers and cargo by steamboat across Nicaragua via the San Juan River and Lake Nicaragua, across the Rivas peninsula by stagecoach and then to California by steamboat.

The "Forty-niners" traveled through Nicaragua by the tens of thousands, leading the English to impose a duty on cargo carried by Vanderbilt's company. But Vanderbilt refused to pay a dime. In response, an English warship fired across the bow of Vanderbilt's steamship *Prometheus* in order to force the American crew to pay the toll. The American press whipped up war fever against the hated English, but Washington and London blinked before going to war against each other. Tensions boiled over again in 1854 when a Greytown mob roughed up an American diplomat. In retaliation, officers of the American sloop *Cyane* ordered the evacuation of Greytown, then bombarded and burned the English port to the ground. It was the first time American servicemen fired on Nicaraguan soil.

The Nicaraguans viewed the Americans as their saviors from English imperialism. U.S. Chargé d'Affaires Ephraim George Squier received a hero's parade when he arrived in the country, after which he negotiated remarkable concessions from the Nicaraguan authorities on Vanderbilt's behalf. The American magnate's transit company was to pay the Nicaraguan government $10,000 and 10 percent of annual net profits for perpetual rights to transisthmian transit. Squier later wrote a popular two-volume travelogue in which he described the Nicaraguans this way:

> [The Nicaraguans] concurred in representing the present unsettled state of public affairs as in a great measure due to foreign intervention and intrigue. . . . It was not unnatural that, distracted within, and subjected to unscrupulous aggression from without, the U.S. should be looked to as a conciliator . . . a friend, and a protector.

As American domestic politics slid toward civil war by the mid-1850s, U.S. policy toward Central America was, in effect, hijacked by private citizens, soldiers of fortune dreaming of a Caribbean slave-based plantation empire ruled by an ascending American Confederacy. The most formidable of these adventurers was Tennessean William Walker, a gray-eyed former newspaper editor who dressed in black.

Hearing of Walker's military expeditions in northern Mexico, members of Nicaragua's Liberal party approached him to fight by their side to overthrow the Conservative government in return for 20,000 acres of land. In May 1855, Walker's force of fifty-eight mercenary misfits and proslave fanatics, many of them unsuccessful gold diggers, stole one of Vanderbilt's steamboats and seized Granada from the Conservatives. Holding many of Nicaragua's most distinguished families hostage, Walker executed the country's foreign minister and grabbed power. Walker ended Nicaragua's civil war, then handpicked a half-senile Liberal party customs official as president and appointed himself commander of the armed forces.

In his time, Walker was a great American hero. American newspapers and magazines boosted his exploits. A Broadway musical called *Nicaragua, or General Walker's Victories* opened at Purdy's National Theater in 1856; according to historian Karl Bermann, "Its cast of characters included 'General Walker, the Hope of Freedom,' and 'Ivory Black, a superior nigger.'" *Harper's* magazine called Walker "one of the most remarkable men of the age." He had strong allies in the Franklin Pierce administration, including Secretary of War Jefferson Davis, and Washington immediately recognized his government.

Later, President James Buchanan invited Walker to the White House and quietly helped him overcome Neutrality Law restrictions to supply his army. With such support, Walker fixed an election to become president of Nicaragua himself. He then legalized slavery, encouraged American colonization, and declared English the official language—to the astonishment of Nicaraguans, who quickly came to hate him.

Walker's downfall came when he got enmeshed in the Wall Street battle for Vanderbilt's Accessory Transit. Two conspiring Accessory Transit corporate officers bribed Walker with $20,000 to confiscate Accessory Transit from the Commodore and transfer the company's transit rights to them. But Vanderbilt struck back. He joined London in financing and supplying a Costa Rican–led Central American force to challenge Walker's government. Walker was defeated in the Nicaraguan town of Rivas by the joint Central American force in 1857. Over the next three years, he tried to conquer Nicaragua two more times before he was captured by sailors of a British frigate, handed over to the Honduran authorities, and executed by firing squad. Walker has been a hated symbol of Yankee imperialism ever since.

But it was a 1893 coup led by Liberal Gen. José Santos Zelaya that changed the political face of Nicaragua forever. The son of a prosperous coffee grower and former philosophy student in France, Zelaya would rule for sixteen years, construct a railroad network with European capital, build public schools, and encourage the production of coffee. He constructed the first national army of 4,000 men, and he made war on Honduras and Guatemala in unsuccessful efforts to unite Central America under Liberal party rule.

Zelaya is best remembered—as a hero on Nicaragua's Pacific coast and as a villian on the so-called Atlantic coast—for his role as the first ruler to govern all of Nicaragua. His troops launched an attack in 1893 and occupied the Atlantic port of Bluefields. In a direct challenge to the English, he declared martial law across the Atlantic coast. London anchored the warship *Cleopatra* off Bluefields as if the Royal Navy would resist, a move that spurred their Miskito allies to rebel. But the Miskito forces fell in days as the English fleet did nothing.

Zelaya first ingratiated Washington by driving the English from the Mosquito Coast and granting huge concessions to American companies that would dominate the country's lumber industry, banana fields, and mines for the next seventy-five years. But his relations with Washington soured by 1903 when President Theodore Roosevelt and Congress unexpectedly chose Panama instead of Nicaragua for a canal. Zelaya sent out diplomatic feelers to Japan and Germany to build a competing canal, deeply alarming Washington. President William Howard Taft decided to intervene after representatives of the Conservative party approached him about a coup. In 1909, Taft deployed four hundred marines to overthrow Zelaya.

Following Zelaya's fall and the subsequent U.S. military withdrawal in 1910, chaos overwhelmed Nicaraguan politics. Conservative and Liberal leaders swung in and out of power until Conservative President Adolfo Díaz invited the United States to return with troops to reestablish order. Taft rushed 2,600 marines to Nicaragua in 1912, for an occupation that would last through the Wilson, Coolidge, and Hoover administrations.

Taft's force was met by riots in León and several other towns. Liberal General Zeledón, carrying the banner of the Zelaya revolution, resisted American forces in the streets of Masaya for about a week. Marines and navy "bluejackets" swarmed the Pacific coast town with their heavy firepower, killed scores of Nicaraguans in combat, captured Zeledón, and then handed him over to Díaz's men for execution. National myth has it that a teenager named Augusto César Sandino burned with rage when he saw Díaz's troops kicking Zeledón's lifeless body in the street.

THE FIRST SANDINISTA REVOLUTION

In 1925, following the election of what appeared to be a stable government, President Calvin Coolidge withdrew the marines. As soon as they left, Conservative chief Emiliano Chamorro seized power in a coup and unleashed a civil war. The deposed Liberal vice president, Juan Sacasa, fled to revolutionary Mexico and convinced its government to outfit him with an army to retake Managua. Perceiving a challenge from "Bolshevik" Mexico, Coolidge redeployed several thousand servicemen to Nicaragua in 1926.

Eager to get the intervention over with quickly, Coolidge dispatched former Secretary of War Henry Stimson to mediate the dispute between Chamorro and Sacasa. With a young Liberal named Anastasio Somoza García as his interpreter, Stimson forced Chamorro to step down from power. In the Tipitapa peace treaty Stimson negotiated, Liberal and Conservative generals agreed to jointly participate in a new constabulary to be founded, trained, and commanded by the United States—the National Guard of Nicaragua.

There was one hitch. One general, Augusto César Sandino, described by a contemporary journalist as "a magnetic wisp of a man," messaged back to Liberal headquarters in May 1927: "I am not for sale"—and he took to the mountains of northern Nueva Segovia province with 150 men. Sandino believed that Nicaragua could never be free as long as U.S. soldiers occupied his native land. For the next six years, Sandino's Army for the Defense of Nicaragua's National Sovereignty fought a war of maneuver, evasion, and raw terror that forced both the marine forces and the U.S.-founded Nicaraguan National Guard to a standoff.

Born in 1895 as the illegitimate son of a well-to-do coffee man and a servant, Augusto lived a youth of pain in the southeastern town of Niquinohomo. His father abandoned him and his mother, Margarita, forcing her into a life of abject poverty. As a young man, Sandino organized a cooperative market association in Niquinohomo, causing resentment among competing merchants from nearby Granada. Sandino got into a gunfight and wounded one of the merchants. To escape the law, he fled to the hills to mine gold, and finally to Tampico, Mexico. There, as a bookkeeper for an American oil company, he was exposed to the radical unionism and anarchism of the Mexican revolution. Sandino returned to Nicaragua in 1926 to organize "an army" of about thirty disgruntled Nueva Segovia mine workers, appointed himself a general in Sacasa's Liberal revolt, and fought against Chamorro's regime.

From his El Chipote headquarters deep in the mountains of Nueva Segovia province, Sandino patiently picked his targets—an American-owned mine company, or a local National Guard outpost—and mastered the element of surprise. His "anti-imperialist war" took the lives of 900 Nicaraguans and 136 U.S. Marines, not a small conflict in a country with a population of 700,000.

Sandino became a Robin Hood figure who spoke of national purpose, land cooperatives, and pride in his Indian blood. His ideology was vague and often contradictory, but his underdog image, ingenuity, and guts struck a chord among Nicaraguans. Above all, Sandino was a nationalist; he rejected not only the Americans but also internationalist Communists, like his secretary Agustín Farabundo Martí, whom he fired after the Salvadoran radical sought to infiltrate and dominate his movement. "There is no need for the class struggle in Nicaragua," Sandino once explained, "because here the worker lives well; he struggles only against the American intervention."

But the Coolidge administration, like so many of its successors would be, was obsessed with communism. The State Department issued a White Paper on Soviet involvement in Latin affairs that made the overwrought charge that the Nicaraguan Liberal party was engaged in a grand conspiracy directed by Moscow, operating through "Bolshevik" Mexico. Many U.S. newspapers mocked the White Paper, and Nicaragua became the most controversial foreign policy issue Congress debated in the second half of the 1920s. After narrowly defeating a cutoff of funding for the intervention in 1929, the Senate passed an amendment halting it in 1932. The popular satirist Will Rogers helped bring attention to Nicaragua by adding the controversy to his comedy routine. "Join the marines and find Nicaragua," he joked. "Why are we in Nicaragua? What the hell are we doing in Nicaragua?"

Impatient to withdraw from Nicaragua, the Hoover administration sponsored a free election in 1932—one that brought to power Juan Sacasa, the Liberal statesman whose revolt in 1926 brought the U.S. Marines there in the first place. Hoover brought home the last of the 4,600 marines occupying Nicaragua as he left the White House. This is how the State Department press release of January 2, 1933, the day of final U.S. withdrawal, depicted the Nicaraguan National Guard the marines left behind:

> American officers and enlisted men have organized and trained an entirely new and non-partisan force, the Guardia Nacional, grounded upon the fundamental precept of service to the country as a whole. During the past five years this force has developed into a well-disciplined and efficient organization with a high esprit-de-corps. The direction of the Guardia has now passed from American to Nicaraguan officers, and it is noteworthy that both political parties have agreed on their own initiative to a plan for insuring the non-political character of that organization.

The press release reflected Washington's best intentions. The construction of the National Guard was to be an exercise of "nation building." But the kind of military force Coolidge and Hoover built in Nicaragua had no authentic native roots. In its first years, all but 15 of the 150 officers in the National Guard were U.S. Marines. The first director of the force, U.S. Army Maj. Calvin Carter, barely spoke a word of Spanish. To make matters worse, the National Guard was an undisciplined force from the beginning; of the Guard's 1,846 men in 1929, 867 either deserted or were discharged for violating U.S. military codes.

The United States made one final mistake before withdrawing the marines: they appointed Liberal Gen. Anastasio Somoza García commander of the National Guard. Somoza made the Americans feel comfortable with his colloquial English picked up from prep school days spent in Philadelphia, and he charmed them with his talents as a rumba and tango dancer. Somoza became a personal adviser to American minister Matthew C. Hanna, and reputedly the paramour of Mrs. Hanna. Historians generally agree that it was the cuckolded Hanna and U.S. Army Gen. Matthew B. Ridgeway, then U.S. director of the Guard, who appointed Somoza as the first Nicaraguan to command the force. President-elect Sacasa distrusted Somoza, but Hanna convinced him to go along with Washington's choice.

With the U.S. Marines gone and the Liberal Sacasa in power, Sandino agreed to disband most of his army. Sandino was willing to retire honorably if he could retain some armed men and had government approval for a cooperative project in northern Nicaragua. Sacasa opened peace talks with Sandino in Managua, and President Franklin Roosevelt's new minister to Nicaragua, Arthur Bliss Lane, blessed the dialogue.

But Somoza wanted power for himself. Contrary to his promises to Lane, Somoza had his Guardsmen ambush and assassinate Sandino on February 21, 1934, following a negotiating session and farewell dinner that Sacasa hosted for the former rebel. That same night, before word of the killing reached Sandino's guerrillas, the National Guard surrounded their Wiwili camp and slaughtered three hundred rebel men, women, and children. It was the worst massacre in modern Nicaraguan history. By then, Sacasa was an irrelevant factor in Nicaraguan politics; Somoza ran the country as chief of the Guard.

Washington's creature became a Frankenstein. In a 1939 "strictly confidential" cable to Secretary of State Cordell Hull, LaVerne Baldwin, the acting U.S. chargé d'affaires in Managua, charged Somoza with using his position in the National Guard to amass a multimillion-dollar fortune and emasculate democratic institutions. "The unpleasant picture," Baldwin wrote, "represents a Government ridden from top to bottom with graft, wasting the substance of a state which needs every centavo in the face of existing world conditions and the ever present extreme poverty of its lowest classes. . . . Continuation of this procedure must inevitably create strong and growing resistance."

But just as Baldwin correctly warned of an eventual revolt against the Somoza family dictatorship, he also expressed the common American apprehension about what might follow. "It may certainly be expected," wrote Baldwin in the same cable, "that any overthrow of his Government will be followed by a Government perhaps not radically anti-American on the surface, but one which will certainly attack any American interests which received its privilege through the efforts of Somoza."

With Sandino and Sacasa out of the way, Somoza snuggled up to Washington. Proclaiming himself an adherent of Franklin Roosevelt and the New Deal, Somoza installed one of the most progressive labor laws in Latin America. During World War II, he confiscated German properties and leased his military facilities to the American armed forces on the most generous terms. Roosevelt was quoted as saying that Somoza "may be a son-of-a-bitch, but he's our son-of-a-bitch." After the war, as the United States and the Soviet Union became enemies, Somoza proved his worth by supplying arms and an airfield to the CIA-backed Guatemalan rebels that overthrew the Jacobo Arbenz government.

While accommodating the United States, Somoza García bought politicians, businessmen, and union leaders and fixed elections for a series of puppet presidents he controlled as chief of the National Guard. He built an economic empire (frequently with American partners) that included large sugar, coffee, and tobacco farms; a shipping line; port facilities; the cement monopoly; farm machinery dealerships; the newspaper *Novedades;* radio stations, and the national airline.

On a Saturday night in September 1956, a radical Liberal party activist (and poet), Rigoberto López Pérez, shot the dictator five times at a party in the city of León before he was killed himself by bodyguards on the spot. The U.S. Air Force airlifted Somoza to the Panama Canal Zone for medical care, but he died a week later.

It was now up to Somoza's two sons, Luis Somoza, thirty-four, and Anastasio Somoza Debayle ("Tachito" until his father's death and then "Tacho"), thirty-one, to sustain the dynasty. Luis, a graduate of Louisiana State University, became president. Anastasio, a graduate of

West Point, became the commander of the National Guard. The two had different visions. Luis, a booster of the Alliance for Progress and the Liberal party, wanted to open up the system for democracy. As a gesture of reform, he passed the presidency to two men outside the family between 1963 and 1967. But Anastasio remained the real power of the land as chief of the National Guard.

By the time Luis died of a heart attack in 1967, the die was cast. Anastasio Somoza would rule Nicaragua for the next twelve years with the active aid of the Nixon and Ford administrations. Somoza smoked big cigars, gambled, partied, and shopped in sprees around the world with his bejeweled mistress Dinorah Sampson. He was an international bon vivant who was more conversant about the Philadelphia Phillies (from his American school days) than about what was happening in Nicaragua. But while the father had a gracious touch and knew the politician's skills of pumping flesh and eating tamales on the stump with the peasants, the son was stiff and essentially uninterested in politics.

A general by occupation, Somoza liked to call himself "a business-man." By 1972, the Somoza family had amassed a fortune estimated to be in the neighborhood of $500 million. Somoza shared opportunities for enrichment with senior National Guard officers, whose perquisites included concessions in drug trafficking and prostitution.

Somoza learned from his father that it was important to remain close to the United States, particularly the CIA. So he opened National Guard bases to the CIA in 1959 to train anti-Communist Cuban exile fighters and flyers. Concerned by critical comments John F. Kennedy made about him and his brother during the 1960 U.S. presidential campaign, Tacho attended the young president's inauguration as a sign of respect. His visit was also a cover to meet with CIA director Allen Dulles. Somoza told *Time* correspondent Bernard Deiderich that his one-hour conversation with the CIA chief concerned the question of whether the new Kennedy administration would go along with the Eisenhower administration's paramilitary invasion plans to overthrow Fidel Castro. Deiderich wrote of Somoza's recollection:

Tacho recalled that the old spy chief had looked quizzically at him and asked, "Now, General, what do you want in return?" Dulles pulled harder on his pipe and let out a cloud of tobacco smoke when I told him, "Not a damn thing, Mr. Dulles." He was very cordial and assured me that the project would continue. Reassuring him, I said, "We are brother officers." Then because of the enormous push Dulles had with the new administration I did say it would be a good thing if someone kept the liberals around Washington from poking at Luis and me.

Having inherited Eisenhower's invasion plot, Kennedy agreed with Dulles to push ahead. But as he entered the White House, the story of the CIA-trained Cuban paramilitary training camps in Guatemala began leaking in the Guatemalan press. Somoza offered to deepen Nicaragua's role in the plan and lend Washington his Puerto Cabezas military facilities as the port from which to stage the invasion instead of Guatemala. Within days, a thankful CIA mobilized unmarked planes to airlift tons of aerial bombs, rockets, and small firearms from Guatemala to Nicaraguan National Guard facilities. Though the Bay of Pigs ended disastrously for the Cuban exiles and the Kennedy administration, Somoza again proved his usefulness. Castro, however, never forgave Somoza and swore he would someday overthrow him.

Prior to the late 1970s, non-Marxist political opposition to the Somoza regime was small and inarticulate. Elections were rigged by buying votes and entire political parties. In the late 1950s and early 1960s, Pedro Joaquín Chamorro, a descendant of a long line of Nicaraguan Conservative leaders, invaded Nicaragua from neighboring Costa Rica a number of times with small bands of Conservative activists. But their offensives were never properly planned or supplied, and Chamorro eventually turned to journalism. Somoza, who said only he could stop communism in Nicaragua, blocked the evolution of democracy— at a time when the economy was expanding and a middle class that would soon demand a share of political power was growing.

Three Marxist-Leninist student leaders—Carlos Fonseca Amador, Silvio Mayorga, and Tomás Borge—took the Cuban model of guerrilla insurrection to heart, split with the nonviolent Nicaraguan Socialist party, and founded a guerrilla movement in July 1961. Their goal was as radical as Castro's: the military overthrow of the Somoza regime and the destruction of all vestiges of Yankee imperialism. Fonseca, the son of a Somoza-allied business manager, studied politics in Moscow, and was the most forceful and brilliant of the three. It was his decision to name the movement after Augusto César Sandino, recognizing the mythic power of Sandino in the Nicaraguan consciousness, personifying the nation's nationalistic and rebellious streak.

Over the first decade of their existence, the Sandinistas lost in one military campaign after another. In 1963, Borge and Santos López, an aging officer from Sandino's original army, led sixty ill-equipped and ill-trained guerrillas across the Coco River from Honduras. They attempted to politicize the Miskito Indians, but speaking neither Miskito nor English themselves, they made no progress. The Sandinistas were driven back into Honduras within a few months, and most sought refuge in Cuba to wait and fight another day.

The Sandinistas picked up little peasant or worker support. According to Sandinista Comandante Omar Cabezas's autobiographical *Fire from the Mountain*, when he joined the guerrillas in the 1960s only "a small [support] network existed, [and] it was very shaky—there were too many stretches, sometimes up to a three-day march, where we didn't have one collaborator among the campesinos."

By 1968, there were only about fifty Sandinistas alive, but of those a new generation had arisen, led by two brothers, Daniel and Humberto Ortega Saavedra. The two Ortegas, the sons of a chemical and textile import broker, were student radicals who started their revolutionary days vandalizing cars outside the U.S. embassy and robbing banks. The Ortega brothers had resented the upper class since their teenage years, not because they were poor but because they were middle-class parvenus. When their father's business went bankrupt in the mid-1950s, the Ortegas were forced to transfer from a ritzy private parochial school to an ordinary public school. Their old upper-class schoolmates snubbed them while leftist Salvadoran exiles teaching in their new school took them under their wing. The outcast Ortegas, seething from their rejection, joined the Nicaraguan Patriot Youth, a radical activist group founded by Fidel Castro's ambassador to Managua.

In this formative time for the revolution, young Daniel was caught by the National Guard robbing a dairy company and spent seven years in a Somoza prison, where he was severely tortured and almost lost an eye. Daniel was shy and softspoken but indefatigable. He organized a hunger strike and other inmate activities, sustained a letter-writing relationship with Monsignor Miguel Obando y Bravo, the future cardinal, read Victor Hugo's *Les Misérables* several times, and wrote poetry, including one inelegant poem entitled "I Never Saw Managua when Miniskirts Were in Fashion." Meanwhile, Humberto trained for several years in Cuba and lost most use of his right arm when he was shot by Costa Rican police in an unsuccessful attempt at freeing Carlos Fonseca from a Costa Rican jail.

The Sandinistas developed into a hardened and resilient vanguard. As Cabezas later wrote, "The new [Sandinista] man began to be born with fungus infections and with his feet oozing worms; the new man began to be born with loneliness and eaten alive by mosquitos; he began to be born stinking. That's the outer part, because inside, by dint of violent shocks day after day, the new man was being born with the freshness of the mountains." Such a vanguard would be ready to strike if somehow, some way, the political conditions of the country changed.

Nicaragua's entire political climate did change, literally overnight, on December 23, 1972, when a massive earthquake leveled Managua, killing at least 10,000 people, injuring 20,000 more, and leaving 250,000 of the city's 325,000 residents homeless. Somoza's National Guard shamelessly took advantage of the catastrophe by looting stores and houses. The regime appeared to be cracking.

But President Richard Nixon never forgot the Somozas' help in operations against Guatemala and Cuba. He ordered the U.S. Southern Command to deploy six hundred combat troops to Managua to bring order and distribute relief. American soldiers pitched their tents in the gardens of Somoza's El Retiro residence as a sign that Washington opposed any ideas of a coup. In the wake of the disaster, Somoza fired a coalition junta, then misused millions of dollars of international relief assistance. He and the top people in the National Guard and Liberal party made millions more on land deals around Managua for the partial reconstruction of the capital. One Somoza aide, Col. Rafael Adonis Porras Largaespada, reportedly bought a piece of land for $70,000 in June 1975, then sold it to the government three months later for more than $3 million.

Somoza's behavior set almost the entire Nicaraguan public, including the business community, against him. When he attempted to channel Church relief through the grass-roots Liberal party apparatus, Monsignor Obando y Bravo, the new archbishop of Managua, spoke out indignantly against the dictatorship. Under Obando y Bravo's cautious but strong leadership, the Roman Catholic church steadily moved away from Somoza and tacitly approved the urban and rural organizing activities of anti-Somoza clergy and lay ministers. With his Liberal party thoroughly corrupted, and the support of the Church and private sector thoroughly eroded, all Somoza had left propping him up was his National Guard and support from Washington.

As the only disciplined military organization in the country, aside from the National Guard, the Sandinista National Liberation Front

(FSLN) was the one political group that could take advantage of the general popular disdain for the Somoza regime. The Sandinistas (with perhaps 150 armed guerrillas in the early 1970s) provided themselves with a major international propaganda boost on December 27, 1974, when they stormed a farewell party hosted by a Somocista businessman for U.S. Ambassador Turner Shelton. Shelton, along with his wife and mother-in-law, had already left the party when the guerrillas arrived, but the rebels still came up with Somoza's brother-in-law and cousin, the foreign minister, the mayor of Managua, and ten other Nicaraguan socialites. Under pressure from his relatives, Somoza decided to deal. In exchange for their fourteen prisoners, Somoza released several Sandinista political prisoners (including Daniel Ortega) from jail and paid a $1 million ransom. As Daniel joined his brother Humberto in Cuba for ideological training, young Nicaraguans began to join the FSLN in larger numbers. After Fonseca was killed in an ambush in 1976, the Sandinistas fractured into three "tendencies," and the two Ortegas emerged as the top comandantes. Believing in bold, immediate action and expanding the revolutionary movement to include the bourgeoisie, they eventually led the Sandinistas to victory.

It was a series of articles in the feisty opposition daily *La Prensa* that eventually brought Somoza down. The 1977 series documented how a blood bank owned by Somoza in partnership with Cuban exile Dr. Pedro Ramos was making a 300 percent profit from buying the blood of poor Nicaraguans to be processed into plasma for export to the United States. Ramos sued *La Prensa* editor Pedro Joaquín Chamorro for libel and lost. Furious, he left Nicaragua for Miami. Weeks later, Chamorro was gunned down by several National Guardsmen while driving his car to the dentist. A hitman later apprehended linked Ramos to the crime. Nicaraguans assumed incorrectly that Somoza had ordered Chamorro's killing. Chamorro's legacy was left to his wife, Violeta.

THE END OF THE DYNASTY

As a rookie reporter for United Press International, I was sent to Managua to cover the businessmen's strike and insurrections that followed Chamorro's killing. Wherever I went, León, Masaya, Rivas, even Managua, people spontaneously complained about Somoza and the National Guard. Driving through Masaya the morning after a Sandinista attack, hundreds of people were milling around excitedly and happily in the streets. A middle-class housewife, speaking excellent English, told me, "Nobody wants Somoza. I just hope I don't lose a son in the process." I was struck by the open rebelliousness of the people, as if the National Guard was more an army to mock than to fear. A middle-aged marketwoman wearing a bright flowered dress told me in English, "Somoza, he's a son of a bitch. Tell your President Carter to get rid of him." This was not a class war.

Somoza had become so isolated from his people, and paranoid of assassination, that he rarely left his Managua National Guard head-quarters, called "el Bunker," an austere aluminum and concrete shelter shielded by an antigrenade steel-wire umbrella.

I got my chance to interview the dictator at the bunker two weeks after the Chamorro slaying. Somoza had me wait outside his office for nearly two hours. While leafing through some military magazines, I spotted Somoza's tall and stocky son, Anastasio Somoza Portocarrero, the new "Tachito" and heir apparent.

Born in Tampa and educated in American private schools before Harvard, Tachito, like his father, was more at home in the United States than in his own country. He liked stylish clothes and cars and especially boating and partying in Miami. Even his English was said to be better than his Spanish. "I love your country," he exclaimed with near solemnity. "The freedom is what I love most."

Leaning against a wall, his hands tucked in the deep pockets of his crisp battle fatigues, young Somoza advised me to be more trusting of his family's good intentions. "Try to understand me," he said. "I want to help the poor. When I was at Harvard I even marched against the Vietnam War. You know what they called me at Fort Leavenworth? The leftist of Leavenworth!" He went into a childish giggle. "How bad a guy could I be?"

Before long, I was called into the president's office. It was the eleventh day of a national business strike that had closed 80 percent of Managua's industrial sector. Relations with the human rights–conscious Carter administration were growing tenser by the day as the State Department came out with a barrage of demands to end martial law and open a dialogue with the democratic opposition.

Somoza seemed to have lost the family touch. In July 1977, he suffered a massive heart attack, forcing him to give up whiskey and cigars and to lose sixty pounds. Scandals throttled his business empire and forced him to imprison two business partners. His elegant wife, Hope Portocarrero, tired of playing second fiddle to his mistress, Dinorah, had just moved to Miami. But the killing of Chamorro was the crucial blow. Chamorro and *La Prensa* had been Somoza's democratic cover to the Carter White House and the U.S. Congress. "Pedro Joaquín and I grew up together," a distracted Somoza told me. "We were friends." Even he seemed to realize how hollow his words sounded.

Somoza appeared particularly gaunt below a framed photograph of himself as the portly self-confident dictator taken before his heart attack. But he still enjoyed sparring with American reporters in the 1950s slang English he picked up at Christian Brothers' Military Academy on Long Island and at West Point. Like his father, he preferred the company of Americans—even those who disagreed with him— over Nicaraguans.

I was looking for a scoop for the next day's afternoon newspapers, but Somoza was obviously in no mood to help me. His answers were curt, rarely more than "yes" or "no," over the first twenty minutes of the interview. Fortunately, he made one interesting comment that made headlines the next day in the United States and Latin America. "The businessmen strikers," he said, "are working together with the Sandinistas." That Somoza made the remarkable charge in public that Marxist rebels and businessmen had found cause to unite was admission of just how desperate his political position had become.

I raised the subject of Chamorro's assassination and asked why anyone would have committed such a crime. Somoza was evasive, and then he suddenly got up as if to signal that the interview, at the time only twenty-five minutes long, was over.

"The murder is a mystery hovering over your head," I commented, perhaps a bit too sharply, as I got up. Losing his patience, Somoza replied sternly, "Yours, not mine." His words literally had no meaning, but I took them as a threat, and my knees almost buckled. I thanked him for the interview and asked if there wasn't anything more he wanted to say.

"Listen, why don't you reverse all the bad publicity and write about our stability?" The word *stability* seemed to lag on his lips and made his voice crack.

"What do you mean?" I answered incredulously. "You just told me 80 percent of the Managua business sector is striking to bring down your government."

Somoza became combative. "I know my country better than you do!" Somoza exclaimed. "Those are a handful of people striking. The farmers aren't striking. The workers aren't striking. The government isn't falling. That's stability!" Again, he seemed to have trouble with the word *stability*, as if the word unhinged his English just for an instant.

By late 1978, Nicaragua's Pacific coast was on the verge of national insurrection. The Sandinistas captured the imagination of the country's urban population that August when a twenty-five-man commando team, led by Edén Pastora and dressed in National Guard uniforms, took the entire national congress hostage.* Somoza wavered, and then gave in to Sandinista demands to free fifty-eight political prisoners, including their most experienced comandante, Tomás Borge, and pay them a $500,000 ransom. Spontaneously, students rose up in arms across Nicaragua's western cities over the next four weeks in an insurrection that exploded faster than even the Sandinistas had anticipated.

I witnessed one of the first of those insurrections, in the hilly cobblestone city of Matagalpa, during the final days of August 1978. The trouble began over a demand by a Sandinista-front student group that a "Somocista" high school principal resign. Tensions flared when one student, attempting to throw a homemade bomb at a National Guardsman, was shot to death. Led by a few adolescents, some 450 high school students furtively borrowed pistols and shotguns from their fathers, put on face masks, and shot up the National Guard *cuartel*. Somoza compared the students to youth gangs that stalk the Bronx, and then ordered the National Guard air force to strafe the city with rockets and machine guns.

All the traffic was going south along the Pan-American Highway on August 30, except for the reporters and relief volunteers driving north to embattled Matagalpa. After the turnoff at the saloon and gasoline station town of Sebaco, where the northern highway splits off the Pan-American Highway for Matagalpa, the southbound lanes were clogged with pickup trucks loaded with Matagalpa families and their rocking chairs, stoves, and animals. Scores of poorer refugees hiked along the road, carrying on their backs sticks of furniture, boxes of clothes, and food.

The frenetic Red Cross headquarters stood near the entrance to the city. Nurses complained that the National Guard was surrounding the

---

*Each commando was given a number; Pastora was Comandante Cero, a nom de guerre that stuck ever after.

city, blocking supply shipments to take care of the wounded. "There will be a massacre," one nurse told me. One of the doctors introduced me to a woman who was a former prisoner at a National Guard jail. The woman showed me cigarette burn marks around her belly and back. She recalled one torture method in which she was interrogated for hours at a time with a metal helmet over her head that worked like an echo chamber. She had been accused of being a Sandinista activist.

"And?" I asked.

"Of course I'm a Sandinista, just like everyone."

The National Guard officer in charge of the coming mop-up operation gave reporters forty-five minutes to go downtown before he would dislodge the armed resistance.

Shrouded by a steady gray drizzle, Matagalpa looked like a ghost town. About five hundred people, afraid to leave the city or remain in their homes, huddled in the San José church, under a roof flying white flags. Red Cross volunteers burned corpses with gasoline to prevent disease as already fattened birds of prey, perched on overhanging tile roofs, looked on. There was no other movement on the streets, which were full of glass spread around as a defensive measure by the muchachos. The whitewashed stucco houses were shut tight, windows were boarded up with planks of wood. At every other corner, teenage boys and girls were manning barricades of sandbags, oil drums, concrete blocks, and wooden planks. They wore red-and-black Sandinista bandanas and chanted "Patría Libre o Morir. Free Country or Death," the slogan of Augusto César Sandino's men.

At first blush it was a ludicrous sight, these children playing their war games on the hilly cobblestoned streets, but with live ammunition. Paradoxically, the younger the fighter, the more fanatical he or she looked. One boy fighter was twelve years old.

A fifteen-year-old girl named Ana stiffly held her .22 caliber pistol behind a barricade. "Don't you realize," I asked her, "that the National Guard is coming in here at any time?"

"We're taking a stand for our country," she replied. "We won't move."

There wasn't much time to talk before I thought it was appropriate to grab a ride in a Red Cross ambulance out of Matagalpa and to safety. We got out moments before the shooting started. The Guardsmen charged behind an armored car fortified with 37mm cannons. With National Guard special forces surrounding the city's perimeter to make sure that Sandinista regulars couldn't slip into town to reinforce the students, it looked as if the kids were trapped.

I couldn't clearly see the battle from my perch on top of a hill overlooking Matagalpa, but I heard loud blasts of automatic weapons fire that seemed to last five minutes at a clip. The return fire was a spurt here and there, completely overwhelmed by the incoming fire of the National Guardsmen's cannon and G-3 assault rifles. But before the National Guard could crush them, most of the student fighters took their masks off and melted into their houses to fight another day.

Frustrated, National Guardsmen burst into the Hotel Soza, a small family lodging house, and opened fire at the reception desk, killing four unarmed civilians. In all, about fifty people were killed and more than two hundred wounded in Matagalpa over five days of fighting, until the young rebels ran out of ammunition.

After the insurrections in Masaya and León that September, it was all downhill for Somoza. The Sandinistas had all the popular support they needed—and only lacked better planning, better arms, and more ammunition to win the war. The revolution reached a turning point in March 1979 when Fidel Castro convinced the comandantes that they needed to unify in order to win his full support. By June, when the urban students rebelled again, they had automatic weapons, and they fought in coordination with regular Sandinista units operating out of Costa Rica and the Nicaraguan central highlands. Armed shipments from Cuba, Venezuela, and Panama were funneled through Costa Rica, and made all the difference to the Sandinistas. They easily overthrew the National Guard only three months after the unification. The undermanned Guard, expanded from a mere 7,500 to 11,000 by the end of the war, was simply overwhelmed. When the Carter administration virtually cut off military aid in 1977, the Guard was left dangling as an occupation force without a sponsor. (During two years of sporadic fighting, about 25,000 people lost their lives in the conflict—a good portion innocent civilians in National Guard air bombings during the final eighteen months of the war.)

Carter's State Department attempted to negotiate a settlement in which Somoza would be replaced by moderates before the Sandinistas could take power. But Carter never dared to push Somoza too hard, largely because National Security Adviser Zbigniew Brzezinski argued that a Sandinista victory would open the way for the Soviets to build a base on the Latin American mainland.

The Sandinista revolution of 1979 was unique. This was not a polarizing conflict. Unlike the military regimes of El Salvador, Honduras, and Guatemala, Somoza's dynasty had few Nicaraguan roots. It was a struggle of virtually an entire population against a corrupt, family-based oligarchy protected by an unprofessional premodern army founded by a foreign power and manned by the most backward peasants of the north-central highlands. More than anything else, the Sandinista revolution gave the country a sense of purpose and unity, even for only a moment. The new Sandinista junta, awaiting its triumphant arrival into Nicaragua, promised to found a democratic government similar to Costa Rica's. The Sandinistas kept their true agenda—the consolidation and expansion of a Marxist-Leninist revolution—a secret.

THE SANDINISTA REVOLUTION

In that precious month of July 1979, virtually every Nicaraguan proudly called himself a Sandinista. When the rotting Somoza dictatorship fell on the seventeenth, and a ragtag column of three hundred rebels dressed in fatigues and berets entered Managua two days later, the poor and privileged alike rejoiced. In an exercise of catharsis, a crowd ripped down an equestrian statue of Anastasio Somoza García, founder of the hated dynasty.

The goodwill spread to the most unexpected quarters. Businessmen took to the radio and television airwaves to pledge their support for the revolution. Special U.S. envoy William Bowdler made a surprise appearance at the Sandinistas' victory parade in Managua on the twentieth, and Archbishop Miguel Obando y Bravo blessed the new ruling junta following its entrance into Managua's crammed plaza atop a fire engine. The crowds, massing 50,000 people, hoisted placards celebrating neither Marx nor Lenin but Augusto César Sandino, a pure nationalist who had resisted outside Communist influence on his movement.

A youthful and shy Daniel Ortega, a member of the five-person junta, sensed what the people wanted to hear. He spoke of his hopes for "political pluralism," "nonalignment," and a "mixed economy," and he assured the crowd that the revolution was Christian in essence. Ortega even conceded that maybe Nicaragua could live with Washington. "We are open," he said, "to friendly, respectful, and noninterventionist policies by the United States in the future."

Sandinista radio warned against pillaging of private property and even ordered militia youth to stop their euphoric firing of rifles in the air. "We understand your happiness," lectured the radio announcer, "[but] the people have won peace and they deserve to have it." Nicaragua's newfound peace was as invigorating as a tropical downpour that steams the heat out of an afternoon. And it was to prove just as ephemeral as Nicaraguans once again looked abroad to make war against each other.

From the very beginning, the FSLN displayed two faces: one ideological, inspired by Socialist dreams and hatred for the United States; the other pragmatic, capable of molding its tactics to whatever political and economic realities it faced. A newsstand in the National Palace displayed the pluralism: copies of *Cosmopolitan* magazine were sold beside the *Complete Works of Lenin.*

The first year of Sandinista rule was one of improvisation. Nicaraguan moderates, who did not belong to the FSLN, like junta members Violeta Chamorro and Alfonso Robelo and the first two presidents of the Central Bank, Arturo Cruz and Alfredo César, played important roles in the government. Indeed, moderates took the reins of economic policy, which encouraged the private sector to remain in the country. Financing was guaranteed for private farmers, who continued to control 80 percent of the land. Foreign exchange was promised for private firms needing to import parts and raw materials. Nearly all Nicaraguans supported the Sandinista government's national literacy and health campaigns mobilized in an attempt to wipe out illiteracy and polio. The Sandinistas were anxious to show the world they were moderates: they pledged to meet the government's obligations to Western banks left from the Somoza days, and they treated their National Guard prisoners with generosity.

There were aspects of the revolution that were downright conservative. The first Defense Minister was a former National Guard colonel. Many Somoza laws were left on the books, including those regulating opposition political parties and labor rights. The revolutionaries took control of the Somoza labor confederation and renamed it the Sandinista Worker Central (CST), which frequently functioned to keep wages down to aid the new government's anti-inflation policy. From 1979 through 1981, the CST repeatedly reoccupied by force private factories that had been taken over by Communist union activists aiming to push the revolution to the left and returned them to their owners. A Trotskyist radio station and newspaper were quashed, while *La Prensa,* which Carter fortified with covert CIA funding, was allowed to publish.

The second decree of the junta provided for the transfer of properties owned by the Somozas and their cronies to the new political elite. By the end of July, comandantes were living in the old Somocista mansions and driving Mercedes-Benz limousines inscribed with the slogan "Property of the People" painted on their sides. Comandante Tomás Borge accumulated currency exchange houses, import-export businesses, hotels, and was even linked to a small drug smuggling operation. Comandante Jamie Wheelock, the Agrarian Reform minister, had a particular flair about his indulgences. While his country suffered a foreign exchange crunch, Wheelock's wife got permission and dollars to import flowers from Europe for her garden while his mother's chauffeur became one of Managua's leading black market currency exchangers.

The Sandinistas put into place two governments: one pluralist, led by the five-man junta; the other Leninist, secretly controlled by the nine-man Sandinista party directorate and profoundly influenced by Cuba. Three days following the victory over Somoza, the directorate met for the first time with members of the ruling junta. The two non-Sandinistas—Violeta Chamorro and Alfonso Robelo—were not invited or even aware of the meeting. The invitation list, however, did include Cuban Ambassador Julián López, who arrived dressed in military fatigues. Junta member Moisés Hassan, a senior member of the Sandinista government between 1979 and 1987, recalled "how surprised I was to see a foreigner in such a position of power."

The main theme of the meeting was how the Sandinistas could consolidate control through organizing a large army, security apparatus, and popular organizations like unions to be controlled by the party leadership. "López had ideas on all of this," Hassan recalled to me in 1989 after he had left the government to found an independent leftist party. "He told us how the Cubans took care of such things." According to Hassan, López lectured the Sandinistas. "You can be sure the United States will be aggressive," he said. "Washington will confront you sooner or later. But don't worry. We will always be behind you."

An erudite man of great charm, as well as a man with direct access to Castro, Ambassador López developed a relationship of trust with Sandinista leaders in the months before the victory over Somoza, when he directed Cuban arms supplies to the Nicaraguan rebels from his diplomatic post in Costa Rica. He positioned himself as a mediator between comandantes of the three traditional tendencies. López stayed out of economic planning, but he was frequently decisive in matters relating to intelligence and security, including decisions on how to handle opposition demonstrations. He also promoted the careers of Sandinistas closely aligned with Cuba, including Carlos Fernando Chamorro, editor of the party newspaper *Barricada,* and Fishing Minister Carlos Coronel. López simply filled the role traditionally played by the U.S. ambassador.

That fall, when the junta voted to condemn the Soviet invasion of Afghanistan, López convinced the directorate to veto the decision. The resulting abstention at the United Nations of a resolution to condemn the Soviet action convinced Violeta Chamorro and Alfonso Robelo that they should resign from the government.

The Cubans were everywhere. Within a week of the victory, the Sandinistas began organizing Sandinista Defense Committees, block associations that served as the "eyes and ears" of the revolution. They were designed with the support of Cuban advisers along the lines of the Committees for Revolutionary Defense founded by Castro in the early 1960s to fight street crime, prostitution, and political dissidence. By the end of 1979, the Cuban contingent of teachers, doctors, broadcasting technicians, and military and police advisers in Nicaragua had reached at least eight hundred. Cuban secret police agents had offices in the most restricted areas of Sandinista facilities and were frequently seen giving orders to Nicaraguan employees. Their major role was instructing Nicaraguan Interior Ministry agents in counterintelligence and various methods of repression, including how to tap telephones, bug offices, and furtively open mail. At the same time, Cuban advisers were highly influential in creating the structure and doctrine of the new Sandinista army.

The early Sandinista reliance on Cuba was rooted in shared beliefs, not necessity; Nicaragua was not as isolated internationally as Cuba had been in 1960. During their first year in power, the Sandinistas attracted $580 million in foreign aid and loans from around the world, including $63 million from the Carter administration. Panamanian leader Omar Torrijos sent police advisers to help Comandante Borge set up his Interior Ministry, but Borge assigned them to lowly traffic duties. Bitterly disappointed, Torrijos removed his police. Similarly, Venezuelan offers to send military advisers were rebuffed. Even the United States, under the Carter administration, offered to send Nicaragua the Peace Corps and military advisers to help the new government. The Sandinistas answered that they were not interested in having "CIA agents" in their midst.

The Sandinistas were not concerned about the interference of Cuba, although the Nicaraguan people—particularly the English-speaking Miskitos and black creoles who live on the Atlantic coast—bridled at their presence. The first popular demonstrations against the Sandinista government, in the towns of Prinzapolka and Bluefields in August and September 1980, were aimed at removing "atheistic" Cuban doctors and teachers. The Sandinista army made a bad situation worse by taking the side of the Cubans, and lodging reinforcements in local Moravian churches—a sacrilege to the Indians—in order to secure the safety of their "internationalist" guests.

The Sandinista comandantes believed deeply in the Cuban revolution. In part, their affection was based on their years of sanctuary there and the important military aid they received from Castro. They considered Cuba Latin America's vanguard and only world-class military power. Having just recently held back the South African army in Angola, Cuba was considered invincible. Some comandantes, particularly directorate member Bayardo Arce, were convinced the United States only backed away from sending the Marines to Nicaragua because of Washington's fear of the Cuban army. But the most powerful attraction was ideological; as the Sandinistas proclaimed in private meetings, their revolution was Socialist and internationalist like Cuba's. The comandantes were young and inexperienced; they believed they needed help and advice from El Viejo, "the old man."

The first anniversary of the revolution represented a watershed, a turn, though a temporary one, away from tactical moderation. Nicaraguans hoped Comandante Daniel Ortega would announce elections, but they were treated to a huge military parade complete with freshly imported tanks and armored personnel carriers instead. The honeymoon was over. Within a month, the Sandinistas banned the broadcast or publication of uncensored news stories relating to economic problems or state security. In August, Comandante Humberto Ortega told army troops that elections would not be held until 1985. He added, "These will not be elections to decide who is in power, because the people hold power, through their vanguard, the Sandinista Front."

November brought a distinctly Stalinist chill. First the Nicaraguan Democratic Movement, a liberal opposition party formed by Robelo, the former junta member, was forbidden to hold a rally, and youthful Sandinistas—known as the *turbas divinas* (divine mobs)—sacked the party's Managua headquarters. Next, the country's most charismatic opposition figure was killed by police.

Jorge Salazar Arguello was organizing an anti-Sandinista movement among the peasants of coffee-growing Matagalpa province, many of whom resented Sandinista efforts to organize them into cooperatives and state farms. His rapid success deeply concerned the comandantes, particularly Borge. Salazar was approached by a Sandinista party officer named Nestór Moncada, who presented himself as a dissident, Moncada told Salazar that there were army units ready to rebel against the directorate. Moncada urged Salazar to get arms from abroad for his sympathizers. Salazar agreed to help. On November 18, Salazar was to meet Moncada at a gas station outside Managua. Instead, the unarmed Salazar was met by police and shot seven times. Sandinista officials later claimed Salazar died in a cross fire between a co-conspirator who had fired first and the police. Moncada was tried by a military court as a conspirator against the government and freed without spending a day in prison.

Sandinista repression swelled as the economy soured and as relations with the Soviet bloc deepened. Both factors were rooted in a secret party-to-party agreement negotiated the previous March in Moscow between the Soviet Communist party and the Sandinista National Liberation Front. The agreement, signed by Soviet Foreign Minister Andrei Gromyko as well as Comandantes Borge, Humberto Ortega, and Henry Ruiz, recognized the FSLN as the "vanguard party" of Nicaragua and pledged that the Sandinistas would be loyal to the Soviet foreign policy cause. For signing the agreement, Managua received $100 million in cash from Libya, East German security personnel, and Russian and Bulgarian economic advisers.

By late 1980, the Russians and Bulgarians, holding key posts in the Nicaraguan Planning Ministry, designed a new, East European–style national economic plan. Their program quickened the pace of confiscation of private property and established government control over 80 percent of internal commerce—complete with ration cards, state cattle slaughterhouses, and state supermarkets. A new state-installed price-control policy designed to benefit poor urban consumers was perhaps the most damaging element of the Russian and Bulgarian planners; tens of thousands of rural farmers, unable to make a profit under the new price structure, stopped producing (causing food shortages) and began migrating to the cities (crowding the slums of Managua).

The Ministry of Internal Commerce (Micoin), the ministry most influenced by Bulgarian and Russian thinking, soon became the most unpopular ministry of the entire government. As circulator of ration cards (through the Sandinista block committees), manager of market prices and supplies, and primary purchaser of basic grains from peasants, Micoin was blamed for all of the country's woes. Its personnel manned roadblocks around the country to block transport of basic goods not sold through government agencies. Its market inspectors, who levied heavy fines and confiscated produce, inflamed the market-women of Managua's Eastern Market and created a huge black market.

Such economic policies inspired by Sandinista Socialist dreams and Soviet bloc advice produced widespread ill will—and crippled the Nicaraguan economy for years to come. According to Sandinista government statistics, labor productivity, real wages, and per capita consumption contracted sharply between 1980 and 1983 even as the gross domestic product grew due to the influx of generous amounts of foreign aid from the West and East. By early 1983, before the Contra war was a dominant factor, Nicaragua's economy was already spinning out of control, with sharply falling production and export of coffee, cotton, and sugar; an inflation rate of 40 percent; rising unemployment; and weekly black market currency devaluations. Before long, supermarket shelves were empty of almost everything but expensive Polish pâté and Bulgarian rabbit.

Arturo Cruz, Jr., a top Sandinista party economic and diplomatic adviser until he defected in late 1982, recalls a private 1982 Sandinista assessment of the economy that predicted disaster unless the Soviets came through with a major bailout. "The foreign exchange gap we were coming out with was in the vicinity of $400 million to $500 million a year beginning in 1983 to the end of the decade," he said. "I was terrified." That May, Daniel Ortega went to Moscow for the first of many trips attempting to deepen the Soviet economic commitment to Nicaragua. He came away with a $100 million line of credit to buy agricultural equipment, not a big deal considering the regime's dire straits. Cruz went to party foreign policy chief Julio López and Comandante Arce to voice his concern. "López and Arce told me, 'Don't worry Arturo, the Soviets will come through in 1985. We have assurances 1985 will be the decisive year.' "

According to Sandinista figures, economic assistance from the Soviet bloc peaked in 1982 at about $250 million, and then leveled off to about $150 million in 1983 and 1984. According to American analysts Jiri and Virginia Valenta, Soviet bloc economic aid to Nicaragua reached a less than overwhelming $600 million between July 1979 and June 1985. The year 1985 came and went, but Moscow never made the economic commitment to the Sandinistas that it made to Cuba in order to construct a Socialist system. Leonid Brezhnev's successors evidentally were too busy in Afghanistan and Eastern Europe to offer the Sandinistas anything more than a safety net.

The Soviet bloc role in Nicaragua was a constant irritant in the always uneasy relationship between Managua and Washington, but it was the Sandinista decision to follow Cuba's lead to intervene in the Salvadoran revolution that caused the decisive break with the United States.

On the first anniversary of the revolution, when Castro made his first public visit to Managua, he organized a tripartite meeting between Salvadoran comandantes, Sandinista leaders, and top Cuban strategists including himself. The Salvadoran rebels claimed that the U.S.-backed junta was on its last legs, and that if they received enough weaponry and supplies in a timely fashion, they could topple the regime quickly. Castro agreed to provide them with all they needed provided the five rebel groups united into one organization. The Salvadorans agreed, and Castro urged the Sandinistas to donate Nicaraguan territory for the supply effort. The Nicaraguan comandantes were sympathetic but asked for time.

The directorate owed the Salvadoran guerrillas a huge debt for siphoning millions of dollars the Salvadoran rebels earned from their kidnappings of the 1970s. As the Sandinistas saw it, the "final offensive" the Salvadoran guerrillas promised would greet the new Republican administration in the United States they anticipated with a revolutionary government already installed in El Salvador. Guatemala, and then Honduras and Costa Rica, would follow, according to the most hopeful scenario. "We had radical ideas, radical dreams," recalled Sandinista junta member Sergio Ramírez three years later. "We thought we could push the Central American revolution faster. All triumphant revolutions think they have no frontiers."

Following Castro's urging, the party directorate met to make their most fateful decision since taking power. On the one hand were the radical dreams, but on the other was a congressional stipulation to the

Carter administration's Nicaragua aid package that the Sandinistas refrain from backing neighboring rebel movements. Tens of millions of badly needed dollars could be lost.

"The nine were all to one degree or another for aiding the Salvadorans, despite an expected North American reaction," Edén Pastora (Comandante Cero), who was called into a directorate meeting for consultation on the issue, told me after he left the government. "I told them the FMLN wasn't ready to take power and I voiced my opposition. Borge was the decisive voice when he said we could use the Salvadorans as a bargaining chip in negotiations with the United States."

The "final offensive" failed, and U.S. intelligence came up with a pile of guerrilla documents in El Salvador verifying the Nicaraguan role in the offensive. The Carter administration was forced to suspend aid. U.S. Ambassador Lawrence Pezzullo, who pushed aid for Nicaragua through a skeptical Congress, took the news of Sandinista involvement in the Salvadoran offensive as a bitter personal offense. Only hours after he received the intelligence cable from Washington informing him of Nicaraguan intervention in El Salvador, he cornered Comandante Borge at a diplomatic cocktail party. Pezzullo was furious. "Tomás, you don't deserve the treatment I've been giving you. This was a dirty deal."

Borge denied any involvement in El Salvador.

"You're lying to me," Pezzullo snapped. "You've lied to me before and you're lying to me again."

Pezzullo let loose with some barely controlled rage. "I never pushed you on your romantic attachment to these people in Salvador," he said. "That's your business, but this is shit." Pezzullo even suggested there could be a retaliation from the Salvadoran army: "If I were a Salvadoran, I'd burn your ass. You're the one sitting around talking about preserving your revolution. You have some goddamn nerve talking about your fucking revolution. Tomás, you're a disgrace."

Borge got the message. The next day, junta coordinator Daniel Ortega came to see Pezzullo at the U.S. embassy to begin a series of conversations on the issue of El Salvador. Although Ortega would never directly admit the Sandinistas were involved in the Salvadoran revolution, the Nicaraguan decommissioned airplanes, closed down a Salvadoran radio station, and stopped the flow of aid from Managua. Negotiations worked.

That very week, Ronald Reagan became president. Pezzullo decided to stay on, despite his opposition to the emerging policy line. Pezzullo was out of step, but he hoped that in time the White House would see that the carrot of U.S. aid could modify Sandinista action. "I told the new bunch that we should pursue these talks with the Sandinistas," Pezzullo recalled. "But of course there was a whole new attitude. They were already in discussions with the Argentines [to establish the Contras]."

The Reagan administration gave the Sandinistas one last chance to demonstrate moderation, then promptly pulled the rug out from under them. In August 1981, before the Contras had become more than a military nuisance, Thomas Enders, then Assistant Secretary of State for Inter-American Affairs, flew to Managua for two days of talks with top comandantes. In a private meeting with Daniel Ortega at the old Managua Country Club, Enders forged a tentative verbal agreement with Ortega: in return for the Sandinistas' promise to curtail their military buildup and stop backing Marxist rebellions elsewhere, Washington would not use force against Nicaragua and would enforce the Neutrality Act to stop Contra training in Florida.

As Enders described the discussion, he told Ortega, "We'll accept your government but not a revolution across the isthmus." Picking up on the concession, the Sandinista leader said, "We're willing to discuss that." Enders and Ortega concluded their talk by agreeing that their two governments would prepare detailed working papers from which a formal nonaggression pact might be worked out. But as so often seems to happen in Central America, otherwise competing political extremes unwittingly conspired to avert peace.

Back in Washington, two of the harshest ideologues of the early Reagan administration, National Security Adviser Richard Allen and his aide Roger Fontaine, rewrote the State Department draft coming out of the Enders-Ortega meeting. As Pezzullo put it years later, "Allen and Fontaine just decided to play hardball with these bastards. You can say reduce your weaponry but to say destroy the T-55 tanks, which is a defensive weapon anyway, was a little brusque. The language was: this is what you have to do." Several comandantes on the directorate found the new draft blunt, arbitrary, and offensive. The perceived slight was the perfect excuse to stall Ortega's peace initiative.

The divided Sandinista directorate debated for weeks on what to do without responding to the U.S. draft or submitting its own. Unable to settle the matter, Daniel Ortega flew to Havana in early September to consult with Castro and Edén Pastora, who by this time had left

Nicaragua and was living in a Cuban protocol house. As Pastora tells the story, Ortega explained the agreement with Enders. Castro reportedly replied, "No chico, you still have time in your favor. You don't have to make a deal yet. Wait." Castro was opposed to the Enders agreement because he believed it showed that the Reagan administration's rhetoric was more bark than bite. He also thought the Salvadoran guerrillas could win their civil war, and he did not want to preclude sending them aid through Nicaragua. "The Salvadorans are like the Russian missiles we once had in Cuba. Don't bargain them away until you have to," Castro concluded.

The Sandinistas never responded to the redrafted Enders agreement. It would prove to be a costly lost opportunity for both Washington and Managua.

THE COUNTERREVOLUTION

Anastasio Somoza's National Guard never entirely dropped its arms, even after the deposed president was assassinated by Argentine guerrillas in Paraguay in September 1980. Those who didn't migrate to Miami became hired guns for death squads in Guatemala, El Salvador, and Honduras or cattle rustlers along Nicaragua's northern border with Honduras. The Sandinistas called the former Guardsmen "Contras," for counterrevolutionaries, and the name stuck.

The new Sandinista government pressed Honduran chief of state Gen. Policarpo Paz García to move against the Contras, who set up camps on the Honduran side of the border with Nicaragua. After a series of talks with Daniel Ortega, Paz García promised he would. But the chief of the Honduran police force, Col. Enrique Alvarez, had another idea. Alvarez decided Honduras needed to help organize a group of former National Guardsmen as a shield to defend Honduras against Sandinista expansionism. The guerrilla band was named the Fifteenth of September League, and it came under the formal command of former National Guard Col. Enrique Bermúdez. According to former aides, Alvarez's ultimate hope was to draw the United States into a war with Nicaragua to rid the region of the Communist threat once and for all.

Without the approval of his superiors or even the knowledge of the U.S. embassy, Alvarez set in motion a policy that would commit

Honduras to aid an insurgency against the Sandinistas for the next decade. Alvarez found ready allies in the Argentine military junta, which viewed Nicaragua as a base for Argentine Marxist guerrillas known as the Montoneros. Meanwhile, he drew himself ever closer to the CIA socially and politically. When it was time for the CIA's Tegucigalpa station chief "Mike Farmer" to select a godfather for his newborn son, he turned to Alvarez.

The Contras' first serious, organized mission occurred in Costa Rica at the behest of the Argentine military regime of Gen. Roberto Viola. Viola was obsessed with a left-wing shortwave radio station—Radio Noticias del Continente—operated in San José by Argentine exiles to transmit a revolutionary message across the hemisphere. Believing that the station's reports on Argentine army torture were a threat to his regime, he reportedly first hired right-wing Salvadoran terrorists to destroy the station. When they failed, he turned to the new Fifteenth of September League to do the job. On December 13, 1980, a Contra commando force led by former National Guard Capt. Hugo Villagra sprayed the station with machine-gun fire. Radio Noticias personnel were heavily armed themselves and drove the Nicaraguans back, wounding two seriously.

In strictly military terms, the mission was a flop. But Costa Rican President Rodrigo Carazo, fearing that his peaceful country might be swallowed by the political violence surrounding it, shut down the station following the attack, and then ordered the Guatemalan guerrilla movement to close its San José office. Reagan administration hard-liners learned from the incident that the Contras could be a useful tool.

In April 1981, "Farmer" escorted Alvarez to Washington so the Honduran police chief could push his plan for building the Contras. "Farmer" opened doors in the State Department, the Pentagon, and, of course, the CIA. Alvarez said the Nicaraguan National Guard could be reconstituted to spark a second insurrection in Nicaragua if only the United States would arm and finance the guerrilla force. He boldly offered Honduras as a base for the counterrevolutionary operation, stating that a majority of Honduran officers believed the Sandinistas were a mortal threat to their country. "Farmer" ushered the Honduran police chief in to see his boss, CIA director William Casey. Casey, who disagreed with Enders over negotiating with the Sandinistas, was a ready listener. The CIA director signed on and promised to relay Alvarez's message to President Reagan.

Still focused on domestic economic policy and the war in El Salvador, the White House modified the Alvarez-Casey plan; administration moderates and congressional leaders convinced the president that Congress would never approve a full-scale covert war against Nicaragua. Once the Enders peace mission to Nicaragua fell through, a compromise was struck, and Reagan penned a National Security Decision Directive on November 16, 1981, authorizing the CIA to spend $19.5 million to create a paramilitary Contra force to interrupt the arms flow from Nicaragua to El Salvador. Within weeks, CIA and Argentine agents were setting up Contra safe houses in Tegucigalpa and training camps around Honduras.

The Contra war was on. The CIA took control, appointing a Contra joint command staff that included Alvarez, former Nicaraguan Guard officers Bermúdez and Emilio Echaverry, Argentine Col. Osvaldo Ribiero and Santiago Villegas, and two CIA men. The CIA would never acknowledge the mistake it made by confusing its perceived need to control with the effectiveness of the force constructed around the puppet leadership. With such a Somocista- and foreign-dominated brain trust, the Contras could never project a nationalistic message or attract support in the Pacific coastal cities that only three years before rebelled against the Somoza regime.

For a time, the CIA hoped Edén Pastora, the famous Sandinista who defected in 1981, would supply the Contras with nationalistic authenticity. Based in Costa Rica and supplied from El Salvador's Ilopango military airport, Pastora grew a long beard to look like Ernesto Che Guevara, but he rarely left San José. Pastora was unreliable. His Democratic Revolutionary Alliance (ARDE) was infiltrated by the Sandinistas, even in the high command, which may explain in part why his forces were so unaggressive in the field. Worse, from the standpoint of the propaganda war in Nicaragua and the United States, Pastora publicly attacked Bermúdez and the other National Guard officers who led the Nicaraguan Democratic Force (FDN) as incorrigible Somocistas. Angered by such criticism of the FDN, the CIA and the Honduran military blocked Pastora from ever forming a northern front based along the Honduras-Nicaragua border.

Aside from its brief flirtation with Pastora, the Reagan administration didn't consider backing any anti-Sandinista force other than those led by former National Guardsmen connected to the Hondurans and Argentines.* Following the thesis of U.N. Ambassador Jeane Kirkpat-

---

*The Argentines quietly removed themselves from the Contra war following the March 1982 Falklands War. It is probable that the Argentines miscalculated, believing that

rick that it was nearly impossible to overthrow Communist totalitarian regimes once they have consolidated, the new administration was in a hurry to press the Sandinistas. The National Guardsmen weren't perfect, but they were militarily ready, loyal, and willing to fight to overthrow their enemies. By the time nonmilitary personnel could be trained, the thinking went, it would be too late.

Proof of the Reagan administration's inability to grasp the importance of the authenticity derived from movements that are home-grown was their treatment of José Francisco Cardenal, a business and political leader with demonstrated popular support inside Nicaragua. Cardenal got nowhere when he attempted to attract Washington's backing in founding a Contra force called the Nicaraguan Democratic Union (ADREN) independent of the National Guard. When he first visited the State Department in July 1981 to meet with the influential Lt. Gen. Gordon Sumner, he said the top hard-liner "told me you must unite under Bermúdez if you want American aid." Desperate for economic support, Cardenal swallowed his concerns and agreed to Sumner's demand, uniting ADREN with the Fifteenth of September League. The U.S.-forged alliance broke up within a month into the Nicaraguan Democratic Union (UDN), and the FDN. Lacking U.S. support, the more moderate but militarily inexperienced UDN faded over the years, leaving Bermúdez's FDN (the new name of the League) dominant for the rest of the war. "Somocismo took over the Contras with Washington's blessing," Cardenal remembered bitterly years later.

"By forcing unity prematurely, the Americans created disunity," former Contra director Edgar Chamorro told me in a 1985 interview. "They should have allowed the movement to grow naturally. Nicaraguans were never in charge of the strategy, tactics, and goals." Between 1982 and 1988, the CIA and State Department reshuffled the Contra leadership a half dozen times and renamed the organization twice, but the National Guard core leadership remained until 1989 when it was far too late.

The Contra war was launched the way foreign interventions have been throughout much of Nicaraguan history—with attacks by the Miskito Indians. On December 14, 1981, a Miskito Indian band

---

Washington would back their claims to the Malvinas in return for their help in Central America.

aligned with the FDN ambushed a twelve-man Sandinista patrol in the northern river port of San Carlos, and killed them all. Over the next two months, Miskito fighters killed some forty-five Sandinista troops in hit-and-run raids in surrounding communities, where they attracted popular support in the form of food and shelter. The Miskitos' CIA handlers named the offensive Operation Red Christmas. The CIA understood, as did the British centuries earlier, that the Miskitos did not identify with the Nicaraguan state and could be used against it.

The Indian war spread through 1982 because the Atlantic coast's 100,000 Miskitos, 8,000 Sumos, and 1,000 Ramas resented the revolution, particularly its Sandinista Defense Committees, its Cuban advisers, and the repression that followed the incipient revolt. But the Pacific coastal cities were different; they were reluctant to participate in a fight against a political party they had overwhelmingly supported and shed blood for less than three years before. The Americans would have been wiser to have taken a lesson from successful Marxist revolutions of the past and advised the Contras to plant the seeds of revolt by doing political work before they struck militarily. Instead, the CIA directed the Contras to destabilize the dominant Pacific coast with sabotage.

Accompanied by Argentine and Honduran advisers, CIA-trained Contra commandos slipped across the Honduran border and marched deep into northwestern Chinandega province in early March 1982. On the night of the fourteenth, two sabotage teams simultaneously blew up two economically important bridges with explosives supplied by the CIA. The attacks briefly cut off all vehicular traffic between Managua and Honduras and sparked the migration of hundreds of Nicaraguan peasants to Contra camps over the border. The blasts were a declaration of war that alerted Nicaraguans and the international press that the Contras were no longer simple cattle rustlers. But the aftershocks of the bomb blasts were politically devastating in Nicaragua and the United States.

The Sandinistas responded to the sabotage of the bridges by immediately declaring a state of emergency. Under its broadened powers, the government suspended most constitutional liberties, censored the opposition newspaper *La Prensa*, prohibited independent labor unions from striking, and terminated all independent radio news broadcasts. (The Sandinistas already controlled the news programming on television.)

The Reagan administration had a tough time convincing Capitol

Hill that destroying two Nicaraguan bridges had anything to do with halting Sandinista armaments destined for El Salvador. Encouraged by moderate dissidents within Nicaragua who distrusted the Contras' National Guard leadership, congressional Democrats, led by House Intelligence Committee chairman Congressman Edward P. Boland, began pushing a variety of bills to halt all funding for the Contras. Boland's efforts to stop Contra aid were blocked, for a short time, by the Republican-controlled Senate led by Senator Barry Goldwater, chairman of the Senate Intelligence Committee. But Congress did adopt the Boland Amendment, which prohibited the Reagan administration from attempting to overthrow the Nicaraguan government. It was a compromise arrangement that infuriated all Nicaraguans, Contras and Sandinistas alike; Washington could legally cripple the Managua government but not destroy it.

Like Calvin Coolidge, Reagan kept the pressure up by making unlikely little Nicaragua one of the top priorities of his administration. In April 1983, before a joint session of Congress, Reagan employed characteristic hyperbole and half-truths to charge: "The government of Nicaragua has treated us as an enemy. It has rejected our repeated peace efforts. . . . The national security of all the Americas is at stake in Central America. If we cannot defend ourselves there, we cannot expect to prevail elsewhere." An increasing number of senators and congressmen felt uncomfortable resisting the popular president on a foreign policy issue he thought was so vital.

Congressional liberals faced inept rivals in Langley, Virginia. The CIA repeatedly misjudged the effects that its policies could have. In early 1984, a CIA-directed Latino force laid "firecracker" mines in Corinto and two other Nicaraguan harbors—to scare away international shipping and impress Nicaraguans with the power of the anti-Sandinista cause. When at least five foreign vessels hit mines, the Contras were instructed to take credit for an operation they had previously been unaware of. Again, the firecrackers caused more damage in Washington than they caused in Nicaragua. Even such Contra supporters as Senator Goldwater worried about an out-of-control CIA duping the congressional intelligence committees and making their own foreign policy. "I am pissed off," Goldwater wrote in an angry letter to Casey. "This is no way to run a railroad." The Senate voted to condemn the mining by a vote of 84–12.

Subsequently, Congress learned of a 1983 psychological warfare manual, written by a CIA contract employee who called himself the

"Priest of Death," that included instructions on "neutralizing" local Sandinista officials. (Assassination of foreign government officials is prohibited by U.S. law.) In protest to the mining and the manual, Congress fortified the Boland Amendment by rewriting it to prohibit U.S. intelligence agencies from supplying or spending money on the Contras. Boland said his intent was to end entirely Washington's support for the Contra war.

When the CIA wasn't bungling the Contra effort, the Contras did it themselves. Between 1981 and 1986, the Nicaraguan Health Ministry reported that the Contras had killed more than 3,600 civilians, mostly teachers, coffee pickers, and health workers. The Contra war was never characterized by the kind of massacres that customarily occurred in El Salvador and Guatemala, but human rights abuses consistently caused the rebels political damage with the U.S. Congress. In 1982, the Contras attempted to promote to the American press an aggressive guerrilla commander who went by the nom de guerre of Suicide, but they were deeply embarrassed a year later when Suicide's forces went on a month-long binge of murder and rape around the northern town of Jalapa. The Contras eventually were forced to court-martial and execute Suicide and three of his deputies. In late 1983, the Contras attracted more bad press when they overran the northern Sandinista cooperative at El Coco, killing fourteen peasants; two women and a sixteen-year-old girl were raped and left dead with their throats cut.

In a particularly humiliating incident in 1985, the Contras executed a prisoner in front of Frank Wohl, a twenty-one-year-old conservative American political activist, who snapped his camera to document the cruelty. Wohl sold his negatives to *Newsweek* magazine, which published a sequence of four photographs showing the victim digging his own grave, then lying in the hole, and finally wincing as a Contra executioner dug a knife into his throat. The final photograph showed the executioner pulling out the knife while a second Contra began filling the grave with a shovelful of dirt. *Newsweek* noted that the photographs "summoned up other grisly images, such as police chief Nguyen Ngoc Loan's shooting of a Viet Cong lieutenant on a Saigon street in 1968." The photographs came out a few weeks before a congressional Contra aid vote and helped delay military assistance for months.

With each confrontation on Capitol Hill, the CIA and State Department handpicked a new set of Contra leaders—always looking for the moderate combination that would improve the Contra human rights record and sell the policy to the American public. The rebels' human rights performance did improve, but they never had a chance to choose their own authentic leaders until Congress finally cut off military aid for good in February 1988—when it was too late. Despite Washington's many errors, the Contras, particularly the FDN, sustained offensive operations in the isolated central highlands between much of 1984 through 1987. Whatever success the Contras had was more a measure of the growing pockets of discontent with the Sandinistas than of the acumen or legitimacy of the Contra leadership or their sponsors in Washington. I saw that for myself when I ventured for an abortive trip inside Nicaragua with a Contra scouting patrol in April 1985.

In broad daylight, a motorboat ferried a seventeen-man Contra patrol and me from the Honduran bank of the brown Coco River to the Nicaraguan side. As we began to climb up a muddy path, we passed entire Miskito and mestizo families crossing into Honduras, carrying their few belongings on their backs. The peasants told us they were escaping a new Sandinista campaign to relocate them into refugee camps away from the war zone. The guerrillas promised that they would someday return to a "liberated" country.

Four hundred yards into Nicaragua, the twenty-four-year-old Contra commander, José Velásquez, spotted the first evidence of Sandinista soldiers—fresh boot prints in the calf-deep mud. He guessed there were a hundred men ahead. In a religious gesture, he nervously slashed a cross in an overhanging vine with a knife. "We'll go on no matter what the cost," he murmured. For five hours we walked up and down back jungle trails. The heat was oppressive, and we took frequent stops for drinks of water.

Once Velásquez thought we had snuck by the Sandinistas, we began to talk. He lay on his back, and pointed to a bullet that could be seen still lodged below the skin on his chest. "I've been shot four times, but I refused to die before we drive the rabid dogs out of Managua," he said with a wide smile he seemed to wear permanently. "I love the chase."

Velásquez challenged me. "You probably think I am some kind of National Guardsman," he said. "You American reporters think we are all Guardia." He said the word like a Sandinista, with genuine distaste.

As I soon discovered, he was far from Guardia. As a teenager, Velásquez had fought against Somoza with Edén Pastora's forces on the southern front—and took his first bullet in the final days of the war. Velásquez joined the new revolutionary army after the victory, and despite his wound, he was sent to Cuba for seven months of military training and political indoctrination. A deeply religious man, Cuban atheism grated on him. "They made fun of us because we wanted to go to church on Sundays," he said, as if still shocked by their apostasy.

But it was not until he returned to Nicaragua in early 1981 that Velásquez turned against the revolution. He discovered the Sandinistas had built a military outpost on his farm overlooking Chinandega without his permission. "It made me sick," he told me. "If they had offered me other land, that would have been fine." When he groused, he was jailed for three months. In time, he fled to Honduras and joined the FDN.

Most of Velásquez's patrol members were poor peasants and workers—several were Evangelical Christians—who said they resented the Sandinistas forcing them into cooperatives or fixing the prices of their agricultural produce at unprofitable levels. Others found their way into the Contras after resisting the draft or the Sandinista block committees. Morale was generally high, although the medic, Genio, complained that the National Guard leadership did not respect human rights. "If only they were all like José," he wished.

To avoid contact with larger Sandinista units, we moved single file and spaced well apart on the narrowest trails, where the driest going was at the edges and we could grab at dripping wet trees to keep our balance. I struggled to keep up and contain my fear. Then, in a clearing of jungle, the Contras spotted the friendly village of Par Par Abajo, a cluster of palm-frond shacks. "Maybe they'll have crackers or even a chicken," José said hopefully. "Or even a dog," one of his men cracked. We had to be satisfied with a few ears of corn and beans, which the people gladly gave us. To my surprise, the men of the village had been organized into a militia in support of the regular Contra forces.

The Sandinistas claimed they led a class war in favor of the poor, but in Par Par Abajo and surrounding settlements the poor hated them. "We want to work our own land," Marcial Rizo, a nineteen-year-old militia member told me. He said the Contras were "the only defense we have for democracy," which for him meant the right "to own your own animals and food and nobody can take them away."

Unconnected by electricity, telephone, or road to the rest of Nicaragua, Par Par Abajo was a pathetic place. I saw children, their bellies swollen with parasites, shiver in the night. All the people wore rags. Mangy dogs guarded the few chickens, cows, and pigs from jaguars that prowled the surrounding upland jungle. Nevertheless, residents said they liked the Somozas better than the Sandinistas for the simple reason that they wanted to be left alone.

The people of Par Par Abajo said they turned against the Sandinistas shortly after the 1979 revolution, when the new regime sent student *brigadistas* to their village as part of the national literacy campaign. "They wanted us to study, to dance, to march," Antonio Vallejo told me. "They said God was a guerrilla." The peasants drove out a Sandinista teacher after she took a stick to children who were slow to learn. Months later, Sandinista troops came and ordered them to form a cooperative out of their small plots of land. The peasants balked and refused to change their ways.

The next morning, a local militia scout reported that two Sandinista columns were operating in the area. For the next two days we were chased through the jungle back to safe refuge in Honduras. This had hardly been a successful military mission, but I returned to the Contra camps more respectful of the individual resistance fighters, thinking that perhaps the rebels might have had a fighting chance had they chosen their own leaders and evolved without U.S. interference.

WAR SANDINISMO

As the Contras were mismanaged by the CIA and handcuffed by Congress, the Sandinistas' first reflex was to use the Reagan administration's proxy war as a pretext to repress the internal opposition. The party directorate's early responses to the Contra war underlined their totalitarian instincts; their principal targets were the troublesome Miskito Indians and the Roman Catholic church.

The Sandinistas initially denied that the Miskito Indians had any genuine grievances; Indian and creole calls for autonomy from the "Spaniard" Pacific coast were roundly characterized as counterrevolutionary. For Sandinista propagandists, the December 1981 Operation Red Christmas was nothing more than an effort to set the stage for a U.S. invasion of Nicaragua. Managua responded to the Miskito raids with terror. The Sandinistas militarized the Miskito port of Puerto Cabezas, arresting more than a hundred Indians identified as sympathizers of the Contra cause. Dozens more Indians disappeared at the hands of security forces (although there were no massacres to compare with those of Guatemala or El Salvador). The worst incident reported was in the village of Leimus, where seventeen Miskitos were seized by Sandinista troops and murdered.

Fearing that Indians living along the Coco River (also the border with Honduras) would feed and otherwise aid the Indian guerrilla army known as Misura, the Sandinistas destroyed several river towns and villages, torching churches, crops, and livestock in the process. The government resettled nearly 10,000 Indians into five army-guarded villages collectively named Tasba Pri (ironically, words that mean "freedom land" in the Miskito language). Adding to the Indians' grief, a Sandinista army transport helicopter overloaded with ninety-three Miskito women and children crashed during the relocation process, killing all but nine. Some 30,000 Miskito Indians (along with members of the far smaller Sumo and Rama tribes) fled in fear for Honduras, where many were recruited or kidnapped into the Contra movement.

The confrontation between the Sandinistas and the Church developed more slowly. Archbishop Miguel Obando y Bravo had openly opposed the Somoza regime and had taken a sympathetic stance to the revolution through its first year in power. Before long, however, the archbishop and the other bishops became troubled by the growing Soviet bloc role in governing the country, the presence of Marxist liberation theology priests in senior cabinet and diplomatic posts (against the explicit orders of the Vatican), and the government's encouragement of the radical "People's Church." On the church's radio station, Obando y Bravo voiced his concerns about the development of "two churches"—the established one and the other led by radical priests in urban barrios who claimed that Jesus Christ was a revolutionary. For their part, the Sandinistas became particularly troubled when the archbishop refused to condemn the Contras.

As the Contra war heated up and the government applied the state of emergency, the Sandinistas challenged the primacy of the Church hierarchy. In an August 1982 defamation operation probably designed by Comandante Borge, a Sandinista mob stormed the Masaya house of a woman being visited by Father Bismarck Carballo, manager of Radio Católica and a close adviser to the archbishop, and dragged the priest through the streets. A *Barricada* photographer and a Sandinista television cameraman were conveniently on hand to record the events. The government claimed Carballo was having an illicit sexual affair. The trick sparked a small rebellion in Masaya, a town that only three years before had been solidly Sandinista. Catholic students rioted, occupied a seminary, and fired guns at local police. Borge's security forces killed three of the students to quash the insurrection before it got out of control.

The feuding came to a head during Pope John Paul II's March 1983 visit to Nicaragua. An outdoor mass in Managua drew half a million people, some waving yellow-and-white Vatican flags, others black-and-red Sandinista flags. The pope criticized the People's Church, championed private parochial schools, embraced Obando y Bravo, and omitted any criticism of the Contras and U.S. policy.

But not even the pope could get away with speaking so provocatively in the new Nicaragua. The Sandinistas gave microphones to their militiamen and members of the Sandinista Defense Committee (CDS) and placed them in the front rows of the audience to drown everyone else out. The militants interrupted the pope's homily with cries of "People's Power" and "We want peace," as John Paul's own microphone was switched off. Daniel Ortega and other comandantes standing on the rostrum led the jeers. Red-faced, the pontiff ordered "Silence!," but to no avail. The humiliating spectacle angered many Nicaraguans—among the most deeply religious Catholics in Latin America—for years to come.

As popular resentment grew, so did the Contra movement, which was beginning to build a permanent popular base in the central provinces of Jinotega, Matagalpa, Boaco, and Chontales. By the middle of 1983, the Sandinistas could no longer rely on poorly trained militias to combat the Contras. The Sandinista army, which had been designed as a conventional army to defend the country against an expected U.S. invasion, would have to be redesigned as a counterinsurgency force. The Sandinistas instinctively turned to the Cubans, who had gained valuable experience in such fighting in Africa.

Castro sent his arrogant but most accomplished counterinsurgency officer, Gen. Arnaldo Ochoa Sánchez, fresh from a successful campaign in Angola, to advise the Nicaraguans. Ochoa broke down Sandinista army battalions to a size more fitting for hit-and-run warfare, improved communications and transportation, and altered the kind of weaponry Managua ordered from the Soviet bloc. He persuaded the Sandinistas that they didn't need the MIG fighters they long desired from Moscow; what they did need were high-speed Hind helicopter gunships. Ochoa persuaded the Sandinistas to remove pro-Contra peasants from remote areas and to build a network of farm cooperatives manned by militiamen in disputed areas to control Contra movements. Ochoa's team of Cuban advisers accompanied Sandinista units on operations, while his helicopter pilots flew in combat.

On at least one crucial point, however, the Sandinistas did not heed Havana's military advice. Castro and Ochoa* explained that the Sandinistas needed a professional army of ideologically trained cadres that could be depended on through thick and thin. The directorate decided that Nicaragua needed a national army and a draft. The Sandinista leadership figured that such a force would serve as a political training ground for Nicaragua's youth.

But the Cubans had been correct. The draft was a lightning rod for anger, especially among Nicaraguan women afraid to lose their sons in a war that they did not comprehend or support. The Church proclaimed the draft immoral, arguing that it was installed to defend a political party and not the nation. An underground railroad emerged around the country to shelter draft-age boys and send them on to Costa Rica and Honduras, where many volunteered or were otherwise forced to join the Contras.

In an effort to deflect growing internal dissent and demonstrate reasonableness to the U.S. Congress, junta coordinator Daniel Ortega announced in December 1983 that national elections originally planned for 1985 would be pushed up to November 1984. The Sandinistas saw the election as an instrument of counterinsurgency and as an insurance policy against a U.S. invasion they considered more likely and threatening following the 1983 Grenada "rescue operation." With the internal opposition chronically divided between the many miniparties that survived the revolution and the Contras outside the country, there was no threat to Sandinista power.

In the midst of the campaign, Comandante Bayardo Arce gave a secret speech to the Nicaraguan Socialist party (which was recorded without his knowledge) in which he revealed that the Sandinista directorate would never have permitted "bourgeois formalities" had it not been for U.S. pressure:

---

*Ochoa was tried and executed on alleged drug charges in Havana in 1989.

Of course, if we did not have the war situation imposed on us by the United States, the electoral problem would be totally out of place in terms of its usefulness. What a revolution really needs is the power to act. The power to act is precisely what constitutes the essence of the dictatorship of the proletariat—the ability of the [working] class to impose its will. . . . For us, then, the elections, viewed from that perspective, are a nuisance, just as a number of things that make up the reality of our revolution are a nuisance.

The campaign could have been more of a nuisance if a conservative opposition coalition promoting former junta member Arturo Cruz had remained in the race. CDS-organized *turbas divinas* broke up rallies for Cruz, one reason he dropped out. (Another is that conservatives in the Reagan administration warned Cruz and leaders of his conservative opposition coalition that the election would legitimize the Sandinistas.)

This was no model election. Dozens of opposition activists were imprisoned or drafted. Farm co-op boards were warned that credit would become scarce if their members didn't vote for Sandinista presidential candidate Daniel Ortega. Opposition access to the media was circumscribed. Under the state of emergency laws, opposition candidates could not hold outdoor rallies, thereby limiting their size. Besides, Sandinista mobs beat up people who dared to participate in opposition rallies. Nevertheless, opposition parties, weak as they were, did have a chance to organize and air their views.

I joined Virgilio Godoy, presidential candidate of the Independent Liberal party, on the campaign trail one Sunday. Godoy donned a peasant's straw hat and marched through the cobblestone streets of Estelí, a generally pro-Sandinista city. While many watched warily from their windows, five hundred citizens came out to hear the candidate. What they heard was like nothing a crowd in Cuba had heard in twenty years. "There are hundreds of East Germans here, to teach our children to be spies," charged Godoy, a former Labor Minister in the Sandinista government. On the controversial draft system, he said, "The boys are not there because they want to be; they are obliged to be there."

Disillusioned with Sandinista harassment of his backers, Godoy dropped out of the race a week before the November 4 vote, but his race and his words signified something larger, something he himself probably didn't understand. The Sandinista revolution was moving away from its totalitarian beginnings—in part because of Contra pressure, but also because of the persistence of the internal civic opposition (particularly the Church and the private sector), and because the Soviet bloc wasn't coming up with the rubles to finance a Socialist transformation.

Though imperfect, the election was an exercise in democracy in view of the tawdry history of elections in Central America. Besides electing Ortega as president and fellow junta member Sergio Ramírez vice president, voters chose a ninety-six-member legislature with opposition representation, which in 1986 adapted a moderate constitution upholding private property and freedoms of religion, assembly, and speech. Ortega suspended most of the civil liberty provisions until the end of the war, but his ascension as president represented a victory for the most moderate and pragmatic leaders of the Sandinista movement.

Slowly but surely, Sandinista tactical compromises became permanent reforms.

Ortega's first priority was to end the war. In the waning weeks of the election campaign, he accepted a peace treaty drafted by the so-called Contadora Group (Mexico, Colombia, Venezuela, and Panama) that would have frozen the regional arms race and banned the stationing of foreign troops and bases in the region. The Reagan administration refused to go along, arguing that the treaty had no teeth to enforce its provisions.

Forging ahead with conciliation, Ortega unilaterally sent a hundred (out of 3,000) Cuban advisers home, then offered a moratorium on imports of new arms systems and U.S. congressional inspections of Nicaraguan military bases—if only Washington would kill off the Contras. Calling Ortega's offers hollow propaganda, and feeling that his pressure tactics were finally working, the Reagan administration responded by declaring an economic embargo on Nicaragua.

Making little progress in foreign policy, Ortega turned his attention to his growing domestic troubles and reversed many past policies. He took some of the sting out of the army draft by allowing draftees to go home after two years. To woo the farmers, the Sandinistas began allowing consumer food prices to rise, paying hard currency (e.g., U.S. dollars) rather than cordobas to growers and cattlemen meeting crop and beef quotas. The Nicaraguan president responded to the economic depression with such un-Marxist moves as shaving public subsidies, devaluating the currency, and imposing a modified austerity program. Although they continued to rail against capitalism, the Sandinistas began to encourage small farmers to sell their produce privately (around the Micoin structure) and ordered higher pay raises for managers to stem the growing brain drain among the middle class. In the northern mountains, where the Contras had much popular support, Ortega's new government moved away from the traditional policy of forming large state farms and cooperatives by distributing land titles to tens of thousands of peasants. The revolution was suddenly as heterodox and quirky as it had been its first year.

Nowhere was the government's new moderation more in evidence than on the Atlantic coast. In November and December, the Sandinistas began secret negotiating sessions with Miskito Indian leaders upset with their CIA managers and began a process of allotting the Indians more economic and political autonomy. Managua allowed the Miskitos to leave Tasba Pri and return to their settlements on the Coco River, which the Sandinista army helped rebuild. Cuban teachers were replaced with English-speaking Nicaraguans, and Miskito Indian fighters were even allowed to return to their villages without surrendering their weaponry. The Sandinistas targeted for special treatment Rama Cay, the center of the nearly extinct Rama civilization. The government donated paint to freshen up the Moravian church, a water pump, an electrical system, and a movie projector. To keep the Rama language alive, the Sandinistas supplied one of the last speakers of Rama with false teeth so her words would be understood by linguists attempting to produce a Rama dictionary.

Both the Reagan White House and the Democratic Congress refused to acknowledge that the Sandinistas had taken a more moderate course. The American administration, feeling it was winning its uphill fight in El Salvador, smelled blood in Nicaragua. While Congress denied the Contras military aid, National Security Adviser Robert McFarlane and his aide Lt. Col. Oliver North saw to it that the Contras received $25 million in aid—most in defiance of the Boland Amendment—from various private and foreign sources between July 1984 and April 1985.

In April 1985, the Democratic House overwhelmingly defeated an administration request for a mere $14 million in nonmilitary humanitarian aid for the Contras, 248 votes to 180, but gradually the terms of the debate were changing. Years of Reagan rhetoric—characterizing Nicaragua as a "totalitarian dungeon" and the Contras as "the moral equivalent of our founding fathers"—wore Congress down.

In one of the more perplexing actions of his career, Ortega snatched defeat from the jaws of victory. He flew to Moscow seeking economic assistance and vital oil within a week after the House vote, thus humiliating Democrats. "He embarrassed us, to be perfectly truthful," snapped House Speaker Tip O'Neill. Senator Jim Sasser, a Tennessee Democrat and strong Reagan critic, called it "an ill-timed and ill-advised trip which I think only serves to underscore the growing East-West conflict in Central America." In fact, Ortega's visit to Moscow represented more than anything else Managua's growing desperation to find cheap petroleum as Mexico threatened to cut off its oil shipments to Nicaragua. (Managua was more than a year behind in its oil payments to Mexico.)

But the public relations damage was done. Three weeks after the House defeat, Reagan escalated his war against Nicaragua anyway by declaring a trade embargo. Congress, still upset with Ortega's Moscow trip, didn't complain. The embargo succeeded in hurting the Nicaraguan private sector more than the Sandinistas, since the government could break the embargo by trading through Panamanian companies in the Colón free zone and were provided subsidized Eastern bloc products anyway. Still, combined with American vetoes of World Bank loans and Contra destruction of the coffee crop, the embargo slowly helped throttle the Nicaraguan economy between 1985 and 1990.

In the meantime, the Ortega trip spurred about twenty-five swing House Democrats to look for ways to help the White House on Nicaragua. These Democrats, led by Dave McCurdy of Oklahoma and Ike Skelton of Kansas, were still too uncomfortable with the Contra National Guard leadership to pass military aid, but they wanted to find some way to pressure a regime they saw as a Communist menace. Advised by neoliberal intellectual activists Bernard Aronson, Penn Kemble, Bruce Cameron, and Robert Leiken, the moderate Democrats proposed that the United States liberalize the Contra leadership and set up a Nicaraguan commission to monitor rebel human rights performance. They argued that the United States should resupply the Contras with humanitarian aid, such as medicines, food, and tents, and later provide military aid—but only if the Contras transformed themselves into a human rights–conscious, democratic force. The administration publicly bought the Democratic policy—as a halfway measure until military aid could be secured.

With the encouragement of the White House and Republican-controlled Senate, the Democratic House reversed itself in June 1985 by endorsing $27 million in humanitarian aid and lifting a one-year ban on U.S. intelligence support. The administration's efforts to liberalize the Contra leadership were more cosmetic than anything else, but the tide in Congress had turned. A year later, Congress renewed military aid, granting the rebels $100 million worth of red-eye antiaircraft missiles, plastic explosives, medical supplies, and intelligence. CIA men and contract people, many of whom were veteran "cowboys" from the Vietnam era, were reassigned to the task of training the Contras to win the political war, the peasants' "hearts and minds," with "civic action" and psychological war techniques. Freshly uniformed, possessing new communications and computer gear, and, most importantly, armed with rockets to shoot down the Sandinistas' powerful Hind helicopter gunships, the 16,000 Contras moved out of Honduras and back into Nicaragua. The Sandinistas responded to the congressional action the old-fashioned way: by closing *La Prensa* and the Roman Catholic church's radio station.

THE IRAN-CONTRA SCANDAL AND ITS AFTERMATH

On October 5, 1986, a young Sandinista recruit lifted his SA-7 rocket-launcher to his shoulder, took aim, and with one lucky shot hit a C-123K arms-cargo plane flying over Nicaragua's southern jungles on a resupply mission to the Contras. One of three Americans on board, loadmaster Eugene Hasenfus, parachuted into the jungle and survived. A veteran of the CIA's Air America operation in Southeast Asia, Hasenfus wasn't new to jungle wars and the espionage business; but once captured, he talked at length in the hope the Sandinistas would be lenient. Hasenfus revealed that U.S. government personnel were involved in a Contra arms air drop operation in direct violation of Congress's Boland Amendment. The Sandinistas found flight logs in the aircraft's fuselage that corroborated Hasenfus's statements and proved Salvadoran and Costa Rican involvement in the secret arms supply operation. "It's going to be a cold day in Washington before any more money goes to Nicaragua," said Dave Durenberger, Republican senator from Minnesota. A Contra leader privately complained, "We were born in Washington; we'll die in Washington."

To make matters worse for the White House, free-lance reporter Mark Fazlollah and United Press International's Douglas Farah managed to coax the telephone records for the house where the American mercenary air crew lived out of the Salvadoran telephone company. Reading off the phone bill printouts, Fazlollah and Farah surprised themselves when they dialed the numbers and reached the offices of Oliver North; Joe Fernández, the CIA's station chief in Costa Rica; and retired air force Maj. Gen. Richard Secord, the man who would later be identified as manager of many covert operations involving Nicaragua and Iran. The telephone records contradicted the statements of Assistant Secretary of State Elliott Abrams before Congress under oath that the Hasenfus plane had nothing to do with the U.S. government.

Hasenfus was linked to a vast, illegal and covert, "off-the-shelf" network developed by Casey and North to forge some kind of relationship with Iran, free the hostages in Lebanon, and make war in Nicaragua. Preliminary investigations found that the Reagan administration had covertly sold arms to Iran as a way to free the American hostages held in Lebanon, and then diverted millions of dollars of profits to arm the Nicaraguan rebels.

Reagan told the Tower Commission, the investigative body he appointed to look into the scandal, that he was unaware of efforts by his National Security Council (NSC) to disobey the Boland Amendment to supply and fund the Contras. He denied knowing that the arms sales to Iran were intended to free the hostages, or that the profits from those transactions bought supplies for the Contras. But North seemed to contradict the president when he said he sent Reagan several memorandums, beginning in February 1986, requesting his approval for the arms deals and use of the profits to supply the Contras.

By the time North was due to testify before a joint congressional committee investigating the scandal in July 1987, the administration appeared to be on the rocks. There was even speculation that the president might be impeached for disobeying the Boland Amendment. *Newsweek* magazine commented: "No matter what Oliver North intends, his testimony this week can only hurt Ronald Reagan. Inevitably, it will be one more sign that this presidency, already in decline, is now essentially history."

Newsweek was wrong. Oliver North possibly saved the Reagan presidency by recasting the hearing into a referendum on the presidential right to defend national security. "I saw that idea, of using the Ayatollah Khomeini's money to support the Nicaraguan freedom fighters, as a good one," North said defiantly. "I still do. I don't think it was wrong. I think it was a neat idea." His homespun style, pugnaciousness, and his pressed marine uniform studded with six rows of Vietnam War decorations made him an instant television star. With maps and briefing papers, he went into an emotional defense of the Contras and White House efforts to outfox the media and congressional opponents duped by Communists. North played over the heads of the committee members to the American people, and despite admitting that he shredded White House documents to cover up his activities, he sparked a groundswell of right-wing superpatriotism. A week after predicting that North would bury the Reagan administration, *Newsweek*'s cover declared "The Fall Guy Becomes A Folk Hero: Ollie Takes The Hill." In the days following North's two-day appearance, congressional committee members received tens of thousands of telegrams and letters applauding North and Reagan's Nicaragua policies, chilling the investigation.

"Olliemania" not only saved Reagan but very possibly Vice President Bush as well. In its panicked rush to complete the hearings, the committee never thoroughly looked into Bush's role in the scandal. The vice president said repeatedly that he knew nothing of the NSC covert operations to supply the Contras, but his chief national security advisers, Donald Gregg (now ambassador to South Korea) and Col. Sam Watson, reportedly did. A memo from Bush's office setting an agenda for a May 1, 1986, meeting involving the vice president and Cuban-American CIA asset Felix Rodríguez said the two were going to review "resupply of the Contras." Watson said those words were a typographical error. When the Hasenfus plane went down, Rodríguez, who aided the Contra resupply effort from San Salvador, immediately called to inform Watson. The congressional committee never called Bush to testify and clarify his position under oath. In the two years following the Iran-Contra committee's investigation, the release of classified documents and North's private notebooks turned up the fact that Vice President Bush met privately with North, lobbied Honduras on behalf of the Contras, and was otherwise active in Nicaragua policy in the months preceding the Hasenfus crash and capture. In the end, the Iran-Contra scandal paralyzed the Reagan administration and its Contra policy, but it did not strike a knockout blow.

Iran-Contra hit Central America as hard as it hit Washington. In El Salvador, President José Napoleón Duarte was deeply embarrassed by the disclosure that Hasenfus's plane—and many other Contra supply flights over the years—had originated in San Salvador's Ilopango Airport. Duarte's charge that the Sandinistas were fueling his nation's revolutionary war was no longer an open-and-shut argument for international support. Judging the new reality in the U.S. Congress, and hoping to win sympathy among congressional liberals, Guatemalan President Vinicio Cerezo publicly accused the Contras of being a "destabilizing guerrilla force." Meanwhile, nationalist sentiments swirled among the Honduran army officer corps to expel the Nicaraguan rebels altogether. The Costa Rican government cried foul over the discovery that the local CIA station was illegally facilitating the refueling of supply flights out of a clandestine air strip located on its territory.

Perceiving a policy vacuum in Washington, Costa Rica's new Social Democratic president, Oscar Arias, went into action. He pushed an ambitious regional peace plan including cease-fires, free elections, broad civil liberties, amnesty for political prisoners, and peace talks between governments and armed oppositions. All the countries of the region were to be included in the plan, but from the beginning the Arias effort was focused on Nicaragua. Arias had long voiced disdain for the militarism and human rights records of both the Contras and the Sandinistas, and perceived that there was a more efficient way to bring moderation and stability to Costa Rica's northern neighbor. President Reagan called the plan "fatally flawed" because it was not backed by military force, but the U.S. Congress and most other Central American leaders enthusiastically endorsed the effort.

With the agreement of the Sandinista directorate, President Ortega surprised the world by agreeing to sign a regional peace agreement based on the so-called Arias Plan at an August 7, 1987, conference in the town of Esquipulas, Guatemala. Ortega made astonishing concessions. By pledging to hold free elections in the not-too-distant future, end press censorship, and begin talks with the Contras, Ortega opened the Sandinista National Liberation Front to the greatest challenges the movement had faced since defeating Anastasio Somoza.

True to his word, Ortega allowed *La Prensa* to reopen and publish without prior censorship. The Sandinistas opened a dialogue with the Church hierarchy, allowed exiled priests to return to Nicaragua, and appointed Cardinal Miguel Obando y Bravo head of a commission to monitor Nicaragua's compliance with the peace process.

In the coming months, the Sandinistas went still further, ending the state of emergency prohibitions on certain civil liberties, releasing 985 political prisoners (about one-third of those in the country), reintroducing habeas corpus, and dissolving kangaroo courts known as the Popular Anti-Sandinista Tribunals. Most remarkably, the Sandinistas sat down with the Contras. The two sides agreed to a cease-fire in May 1988 that brought relative peace to the countryside and assured a suspension of U.S. military aid to the Contras through all of 1989.

Compromising on the most cherished tenets of Leninism by promising to broaden political space to an unprecedented degree, Ortega revealed how worried he was about the troubles his revolution faced. Despite the scandal in Washington, the Contras were doing better than ever in central Nicaragua, and Ortega wanted to assure that once the $100 million aid package was used up Congress would cut them off once and for all. The war had destroyed the country, causing more than 25,000 deaths, 700,000 displaced people and refugees, and $1.8 billion in government expenses. Having defaulted on its international debt, with $800 million in imports quadrupling the value of its exports every year, Nicaragua was ever more dependent on the Soviet Union.

But Mikhail Gorbachev, believing that the Soviet Union was overextended anyway, was unenthusiastic about Central America. Moscow shocked Managua in early 1987 by refusing to increase oil shipments, even as Mexico cut off supplies. (Managua had fallen still further behind in paying its bills to Mexico City.) Sandinista moves in favor of conciliation and democracy won encouragement from Soviet Ambassador Valeri Nikolayenko. He pronounced Nicaragua's revolution "pluralist" in contrast to the "socialist" label Soviet officials attach to Cuba's, and he privately encouraged the Sandinistas to loosen up on their economy and look to the West for credits and trade. He also publicly pronounced that Moscow had no intention of ever building a military base in Nicaragua.

While negotiating with the Contras, the Sandinistas also showed renewed ideological flexibility in dealing with its bankruptcy and hyperinflation. In February 1988, the government announced a new economic policy that had the look of an International Monetary Fund (IMF) austerity plan. The government reissued the national currency, taking 15 percent of the total number of córdobas out of circulation while devaluing the currency 3,000 percent in the process. Government spending was cut 10 percent, several public agencies were combined to increase efficiency, 10,000 government workers (out of 70,000) were fired, and nearly all housing and food subsidies were eliminated.

The Sandinistas no longer favored the economic advice of the Bulgarians in this age of *glasnost.* Instead, they turned to MIT economist Lance Taylor. Under Taylor's prescriptions, Managua kept its foot on the monetarist brake through 1989. The Taylor policies were successful though harsh, bringing the 1988 inflation rate of 35,000 percent (the highest the world has seen since Weimar Germany) down to a more manageable 1,700 percent in 1989. The economic reforms also marked the worst downturn in the economic well-being of the Nicaraguan people in history, as gross domestic product (GDP) fell 8 percent in 1988 and 6 percent in 1989. Per capita annual income, which amounted to $900 prior to the revolution, had fallen to $330 in 1989 (adjusted to 1980 dollars).

Perhaps the human cost of the revolution could best be seen in Managua's garbage dump at Acahualinca, where thousands of people—known locally as "vultures"—came every day to pick for food. One steamy August afternoon in 1988, I spent twenty minutes at the dump. Any longer would have been more than I could bare; the smell was so putrid I gagged. I saw dozens of people poking sharp sticks and fine-tooth hoes through piles of rubbish for silverware, plastic bags, half-eaten ears of corn, bottles, and cans. Each time a garbage truck arrived at the dump with a fresh load, people would flock from older piles to pounce on the new pickings.

Juan Quesada, age eighteen, found half of a damp bread stick to eat. "This is food," he told me as if he were as surprised as I was that he could eat garbage. We talked for a moment. "Is there a revolution," he asked me acidly, "so I can live like a crab?" A forty-two-year-old woman named Juana told me "life gets worse and worse."

Nicaragua had become a tableau of despair and resentment. Hunger, disease, and crime—symptoms of a societal breakdown—reached levels far higher than those recorded before the revolution. There were signs everywhere that the revolution had lost its dynamism. *La Prensa* far outsold two Sandinista newspapers while opposition priests drew far larger congregations to their churches than did the progovernment liberation theology priests. The Sandinista Defense Committees, Cuban-style block organizations designed to distribute food ration cards and patrol the streets, had broken down because few citizens would participate anymore. Meanwhile, a half million Nicaraguans had left the country (the rate of emigration curiously picked up after the Contra war ended), including most of the professional class the country needed for development.

From a survey pool of several hundred Managua residents, a poll conducted by the progovernment Catholic University in June 1988 found that only 28.3 percent of the people identified with the FSLN, while 59.6 percent identified with no political party at all. Clear majorities disliked the Sandinista draft, official economic policies, and property confiscations. (At the same time, a full 85.9 percent said they didn't want the U.S. Congress to pass any more military aid to the Contras, and 57 percent said they hoped the Contras could be reincorporated into the country as a political party.)

"There's a lack of consciousness among the people, to comprehend *the reality*," complained Olga Orozco, the twenty-nine-year-old supervisor of forty-six Sandinista Defense Committees in Managua's giant Mercado Oriental, or Eastern Market, in August 1988. "People think the government is at fault for their problems. Many don't see the gringos behind the aggression. Worse still, *militantes* [party activists] used to work twenty-four hours, day and night. Now *militantes* are falling into comfort. It's easier to go to the beach or to the movies than work in the barrio. . . . People think by being a *militante,* or by being a member of the CDS, they'll get a house or a job. There are party members who come here and think they don't have to pay for the food in the market. It's an abuse of authority."

Whoever was to blame, professionals and poor people alike poured out of Nicaragua by the scores of thousands in 1988 and 1989, mostly because of the miserable economy. It soon became clear that the drain of trained talent could cripple the country for years, if not decades. Of the 750 engineers residing in Nicaragua in 1985, only 220 remained in late 1988. More Nicaraguan architects lived in Los Angeles than in Managua.

The Sandinistas demonstrated that they were highly sensitive about the problem of massive defections. When César Estrada Sequeira, the artistic director and popular jazz disc jockey of Radio Sandino, quit in June 1988 to live on Ronald Reagan Avenue in Miami, the station continued to play his recorded voice to make it seem as if he had never left.

The Esquipulas Agreement hastened the Sandinista revolution's inevitable arrival at the ideological divide between a pluralist democracy and one-party totalitarianism. The Sandinistas faced the same Hobson's choice Socialists faced throughout the world in the late 1980s. How far can a Leninist party go before its tactical compromises become incompatible with its very purpose for being? As historian Martin Malia described in a 1990 *Daedalus* essay on the future of Soviet-style Socialist rule: "Civil society under the rule of law is incompatible with the preservation of the lawless role of the party."

Sandinista liberalizing concessions to other Central American countries, the United States, and, to a lesser extent, its domestic political opposition and private sector, were meant to preserve party control not destroy it—but at some point *perestroika*-type policies sharpen rather than soften what Marxists like to call "the contradictions." When I suggested as much to Arias during two interviews in 1986 and 1987, he merely smiled. He would not confirm what I firmly believed: that his peace plan was no less an attempt to overthrow the Sandinistas than was the Reagan administration's Contra policy. Whatever were Arias's original intentions, the Sandinistas came under increasing political pressure, and they responded in ever more contradictory and disjointed fashion in the two years leading up to the February 1990 presidential election.

The Sandinistas were in a box. They wanted to demonstrate moderation to beat Contra aid in the U.S. Congress once and for all, and they wanted to rebuild trade and diplomatic bridges outside the Soviet bloc. But they also wanted to keep the lid on internal dissent so as to guarantee their predominant political position. In the end, the Sandinistas found that too much liberalization was dangerous to their hold on power. Popular distress grew, and the Sandinistas' new openness was increasingly tested. While Ortega's moderation was most in evidence during the late 1980s, the harsh hand of Interior Minister Comandante Tomás Borge was also much in evidence. Nicaragua was generally far more open than in earlier years of the revolution, but the more selective repression of the late 1980s was frequently more flagrant and brutal.

An antigovernment riot broke out in the city of Masaya in February 1988. A mob burned two police cars and threw stones at the local police station. Sandinista police, afraid to provoke further unrest, remained in their station. Comandante Borge was deeply distressed that his men were soft before the traditionally rebellious people of Masaya, and apparently decided he needed to send a different message next time. A month later, when the Social Christian party–affiliated Mothers of Political Prisoners marched in Masaya, the Sandinistas bused in a Sandinista *turba* mob to attack them. Sandinista police stood by without interfering. *Miami Herald* reporter Sam Dillon wrote in a March 7 dispatch: "hundreds of club-wielding Sandinista activists attacked an anti-government demonstration . . . , pelting outnumbered opposition marchers with rocks and singling out panicked protesters for mob beatings."

Popular protests, including hunger strikes and work stoppages, picked up steam anyway. Opposition activity peaked on July 10, 1988, in the town of Nandaime, when the Coordinadora opposition coalition gathered about 5,000 people for an anti-Sandinista rally to test the government's pledge to guarantee dissent under the Esquipulas Agreement. A march around Nandaime was peaceful and enthusiastic, but once public speeches were about to begin in the central plaza, uniformed Sandinista police moved into the crowd to break up the rally. The people fought back with ferocity, even attacking the police with sticks and stones. The police retreated, but returned within minutes with riot gear and overcame the spontaneous resistance. Dozens of police and citizens were hurt in the fracas. Later, police mounted buses and other vehicles leaving Nandaime and arrested thirty-nine leaders of the rally, who remained in jail for six months. Then, compromising its Esquipulas commitment to freedom of the press, the government briefly closed *La Prensa* for publishing stories and pictures describing the Nandaime police riot. Managua blamed the entire episode on the U.S. embassy, and expelled U.S. Ambassador Richard Melton and seven other American diplomats the following day.

After Nandaime, it appeared that while the Sandinistas might continue to loosen up when they needed to be tactically creative, their power was ultimately unconditional and irreducible. Certainly that was the message sent by the government to the business community when later in the year the Sandinistas confiscated the largest private enterprise in Nicaragua, the San Antonio sugar plantation and refinery. In speeches through the rest of the year, President Ortega announced that Nicaragua was a Socialist country.

Whether Socialist or not, the Sandinistas were no friendlier to independent labor unions. Blaming dissident union activity on U.S. imperialism, the Sandinistas broke a series of strikes in 1988 and 1989. When management at the privately owned Toña beer factory in the middle of Managua wanted to lay off forty-seven people, the Sandinista union went along without argument. In response, the factories' 480 workers voted to disaffiliate from the Sandinista union in June 1988 and join a Communist party–affiliated union instead. With the aid of *turba* members from other factories, Sandinista unionists occupied the plant and threw out the majority insurgents.

The Sandinista security forces were most heavy handed in the remote mountain ranges of Matagalpa and Jinotega, where Borge's Interior Ministry State Security police and the Sandinista army systematically murdered civilian Contra collaborators. Americas Watch documented seventy-four murders and fourteen disappearances from 1987 through the first months of 1989—the worst spree of death-squad-style operations since the 1982 repression of the Miskitos.

At the entrance to the Sandinista army base outside Puerto Cabezas, a sign read: MEN ARE BORN AND DIE. THE [SANDINISTA] FRONT IS IMMORTAL.

It was Army Day, September 2, 1988, and the 375 Sandinista troops at the base looked sharp for an official visit by Comandante Tomás Borge. Their formation was straight and proper; their uniforms were crisp, their faces confident and smiling. The local commander made the expected perfunctory remarks introducing Borge and ended his speech with the usual militaristic rhetoric:

"National Directorate!," cried the commander.

"Ordene! [Order us!]," was the screaming reply of the men in unison.

The sole surviving founder of the Sandinista party devoted his speech to reminiscing about another original Sandinista comandante, Germán Pomares, who died in the war against Somoza when most of these recruits were only children.

As he spoke, the elflike Borge bounced defiantly on the balls of his feet, then he would pause to make a point, staring at the audience with intensity. "Germán always said Nicaragua would need a large, strong army," Borge claimed. "How was he so intuitive about history? He knew when you substitute one social class for another you have a revolution and you confront imperialism. By the laws of nature, the workers and peasants have taken power. They need the army to preserve that power against an enemy out to liquidate the revolution." It was Borge's way of saying that the Sandinistas had no desire to demilitarize the society, even after the Contras are finally defeated.

That night I felt confused about where the revolution was going. The Ortegas were on a diplomatic offensive and promising new elections in 1990, but here was Borge pledging that the Sandinistas would not budge from their original principles. "What kind of revolution is this?" I asked Cuban Ambassador Norberto Hernández Curbelo, who was Borge's guest on the trip, as we drank together at the Cayuca, a Sandinista army discotheque in Puerto Cabezas.

Ambassador Hernández took a swig of cold beer and thought for a moment. "The political leadership of this country is fighting for the same principles as the leadership of Cuba. Only the methods are different," said the husky blond ambassador. "I'm not against elections here, because I understand the tactics. They need a good image in the international community to get aid. This government will never let power be put in dispute. That's Marxist principle."

The Arias Peace Plan marched on, however, and events quickly got out of Ambassador Hernández's and even Borge's control. In February 1989, President Ortega and the other Central American leaders signed another accord in which Nicaragua agreed to reschedule elections almost a year sooner than originally planned in return for the voluntary dissolution of the Contras. The Contras refused to disband, and continued to survive with the help of Honduras and the United States. The Bush administration proved to be far more agile in its dealings with Congress than the Reagan administration had been. Secretary of State James Baker worked out a deal with congressional Democrats whereby he agreed not to seek military aid for the Contras in return for Democratic approval of humanitarian aid—uniforms and food, for example—to keep the Contras alive as a potential threat in case Managua did not live up to the commitments it negotiated with its neighbors.

Still, as the scheduled February 1990 national elections approached, the Sandinistas scurried to regain popular favor by further liberalizing their policies. They liberated all remaining political prisoners, accelerated the distribution of land to individual peasants, dropped the word *socialism* from the party platform, suspended the draft, and permitted religious services to be held for the first time on Sandinista army bases. But no matter what they did or said, the Sandinistas could never make up for the economic mistakes they made in their early years, nor could they vanquish the general feeling that they were responsible for bringing the Contra war and U.S. trade sanctions down on them.

When I headed on the campaign trail in December 1989, I found a country desperate for change but as nationalistic as ever. Daniel Ortega campaigned on the slogan of "Everything Will Be Better," as if he were the opposition candidate offering an alternative. Violeta

Chamorro, the leading contender, ran promising to end "Sandinista treason."

I followed the Ortega campaign to the city of Masaya, a cradle of the revolution, where a freshly painted mural reminded the people that they had fought for rebel leader Benjamín Zeledón against the Yankees in 1912 and against the Somoza dictatorship only a decade before. The crowds waiting for Ortega and Vice President Sergio Ramírez were large and young, mostly from local high schools. This was obviously a well-financed, well-organized campaign. Hundreds of people wore Daniel T-shirts as they danced to music performed by salsa bands paid for by the local party organization. Twenty parked buses indicated that the Sandinistas had brought people in from around the countryside. The city's older citizens generally didn't come out. "These young people are fooled the way we were," said nightwatchman Juan Mercado Calero, seventy-nine, who observed the crowd from a side street. "Our fight against the Guard accomplished nothing."

After arriving in a motorcade, Ortega spoke to a crowd of 10,000 people with more humor and energy than I had ever seen him display before. He had discarded his eyeglasses and exchanged his army fatigues for tight black pants and a cream-colored shirt. This was the new Daniel Ortega, a youthful, more human image, a dancer not a fighter. "What do you want?" he asked the rally. "Peace!" was the answer. Ortega didn't make any promises about improving the country's social and economic problems. He didn't even mention his main opponent, Violeta Chamorro, by name once. Instead, he concentrated on foreign policy and the alleged connections to Washington of the National Opposition Union (UNO), a coalition of fourteen opposition groups.

"The Yankees invented the National Guard and the Nicaraguan people destroyed them, the Yankees invented the Contras and the Nicaraguan people destroyed them, and now the Yankees invented UNO—and the Nicaraguan people will destroy them, too," he said. His message was mixed with a threat: "Don't mix yourself up with the UNO, or you'll fall. Defend Nicaragua against the Yankees! Remember, on one side is Bush and on the other is Daniel. A vote for UNO is a vote for Bush and a treason committed against Nicaragua!"

Ortega's claims didn't fly. As the widow of the beloved and martyred newspaper publisher Pedro Joaquín Chamorro and a member of the original Sandinista junta, Violeta Chamorro represented the 1979 revolution as much as anyone. She personified what the majority of

Nicaraguans wanted all along, a democratic revolution that would bring the kind of system enjoyed by Costa Rica. She was seen as a conciliator, a woman who managed to keep her family together despite the wide political gulf between her four children, two of whom held prominent positions in the Sandinista party and government while the other two were active in the opposition. Her vice presidential candidate running mate, Virgilio Godoy, had been the first Labor Minister of the Sandinista government. Both UNO and the Sandinista Front were parties of the Nicaraguan revolution.

Chamorro's campaign could not have been more different from Ortega's. Ortega was young and virile; Chamorro was graying and braced in a wheelchair suffering from knee and bone problems. Ortega's crowds were generated by organization, Chamorro's by spontaneity. Her symbols were traditional; she wore yellow and white ribbons in her hair honoring the Vatican colors; her rallies began and ended with the national anthem (Ortega's featured the Sandinista party anthem); she prayed to God and her husband. But Chamorro refused to yield the banner of nationalism to the Sandinistas. Referring to the nineteenth-century rebel leader who defended Nicaragua against invading Mexican forces, she told one rally in the town of Diría, "Our hero is Diriangen, who gave his blood for this country against the foreigners."

As Chamorro spoke in the city of Camoapa, in the middle of the pro-Contra province of Chontales, a Sandinista army helicopter flew around the rally threateningly. The crowd of 8,000 shook Nicaraguan flags at the helicopter and chanted "Qué Se Vaya. Be Gone. Qué Se Vaya!" Chamorro picked up on the tension. "They imposed the war on us with their ideology. We aren't interested in their foreign advisers. We are Nicaraguans!" Chamorro had quickly understood that the helicopter buzzing was an attempt at intimidation. "Don't forget," she screamed. "The ballot will be secret. They can't impose anything on us."

The Sandinista attempts to harass and intimidate the opposition were sporadic. I witnessed the worst incident of campaign violence, on December 10, a blazing hot day, in the town of Masatepe. Sandinista mobs attacked an UNO rally after some youthful UNO supporters tore down some Sandinista campaign posters. One Sandinista activist swung a machete in the middle of the crowd and chopped a man's arm off. In the melee that followed, one young man died and twenty more people were injured. What impressed me most about the incident was the anger of the crowd. Young boys broke stones and handed them to older boys who threw them at Sandinista supporters to protect Chamorro's rally. There was pure hatred in their young faces. As they left the rally, they descended on a local Sandinista party headquarters, looted it, and burned it to the ground. I came away feeling Nicaragua was in another preinsurrectionary moment, similar to 1977 or 1978.

But under the guise of more than 2,000 international observers, including former President Jimmy Carter, the campaign proceeded peacefully after Masatepe, even though the Sandinistas attempted several minor harassments. For the final UNO rally of the campaign, for instance, the Sandinistas rerouted trains away from Managua and programmed the movie *Batman* and the Mike Tyson–James Douglas fight on Sandinista television at the time of the event to keep attendance down. The Sandinistas also financed minor opposition campaigns to draw votes from UNO, and threatened local UNO candidates with the loss of their jobs and worse. But by Central American standards, it was a clean campaign and election. Buoyed by American polls showing they were way ahead, the Sandinistas couldn't believe they would lose.

Ortega opened the system in the hope that at minimal risk he could get his election victory certified, lift the U.S. trade embargo, end the Contra war, and attract hundreds of millions of dollars in Western European and Japanese aid. Sandinista campaign manager and directorate member Bayardo Arce privately told a Mexican reporter, "First we have to win the election and retain power; then we can push our Socialist ideals later when the correlation of forces has improved." But when it came to election day, February 25, 1990, the Nicaraguan people didn't forget the years of repression, want, and pro-Soviet rhetoric they never quite understood. They came out massively and voted Ortega out of office in a landslide.

The two-month transition period leading to Chamorro's April 25 inauguration appeared to be more a transition to chaos than to democracy. The Sandinistas distributed guns to thousands of their supporters around the countryside "to defend the conquests of the revolution." They coordinated a series of public and private sector union strikes that crippled vital industries. They stole millions of dollars worth of property from ministries, including scores of automobiles and trucks, not to mention most of the government's cutlery and typewriters. The thieves had nothing to worry about since the Sandinista-controlled National Assembly passed a law pardoning all officials for any illegalities committed between the 1979 Sandinista takeover and Chamorro's inauguration.

To make matters worse, the Sandinista newspaper *Barricada* published a series of editorials saying the security forces should not obey the new government, while the Contras swore they would never drop their arms as long as the Sandinistas controlled the military.

Vice President–elect Virgilio Godoy and the more conservative sectors of Chamorro's UNO coalition argued to fight fire with fire. They advised her to unleash the Nicaraguan masses into the streets and encourage desertions from the army to force the Sandinistas out of the barracks. A display of "people's power," they argued, could split the Sandinista army and party and break the revolutionary movement once and for all. Chamorro wasn't so sure; the Front had still won 41 percent of the vote and was still the best-organized political force in the country. Her chief advisers counseled caution; they urged her to appoint Defense Minister Humberto Ortega as the army chief of staff.

Her decision to keep the outgoing president's brother in the government was widely criticized as appeasement. Several political groups in her coalition threatened outright rebellion. Two appointed cabinet ministers resigned before taking office. The Bush administration rushed Bernard Aronson, the Assistant Secretary of State for Inter-American Affairs, to Managua a week before the inauguration to urge that she drop Ortega or risk losing much of the $300 million economic aid package being ushered through Congress. (The Sandinistas had left Chamorro $3 million in the treasury and an $11 billion debt.) Meeting in the study of her Managua residence, among the memorabilia of her martyred husband, Chamorro told Aronson her appointment of Ortega would isolate the radicals like Borge. "Don't worry," she said. "We can handle the Ortegas better inside the tent than outside the tent." Besides, she said, she needed to demonstrate her independence from the United States. As Aronson left for the airport empty-handed, he was intercepted by an angry Sandinista mob that rocked his car as police looked on.

The polarization that threatened to lead the country into yet another civil war was vividly displayed during the inauguration-day festivities, which took place in a Managua baseball stadium. On the third-base side sat the Chamorro supporters; on the first-base side sat the Sandinista supporters. The Sandinistas jeered and threw garbage and water balloons as Chamorro entered the stadium in an open car.

Not unexpectedly, they saved their most strident invective for Vice President Dan Quayle, one of the visiting dignitaries. Thousands chanted "Murderer, Murderer" as Quayle and his wife, Marilyn, gamely took their seats for the swearing-in ceremony.

4
Honduras:
The Ultimate
Banana Republic

On a sticky June night, the slow, hot salsa on the jukebox at the Toucan Club urges the American troops and Honduran women to dance closer. The loud music and the language gap make heavy petting the only communication available, and dozens of locking bodies take full advantage. "You like? You like?" a dainty young Honduran woman wearing high heels and a sheer white blouse asks her muscular dance partner, gasping for air. The young soldier responds in a thick, Southern twang: "Bueno, Bueno, B-u-e-n-o!"

The Toucan Club is located on the Soto Caño Air Base, which is officially a Honduran military facility but is run by and for the United States. Soto Cano is the headquarters for an ongoing series of U.S. military maneuvers that were designed to intimidate Honduras's southern neighbor, Nicaragua. It is also the launching site for top-secret U.S. Air Force unmanned, remote-control spy flights that keep track of guerrilla positions to the west, in El Salvador, and to the north, in Guatemala. What little recreation there is for the 1,500 American servicemen stationed on Soto Caño comes when the busloads of perfumed and rouged Honduran señoritas arrive at the Toucan Club for bingo, pizza, and disco Thursday and Saturday nights. It has been that way since American troops were restricted to the base after an August 1987 guerrilla bombing of a nearby Chinese restaurant that left six American soldiers wounded.

The Americans call the ritual "Bimbo Bingo" and "The Leg PX." On benches outside the club, the American soldiers were sometimes so sexually aggressive that Honduran soldiers felt obliged to step in. But to hear the Honduran women tell it, the American soldiers would make perfect husbands.

"I would like to find an American man to take care of me," Cleopatra Guillan, a twenty-seven-year-old secretary from the nearby city of Comayagua, told me as we watched the dance floor fill with couples. Angélica Suezo, thirty, gave birth to a girl fathered by an American soldier who has long since abandoned her, yet she still thinks the Yanks are superior to Honduran men. "Americans are just nice. You see that medical clinic over there?" Angélica asked, to make her point. "American doctors deworm dozens of Honduran children there every day. The Americans help us. We are poor and we need them."

Something is wrong at the Toucan Club, and in Honduras itself. The disparity of expectations between the soldiers and their dates is part of what makes the ever-close Honduran-American relationship so unhealthy. While the Hondurans have the highest opinion of the United States of any people in Central America, they have the lowest self-esteem and, ironically, receive the most disrespectful treatment from Washington.

U.S. Army Sergeant Noel Sánchez expressed an intolerance for the evening's proceedings. "This entire base is like the big white plantation house, and the rest of Honduras is one big Chiquita banana field," he complained. "As a Latino, frankly, I'm embarrassed to say this is still a banana republic."

That very day, the daily newspaper El Heraldo ran the second in a series of articles entitled "Who Are We Hondurans Really?" with one subheadline that read "Are We a Nation of Loafers?" One of the Honduran authorities quoted in the articles, psychiatrist Carlos Sosa Coello, claimed that the country is "depressed" because "we are people who don't have our own solutions to our own problems. The only answers that we think are good are those proposed by AID [the U.S. Agency for International Development], the World Bank, or the European Common Market." Compared to other Central Americans, according to another expert cited, sociologist Ramón Oquelí, Hondurans are "apathetic and without initiative."

The deep Honduran feelings of powerlessness, dependency, and self-deprecation are rampant. This is not a new or inexplicable phenomenon. Such feelings of inadequacy are rooted in the fact that Honduras has failed to build a modern state, a unified national economy, or a national identity—three characteristics that U.S. policy unwittingly discourages though all are necessary for healthy political and economic development.

Most of the governments in the region obey Washington's will because they need U.S. economic and military aid. But none of the countries are asked to grovel before Washington the way Honduras is. No other Central American country would have given a considerable amount of its territory to provide the Contras with a base of operations. The Guatemalans would rather fight an interminable dirty civil war with limited U.S. military aid than accept U.S. human rights conditions. Nicaragua spent a decade asserting its distance from the United States. Costa Rica resisted Reagan administration demands that it sacrifice its neutrality to promote the Contras.

When the Kissinger Commission came to Honduras in 1984, during its tour of the region, the government of Roberto Suazo Córdoba suggested that the United States should either make the country a full-fledged protectorate or station troops in the country permanently. The Honduran newspaper *El Tiempo* responded to the proposal in an editorial claiming that "now we have lost everything, even our honor."

The disgrace and embarrassment fester at the top and seep down the society. "We don't have pride," then–Vice President Jaime Rosenthal, a descendant of Jewish immigrants,* told me. "When we have an economic crisis we do nothing but hope the United States will come to our rescue. We say, 'Our economic policy may not be good, but we are good to the Contras.' The problem comes down to dependency." Honduran art critic Leticia Oyuela openly claims that "If the Peace Corps doesn't come with food, our people starve. We are a nation of beggars." She adds, "We can't build a house without importing the

*A small Jewish community is influential in Honduras, especially in the city of San Pedro Sula.

materials. We don't even have our own foreign policy. Unlike El Salvador or Guatemala, our bourgoisie always failed to lead us and give us a national identity and purpose." Many of the Honduran elite simply leave their country, usually for the United States and Europe.

Nelsón Merren, a leading Honduran poet who lives in Greenwich Village, New York, left Honduras twenty years ago because, as he put it, "I just couldn't stand it anymore. It is too hard to develop yourself there." His analysis of his country is bleak: "Honduran culture is the weakest in Central America. Children's folktales have been replaced by Donald Duck and Superman. The marimba, our national instrument, has gone the way of the dinosaur, replaced by American instruments. . . . Even our bakeries have been replaced by Dunkin Donuts." His explanation: "A great many Hondurans are *Malinches,*" about as acidic an insult as one finds in Latin America. Malinche was Hernán Cortés's Mexican Indian mistress and interpreter who aided him in the conquest of her own land.

At first blush, Washington doesn't appear to have a care in Honduras. But there is a backlash brewing. Once in a while the Hondurans bridle like a horse rebelling against its rider. Some 1,500 students attacked the U.S. embassy and burned an annex to the ground in April 1988. A small Honduran guerrilla band strafed a bus full of U.S. Air Force servicemen twelve miles north of Tegucigalpa, leaving seven wounded, in March 1990. Honduras in some ways resembles Panama, another country where the people usually demonstrate great affection for the United States, but occasionally turn nationalistic and anti-American. As in Panama, drugs and corruption are rife in Honduras. Also as in Panama, much of the malfeasance can be linked to dependence on Washington.

For all the misery, Hondurans have reasons to be proud of their country. Honduras is an exquisite country of vast natural diversity, from the great pine forests of central Olancho province, to the flat savannas of the eastern Mosquitia, to the endless acres of banana fields on the north coast, to some of the hemisphere's most spectacular coral reefs surrounding the Bay Islands on the Caribbean. By Central American standards, it is a peaceful and stable country with a working two-party system. Honduras doesn't suffer the racial violence that has racked Guatemala, El Salvador, and Nicaragua, because it is overwhelmingly mestizo. Its army has traditionally been one of the most tolerant and least violent in the region. Honduras is poor, but what wealth it has is more equally distributed than in any other country in Central America.

Perhaps Honduras is best characterized by its capital, Tegucigalpa, which as recently as 1965 lacked even a road to connect it with the rest of the country. Hilly, windy, cobblestoned Tegucigalpa is a city of tin and cardboard shantytowns surrounding a glassy downtown that hasn't looked modern since the 1950s. The Labor Ministry building is literally crumbling, forcing the minister and his staff to go to the nation's unions seeking handouts. The book collection in the National Library is forty years out of date and molding. Even the widow of a former president sells her husband's clothing to supplement her pension. What middle class there is works in the corrupt and inefficient public bureaucracy. The river that runs through the city is polluted, but the poor still wash their clothes in it.

The only modernity in Tegucigalpa is there for the Americans. The Honduras Maya, Tegucigalpa's only luxury hotel, is a nest of American spies, a Contra rendezvous spot, and a dormitory for American military trainers and soldiers of fortune. The glassy U.S. embassy compound, with its three buildings, is larger in size than the offices of the presidency, the Finance Ministry, and the mayor's office put together. Most of the best homes in town are rented or owned by embassy personnel, American aid consultants, Contras, or Honduran army officers and politicos who have skimmed U.S. military and economic assistance.

Even the capital's most patriotic monument, the equestrian statue of Honduran liberator Francisco Morazán, is an insult. Though Morazán's name is inscribed on the statue's base, it is really the likeness of Marshal Michel Ney of France that graces Honduras's central plaza. As legend has it, the Honduran board responsible for commissioning the monument stole so much money it was obliged to acquire the French statue on the cheap to avert a public scandal. The cover-up eventually leaked, but the Honduran government never felt compelled to honor in a more appropriate way the man who attempted to unite all Central America in one nation. A French Morazán would do.

FROM PRIDE TO DEPENDENCY

The intellectual center of the classical Mayan empire was the city of Copán, located in what is today western Honduras. Copán's astronomers were centuries ahead of their European counterparts in charting the heavens, while its sculptors fashioned giant statues whose modernistic, surreal designs would not be equaled in the West until Picasso's day. These first Hondurans were anything but *malinchista;* they were strong and independent.

For the better part of the sixteenth century, Honduras flowered as an important Spanish colony due to the discovery of major veins of silver in the central highlands. The silver boom created the need for meat and leather sacks, and a strong cattle industry developed around the mining centers of Tegucigalpa and Comayagua. But the metal boom climaxed in the mid-1580s, because Honduras's tough mountainous terrain and labor shortage—the Indian population dropped from an estimated 500,000 to less than 40,000 due mostly to European disease—made mining expensive relative to Peru and Mexico. Honduras never fully recovered from the depression that lasted through the seventeenth century.

Upon independence in the 1820s, Honduras was the most backward country in the region, and it was regularly manipulated by the leaders of neighboring El Salvador, Guatemala, and Nicaragua. The Royal Navy even occupied ports on the north coast in the 1840s and 1850s to oblige debt payments. The Americans began to fill the political void. The U.S. Chargé d'Affaires Ephraim George Squier was personally planning the future development of the country. Arguing that railroads were the path to modernity, Squier convinced the Honduran congress in 1853 to grant him the exclusive right to lay track for a national railroad to connect Tegucigalpa to the north coast. Washington granted the Honduran government $20,000 to begin financing the project, money that Tegucigalpa funneled into a border war with Guatemala.

The elites of all the other nations of Central America developed their countries using coffee revenues as their engine of growth. Unlike

Guatemala, El Salvador, Nicaragua, and Costa Rica, Honduras is not volcanic, and it therefore lacks the rich soil needed for coffee cultivation. Honduras was forced to choose a different road to development: bananas.

Victor Bulmer-Thomas, an economic historian at London University, has pointed to several differences in the divergent Central American models of development based on bananas and coffee. According to his book *The Political Economy of Central America*, the fruit companies preferred owning everything that had to do with their business, from top to bottom, including the banana lands, railroads, and port facilities. While the banana industry was vertical, the coffee industry was horizontal, meaning the growers, exporters, and builders of transportation infrastructure tended to be different people, and frequently they were nationals. The foreign fruit concerns generally did their banking in the United States rather than locally, thus further retarding the development of a modern economy in Honduras. While the railroads that helped develop the coffee industry were built by the Guatemalan, Salvadoran, and Nicaraguan governments and tended to link their cities with their countryside, the railroads built by the American fruit companies in Honduras served the fields alone. Each fruit firm transported its own bananas on its own railroads to be exported out of its own ports on its own ships. Even the police forces organized by the banana companies in their respective zones wielded more power on the Caribbean coast than did the Honduran army.

O. Henry, the American writer who lived in Tegucigalpa's Hotel Lincoln for eight years to avoid bank embezzlement charges in the United States, witnessed the first years of the banana bonanza. He ridiculed Honduras as an opéra bouffe in his best-selling 1904 novel *Cabbages and Kings*, forever brandishing the country as the quintessential banana republic. Honduras, O. Henry wrote, was a nation of greedy rulers, compliant bureaucrats, and innocent peasants; a place where brave Yankee bananamen could make quick, easy fortunes and wield power. O. Henry painted a picture of the bananamen as the new American explorers, heroes of enterprise and initiative, who spread the beneficence of American culture and principles to Third World primitives. Hondurans overlooked O. Henry's insults and built a monument honoring him in the port of Trujillo.

Between 1910 and 1930, United Fruit won control or leased nearly 400,000 acres of Honduran land, again mostly in the form of railroad concessions offered by national governments too poor to build their own. United's chief Honduran subsidiary, the Tela Railroad, in turn built an ice plant, generators, a hospital, and a 1,000-foot wharf in Tela, which by 1920 was the leading banana port in the Caribbean. Tela, Puerto Cortés, La Lima, and El Progreso were practically company towns; Hondurans from around the country flocked to them and the benefits the fruit companies offered—further eroding Tegucigalpa's rule.

United Fruit hired scores of Honduran officials and consistently got the sweetest deals from the Honduran government over the years. The company agreed to pay a mere one-penny tax for each stem of bananas it exported—and only after the government pledged that United would never have to pay more than the lowest rate agreed to by competing firms. Nearly half of the company's landholdings were obtained at no cost, due to Honduran government subsidies it earned for constructing railroads. And when the workers got uppity, United Fruit invariably relied on the authorities for support. To break a strike at United Fruit's Trujillo Railroad subsidiary in the early 1930s, company director John Turnbull bribed a union official to acquire a secret list of militant labor leaders. Turnbull turned the names over to Honduran army Gen. Salvador Cisneros, who dutifully arrested the men identified.

The banana age was personified by Samuel Zemurray, "Sam the Banana Man," who carved out his own personal Caribbean empire. Born to a modest Russian Jewish family in 1880, Zemurray immigrated to rural Alabama as a child, but he spoke English and Spanish with a Russian accent all his life. One afternoon, while young Zemurray was tending his uncle's country store, he met a banana salesman with a talent for spinning yarns about his adventures on the road. Inspired, Zemurray made his way to Mobile, where he began a fruit import business. He saved enough money by 1905 to sail to Honduras and establish the Cuyamel Banana Company. Within five years, Cuyamel had acquired banana lands stretching from Tela east like a checkerboard for seventy square miles, even crossing Honduras's disputed border with Guatemala.

At the time, Washington's policy toward Honduras was called "Dollar Diplomacy." Seeking to decrease European influence in Central America, Washington wanted to replace the $70 million British railroad debt with American financing. With the Taft administration's blessings, Honduran President Miguel Dávila contracted J. P. Morgan and other U.S. bankers, placed the Honduran customhouses under

Washington's control, and terminated tariff exemptions until the debt was paid off. But Zemurray had a distinct approach to Honduras. He wanted the American banana interests, not the bankers, to finance the Honduran government as a way of guaranteeing their overwhelming political influence. And he vehemently defended the tariff exemptions, which allowed him to bring machinery and spare parts into Honduras for his operations.

Zemurray decided that Honduras needed a new president. He enlisted former Honduran President Manuel Bonilla and provided him with a surplus U.S. Navy gunboat, the *Hornet,* and money to organize a rebel army to overthrow Dávila. Zemurray also hired Lee Christmas, a black American mercenary and former banana train engineer in Guatemala, as military leader of the "revolution." Christmas, who was known to bite into the rims of drinking glasses for party fun, introduced the machine gun to Central American warfare with his successful assault on Trujillo in January 1911.

At first the Taft administration attempted to stop Zemurray's plot, and the *Hornet* was forced to take evasive action around the coast guard as it sailed out of New Orleans harbor on December 24, 1911. But within two weeks, Christmas had reinforced his foothold in Trujillo. Washington withdrew its diplomatic support from Dávila. State Department representative Thomas Dawson selected Dr. Francisco Bertrand as interim president from a list of six candidates drawn up by the Zemurray forces. Bertrand governed for a year with loans granted by Zemurray, and then reportedly fixed an election so Bonilla could return to the presidential palace. Once back in power, Bonilla deepened the influence of private Americans on Honduran affairs by appointing mercenary Lee Christmas commander-in-chief of the Honduran army and a former New Orleans policeman, Guy "Machinegun" Maloney, as his chief lieutenant in charge of putting down labor organizing in the banana fields.

Zemurray, having noted that bribery was so cheap in Honduras that "a mule is worth more than a congressman," financed the Liberal party, while United built up the Conservative party (soon to be renamed the National party). Foreign domination of the democratic system diluted whatever ideological and policy differences that might have developed between the two parties. Civil war broke out in 1925 between Honduran forces, one representing the commercial interests of Zemurray's Cayumel and the other representing United Fruit, for the use of a Honduran railroad.

Honduran feelings toward the fruit companies were mixed. They appreciated the railroads, health clinics, and company stores, but they resented the working conditions and strike-breaking goon White Guard. A most eloquent Honduran protest of the banana companies came years later from novelist Ramón Amaya Amador, who as a young man had worked for nearly a decade as a banana worker and striker. In his classic 1950 novel *Green Prison,* Amaya Amador recalled plantation working conditions in bleak tones:

> Amid all the confusion of workers and banana trees, sun and affliction, sweat and machines, creeks and malaria, cried out the conceited voices of the foremen, the whistling of the supervisors, and the arrogant, cocky gringo slang. That's the way it was all day long. The exhausting work of the peasants stretched out until dusk when, their legs weary, they quit the green prison of the banana fields only to face the joyless, soulless barracks they had to live in.

For over two decades Honduras was plagued by occasional labor unrest that was climaxed with a national general strike of 55,000 workers in 1954, inspired by the semi-clandestine Honduran Communist party and labor leaders trained in Guatemala, which at the time was ruled by the Socialist Jacobo Arbenz. The uprising began over a relatively small issue: United Fruit had refused to pay its employees double time for work done on Easter Sunday, as stipulated by Honduran law. The strike began in Puerto Cortés and quickly spread to Tela, El Progreso, and La Lima; demands escalated. The strike's crucial moment came in Tela, when banana company stevedores and hospital workers gave United Fruit a forty-eight-hour deadline to reply to their demand for a 50 percent salary increase. When the company requested a thirty-day cooling-off period, the workers walked. Eventually, workers at the American Rosario Mining Company and British-American Tobacco Company joined the strike in solidarity as public workers cut telegraph lines. The strike faded after ten weeks over divisions between Communist labor leaders, who looked to Guatemala City and Moscow for ideological direction, and more moderate labor leaders. In the end, the Honduran workers demonstrated that the national instinct for reconciliation was stronger than any instinct for hate or class struggle.

Though the workers compromised for smaller wage increases than they demanded, and the companies cut their payrolls substantially in the following years, a national labor movement came out of the 1954 experience that remains a key to worker rights and social stability to this day. With the backing of the AFL's American Institute for Free Labor Development (AIFLD), the State Department's AID, and most probably the CIA, the moderates came to dominate the labor movement and work out a mutually beneficial alliance with the military governments of the 1960s and 1970s.

HONDURAS AND THE COLD WAR

Honduran President Juan Manuel Gálvez shared Washington's worry about the Socialist experiment in Guatemala, but he was reluctant to join in a CIA plan to destabilize Arbenz. The Dulles brothers reportedly assigned the task of arm-twisting to Whiting Willauer, a dashing, patrician career diplomat who had flown as Gen. C. L. Chennault's first officer in the Flying Tigers against Communist China in the early 1950s. A varsity football and lacrosse player at Princeton, a top-of-the-class graduate of Harvard Law School, and an accomplished ocean diver, Willauer had the perfect can-do disposition for covert operations.

Willauer's conversations with President Gálvez were heated, as Tegucigalpa wanted assurances of U.S. protection from Guatemala if the invasion failed. Before a Senate subcommittee in 1961, Willauer revealed, "I certainly was called upon to perform very important duties, particularly to keep the Honduran government—which was scared to death about the possibilities of themselves being overthrown—keep them in line so they would allow this revolutionary activity to continue, based in Honduras."

From his office at the U.S. embassy, Willauer supervised the supplying of the two-hundred-man National Liberation Movement army, as it waited on the border to move, by contracting private flights out of Tegucigalpa's Toncontín Airport to do the job. He helped organize the Liberation movement's radio station (one of its two Honduran transmitters was located in the U.S. embassy in Tegucigalpa). Meanwhile, a CIA officer who went by the name of "Colonel Rutherford" trained Guatemalan rebels along the border and openly recruited exiles and mercenaries in Tegucigalpa. When it came time for the invasion to overthrow Arbenz that June 19, Willauer reportedly commanded the Liberation air force himself. The Willauer-directed bombings and strafings of Guatemala City paralyzed Arbenz and persuaded the army to desert him. Through it all, and after, the Honduran government denied to its people and the United Nations that Honduras had anything to do with the anti-Arbenz coup. Honduras had become a country for lease in Washington's cold war.

Honduras also played a supporting role six years later in the U.S.-backed Bay of Pigs Operation for invading Cuba. Honduran President Ramón Villeda Morales donated a remote little island in the Caribbean, Swan Island, as a transmitter base for broadcasting propaganda and combat instructions to Cuba before and during the invasion. While the Swan Island transmitter was unknown to Americans, it was an open secret to Hondurans. The only hitch for the CIA's operation came one Sunday afternoon shortly before the Bay of Pigs invasion, when a boatload of Honduran students disembarked on Swan Island to assert their country's sovereignty. The CIA security officer radioed communications officer David Atlee Phillips and asked what he should do. As Phillips recounted in his 1977 book *The Night Watch,* he personally cabled to the security officer to stall for time. Following "a series of flash messages" from the CIA man, Phillips cabled the agent: "Give them plenty of beer and protect the family jewels." Which is exactly what the agent did; he and the students drank an undisclosed amount of chilled bottles of beer and presumably debated the pros and cons of the Castro revolution. The Honduran students agreed to leave after the agent granted them permission to lay cement lettering that read "This island belongs to Honduras." After he himself saluted the raising of the Honduran flag, the agent messaged back to Phillips: "Swan to Hqs. Students have embarked Honduras. Liquor supply exhausted. Family jewels intact." The destroyer went on its way. Radio Swan changed names from time to time, but it continued to broadcast anti-Communist propaganda from southern Mexico to northern South America for years to come, even after Washington returned formal control of the island to Honduras in 1971.

President Villeda was an anti-Communist progressive who viewed President Kennedy as a soulmate. While he took a hard line against the Castro revolution, he also pushed an aggressive land and labor reform program with U.S. funding and growing revenues from trade spurred by the new Central American Common Market. With the aid of the AFL-CIO's Latin American arm, AIFLD, Villeda in 1962 sponsored a mass peasant union, the National Association of Honduran Peasants (ANACH), to demand higher rural wages. He encouraged the growth of rural cooperatives and condoned the invasion by 35,000 peasant families on 75,000 acres of idle land, much of it owned by the American banana companies. The Honduran army backed Villeda's progressivism until he stepped over the line by disbanding the National Police and replacing it with a popular militia independent of the army. The high command staged a coup to overthrow the Villeda government in 1963.

Anywhere else in Central America, an entering military ruler would clamp down on the labor and peasant organizations and otherwise repress dissent. Not Honduras. The new military dictator, Gen. Oswaldo López Arellano, sent most of the Liberal party leadership into exile in 1963 and fixed his own election as National party presidential candidate two years later. He also imprisoned the leadership of the radical National Federation of Honduran Peasants (FENACH), but he was otherwise a modernizer who believed Honduras needed to work with moderate labor leaders, continue to diversify its economy, develop trade with its neighbors, and attract new foreign enterprises. A son of peasants, López Arellano is one of the more intriguing personalities in Honduran history. Venal and sometimes repressive, he could also be generous and tolerant. Though a military man, López Arellano was cautious not to ally himself too closely with the harsher military dictatorships of Guatemala, El Salvador, and Nicaragua, and even allowed the Sandinistas to use Tegucigalpa in the 1960s as an early point of refuge and organization. He pressed ahead with the Villeda reforms and made a unique alliance between the military and the national labor movement throughout his era in power, which stretched from 1963 to 1975 (with one twenty-three-month interlude in 1971 and 1972). He liked to say that he "seized the banners of the left and made the revolution peacefully."

The Honduran leader, however, was corrupted by his close ties to the banana companies. He was forced to resign in May 1975 following the allegation by the U.S. Securities and Exchange Commission (SEC) that he or some other top official in his government had accepted a $1.25 million bribe from United Brands (the renamed United Fruit Company). It was a messy affair. Eli Black, the president of United Brands, heaved his attaché case through the window of his forty-fourth-floor Manhattan office and jumped to his death rather than face professional ruin and likely legal trouble.

No sooner was López Arellano gone from the presidential palace, than there was a spurt of violence. Confronting little interference from

López Arellano, peasant organizations had mounted scores of land invasions in the preceding months, alarming conservative farmers and right-wingers in the military. During a peasant march to the capital that June, Olancho province cattlemen and the provincial military commander conspired to block the demonstration. Gunmen raided a Church-run union training center, captured nine activists, and then cooked them to death in bread ovens. The so-called Los Horcones massacre was so shocking for Hondurans that it chilled the activism of the peasantry and the Roman Catholic Church in most of the country for at least five years.

But when the Sandinistas defeated Anastasio Somoza in July 1979, an event that rumbled like an earthquake across Central America, Honduras could not contain the tremors at its borders. To the south, in Nicaragua, a radical social revolution was taking place that challenged everything the ruling Honduran generals held dear. To the west and north, in El Salvador and Guatemala, other Marxist insurgencies were growing, sending tens of thousands of peasant refugees across their borders into Honduras. By the end of the year, corrupt Honduran officers were aiding the insurgencies by allowing Panama and Nicaragua to send weapons overland through Honduran territory. Tegucigalpa then stood by helplessly as hundreds of Somoza National Guardsmen escaped across the Honduran border and set up camps from which, by late 1980, they began attacking Sandinista positions.

Honduras appeared to have escaped the instability of its neighbors until one Friday night in September 1982, as the Chamber of Commerce and Chamber of Industries met in the city of San Pedro Sula. Jane de Martel, a Banco Atlantida executive, was speaking to an audience of 107 people, including the nation's top businessmen, Honduras's Central Bank president, and two cabinet ministers, telling them of the virtues of increasing the nation's savings rate. As she spoke, a dozen Honduran guerrillas broke through the door of the Chamber of Commerce building, their AK-47 assault rifles blazing. "Everybody on the floor!" screamed the rebel commander over the wail of one businessman shot through the kidney. "We are the Cinchonero Popular Liberation Movement!"*

The commander of the rebel force, who kept his face covered, was an able leader, and his conduct suggested he had received military

---

*The group was named for a minor nineteenth-century peasant revolutionary nationalist.

training. He called himself "Uno," as if to link his mission to the famous takeover of the National Palace in Nicaragua by Sandinista forces led by Comandante Cero four years before.

Uno almost immediately released more than a dozen hostages, mainly the sick and wounded. But he had a shopping list of demands for the Honduran government before he would release the rest: the expulsion of American, Israeli, and Argentine military advisers and of the Contras from Honduran soil; and the release of dozens of political prisoners. The chief Cinchonero demand was the release of Salvador guerrilla Alejandro Montenegro, the military genius who led the devastating attack on Ilopango Airport destroying the Salvadoran air force the year before. On a tip from the CIA, Montenegro had been picked up the month before by the Honduran security forces as he traveled from Nicaragua back to guerrilla zones in El Salvador.

Christopher Dickey of the *Washington Post* and I happened to be traveling together on the same flight from Mexico City to San Pedro Sula on the Saturday morning of September 19, rushing to the scene of the crisis as fast as we could. We wondered if Honduras was finally going to fall into the same process of polarization and violence as its neighbors.

After landing, we took a taxi to the hostage scene, not quite knowing what we'd find after paying our fare. When we got out of the car, we witnessed a curious scene. Entire families had gathered around the Chamber building. Merchants had set up kiosks to supply onlookers with fruit, sugary slurpies, and tortillas, as if this were a country fair. The presence of the Honduran antiterrorist Cobras didn't interrupt anybody's good time. For eight days, about twenty-five foreign journalists staked out the building.

Demonstrating the conservatism of San Pedro Sula, more than 20,000 people staged a demonstration *against* the guerrillas. Protestors chanted: "Honduras sí, Terrorismo no!" The demonstration seemed to demoralize the rebels, and after the army cut off water and telephone communications, the guerrillas dropped one demand after another. Inside the building, the hostages and their keepers coexisted well. The hostages elected representatives, and after a while they played cards and told jokes with the rebels. "These weren't the kind of guerrillas you find in El Salvador and Guatemala," recalled former hostage Enrique Morales, the local manager of a Swiss roofing company, seven years later. "They didn't insult, offend, or abuse anyone physically. Hondurans are kind, open people."

Then Honduran authorities revealed that they had already turned

Montenegro over to Salvadoran authorities, who steadfastly refused to release him, and the hostage affair became pointless. With the mediation of the Honduran church, the Venezuelan ambassador, and Panamanian military chief Manuel Antonio Noriega, the guerrillas finally dropped all demands in exchange for a plane and free passage to Cuba via Panama. The Cinchoneros never managed a respectable encore.

The two other major Honduran rebel groups—the Popular Revolutionary Forces "Lorenzo Zelaya"* (FPR) and the Revolutionary Party of Central American Workers–Honduras Chapter (PRTC-H)—have had even less success. The PRTC-H, one of whose leaders was an American chaplain, was wiped out in the mountains of Olancho province soon after it crossed into Honduran territory from Nicaragua in July 1983. Local peasants would not cooperate with their would-be liberators; they instead revealed the guerrillas' positions to the army. The FPR picked up some peasant and worker support in the early 1980s, staged a series of bombings, then evaporated in early 1987 when the armed forces captured its two top leaders.

Thus, Honduras offered the United States a steady platform for making war in neighboring El Salvador and Nicaragua, and the Reagan administration seized the opportunity, putting Honduras's national interests behind its own. Honduras was made a less secure, more dependent, and more corrupt place.

THE U.S.S. HONDURAS

Under Washington's prodding, the Honduran army allowed civilians to take the presidency and cabinet. But at the same time the United States allied itself with the most undemocratic sectors of the society. The army high command remained in true control—and the man who wielded power more ruthlessly than any dictator in Honduran history was the commander of the armed forces, Gen. Gustavo Alvarez Martínez. A hardcore anti-Communist with a Prussian bearing that compensated for his slight build, Alvarez believed that war between Honduras and Sandinista Nicaragua was inevitable. He thought that Honduras's only hope was to tighten its alliance with the United States, and then draw American troops into a war with Managua.

*Named after a peasant leader of the 1960s.

Alvarez posed as a nationalist, but his career mirrored the history of his country. He always looked to ally his fortunes with foreigners, and he picked up his repressive politics and methods in Argentina, where he trained as a cadet. Alvarez rose to the rank of lieutenant colonel and commander of the Fourth Army Battalion in La Ceiba, where records show he received "special payments" of at least $2,850 from Castle & Cook (Standard Fruit and Steamship became a wholly owned subsidiary of Castle & Cook in 1968) in October 1976, shortly before he arrested two hundred members of the competing Las Isletas banana cooperative. Alvarez broke the cooperative when its members refused to accept bribes from Castle & Cook to set a price on their fruit so as not to undersell farms owned by the American company.

From his experience in banana politics, Alvarez moved on to become chief of the Public Security Forces (FUSEP) national police force. As soon as the Sandinistas took Managua in July 1979, Alvarez invited members of the broken National Guard to come organize in his country, under his protection. Without the approval of his superiors, Alvarez set in motion a policy that would commit Honduras to aid an insurgency against the government next door. When Roberto Suazo Córdoba, the Liberal party candidate who won the first presidential election in over a decade, was inaugurated in January 1982, the U.S. embassy and CIA pressed him to appoint Alvarez as commander of the armed forces. Suazo Córdoba agreed, in perhaps the most important decision of his presidency. The third member of the governing triumvirate was the Reagan administration's ambassador, a shipping family scion and Yale graduate named John Negroponte, who went about his duties in the Whiting Willauer mold. Negroponte's wall was decorated with paraphernalia from his days as a political officer in Saigon and with an autographed photograph of Secretary of State Alexander Haig that read: "Good luck in your challenging new assignment."

Shortly after his appointment as chief of the armed forces in early 1982, General Alvarez held a meeting with leaders of the main Contra group, the Nicaraguan Democratic Force (FDN). They agreed to work together to wipe out the Marxist threat in Honduras, including the Salvadoran and Sandinista arms trafficking network and Honduran leftist groups. Contra agents typically stalked suspected leftists to learn their habits and identify their friends; they took notes all the time in little red notebooks handed out to them by the Honduran military. The Contras submitted their reports to a Honduran death-squad unit (first known as Dirección de Investigaciones Especiales, and later shortened to Battalion 316) that Alvarez had set up with the help of Argentine and CIA advisers. Suspects were picked up by Contras dressed in Honduran police uniforms or off-duty Honduran police, tortured, and frequently never seen again.

The death squad's activities loosely corresponded to the Contras' original mission as outlined in a 1981 Reagan intelligence finding: the Contras were supposed to interdict arms that flowed from Nicaragua through Honduras into El Salvador. How much Washington knew of the Contra-Honduran death squad is a matter of dispute.

A Honduran defector from the death-squad operation, Florencio Caballero, told the InterAmerican Court on Human Rights that he had been trained as an interrogator by the CIA. He told a reporter that he hid his death-squad activities from the CIA, although it is generally believed that top officials in the U.S. embassy and agency station knew what was happening but looked the other way. Honduran Maj. Ricardo Zuñiga reportedly revealed an even deeper CIA involvement in Battalion 316 to U.S. congressional staff members in 1984, but his stories could not be confirmed because he was murdered soon afterward by a business partner who owed him money.

Some 250 people—nearly half of whom were Salvadorans or Nicaraguans—were picked up and killed by the Nicaraguan-Honduran death-squad network between late 1981 and 1984. Though not comparable to the mass death-squad slaughters in Guatemala and El Salvador, this was the worst rash of violence in the modern history of Honduras. What made the turn in the human rights situation particularly grim was that it had occurred under the rule of a civilian president.

In a November 1982 interview I had with U.S. Ambassador Negroponte in Tegucigalpa, he denied that there was a human rights problem in Honduras. He proceeded to personally arrange an appointment for me with a National Police official, who said charges of abuses were mostly Communist propaganda. It was hard to believe that Negroponte, with the intelligence resources at his disposal, did not know about Alvarez's clandestine prisons and the role the Contras played in this Argentine-style repression.

Some junior Honduran army officers, however, grumbled increasingly about Battalion 316 and the general's dictatorial style. On March 31, 1984, while Alvarez presided over a meeting in San Pedro Sula of an ultraright business association, Col. Roberto Martínez Avila of the Honduran army's Second Brigade took the general into custody. Col. Martínez had his men handcuff the general and, at gun point, demanded that he sign a letter of resignation. Alvarez refused. The troops threw him to the ground, kicking and punching him repeatedly. Alvarez wouldn't resign, and Martínez finally halted the beating. After spending the night at a Honduran air force base to recuperate, Alvarez was flown to Costa Rica and subsequently spent his exile living in Miami.*

The young officers handed power to the commander of the air force, Gen. Walter López, a hero of the 1969 Soccer War with El Salvador, when Honduras rebuffed El Salvador's territorial advances. López reinstalled the traditional parliamentary style of the officer corps, ended the U.S. military training of Salvadoran troops on Honduran soil, and initiated an investigation into the human rights violations of the Alvarez years. The Honduran army's own investigators linked the Honduran military and the Contras in death-squad activities. López did not have the power to destroy Battalion 316, but at least he succeeded in keeping it quiescent.

Ambassador Negroponte and the CIA station were surprised by the turn of events in San Pedro Sula; the tenor if not the nature of the U.S.-Honduran relationship changed. General López was quick to swear allegiance to U.S. policy and guarantee the continuation of U.S. military maneuvers, but his commitment to the Contras was softer. Unlike Alvarez, he never believed the United States would follow the Contras into Nicaragua to smash the Sandinistas. It made more sense to him for Honduras to keep the peace with Nicaragua through negotiations than risk having a foreign irregular military force on its territory. During a series of interviews over the years, López told me he worried that the United States would abandon the Nicaraguans in Honduras and leave something behind akin to Lebanon.

But by the time López took over the military that March 1984, the Contras were already an established military organization with the full support of the Reagan administration. López contained the spread of the FDN Contras, confining them to the Las Vegas salient, a finger

---

*Alvarez returned to Honduras four years later to preach his newfound evangelical faith until he was assassinated on the outskirts of Tegucigalpa by unidentified gunmen in January 1989. However, Capt. Alexander Hernández, the reported commander of the death-squad battalion during the Alvarez years, remains on active duty in the army and has been promoted to the rank of colonel.

of Honduran territory pressed into Nicaragua. Once, in 1985, López even threatened to bomb Contra positions in order to move them from Honduran population centers. But the Honduran general could never muster enough power, not even within his own armed forces, to turn on the Reagan administration and oust the Contras.

"I used to worry," López said years later, "that I would be assassinated—not by leftist guerrillas, but by the CIA."

What emerged from Alvarez's downfall was a Honduran policy of benign ambivalence toward the Contras, a policy of not having any policy. Every six months or so, Honduran military officers would make moves against the Contras, but they would never amount to anything more than a heavy-handed play for yearly increases in economic and military assistance from Washington. At the time, one Honduran officer grumbled to a *Los Angeles Times* reporter that "We've become a whore who doesn't know how to sell herself." But in the end, there were too many officers skimming off the aid to kick the Contras out.

From 1982 through 1989, the United States pumped more than $1.2 billion of economic aid into tiny Honduras—an enormous amount of money considering the country has a population of only 4.4 million. U.S. assistance accounted for more than 50 percent of all Honduran government revenue. The Peace Corps contingent was more than tripled to 350 volunteers to become the largest in the world as advisers from AID fanned out to farms across Honduras. This vast economic aid program was designed to promote exports, privatization, foreign investment, and jobs. Yet the combined rate of unemployment and underemployment (a category that includes the street vendors of toilet paper and chewing gum) remained steady at 40 percent throughout the decade. Consumer purchasing power shrunk. The current account trade balance worsened between 1985 and 1988.

The only thing that expanded was dependence on American handouts, and that was, in large part, because U.S. military policies in Honduras conflicted with its economic development. Pushing Honduras into the Contra war—especially in the years following the fall of Alvarez—eroded both domestic and international investor confidence. Meanwhile, Washington's buildup of the Honduran army and military maneuvers, though mostly paid for by U.S. taxpayers, expanded the Honduran defense budget and the government's fiscal deficit. The lost opportunity to encourage economic growth may become a destabilizing factor in the future.

U.S. military aid was multiplied by a factor of ten, comparing the $16 million the Pentagon sent to Tegucigalpa between 1975 and 1980 and the $170 million it dispensed over the following five years. The U.S. Joint Chiefs of Staff took particular interest in Honduras in the hope that the building of a military infrastructure, the warehousing of hardware, and the series of joint U.S.-Honduran battle maneuvers would frighten the Sandinistas to behave themselves. U.S. troops participated in the building of military runways across Honduras (at least one was eventually used to supply the Contras).

By early 1983, the military maneuvers were almost constant. That February, the Big Pine I exercise air-dropped 1,600 American soldiers into the grass and pine savannas of the Honduran Mosquitia, only twenty-five miles from the Nicaraguan border, with the mission of defending the territory from an attack by the "red army." Big Pine II, which came in August and lasted through February 1984, airlifted 5,500 American troops to Honduras—the biggest single U.S. military operation in the history of Latin America until the 1989 invasion of Panama. Big Pine II was designed to train the Honduran and American armies in counterinsurgency techniques, and it serendipitously coincided with the invasion of a hundred Honduran PRTC guerrillas from Nicaragua into Olancho province. Under the command and control of U.S. advisers, the Honduran army wiped out the rebels. American and Honduran troops also built an 8,000-foot stone and dirt runway at Aguacate, which became a secret base for resupplying the Contras over the next three years.

The epicenter for all this military presence, known as Joint Task Force Bravo, was the Palmerola Air Force Base—it was renamed Soto Caño in 1988—outside colonial Comayagua. G.I.s assigned to Joint Task Force Bravo were technically on temporary duty, though their massive facility—with its own weekly newspaper, television station, tennis court, fast-food stands, movie theater, and huge ammunition depot capable of supplying an invasion—took on a look of permanence. While hundreds of Honduran civilians came to the base every week for free dental and medical treatment, U.S. military civic action teams streamed out of the base to build roads, bridges, latrines, schools, and health clinics and to dispense veterinary treatments around the country. By 1989, the U.S. military took credit for deworming over 25,000 children and pulling more than 20,000 teeth.

For all the goodwill they spread, the American soldiers were social misfits in Honduras; few spoke Spanish or knew anything about the country in which they were stationed for tours lasting an average of six months. Often tall and blond, and most importantly earning a wage four times higher than the average Honduran's, they attracted hundreds of prostitutes from around the country. A dirt street of pastel adobe houses, full of cantinas and brothels became known as the *zona roja;* the whorehouse most popular among the G.I.s went by the name White House. Such excess, and the appearance of the AIDS virus in Honduras for the first time, played into the hands of the Honduran leftist opposition.

While the Reagan and Bush administrations continued to pay lip service to the Carter administration's push for democratic rule and civilian control, the U.S. agenda for Honduras always transcended borders. The United States was more interested in Honduras the base than Honduras the country. The Honduras-based Contras, flush with loosely audited U.S. aid, made perfect accomplices for Honduran officers with a taste for Chilean wines and New Orleans real estate. American agents and officers, eager to avert controversy and other complications for their covert war against Nicaragua, generally looked the other way.

The malfeasance ranged from the petty to the grand, from the CIA's bribing of Honduran newspaper and radio reporters to give the Contras good publicity to Honduran military officers taking a cut of Contra supply shipments and then selling hundreds of thousands of dollars worth of loot on the black market. Honduran military officers who helped the Contras stay in their country and receive supplies came to believe Washington would support them no matter what they did. Such was the message the Reagan administration sent in the case of Honduran Gen. José Bueso-Rosa, a liaison officer between his army and the Contras. Shortly after he was demoted in a 1984 military purge, the retired general and two Honduran businessmen plotted, in Miami, the assassination of President Suazo Córdoba and the takeover of his government during the civil unrest that followed. Their plans were foiled by the FBI, which linked 345 kilos of cocaine worth $20 million confiscated in south Florida to the plot. Bueso-Rosa received a sentence of five years at Eglin Air Force Base federal prison camp in Florida. Documents released during the 1989 Oliver North trial offered a few clues as to why his punishment was so light: to keep Bueso-Rosa from disclosing secret Contra arrangements in Honduras, North and Duane "Dewey" Clarridge, the CIA's chief operations officer in Latin America, sent memos to the State and Justice departments seeking leniency. North's memos warned that Bueso-Rosa "could start singing."

Among those convicted with the Honduran general was Gerard Latchinian, a Honduran arms dealer and onetime business partner of Felix Rodríguez, a Cuban-American former CIA asset who worked with William Casey and Oliver North to covertly supply the Contras. Latchinian, who was sentenced to thirty years for the attempted assassination and narcotics charges, said he thought he was working for the U.S. government during the plans to assassinate the Honduran president. His defense attorneys surmised that the Reagan administration planned the plot as a ruse to call off at the last moment as a way to frighten and then curry favor with Suazo Córdoba. By this theory, the FBI blew the whole thing when it followed a tip and seized the cocaine. In any case, in their haste to overthrow the Sandinistas, North and others never seemed to care about the risks its policy brought down on Honduras.

Narcotics have frequently been linked to the U.S. Contra policy. U.S. congressional investigators found that the State Department and the Contras contracted an air transport company as the Nicaraguan rebels' principal carrier despite the fact that it had been established by drug trafficker Juan Ramón Matta Ballesteros a few years earlier to move narcotics. The company, named SETCO, carried a million rounds of ammunition, food, uniforms, and other military supplies for the Contras between 1983 and 1985, according to congressional investigators. The investigators found that one of SETCO's Contra supply flyers was Frank Moss, a man who had been under investigation by U.S. antinarcotics agencies for nearly a decade for alleged trafficking. In 1985, Moss established his own flying company, Hondu Carib, which also transported supplies to the Nicaraguan rebels.

A direct connection between the mainline Contra groups based in Honduras and drugs has never been established with hard evidence, but it is clear that the Reagan administration was willing to further enrich the flyers and aircraft owners involved in trafficking in exchange for their helping the Contra cause. Whatever the links, Honduras has become a major transshipment point for the Medellín Cartel's cocaine trade from South America to the U.S. market since 1985, partially replacing Panama in that role as Gen. Manuel Noriega came under increasing pressure from the U.S. government. According to some estimates, as much as three to four tons of cocaine passed through

Honduras every month. Critics of U.S. policy in Honduras have pointed out that the Drug Enforcement Agency's (DEA) closing of its Tegucigalpa office in the early 1980s served as a green light for the military to assist in the trafficking.

While Honduran officials denied that Contras were even present in their country, the Nicaraguan rebels continued to travel around the countryside with special identity cards. That way, when they were stopped at Honduran military roadblocks, they could pass securely with their heavy automatic weaponry. Within the two-hundred-square-mile Las Vegas salient, from 1984 to the end of the decade, the Contras set up a virtual independent republic that some called "New Nicaragua." Aside from the fifteen or so Honduran soldiers stationed in the town of Capiré on the edge of the salient, between 10,000 and 20,000 Contras (along with 50,000 members of their families) settled in a series of camps—complete with health clinics, target ranges, and everything else a regular army would need.

Aside from a few hundred Honduran merchants who set up general stores around the Contra camps, the massive presence of the Contras created resentment among the local population. The Nicaraguan rebels displaced 16,000 Hondurans, who then watched from hillside huts as trucks brimming with U.S.-financed food and clothing rolled past the town of Las Trojes toward the Contra camps. By 1984, nearby coffee producers and cattle ranchers, who originally welcomed the Contras, began to denounce the rebels' control of the salient as hundreds of acres of their land became a war zone. Minings and artillery barrages, as well as the periodic incursions of Sandinista troops into the area, made it impossible to harvest some of Honduras's best coffee lands.

A few Honduran army officers grumbled, particularly after the U.S. House of Representatives cut off all Contra aid in October 1984 and reinforced the Boland Amendment prohibiting both direct and indirect aid to pursue military or paramilitary programs in Nicaragua. Seeking some cover, the Honduran military began secret contacts that October with Nicaraguan President Daniel Ortega and Defense Minister Humberto Ortega. The militaries of the two countries began sharing information about the maneuvers of their forces so as not to inadvertently fall into war.

A stiffened General López publicly criticized the Contras as a challenge to Honduran sovereignty. For his part, Suazo Córdoba, a lame duck who was legally prohibited from seeking reelection in 1985, schemed to exploit the Contras as his trump card with the United States to prolong his own rule. What followed, according to documents released during the North trial, was a two-year covert effort by the National Security Council's John Poindexter and Oliver North, Vice President Bush, and President Reagan to cajole a reticent Honduras into sustaining its support for the Contras.

With a CIA assessment in hand arguing that continued support from Honduras was vital to the survival of the Contras, North and McFarlane flew to Honduras following the December 1984 vote. In a session attended by McFarlane, Southern Command commander Gen. Paul Gorman, Ambassador Negroponte, and the top Honduran military brass at the Honduran air force officers' club, sparks flew between McFarlane and López.

"What guarantees do we have that we won't be left isolated?" asked López. "What guarantees do we have that the Contras can win? How will they win?" López also demanded a doubling of U.S. economic and military aid and twelve F-5E combat jets to bolster his air force. The blunt and prepotent McFarlane responded in an ill-tempered burst. "You have no alternative but to support the Contras," he said. "You have to choose between the Soviet Union and the United States." General Gorman, who was the principal planner of military exercises in Honduras, stepped in to take some of the heat out of the discussion. "You don't have the military capacity to stop the Sandinista army, so we need each other," said the general.

On February 7, 1985, the Crisis Pre-Planning Group (CPPG)— including top officials of the CIA, Defense Department, State Department, National Security Council (NSC), and military Joint Chiefs of Staff—agreed to a modified Honduras policy designed to offer several carrots to Tegucigalpa in order to guarantee their continued support for the Contras. Though the administration could no longer provide military support to the rebels under Boland, the Hondurans had to be convinced to allow the Contras to continue to inhabit their territory, as well as receive private aid in a timely fashion. Suazo Córdoba and López had to be reassured that the administration would continue to press Congress to reinstall military aid, and that eventually it would succeed. The policy planning group suggested that President Reagan write a letter to the Honduran president guaranteeing Washington's support in case Honduras were attacked. It also recommended that the administration offer to release $75 million of $174 million in economic aid that Washington had been holding up for several months awaiting tax reforms, devaluation of the Honduran lempira, and an end to Suazo Córdoba's attempts to perpetuate his rule.

A U.S. government–prepared synopsis of the documents stated that the CPPG "was in agreement that transmission of the letter should be closely followed by the visit of an emissary who would verbally brief the 'conditions' attached to the expedited military deliveries, economic assistance, and other support. CPPG did not wish to include this detail of the quid pro quo arrangement in written correspondence." A memo drafted by North for McFarlane to submit to Reagan emphasized that the "discreet" envoy "would advise Honduran officials of U.S. government expectations concerning support for the [Contra] Resistance."

The White House accepted the recommendations, including the cabling of a note from Reagan to Suazo Córdoba that read: "As we face the challenges ahead, we must continue to work together to achieve security in your country and throughout Central America. I hope that your government will continue to do all in its power to support those who struggle for freedom and democracy."

Less than a month later, following the March 16 inauguration of Brazilian President José Sarney in Brasilia, Vice President Bush stopped at Palmerola Air Base in Honduras en route back to Washington. There Bush was met by President Suazo Córdoba and General López. A motorcade was assembled, including much of the U.S. embassy and nearly the entire Honduran cabinet and military high command, to accompany Bush to Suazo Córdoba's hometown of La Paz, an easy fifteen-mile drive from the base. A country doctor by education and a crafty machine politician by predilection, the Honduran liked to bring international figures to his modest colonial home, where he was born. La Paz gave Suazo Córdoba a chance to show himself and his country at their best; thanks to the president's largesse, the town was suddenly coming of age with a new hospital, a teachers' college, three major boulevards, and a soccer stadium.

As Suazo Córdoba and Bush drove together through the newly paved streets of La Paz, thousands of Hondurans enthusiastically cheered them, waving American flags as if they were their own.

Following a general meeting, in which Hondurans said they wanted an explicit security arrangement with Washington similar to one the United States has with Israel, Bush and Suazo Córdoba met alone in the Honduran president's study. When the released North trial documents indicated that a ranking emissary was to be dispatched to pressure the Hondurans just before he had visited La Paz, Vice President Bush denied that he ever suggested a quid pro quo. Suazo Córdoba refuses comment on the meeting. But U.S. government documents indicate that Bush did inform Suazo Córdoba that Reagan had decided to release withheld economic aid and to "enhance" several security programs. After the Bush visit, more than $70 million in U.S. aid was released, and CIA funding for several secret projects were enhanced by $4 million. In exchange, the CIA reported to the White House, the Honduran military expedited the movement of weapons to Contra units.

The Senate passed $14 million in Contra aid on April 23, but the next day the House refused to follow. The Hondurans became skittish, and the Honduran army stopped an ammunition shipment from arriving at the Las Vegas base two days after the vote. McFarlane quickly drafted a memorandum advising Reagan to call Suazo Córdoba immediately. "It is imperative," McFarlane wrote the president, "that you make clear the Executive Branch's political commitment to maintaining pressure on the Sandinistas, regardless of what action Congress takes. President Suazo will need some overt and concrete sign of this commitment in order to forestall his military in taking action against the FDN."

Reagan made the call, as implausible as it may seem that an American president would personally call the leader of a tiny country about releasing some held-up ammunition. The conversation indicates how deeply involved Reagan was in affairs leading up to the Iran-Contra scandal. During the April 25 telephone conversation between the American and Honduran presidents, Suazo Córdoba promised to speak to the army about releasing the Contra munitions shipments and Reagan promised to increase aid programs, including CIA operations.

But a secret memo written by McFarlane for Reagan on May 21, 1985, indicates that bilateral relations were still touchy. The memo, which briefed the president for an upcoming visit by Suazo Córdoba to the White House, noted that "Honduras has been key to our ability to project power in Central America and bring pressure on Nicaragua. . . . But in the past year, the Hondurans have become restive over what they see as a one-sided relationship." He added, "In response to recent Sandinista artillery and ground attacks on FDN positions in Honduras, Suazo ordered the immediate removal of the main FDN base camp to a remote and untenable site." (A second secret May 21 White House memo, written by Oliver North and fellow NSC aide Raymond Burghardt, noted that the Honduran move to force the Contras out of the Las Vegas camp "had a serious effect on medical treatment and morale in the FDN.")

At the May 21 White House meeting, Suazo Córdoba, who had long requested a formal military treaty with Washington, got part of what he wanted. According to his written "talking points," also released during the North trial, Reagan told the Honduran president: "In case of an armed attack against Honduras, the United States will take appropriate measures . . . to consult with and support in a timely and effective manner the Government of Honduras in its efforts to defend its sovereignty and territorial integrity against Communist aggression." Reagan's security commitment and the U.S. Congress's June 1985 passage of $27 million in humanitarian aid for the Contras briefly shored up the Reagan policy in Honduras.

With the encouragement of the U.S. embassy, and especially the CIA, the military replaced General López with Capt. Humberto Regalado, commander of the Honduran navy, as chief of the armed forces. According to several sources, in his former post, Regalado was known to U.S. intelligence as a corrupt officer who skimmed payoffs from fishermen as well as proceeds from the flagging of civilian ships. In his new post, he was reportedly known to take kickbacks on construction projects and to pad brigades to receive the pay of nonexistent officers. Regalado was to stay in the post for one year, but he and his thuggish officer staff decided they liked their jobs so much they stayed until 1990.

The Honduran government that Regalado shared with the newly inaugurated President José Azcona had no more success in making a coherent foreign policy than its predecessor; it responded to the whims of the Reagan administration and the troublesome Democratic Congress. On March 20, the House of Representatives voted down a $100 million aid proposal, a move that sent Assistant Secretary of State Elliott Abrams immediately down to Tegucigalpa to reassure Azcona and Regalado that the White House would win congressional support in the end. Following the old script, Abrams offered increases in military aid for continued Honduran support.

Two days later, the Sandinista army crossed the border to fight the Contras, as they had done repeatedly. U.S. Ambassador John Ferch went to Azcona's house early in the morning of the twenty-fifth to advise him to publicize the Nicaraguan "invasion" and to request $20 million in emergency military aid. "You don't have a choice," Ferch told Azcona. "You've got to get a letter up there [to Washington] right now. They're going bonkers up there. This is absurd but you've got to do it." Azcona dutifully drafted a letter for the White House, but then took a long weekend at the beach to demonstrate to his countrymen that there was really no danger.*

Few people in Washington believed Nicaragua was about to invade Honduras with the objective of taking territory, as the Reagan administration implied. But in June, Congress reversed itself anyway, and passed the $100 million Contra aid package (including sophisticated military hardware and renewed CIA support). With such congressional support, Regalado and Azcona proved to be more reliable to Washington's will—until the Iran-Contra scandal crippled the Reagan administration's Contra policy for good four months later.

Flush with new funds, which began flowing weeks before the scandal broke, the Contras began a massive invasion of Nicaragua. The Sandinistas mined the border and amassed troops along the river frontier to try to stop them. On December 8, 1986, the Nicaraguan army broke a tacit agreement between the two countries by attacking a Honduran army position and killing two soldiers. The Nicaraguan attack was probably a mistake, aimed instead against the Contras. But with the public praise of the U.S. embassy, the Hondurans retaliated three days later by unleashing the most serious air attack between Central American countries in twenty years. New U.S.-made supersonic A-37 Dragonfly bombers, protected overhead by aging French-made Super-Mystéres, strafed and bombed Sandinista and Contra positions inside Honduras, then crossed the Nicaraguan border to drop bombs over the villages of Wiwili and Murra, leaving seven Sandinista soldiers dead and two children wounded. Still, Tegucigalpa and Managua stayed in constant contact during the crisis to avert a war, as they had during previous military clashes. "This is not really our battle," a Honduran carpenter told me hours after the bombing of the two Nicaraguan villages. "It's yours."

Corruption, and the dissent it created within the army, grew more serious under Regalado's command. Take the case of a Tegucigalpa grocery store named Hermano Pedro, which was a principal provider

*Soon after, Ferch was forced to resign his post because of his poor relationship with the CIA station and the Contras.

of food and other supplies to the Contras by virtue of the fact that its owner, Rodolfo Zelaya, was a politician with close ties to several colonels. Hermano Pedro served as a front for military officers milking the Contra supply operation for profit. According to one account, the store also illegally avoided paying Honduran taxes on about $4 million in U.S. and Contra payments. Moreover, at least one shipment of uniforms, for which Washington paid Hermano Pedro $325,000, existed only on paper and the money disappeared.

Reporting on Hermano Pedro, *Miami Herald* reporter Sam Dillon wrote: "A U.S. official with knowledge of Contra operations said U.S. authorities apparently tolerated these dealings in recent months as a way of rewarding key Honduran army officers for cooperation with the Nicaraguan rebels."

Hermano Pedro became a plum to be fought over by competing officers. On the morning of August 8, 1986, heavily armed troops of the Cobra police counterinsurgency force blasted their way into Zelaya's home. No one was wounded in the attack, but Zelaya, along with his wife, his mother-in-law, daughter, and four security guards were arrested, gagged, and forced to walk into the street in their nightclothes. Zelaya later accused the Cobras of stealing $36,000 worth of jewelry. He refused to confirm or deny allegations that army officers with close ties to the Contras owned a piece of the business, but accused intelligence chief Col. Roberto Núñez of attempting to pressure him into relinquishing his Contra supply operations. Zelaya went out of business and sought refuge in Miami. The affair led to the dismissals of two ranking colonels, tank corps commander Tomás Said and intelligence officer Héctor Aplicano, Zelaya business associates and important allies of the Contra cause within the armed forces.

Drug scandals have hit the Honduran military hard and frequently since Regalado took over. In November 1987, Medellín Cartel kingpin Jorge Ochoa was arrested in Colombia. At the time he was driving a brand-new Porsche Turbo that was owned by Honduran Col. William Said Speer, Tegucigalpa's military attaché in Bogotá for a little over a year. Said Speer lamely denied knowing Ochoa, even as Honduran newspapers raised the question of how an officer earning $30,000 a year could buy a car that was worth $100,000 at the time in Colombia. In May 1988, Honduran Col. Rigoberto Regalado Lara, the ambassador to Panama and half-brother of the commander-in-chief of the armed forces, was arrested and held without bond when Miami customs agents found more than twenty-five pounds of cocaine stuffed in bags of coffee in his designer luggage.

Col. Alvaro Romero, an outspoken army reformer and director of the Honduran military academy, does not discount the possibility that General Regalado had his own ties to the drug cartels. "I understand," Colonel Romero told me in a 1989 interview, "that the DEA is investigating Regalado and they are not investigating him for nothing." Romero said there was a connection between the U.S. Contra policy and the army involvement in drugs. "Because it is the American army, and not the Honduran army, that actually confronts the Nicaraguan threat, our army has no well-defined purpose. A bureaucratic army easily becomes mired in intrigue and corruption."

In March 1988, the *New York Times* exposed Juan Ramón Matta Ballesteros as a drug kingpin who worked with the Medellín Cartel and had close ties to the Honduran military. Only a month later, competing reformist Honduran military officers surrounded the trafficker's Tegucigalpa house, seized him in the presence of U.S. officials, and put him on the next plane flying to the Dominican Republic. At Santo Domingo's airport, waiting Dominican police turned Matta over to U.S. marshals who took him in custody and flew him to New York to stand trial.

(Matta was convicted in a Pensacola, Florida, federal court on charges arising from a 1971 prison break, and incarcerated in the federal penitentiary in Lompoc, California. In July 1990, a Los Angeles jury found Matta guilty of racketeering, kidnapping, and conspiracy in connection with the 1985 abduction and killing of DEA agent Enrique Camarena Salazar in Mexico. Matta was found to be an intermediary between the Medellín Cartel and Mexican drug mafia.)

It is a sad commentary that the greatest Honduran activism against U.S. policy was sparked by the arrest of Matta, an action roundly criticized by the public and politicians as breaking a constitutional statute making extradition illegal. A broad array of Honduran society found themselves in accord: Carlos Montoya, the speaker of the legislature, immediately denounced Matta's seizure as "a public kidnapping." Military officers aligned with Matta felt suddenly vulnerable. Ramos Soto, rector of the national university and prospective National party presidential candidate, made a speech on campus urging the students to protest the Matta affair. Soto's behavior was particularly provocative, since he had always worked to discourage political activity on campus in the past. The brouhaha over Honduras's stolen sovereignty led to perhaps the most striking event in the history of U.S.-Honduran relations.

Two days following Matta's seizure, a few hundred students set off on foot from the university to march across town to the U.S. embassy. The protestors told reporters they were demonstrating their determination to protect Honduran sovereignty and rules of law. By 7:30 P.M., a crowd of mostly 1,500 students, including activists of the left and the right, amassed in front of the three-building U.S. embassy complex and sang the Honduran national anthem. A few rowdy students began smashing parked embassy vehicles with rocks and clubs, which led to the burning of an American flag, and finally the torching of the seven-story embassy annex itself.

American lives were not at stake, but U.S. Ambassador Everett Briggs telephoned the chief of the FUSEP military police force to ask why Honduran forces had not been deployed to keep order. Col. Leonel Riera Lunatti would not come to the phone. Briggs called President Azcona, and then General Regalado to ask for help, and again, neither would come to the phone. Briggs then called Washington, to alert policymakers that they might have to deploy U.S. troops from Palmerola. Two hours after the riot began, police had still not arrived on the scene—potentially risking the embassy's top secret files should the students ransack the entire diplomatic complex. As the American troops outfitted to move on Tegucigalpa, the Honduran police finally arrived at the embassy to disperse the students. One student died in the flames and four other students were killed from gunfire that witnesses claimed came from the embassy. Both the Honduran police and U.S. security guards denied they were responsible for the deaths. In a separate incident, a mob beat up an American resident for no other reason than that he was an American.

Washington was shocked by the riot, which caused almost $6 million in damages, and by the official Honduran reaction to the incident. State Department spokeswoman Phyllis Oakley said, "We do not understand the slow response. We are highly concerned." A top State Department official admitted a year later that Washington had no idea that Hondurans would react so strongly to "a legal technicality." He added, "Various sectors of the military and government were using the occasion to demonstrate that they were fed up with us."

There are a number of theories as to why the Honduran authorities didn't accept their responsibility to protect diplomatic missions. Riera was later said to have had links to Matta; he was also said to be sore at the United States for blocking his rise to commander of the armed forces. Some Honduran officers were miffed at the Reagan administration's pressing for the Honduran armed forces to continue logistical support of the Contras even after Congress cut off military aid to the rebels a third time in February 1988.

Whatever the reason, there is also evidence that the Honduran military, or sectors of the armed forces, actually took part in the riot. An American Peace Corps volunteer reported to the embassy a story she was told by a friend whom she considered utterly reliable. He told her that FUSEP policemen had entered the facilities of his night school and, in the middle of a reading exam, ordered the thirty students to march on the embassy. Vice President Rosenthal told me he thought the military had inspired the riot in the first place. If that is so, the officers were most probably split over what to do. Three days after the riot, Roger González, the student leader who was filmed burning the American flag, disappeared and has not been seen since.

Honduran tempers calmed quickly, and with the exception of three or four unsuccessful terrorist actions on American servicemen over the next two years, expressions of anti-Americanism remain rare. Tegucigalpa continued to do Washington's bidding by granting the Contras safe refuge even after Azcona signed a 1989 accord with other Central American presidents calling for the dismantling of the Contras. "It's a funny place," a middle-ranking U.S. official told me in July 1989. "One day they burn down our embassy, the next they are our friends. Don't ask me what's going to happen tomorrow."

5
Costa Rica:
Central America's
One Democracy

In the 1980s, while the rest of Central America waged war, Costa Rica's Legislative Assembly passed endless resolutions condemning all kinds of violence, made the wearing of seat belts mandatory in all moving vehicles, and banned smoking in public buildings. What made the laws especially notable was not only their passage, but that they were obeyed, not dodged and derided as they would have been anywhere else in Central America.

I visited the Legislative Assembly, a neat colonial-style stucco building in downtown San José, in August 1988 much as an American civics student would drop in on a session of the House of Representatives. The hot issue of the day was a financial reform bill proposed by President Oscar Arias designed to boost the private banking industry and meet the requirements of the World Bank to qualify for a vital $100 million loan. The organized left, including a wing of the governing National Liberation party, viewed the bill as an attack on the nationalized banking system, a cornerstone of Costa Rica's social democracy. About twenty students and activists assembled in the gallery and taped radical posters on the glass divider between their seats and the assembly chamber for all the deputies to see. A single security guard looked on wearily.

The mostly young demonstrators got a chance to cheer when it came time for the Popular Vanguard party's deputy, Humberto Vargas, one of two Marxists in the fifty-seven-member chamber, to speak. "This is an outrage!" bellowed Vargas, who looked more like a banker than a revolutionary in his matching gray suit and tie. He hammered away against private finance, punctuating his speech with hyperbolic waves of his pencil. "We can't return the country to the hands of the oligarchy! How will we explain this to the peasants and workers?" Vargas's more conservative colleagues made telephone calls and read the afternoon newspapers at their desks as if his diatribe was nothing more than bombast. Although their reception to his remarks was cool, Vargas could drive home later without worrying that a death squad might assassinate him in some dark alley, which could easily happen if he voiced his views in El Salvador or Guatemala.

Unlike its neighbors, Costa Rica has developed resilient political institutions and has fostered a remarkable tolerance for minorities. Political parties—the two largest, the National Liberation party and the Social Christian Unity party, are both social democratic in orientation—compete over nuances, not over fundamental shifts in ideology and power. While Central American election campaigns are often marked by fraud and bloodshed, here in Costa Rica they are publicly financed, open and lightheartedly called civic fiestas. The February 4, 1990, election of Rafael Angel Calderón as president marked the tenth consecutive peaceful transfer of power in Costa Rica since 1948.

Costa Rica has wrestled with and answered the basic political question facing all societies—What is the proper role of the state?—with more success than any country in Latin America. Throughout Costa Rican history, the government never exclusively benefited the wealthy; power has always, to one degree or another, been wielded on behalf of the community. Today, there is national health insurance and virtually free medical care. The government provides free breakfast and lunch to children and pregnant women in schools and health clinics.* The government finances or subsidizes seven universities and three

---

*The infant mortality rate of 15 per 1,000 is half Guatemala's rate. Life expectancy is seventy years, about a decade more than El Salvador's.

symphony orchestras. Most recently, the government contracted IBM to install computers in scores of public elementary schools to train the new generation in modern technology. Public ecologists protect two-thirds of the country's forest lands in sprawling national parks.

Most noteworthy of all is that in a region marked by guns going off and dissidents disappearing in the night, Costa Rica has no army. The 8,500 men who make up the Civil and Rural Guards, along with the handful of other police forces, are appointed after every presidential election. There are no more than one hundred professional military-men in the entire nation of 2.8 million people. There isn't a piece of heavy artillery or a jet bomber in the country. The security forces are so poorly equipped that when they were deployed to the southwestern port of Golfito in 1986 to keep order during labor disturbances, they were forced to hire taxicabs for transport.

Costa Rica disproves the thinking of Frederick the Great, who stated that diplomacy without weapons was like music without instruments. Without a single warplane or tank to order into action, President Arias not only effectively crusaded for a peaceful settlement to the civil war in Nicaragua (for which he won the 1987 Nobel Peace Prize), he also successfully stood up to the Reagan administration's persistent attempts to use Costa Rican territory for its Contra war.

The Costa Rican psyche, reflected in linguistic expressions found nowhere else in Latin America, is defined by a deeply embedded desire to sustain the country's social peace. Costa Ricans call their inclination to socialize without friction *quedando bien*— literally "staying good," or "staying relaxed." Costa Ricans have an expression that goes: "Mejor un mal arreglo que un buen pleito," meaning "Better a bad deal, than a good argument." They customarily reduce the possibility of offending by employing the diminutive form to their nouns in order to soften their speech. (Hence Costa Ricans call themselves "Ticos," the diminutive form of "Costa Ricans.")

Actions speak louder than words, and Costa Rican actions resist offending. At beauty contests, all contestants win some prize so as not to insult anyone. At bullfights, which are known to be particularly bloody affairs in the rest of Central America, the bull is spared from the sword (and all who are brave enough get a chance to be matador). As American historian Charles D. Ameringer noted, Costa Ricans "do not like unpleasantness and shun extremes and fanaticism. Disputes are resolved *a la tica*—that is, the tico way: with civility and without rancor."

Always conscious and proud of their separateness, Costa Ricans are by nature a pacific people with strong egalitarian tendencies. Conspicuous accumulation of wealth, the norm among the rich of Guatemala and El Salvador, is frowned upon in Costa Rica. President Arias, for example, sat beside his driver rather than ride in the backseat. Community volunteer associations, which sweep the streets and construct public works, attract broad participation. Ticos describe their social harmony with one word: *convivencia.*

No society is perfect, and neither is Costa Rica's. A drug and corruption scandal in 1989 tainted three Supreme Court justices, the homicide chief of the judicial police, a congressman, and a presidential contender. More than 200,000 Nicaraguan, Salvadoran, and Guatemalan refugees have taxed the nation's social services in the last five years. There is significant street crime (in part because the police force is so unprofessional), alcoholism, and family violence, especially in the cities. But because an astounding 93 percent of the adult population is literate, there is a notable degree of social mobility—a fundamental root of *convivencia.* The Costa Rican poor, generally, have a different appearance than the disadvantaged do anywhere else in Latin America. Their homes, even those with dirt floors, are usually tidy, with clothing neatly folded in cardboard boxes. The typical Tico house has a potted plant on display beside the front door; a symbol of the pride Costa Ricans take in their homes.

One Sunday afternoon in August 1988, I was walking along one of Costa Rica's innumerable nature trails in Cahuita National Park on the southeastern Caribbean coast. I was searching into the palm fronds looking for iguanas and white-faced monkeys, when I was approached by a friendly black teenager.

"Hey mon," was Ernie Tabash's exuberant greeting in his Jamaican-accented English.* Ernie, who was nineteen, wanted to take me fishing or horseback riding. I had to catch a bus back to San José, but we talked. His tale, in some respects, wasn't altogether different from what I'd heard from impoverished youth elsewhere in Central America. Ernie said he couldn't make a decent living diving for lobsters, his main job. "Some nights, I go without eating." Still, there was no sense of resentment or self-pity.

*Costa Rica is perhaps the most homogeneous nation in Central America. More than 95 percent of the population is white or mestizo, 3 percent is black, and less than 1 percent is Indian. Homogeneity is certainly another reason for Costa Rica's tranquility.

With a twelfth-grade education, Ernie was bright and hopeful about the future. Smiling widely, he reflected on his country. "We Costa Ricans love peace and freedom so much, we don't fight like the Nicaraguans always do," he said. "I like Costa Rica because it is a free country. Anything you want, you can do in Costa Rica. There is law, but you can walk around without your shirt on. You can't do that in Panama."

"F-r-e-e-d-o-m." He savored every syllable. "N-i-c-e!"

A DIFFERENT HISTORY

In 1839, President Martin Van Buren dispatched diplomat and naturalist John L. Stephens to Central America to establish relations with the United Provinces of Central America and to assess the political situation while the five infant states attempted to form a political union. Stephens found chaos and venal, militaristic dictators wherever he went—except in quiet Costa Rica. In his classic two-volume travelogue entitled *Incidents of Travel in Central America, Chiapas and Yucatán,* Stephens wrote:

> The State of Costa Rica enjoyed . . . a degree of prosperity unequalled by any in the disjointed confederacy. At a safe distance, without wealth enough to excite cupidity, and with a large tract of wilderness to protect it against the march of an invading army, it had escaped the tumults and wars which desolated and devastated the other states. . . .
>
> [President Braulio Carrillo Colina] was about fifty, short and stout, plain, but careful in his dress, and with an appearance of dogged resolution in his face. His house was republican enough, and had nothing to distinguish it from that of any other citizen; in one part his wife had a little store, and in the other was his office for government business. It was no larger than the counting-room of a third-rate merchant. . . ."

Such images of an idyllic, classless society have been recorded by chroniclers since the earliest colonial days. Costa Rica has always been the jewel of Central America. The question is why.

Costa Rica is different from the rest of Central America, indeed from the rest of Latin America, because its people distribute their wealth, land, and power far more equitably. Its social welfare system and parliamentary democracy have no equal. This is not a new development; rather, it is the result of an enduring consolidation and deepening of social patterns that originate from the earliest colonial days, and the result of unique geographical and cultural factors. "Costa Rica shows itself the 'happy exception,' or perhaps a fortunate accident," wrote Costa Rican historian Hector Pérez-Brignoli. "It is without question the product of a long historical process."

Costa Rica, to its everlasting good fortune, was the most neglected province of colonial Central America, in large part because it was farthest from the colonial governors based in Guatemala. As large-scale colonization began elsewhere, only 330 Spanish colonists claimed lands in Costa Rica by 1611, because it had neither of the two things the Spanish conquistadores wanted: mineral wealth (gold and silver), or an abundant Indian population to work their haciendas. Out of Costa Rica's isolation arose a small, homogeneous, and autonomous society that began holding local elections as early as the eighteenth century.

With few Indians to conquer and exploit, greedy soldiers, colonial bureaucrats, and Catholic priests—all enemies of tolerance—went to different provinces for booty, taxes, and souls. Meanwhile, the absence of mines and indigenous workers meant that settlers worked their own land—and there was plenty of it to go around for centuries—to form a huge middle class of yeoman farmers. Even for those without land, labor shortages usually assured the highest wages in the region, which in turn further discouraged the formation of large estates. Costa Rica has been largely spared the legacies of ethnic and class conflict.

"Frontiers breed equality and individualism. Class resentments arise in a developed and stratified economic order," noted American historian Arthur Schlesinger, Jr., in a 1989 essay on the age of Andrew Jackson. It was the more densely populated, economically sophisticated eastern United States, not Jackson's west, "that had the bitter experience of shrinking opportunity, growing inequality, and hardening class lines." Schlesinger's analysis holds equally well for Central America. Guatemala and El Salvador, the political and economic centers of colonial Central America, with their abundance of native Indian labor and good soil, developed the most stratified and polarized societies. Honduras and Costa Rica, the frontiers of the colony, became the most egalitarian nations in the region.

· · ·

Like Guatemala and El Salvador, Costa Rica was transformed by coffee in the nineteenth century. The brown bean attracted foreign capital and immigrant merchants, and promoted road and railroad development. But Costa Rica's more equitable land tenure patterns and the absence of Indian-Ladino racial tension averted the class warfare and growing militarism that accompanied the coffee booms in some of its neighbors.

Coffee did generally widen the gap between classes as large land-holders bought out small landholders. Accumulating real wealth for the first time, upscale Costa Ricans established a consumer society, complete with imported champagne and cognac. The elite looked to Europe for its culture as well as its capital and built the rococo National Theater in downtown San José as a small-scale replica of the Paris Opera House. But Costa Rican society provided a social cushion to absorb the shocks. Upper-class families, in Tico fashion, showed a common touch and an interest in promoting their country. President Juan Rafael Mora and his cabinetful of coffeemen, for instance, regularly frequented the popular San José cockfights in the 1850s, and bet along with the workers and peasants. The coffeemen who controlled the presidency through the later half of the nineteenth century spent the country's coffee wealth lavishly on improved urban sanitation, public schools, and transportation.

The greatest of the modernizers, President Tomás Guardia Gutiérrez, approached American engineers in 1871 to propose building a railroad from the settled central plateau over the rugged mountains to Puerto Limón on the Atlantic. Minor Cooper Keith, once described as "an apple-headed little man with the eyes of a fanatic," won the railroad concession. He first recruited Chinese and Italian workers, and when they died by the thousands of malaria and yellow fever and walked out on strike, he imported Jamaican workmen. In one of the major engineering feats of the age, Keith completed the San José–Puerto Limón railroad in 1890 and built himself a Costa Rican banana empire in the process. Keith connected the U.S. fruit centers of New Orleans and Boston with San José, and from Costa Rica expanded his United Fruit Company to Guatemala and Honduras.

United Fruit developed an imposing influence in Costa Rica. The company ran the railroad and banana lands and funded much of the national debt. But the society stood up to "the Octopus," as it was called, better than either Guatemala or Honduras. American banana-men never dictated public policy. They never strangled democracy as they did in Honduras, and in 1889, Costa Rica held its first freely contested national election in which nonproperty owners and the uneducated could vote.

The nation's strong labor movement built muscle on the United Fruit plantations during a series of bitter strikes that began in 1913 and continued through the 1930s. The Communist Popular Vanguard party, founded in 1931, led several strikes but failed in its attempt to use United Fruit as its foil to ignite revolution. The party, however, has been credited with helping to limit the American company's power over the country without polarizing the society as Communist parties have done elsewhere in Central America.

There was one aberration in what was otherwise a period of stability and development. During a sharp downturn in coffee prices during World War I, President Alfredo González Flores handled the economic crisis poorly and incensed the population by proposing an income tax. His Defense Minister, army Col. Federico Tinoco, did the unthinkable: he launched a military coup. For two years Tinoco administered a heavy-handed regime that shred the principle of due process and free expression. Tinoco was eventually forced to resign under mass popular protest. Free elections were quickly restored.

Several Latin American governments flirted with Fascist Germany and Italy during World War II. Again Costa Rica was different. President Rafael Angel Calderón Guardia, a mild-mannered pediatrician, declared war on Germany even before the United States, and then confiscated major German properties in coffee and banking.

Calderón's anti-Fascist policies led him into a "United Front" political strategy that sparked a revolution and forged modern Costa Rica. Inspired by the Catholic church's new progressive social doctrines and Chile's social reform, Calderón pushed major initiatives to expand health care and labor rights, including an eight-hour work day and a minimum wage. His social security system offered unemployment insurance as well as disability, accident, and old-age benefits otherwise unheard of in Central America.

While implementing social reforms, Calderón made alliances with such motley political bedfellows as Roman Catholic Archbishop Victor Manuel Sanabria and coffee heir Manuel Mora, leader of the

Marxist Popular Vanguard party. The Communists used their position in the government to strengthen their hold on the banana union, which would fight a virtual war against United Fruit over the next three decades. As World War II and the days of United Front politics drew to a close, the administration of President Harry Truman cut military aid to Calderón's handpicked successor and puppet, President Teodoro Picado, because of the government's perceived reliance on Communist support. Meanwhile, a moderate left opposition emerged that favored modernizing the country but excluding the Communists from the process. This movement, which came to be known as the National Liberation party, was led by the charismatic José "Pepe" Figueres, who would dominate Costa Rican politics for much of the next four decades. The son of a Spanish doctor, Figueres was a coffee grower, an admirer of Franklin Roosevelt, and a Massachusetts Institute of Technology dropout who taught himself politics and literature at the Boston public library. As a social democrat, Figueres was offended by Stalin's Soviet Union, and he was thoroughly anti-Communist. He was a pragmatist who made an alliance with more conservative coffee growers and detested the sweeping social programs and high taxes initiated by Calderón. Tensions reached a climax with the hotly contested presidential election of 1948. Otilio Ulate, a conservative opposition newspaper publisher running for president against former President Calderón, won 54 percent of the vote. But Calderón's forces in Congress nullified the election and arrested Ulate in what was in effect a coup d'état.

Figueres assembled a small army and rebelled. The six-week-long civil war, during which cadres of the Communist party occupied downtown San José with guns, took a total of 2,000 lives. Disgraced in defeat, Calderón and Picado were exiled to Nicaragua, where Calderón's wife gave birth to the current President Calderón.

The Truman administration played a pivotal role in the war's outcome. Picado made several requests to Washington for military aid in order to beat back the Figueres forces. But U.S. Ambassador Nathaniel Davis deeply resented the Communist presence in the government, and advised the State Department against backing San José. Instead, Washington implicitly supported Figueres. Five U.S. warships were anchored outside Puerto Limón but never fired a shot. Their very presence deterred Picado from sending forces to put down Figueres's army on the Caribbean coast.

For the following eighteen months, a junta led by Figueres ruled

Costa Rica, shutting down the Communist party and the unions, and purging the government bureaucracy of hundreds of leftists. But once Figueres purged the extreme left, he quickly betrayed his conservative supporters and moved to deepen and consolidate Calderón's social democratic reforms. The junta granted full voting and civil rights to women and blacks and broadened social security benefits and public health care. Perhaps most important, Figueres abolished Costa Rica's tiny army and converted the Ministry of Defense building into the National Museum. The Figueres junta reconvened regular and clean national and local elections in 1950, and ultimately Figueres was elected president for three unconsecutive four-year terms.

The personal political battle between Calderón and Figueres was a matter of power more than policy. Ever since 1948, all major Costa Rican presidential candidates have voiced support for the public programs launched by those two rivals of the 1940s and 1950s. Figueres's other personal rivalry, with Nicaragua's dictator Anastasio Somoza García, forced his nation into periodic sparring with its northern neighbor and stretched Costa Rica's neutrality. Somoza began the grudge match when he sent five hundred National Guardsmen into Costa Rica to back Calderón in the 1948 conflict. When that operation failed, the Nicaraguan dictator supported a Costa Rican conspiracy to topple the Figueres junta later that year. Figueres would never forgive and forget; he struck back in 1953 and again in 1960 by giving safe haven and logistical support to Nicaraguan guerrillas fighting the Somoza dictatorship.

Figueres seemed to lose his sagacity with age. He was reckless enough in his final presidential term in the early 1970s to grant asylum and even welcome outlaw American financier Robert Vesco. Vesco brought millions of dollars into the country, but he also gained undue influence by allegedly paying off officials of two National Liberation governments. Vesco reportedly offered unsecured loans to several influential Costa Rican politicians and organizations, including one for $2 million to a company linked to Figueres. Vesco's private plane would come and go at San José's Juan Santamaría Airport without undergoing normal customs searches.

Popular rage over Vesco led to the 1978 election of opposition Unidad party candidate Rodrigo Carazo. Carazo forced Vesco out of Costa Rica, but he continued and intensified Figueres's active policy opposing the Somoza dictatorship. Upon taking office in 1978, Carazo pardoned a top Sandinista commander, Plutarco Hernández, who was imprisoned in a Costa Rican jail charged with arms trafficking. A couple of weeks later, by coincidence, Hernández and Carazo came across each other at a restaurant outside San José. Hernández, who was a Costa Rican citizen by birth, seized the moment and requested direct aid from the Carazo government for the Sandinista cause. Carazo agreed to "tolerate" Sandinista activity inside Costa Rica, and told Hernández to see Minister of Public Security Juan José "Johnny" Echeverría. Thus began an exceedingly dangerous period in Costa Rican history, lasting until 1986, when the country's fortunes became intertwined with those of revolutionary Nicaragua.

The public security minister became the point man in a complex international arms network including the governments of Venezuela, Panama, and Cuba that used Costa Rica as a springboard for supplying the Sandinistas. As the Carter administration and the rest of Latin America looked the other way, the Carazo government also allowed the Tercerista faction of Sandinistas, the one led by the Ortega brothers, to construct several camps in Guanacaste province. It was from here that the Ortegas launched their final offensive in 1979. Somoza repeatedly threatened to send his National Guard across the border to clean the rebels out, but he backed down when Panama and Venezuela promised to come to Costa Rica's aid in case of an invasion.

At the time, believing that Somoza was the real threat to their democracy, the vast majority of Costa Ricans supported Carazo's policy of backing the rebels. Scores of idealistic Costa Ricans fought side by side with the Sandinistas to install a democracy like their own. But by 1980, when the Sandinistas began to demonstrate their radicalism, Costa Ricans felt betrayed and they turned on Carazo, blaming him for bringing the Sandinistas to power.

There was cause for Ticos to be concerned. Persistent reports circulated in political circles that government officials, particularly Echeverría, received Sandinista payoffs for their help. The charges of corruption were never proven, and neither were suggestions by American intelligence that Echeverría was an asset of Cuban intelligence.

Whatever Echeverría's agenda, Costa Rican affairs took a turn for the worse at the beginning of the 1980s. As the Sandinistas consolidated their power, and as violence spread in El Salvador and Guatemala, sporadic terrorism and militant labor strikes shook Costa Rica. To make matters worse, a world coffee price bust seriously drained the country (payments on the debt reached 70 percent of exports by 1982), and forced the government to cease payments on its international debt and trim its social welfare programs. This was the beginning of a period that would test the foundations of Costa Rican democracy.

DEMOCRACY THREATENED

Following long reporting stints in El Salvador and Guatemala during that horrible year of 1980, I moved to San José hoping to find a bit of peace and quiet. I only knew of Costa Rica from the tourist brochures—"The Switzerland of Central America"—and that's exactly what I wanted to find. Costa Rica would become a secure base, a home away from home, as I traveled the isthmus as a roving free-lance correspondent.

During my first weekend in the country, visiting Poás volcano, I looked out a car window at misty mountain pastures and thick coffee fields. My hopes were confirmed: the houses in the rural highlands did look like Swiss chalets, with their gingerbread roofs and charming wooden window shades. Their bright pastel colors were Latin, making what seemed like a perfect mix of order and zest.

But my arrival in Costa Rica coincided with the country's greatest crisis since 1948. With coffee prices down and fuel prices up, the unemployment rate doubled between 1979 and 1981 to over 8 percent. Inflation was beginning to skyrocket. Costa Ricans, at least at the fringes, appeared to be headed toward polarization. Hundreds of workers were arrested in several labor incidents on the Atlantic coast that year, and during a strike on the Pacific coast, a Civil Guardsman killed a banana worker. A small leftist guerrilla group was beginning to stage small attacks around San José, and there were reports that armed rebels were visiting remote villages preaching revolution. Right-wing paramilitary groups, fashioning themselves after the death squads of northern Central America, were beginning to collect weapons.

On a shopping trip in downtown San José one afternoon, I came across a student demonstration against newly announced austerity policies. Police lines swept down the street, throwing tear-gas canisters to disperse the crowd. I escaped into a bank lobby with several other pedestrians, but not before getting a nauseating whiff.

For a time, incidents of violence came hard and fast. The first crisis brewed in the town of Grecia, fifty miles northwest of San José. The

Nicaraguan Contras unsuccessfully attempted to blow up the short-wave radio station, Radio Noticias del Continente, which was owned by a Costa Rican corporation dominated by leftist Argentine exiles and had been transmitting a revolutionary message from Grecia as far as South America. Several Contras were jailed for their participation in the attack. They were freed a year later when other Nicaraguan rebels hijacked a Costa Rican plane and traded their hostages for the Contras.

Reactionary violence from El Salvador also spilled over into Costa Rica. Following the 1980 slayings of two American land reform advisers and a Salvadoran labor leader at the Sheraton Hotel in San Salvador, El Salvador's junta appointed one of the two military men involved in the crime, army Capt. Eduardo Ernesto Avila, to the position of military attaché to Costa Rica. Avila, however, couldn't keep his powder dry. He allegedly ordered the bombing of a car rumored to be driven by a romantic rival. When San José expelled Avila from the country, he claimed the vehicle he destroyed had been used by leftists to traffic arms to El Salvador.

To a majority of Costa Ricans, the violence that came from the left was more disturbing than that from the right. On March 17, 1981, gunmen rocketed a U.S. government van in San José, injuring three U.S. Marine embassy guards; an hour later, a bomb went off and destroyed the small Honduran embassy. The Commander Carlos Aguero Echeverría Command, a group named after a Costa Rican who died fighting with the Sandinistas against Somoza, took credit for the attacks. In response to the incident, Unidad and the National Liberation party together sponsored an antiterrorism rally, which was ominously disrupted by right-wing thugs.

Three months later, four policemen patrolling San José became suspicious of two men changing the license plates on a yellow Datsun sedan. One of the men opened fire on the officers with a .38-caliber revolver and the ensuing gun battle left three policemen, one militant, and one taxi driver dead.

Established Marxist parties, which receive usually between 2 and 5 percent of the Costa Rican national vote, condemned the violence. Fearing that the guerrillas might spur a rightist reaction, a group of leftist politicians appeared at a meeting of University of Costa Rica activists. The scene of Marxist leaders urging several hundred students to remain peaceful would have delighted U.S. diplomats in Guatemala or El Salvador. "The revolutionary process will be carried through by the masses, not by a group of adventurers or supposed heroes," Socialist party leader Dr. Alvaro Montero Mejía intoned. "The democratic process of this country—its press freedom, freedom of speech, elections, even with their imperfections—can be used to liberate the country."

Imperfections in the seams of Costa Rica's social fabric appeared to be growing. One of twelve suspects captured in the police roundup of leftists following the ambush, a young woman named Viviana Gallardo, was executed in the custody of the Costa Rican special police, the Organismo de Investigaciones Judiciales (OIJ). Gallardo's slaying had the markings of a death-squad killing—something almost unheard of in recent Costa Rican history.

I had an appointment with President Carazo the afternoon of the Gallardo killing, which, in retrospect, I'm surprised he kept. The presidential palace was still and very tense as I negotiated my way past the palace guards and the secretaries who staffed the front desks. All faces were sulking or stern or fearful.

Carazo pretended to be relaxed, opening our interview session with a humorous crack: "As president of the republic, it is illegal for me to speak to you in a foreign language on Costa Rican soil." He was telling me this in English, and after we both chuckled, we switched to Spanish. I was pleasantly surprised by Carazo, a fair and rotund man with a toothy smile and wavy, ginger-speckled brown hair. Given that his popularity was at an all-time low, and rumors of his allegedly corrupt relations with the Sandinistas were all over San José, I had come to his office with skepticism. But he began to win me over a bit when I noticed that his brown suit looked like something off the rack of J. C. Penney's. His laced shoes appeared to be Costa Rican–made, with unfashionable square toes. I was new to Costa Rica and not yet aware of the national tradition of the ruler's modesty in displaying privilege. I was impressed when his white-jacketed servant came into the office to serve us a demitasse of rich coffee and called the president by his first name.

I questioned Carazo about the Gallardo case, but he said it would be inappropriate for him to discuss it with the foreign press at that early point. He resorted to humor to mask his discomfort. "When a sexy dancer goes to a nightclub nobody takes notice," Carazo told me, "but when a nun goes to a nightclub everyone gets concerned because it's not normal. People are accustomed to seeing us live in peace." Carazo said his main concern was the economy, "because the price of coffee is at hunger."

Carazo turned out to be right. Costa Rica's violence was for the most part over by the following year. The security forces easily cleaned up the commandos' safe houses before an all-out guerrilla war broke out, and they did it without militarizing the country. It was the economic crisis—the triple-digit inflation rate and precipitous slide of the colón (from 8.54 to the dollar at the end of 1979 to 35.50 in January 1982 to 64 by June)—that assured the easy defeat of Carazo's Unidad party by National Liberation candidate Luis Alberto Monge in the presidential elections of 1982. (Carazo went on to found Costa Rica's University for Peace.)

With his government unable to pay most interest on its $2.6 billion debt (now swollen to over $5 billion), Monge felt he had no alternative but to strengthen ties with the United States and gain its financial backing. Monge saw Contra aid as his ticket on the White House gravy train. In effect, Monge rented part of his country to the Contras' fledgling southern front as a base and supply route in exchange for aid to cushion Costa Rica's steep economic slide.

Through 1982 and 1983, Contra commander Edén Pastora and his Democratic Revolutionary Alliance (ARDE), set up armed headquarters and radio communications in San José and in camps on either side of the San Juan River border. When they wanted to cross back to the Costa Rican side of the frontier, they simply flicked their flashlights in code to Costa Rican border guards to let them know they weren't Sandinista invaders. Contra supplies and wounded rebels were flown back and forth across the Nicaraguan–Costa Rican border from airstrips on Costa Rican soil, frequently to and from farms owned by an Indiana-born rancher and CIA asset named John Hull.

(Hull was charged and held in a Costa Rican jail in 1989 for allegedly smuggling drugs and weapons to the Contras between 1982 and 1984. While free on $36,000 bail, he fled the country. Hull denied the charges to me in a 1988 interview on his ranch, but he admitted helping to transport food and medical supplies to the Contras, as well as hosting at least one Contra leadership meeting. He was later implicated by a Costa Rican prosecutor in a 1984 murder attempt on Edén Pastora.)

For Monge's services, Washington came through with one of the biggest American aid programs in the Third World, including the transfer of more than $125 million in economic support funds in 1983 alone. With Washington's backing, Costa Rica also received that year a $100 million standby loan from the International Monetary Fund (IMF). By guaranteeing credit to the private sector and subsidizing imports, U.S. economic assistance permited Costa Rica to keep up with its debt payments and to sustain politically acceptable living standards. According to one estimate, U.S. economic assistance between 1983 and 1985 was equivalent to more than one-third of the Costa Rican government's operating expenditures and 10 percent of the country's gross domestic product (GDP).

By late 1985, the Costa Rican economy had begun to turn around. Inflation had fallen to 15 percent from a high of more than 100 percent in late 1982. The colón had stabilized in the low forties to the dollar. Meanwhile, imports had been cut by 50 percent.

It is arguable that Monge's deal with Washington saved his country's economy and its welfare state. But the Costa Rican president never quite made the Faustian bargain with the Reagan administration that his Honduran counterparts did. Indeed, by striking a tougher negotiating stance, he earned far more for his country than did Honduran President Roberto Suazo Córdoba—a fact that infuriated Tegucigalpa. While he was helpful enough to the rebels to secure American economic aid, he never gave the anti-Sandinista forces his total support.

"It was clear to me that the Monge administration didn't want to go along with everything the United States wanted," Contra leader Alfonso Robelo, a longtime resident of Costa Rica, told me years after Monge left office. "They would not allow an open military operation based in Costa Rica. The rules of the game were, more or less, complete freedom for the Contras to pursue political, humanitarian, and nonlethal activities like buying food, treating the wounded, communications." Robelo paused. "Contra military activity—" he paused again. "Yes, but very clandestinely, very discreetly, very cautiously. The Americans wanted more than Monge would allow."

When Contras were caught carrying weapons or training in Costa Rica during the Monge years, Robelo and other rebels said, they were arrested by the Rural Guard or Civil Guard and imprisoned for weeks at a time. At different times even Contra leader Edén Pastora, perhaps the only prominent Nicaraguan to have a popular following in Costa Rica, was imprisoned and deported. Miskito Contra leader Brooklyn Rivera complained that hundreds of pounds of equipment and supplies intended for him were confiscated by Costa Rican authorities in the early and mid-1980s and never returned.

The uneasy, ambivalent relationship between the Contras and the Monge administration created awkward situations for both sides. During the second half of 1983, a unit of Contras under Pastora's command upset the quiet life of the cacao farmers and merchants in the town of Upala, ten miles inside Costa Rica. In all, at least six Upala residents died at the hands of Costa Rican or Contra death squads, and several others received death threats. The victims apparently were selected for their opposition to Contra presence in the Nicaraguan border area. Under Monge's orders, Civil Guard units were beefed up in and around the border town by late 1983, and the Contras eventually cut out their violence (apart from the occasional macho drunken gunplay on Saturday nights).

The Upala murders strengthened the hand of several high-level doves in the National Liberation party who wanted no part of the Contra war. Minister of Public Security Angel Solano Calderón, Ambassador to Washington Fernando Zumbado, former President Figueres, and the rising party secretary general Oscar Arias pushed Monge to criticize the U.S. invasion of Grenada as a sign of Costa Rican independence. That was the first in a series of victories for the doves. The doves were further strengthened by Monge's sensitivity to Latin criticism that he was acting like a tool of the gringos.

On November 17, at a solemn ceremony in the National Theater before government officials and the diplomatic community, Monge proclaimed Costa Rica's "perpetual, active and unarmed neutrality." To emphasize that this proclamation represented a real change of policy, Monge fired pro-Contra Foreign Minister Fernando Volio and declined a U.S. offer to supply as many as 1,000 army engineers to build roads and bridges near the Nicaraguan border.

The U.S. ambassador to Costa Rica at the time was Curtin Winsor, an ultra-right-wing former West Virginia coal magnate who repeatedly offended Costa Ricans with his loud mouth, awkward manners, and bad Spanish. Given to blurting out whatever was on his mind, Winsor began to publicly criticize the Costa Rican government and its social welfare policies. Winsor was not subtle about making the link between the interests of the Contras and the still expanding U.S. aid project in Costa Rica. Members of Monge's government who backed the Contra war, particularly Vice President Armando Arauz and Interior Minister Alfonso Carro (commander of the Rural Guard), got ready access to U.S. officials and funding for their projects. Known anti-Contra forces in the cabinet got Uncle Sam's cold shoulder.

Washington developed a multifaceted campaign to reverse Costa Rica's neutrality proclamation and heat up the southern front. CIA agents passed out bribes to Civil and Rural Guard commanders in areas where Pastora's forces operated, helping to assure that at least some of the Contras could function around the border. The CIA also paid off local journalists to write articles favorable to the Contras, an effort to build popular support for the force.

The CIA tactics, which contradicted Washington's publicly stated policy of fostering democracy in Central America, had an impact. Anti-Sandinista feelings grew among the Costa Rican public in 1983 and 1984, due to a flurry of border skirmishes between Sandinista army regulars and Costa Rican Civil Guardsmen. Costa Rican authorities later concluded that these flareups had been instigated purposefully by the Contras with the apparent urging of the CIA.

Typically, the Contras would openly attack from the Costa Rican side of the border to provoke Sandinista mortar fire into Costa Rica. Five years later, an American intelligence officer stationed in San José told me that hard-liners in the Reagan administration "would have liked nothing better" than to have the Sandinistas invade Costa Rica. "That would have been the perfect pretext to clean up Managua once and for all."

According to Solano, who supervised the Costa Rican intelligence service as minister of public security, CIA station chief "Felipe Papas" bribed and directed agents throughout the Costa Rican government. Every week or so, "Papas" assembled his fifteen primary Costa Rican agents—known collectively as Los Babies—in a private dining room in the rear of a noisy Spanish-style grill restaurant called El Escorial in downtown San José. There, over bottles of scotch and rum, "Papas" directed his men, all well-placed officers in the Costa Rican security forces, to work around their superiors and aid the southern-front Contras. They were also instructed to pick up embarrassing personal information about targeted government officials for possible future blackmail. Of particular interest to "Papas" were facts about Monge, Solano, and a number of well-placed vice ministers.

After several months, one of the fifteen agents reported the network's espionage in early 1985 to Solano, who relayed the information to Monge. The Costa Rican president fired all fifteen from the government and complained bitterly to the U.S. embassy. (The double agent who blew the whistle was allowed to change his name and retire quietly to a farm in the provinces.)

"Papas" was quietly shuffled to another posting, and Winsor was soon removed from San José at Monge's insistence. The full extent of the CIA's infiltration of the Rural Guard, the Civil Guard, and the other security forces may never be known, but suspicions of CIA linkage were so sweeping that Oscar Arias purged dozens of Costa Rican professional officers when he took over the presidency a year later.

"The United States embassy was a criminal outpost," complained Monge's Information Minister, Armando Vargas, in a 1988 interview, "breaking United States law, Costa Rican law, and international law—just to open a southern front."

Between 1982 and 1986, the CIA treatment of Costa Rica was imperious, as if it were an unruly colony. Nicaragua was an obsession in the Reagan White House, and the interests of developing democracy in El Salvador and Honduras and sustaining democracy in Costa Rica were forgotten. Indeed, while the Tower Commission and the congressional intelligence committees touched on Costa Rica in their Iran-Contra investigations, the full implications of the administration's espionage activities in Costa Rica were never addressed. A weaker democracy than Costa Rica's might well have collapsed under similar pressure.

Several leaders of the National Liberation party deeply resented the Reagan Central America policy, but Monge kept his criticism of U.S. espionage private. Indeed, during his last two years in power, Monge partially reversed his Nicaragua policy again, this time in favor of the Contras. In part, Monge was reacting to the Sandinista regime's repression of Nicaraguan labor leaders the Costa Rican president personally knew and admired. But Monge's posture also had a lot to do with the pressures from the right in his own party, from the conservative domestic press and business community, and the U.S. embassy.

If there was a turning point in the Monge government's attitude, it came with two skirmishes between Costa Rican and Nicaraguan border forces in late April and early May 1984. Rattled by the obvious inability of the Civil and Rural Guards to defend the border from either the Sandinistas or the Contras, Monge put in a secret urgent request to Washington for an increase in military aid from $2.15 million to $9.6 million. Those are minuscule numbers even for Central America, but the request included some deadly weaponry: $3 million for 4,000 M-16 assault rifles and $2 million more for several hundred grenade-launchers and mortars. Costa Rica hands in the State Department were ecstatic. According to a secret State Department report dated May 5 that was obtained by the *Washington Post,* the request for aid "provides an opportunity to help shift the political balance in our favor on Nicaragua's southern flank. . . . It could lead to a significant shift from [Costa Rica's] neutralist tightrope act and push it more explicitly and publicly into the anti-Sandinista camp."

In early August 1984, while Monge was touring Western Europe and his pro-Contra Vice President Arauz was governing in San José, the tensions building between the two factions within the National Liberation party finally erupted. Aware that his anti-Contra position within the government had eroded and perceiving that he was surrounded by spies compromising his control over the Civil Guard, Public Security Minister Solano panicked. In an off-the-cuff remark to a local television reporter, Solano claimed the government was close to being overthrown in a coup d'état. Solano later said it was all a joke, but Monge dismissed him anyway.

The Costa Rican president then preserved party unity by firing pro-Contra Interior Minister Carro along with the anti-Contra Solano. Monge filled the Public Security Minister post, which commands the Civil Guard, with pro-Contra Benjamín Piza Carranza and the Interior Minister post, which commands the Rural Guard, with anti-Contra Enrique Obregón. It was a mirror image of the previous arrangement, but the Contras came out ahead since they now had the support of the Costa Rican security force that was directly in charge of the border area.

Christmas is usually an uncommonly tranquil time in Central America, but the 1984 holiday season was tumultuous for Costa Rican–Nicaraguan relations. On a dry, cool evening on December 24, 1984, Sandinista police entered the grounds of the Costa Rican embassy in Managua and grabbed a Nicaraguan student draft dodger seeking asylum. While Costa Ricans demanded respect for its embassy and the right of asylum, the Sandinistas were more interested in making the point that draft dodging is a criminal act, not a political protest worthy of diplomatic protection.

Monge removed his ambassador from Managua and refused to participate in the Contadora peace process led by Mexico, Venezuela, Colombia, and Panama until the Sandinistas freed their prisoner—a year later. The Sandinistas would not allow the Costa Ricans to monopolize the moral high ground; they lumped Costa Rica together with Honduras and sued both countries (along with the United States) in the World Court for committing aggression by harboring the Contras on their territory. Managua's challenge of Costa Rica's beloved neutrality deeply embarrassed and angered Monge, and served only to sour relations even further.

By mid-1985, Monge was widely considered a lame-duck president, and his heavy drinking was a common topic of gossip in San José. To some in the inner circle, Monge appeared unbalanced and unfocused. The new Minister of Public Security Piza, an ally of the new CIA station chief Joe Fernández (known as "Tomás Castillo"), exploited Monge's personal troubles to take charge of defense policy. Without Monge's knowledge, Piza devised a training assistance plan with the American embassy and then requested twenty U.S. Army Green Beret advisers to train seven hundred Civil Guardsmen in Costa Rica over a period of six months. Monge was upset and worried by Piza's move to militarize and draw closer to the Pentagon, but he dared not risk offending the United States by rescinding the request.

This was a time when the U.S. Congress was cutting Contra aid one month and reviving it the next, and the Costa Rican appeal for military aid played into the hands of an administration attempting to demonstrate an urgent Sandinista threat.

Monge was asked in Washington, Europe, Latin America, and at home whether he favored U.S. aid to the Contras; he wavered in his answers, refusing to fully commit himself. His double-talk may have succeeded in confounding Nicaragua and the United States, and in keeping his party united for the February 1986 presidential elections; but his inelegant public obfuscations made him look pathetic on the world stage.

Monge did manage to get the objectionable U.S. Ambassador Winsor replaced. But Winsor's successor, Lewis Tambs, was only slightly smoother in style and no different when it came to policy. He was told by Elliott Abrams, Oliver North, and CIA Latin-operations director Alan "Cliff" Fiers "to form a Nicaraguan Resistance southern front," according to documents included in the Tower Commission report.

By mid-1985, it became clear that the unpredictable and disorganized Pastora was going nowhere. The CIA brusquely abandoned him. Several in the agency came to believe that Pastora was a Sandinista double agent. Pastora's replacement, Fernando "El Negro" Chamorro, took charge of the southern front in late 1985, but he alternated between undue caution and utter recklessness. Though daring and committed, Chamorro nevertheless proved unable to hit the Sandinistas in any sustained way, and soon lost the confidence of his men and his patrons at the CIA.

Had the southern-front Contras shown themselves to be more effective fighters, Monge might perhaps have taken a firmer position on their behalf. The southern-front leaders—including Pastora, Chamorro, Arturo Cruz, Alfonso Robelo, Alfredo César, and Pedro Joaquín Chamorro, Jr.—had longtime close relations with Costa Rican political society. Monge and some of his other advisers openly sympathized with their social democratic ideals. The problem, as most Costa Ricans well understood, was that the liberal Contras of the southern front were insignificant in number and influence compared to the archconservative Contra forces based in Honduras and dominated by former National Guardsmen.

The Contra liberals attempted to use what influence they had in Costa Rica to gain leverage in their constant political squabbles with former National Guard Col. Enrique Bermúdez and the rest of the FDN military leadership based in Honduras. If they could only get their war off the ground in Costa Rica, the southern-front Contras thought, they could challenge the conservative FDN and its former National Guard commanders. Time after time, they were frustrated.

Once Robelo tried to do a personal favor for Adolfo Calero, his archrival within the United Nicaraguan Opposition (UNO) Contra directorate, by requesting that San José grant Calero a visa. It had been Monge's policy to prohibit Calero's entrance on the grounds that he was officially commander-in-chief of the FDN army. Robelo's idea was to expose Calero to the influence of Costa Rican liberal democratic ideals as a way of strengthening the principle of civilian control over the Contra army. (Calero had a different idea; for years he hoped to open up a southern front for the FDN in Costa Rica. Monge wouldn't allow it.)

Monge knew ahead of time that he would deny Robelo's request, but he wanted to be gracious to his old friend. The Costa Rican president invited the Contra leader over to his house on the morning of September 15, 1985, the last Central American Independence Day Monge would celebrate as president.

When Robelo arrived, Monge was just getting back from church. Monge greeted his Contra friend, breathing heavily and sweating, visibly uncomfortable in his dark dress suit. "I'm very overheated," Monge said. "I need to refresh myself. Why not come along, and we'll talk in the bedroom." Robelo was touched by Monge's simplicity and open friendship. Lyndon Johnson used to take his associates into the bathroom to evoke or force intimacy and intensity whether he wanted to cajole or otherwise manipulate them. Monge was doing much the same with Robelo, granting the Nicaraguan exceptional access, and even friendship, to console him without making a commitment of any kind.

Robelo found himself in the uncomfortable position of staring at the president's strange figure—his abdomen was huge and totally out of proportion to his skinny legs and arms. With Monge sitting in a stuffed chair in his boxer shorts and bathrobe, preparing to dress himself for a series of public holiday events, Robelo made his case for Calero.

"In his typical suave way of doing things," recalled Robelo, "Monge said he agreed with me but there were members of his party who wouldn't go along. He said he'd think about it."

Monge gave the Reagan administration two final gifts in his last months in office that made up for his decision to bar Calero: permission to open a clandestine communications station run by American agents for the Contras, and permission to build a mile-long air strip designed for the refueling of planes flying to resupply the Contras. The Santa Elena air strip played a central role in the administration's covert effort to skirt the congressional ban on arming the Contras, and it came to illustrate the White House's inattentiveness to, if not disdain for, Costa Rica's civilian democracy.

According to the findings of the congressional committees investigating the Iran-Contra scandal, Lt. Col. Oliver North flew to Costa Rica on August 10, 1985, for meetings with Ambassador Tambs and CIA station chief Fernández to discuss the secret airfield "that would permit moving all Contra military operations inside Nicaragua for resupply by air." A few days later, North sent Robert Owen, a former Senate aide to Dan Quayle, as his personal emissary to survey the Santa Elena site with the CIA's Fernández. As soon as North was satisfied with Owen's photographs and maps, he, Fernández, and Tambs brought together the contractors, landowners, and security men to make the operation possible. Retired air force Maj. Gen. Richard Secord, a key founder of "the Enterprise" and controller of the covert network's Swiss bank accounts, paid out $190,000 in expenses. On North's instructions, Secord contacted Minister of Public Security Piza to guarantee Civil Guard cooperation with the airfield's operations.

Construction of the Santa Elena airstrip between September 1985 and February 1986 encouraged administration hard-liners to think that pressuring Costa Rica just might help invigorate the southern front. But as the airstrip was being built by American and Costa Rican personnel, a sea change in Costa Rican public opinion on Nicaragua occurred.

National Liberation party presidential candidate Oscar Arias and Social Christian Unity candidate Rafael Angel Calderón Guardia were running neck-and-neck until the last weeks of the campaign. Arias, a wealthy introverted intellectual, had little appeal on the stump, but he sensed a popular longing for peace. He began to suggest that the Contra presence in Costa Rica endangered the peace—and even joked that it was too bad Nicaragua didn't have a tenth comandante on the party directorate, since each comandante was worth $50 million in annual U.S. aid to Costa Rica. Ticos responded with laughter, and Arias's crowds began to grow. Calderón's tough anti-Sandinista rhetoric attracted sizable campaign contributions from the Cuban and Nicaraguan exile communities in Miami, but it frightened Costa Rican voters. Arias was elected by a surprise landslide on February 3.

During the race and after, Arias and his top aides were convinced that the CIA contributed money to the Calderón campaign as a way to promote the Contra cause. (A former top aide to Gen. Manuel Antonio Noriega testified to the Senate Foreign Relations subcommittee on terrorism that the dictator, then on the CIA payroll, donated $500,000 to the 1986 Calderón campaign.)

The incoming Arias doves understood that they would face a difficult time in their relations with the United States. In the days following the election, senior members of the transition team debated how to approach the Reagan administration. Incoming Foreign Minister Madrigal Nieto and other conservative party leaders argued against confronting the United States directly. They warned that an abrupt turn from the Monge tightrope walk would jeopardize millions of dollars in economic aid. Arias and the doves around him argued that a continuation of the Monge policies might lead to war with Nicaragua.

The issue came to a head as President-elect Arias prepared for a February 17 appearance on John McLaughlin's "One on One" nationally syndicated PBS television program (three months before inauguration day). Arias decided he would firmly state his position on American television and risk whatever cuts in economic aid that might come as a result. Arias jabbed back and forth with the conservative American journalist before McLaughlin asked him point-blank whether or not he supported President Reagan's $100 million Contra aid package then before Congress.

"If I were Mr. Reagan," advised the forty-five-year-old Costa Rican president-elect, "I would give that money to Guatemala, El Salvador, Honduras, and Costa Rica for economic aid, and not military aid to the Contras. I don't think that with that aid he is going to obtain what he wants. The result of the aid to the Contras has been a more dictatorial, more totalitarian government in the north." To Arias, U.S. Contra aid did little more than serve as "an excuse" for the Sandinistas to abolish personal liberties in their country.

Suggesting that his guest's argument was naive, McLaughlin probed to see if there was a leak in Arias's position. "What would the Sandinistas have to do" to justify Contra aid?

"Why don't you accept my answer?" Arias snapped. McLaughlin backed off and moved on to talk about Costa Rica's debt and efforts to control drug trafficking.

But the Reagan administration refused to accept Arias's answer. Immediately following the Costa Rican leader's provocative television appearance, Ambassador Tambs was called back to Washington for "consultations." When Tambs returned to San José, he appeared on a local radio program and suggested that with coffee prices going up and oil prices going down Costa Rica might not need as much U.S. aid as before. Tambs didn't have to mention Costa Rica's position on the Contras for people to read between the lines.

Such administration heavyweights as National Security Adviser John Poindexter, Assistant Secretary of State Elliott Abrams, Deputy Assistant Secretary of Defense Nestór Sánchez, Southern Command commander Gen. Paul Gorman, and special envoys Harry W. Shlaudeman and Philip Habib were sent to San José over the next few weeks to ask Arias to withhold his criticism of the Contras while the aid issue was before Congress.

Arias never shifted from his stance against military aid to the Contras as he went on to propose a peace plan that won him a Nobel Prize and, more importantly, would force political pluralism in Nicaragua and, to a lesser extent, El Salvador and Guatemala. It was his belief that Costa Rica could only exert moral influence over Central American affairs if it withdrew from its role as a passive participant in the Contra war. The Reagan administration, particularly the CIA and National Security Council (NSC), consistently interfered with Arias's efforts to reassert Costa Rican neutrality every step of the way.

At Arias's festive May 8, 1986, inauguration, which was attended by ten Latin heads of state and then–Vice President Bush, the new Costa Rican president called for the immediate signing of the Contadora regional peace treaty, which would remove foreign military advisers, reduce the size of armies, and end foreign support for guerrilla groups—a position that set him apart from not only the previous Costa Rican government but also from Managua.

Arias refrained from direct criticism of the Reagan administration or his predecessor, but he made it clear that the days of Monge's delicate balancing-act policy were over:

> We will never negotiate when it comes to our national dignity. We tolerate no threats, offense or any other act that would compromise that dignity. We are a nation of reasonable citizens and lovers of peace. But nobody should believe that these virtues . . . weaken our resolve to defend Costa Rica.

Arias's words were for Washington more than for Nicaragua, but the American delegation didn't take heed.

Following the ceremony, Arias invited the Americans to his home for what he knew would be a difficult summit. In the president's living room, Abrams and Gorman attempted to soften up Arias's top aides: the president's brother Rodrigo Arias, who would become Minister of the Presidency; John Biehl, an influential Chilean adviser to Arias; Guido Fernández, who would become ambassador to the United States; and Fernando Zumbado, the incoming Housing Minister. While General Gorman emphasized the military threat that Nicaragua posed to the region, Abrams promised that social democratic moderates in the Contras could take control of the movement with the support of Washington and San José. Zumbado later said that the Americans were talking "fantasy, not of the reality here in Central America."

Arias, meanwhile, met alone with Bush in the president's richly furnished library, appointed with historical treatises and busts of Abraham Lincoln and John F. Kennedy. Bush told his host, "You have to help. Nicaragua is a real danger to Costa Rica. There is no limit to the help we can give you if you help us." Bush, however, stopped short of threatening any cuts in U.S. aid if Costa Rica didn't contribute to the Contra cause.

"I've made my position clear," responded the new Costa Rican president, who was stronger than the American had expected. "Please, don't insist." A few days later, to back up his words, Arias dismissed the Civil Guard colonel who had worked on the Santa Elena project.

Despite his opposition to U.S. policy, Arias was respectful toward Washington. He never revealed publicly the existence of the Santa Elena airfield, despite his likely realization that the airfield operation violated the congressional Boland Amendment restricting Contra aid. Arias privately demanded that the United States close down the Santa Elena air strip. Ambassador Tambs pledged Washington would obey Arias's order, and he cabled North suggesting the air strip be closed. But the Reagan administration never intended to keep Tambs's promise to Arias. According to the Tower Commission report, Tambs repeatedly told Costa Rican officials the airfield was no longer in use when in reality it was.

Only three weeks after the Arias inauguration, the CIA's Fernández called North and insisted that the southern-front Contras needed immediate airdrops. North ordered the air strip put back into action— the wishes of the democratically elected government of Costa Rica be damned.

The first airdrop after the transport flights were resumed in early June almost ended in disaster. The CIA contract flyers were unable to find the supply-starved Contras. The airmen then landed their C-123 transport on the muddy Costa Rican air strip following the failed mission. Their plane got stuck in the mud. Afraid that Arias would find out about their mission, Tambs and Fernández scurried to obtain trucks to free the aircraft from the muck. The plane took off on its own power before the vehicles arrived, and the Americans were temporarily off the hook. But in the end, the Costa Rican government learned of the betrayal when a national park ranger reported that he spotted large unmarked planes taking off from the strip.

Having been lied to by Tambs, Arias decided to reveal the existence of the Santa Elena air strip at a press conference, which would have put the entire "Enterprise" in jeopardy of being exposed (weeks before the Hasenfus plane crash unleashed the Iran-Contra scandal). Through his sources in the Costa Rican government, the CIA's Fernández got wind of the press conference days before it was to occur and informed North and Poindexter of the coming disaster.

As noted in the Tower Commission report: "On September 9, LtCol North informed VADM Poindexter that he had completed a conference call with U.S. Ambassador to Costa Rica Tambs, Mr. Abrams and the Director of the CIA CATF [Central American Task

Force, Alan Fiers] who all agreed that LtCol North would call Costa Rican President Arias to insist the press conference be stopped. LtCol North said that they agreed he would take a tough line with President Arias, threatening to withhold U.S. assistance." North finally left it up to Tambs to call the Costa Rican leader, although he later told Poindexter that he had called Arias himself.

Arias and his closest advisers were in a relaxed mood on the night of September 13; it was the president's birthday and they gathered in John Biehl's house for a party. The president and his aides drank heavily, and Housing Minister Zumbado got so giddy he stripped off his clothes and danced naked on a living room table. At 10:00 P.M., the phone rang. It was Ambassador Tambs. Tambs, who said he was speaking for Abrams, appealed to the president to call off the press conference in exchange for guarantees that the airfield operation would be closed down. He also suggested that a scheduled Arias visit to the White House was in jeopardy if the press conference took place. Arias agreed to delay any announcement of the strip—but only for a week or two.

On September 25, Costa Rican Public Security Minister Hernán Garrón announced that his Civil Guard had closed the air strip, which he said had probably been used by both the Contras and drug traffickers. Garrón said the air strip property belonged to a Panama-based dummy company called Udall Research Corp., but he was vague about what his government knew about the Santa Elena operation. He denied any Costa Rican government involvement in the project, even though the local Civil Guard colonel who had provided twenty-four-hour security for the field and built a locked gate on a road to the strip was fired when Arias took office.

North was incensed by the Garrón announcement, and on September 30 he fired off a memo to Poindexter urging that Costa Rica be punished. Arguing that those in the administration who wanted to keep aid levels to San José high should be blocked, North wrote that "those who counsel such a course of action are unaware of the strategic importance of the air facility at Santa Elena and the damage caused by the Arias government revelations."

But on October 5, 1986, before North could strike back at Arias, Eugene Hasenfus and his C-123 cargo plane flying from a base in El Salvador were shot out of the Nicaraguan skies. The Costa Rican connection to the scandal was in the open once Hasenfus identified the Santa Elena strip as part of the illegal resupply network. Records

captured from the plane wreckage identified Cuban exile Rafael Quin-
tero, a colleague of imprisoned former CIA renegade Edwin P. Wilson, as the man who coordinated the Contra resupply flights from his
headquarters in Costa Rica. Telephone records pertaining to the airmen's San Salvador safe house included calls to the U.S. embassy in
Costa Rica and to Fernández's home.

The covert resupply operation was finished, and Costa Rican authorities wondered what aftershocks might follow the Iran-Contra revelations. Fernando Zumbado, the Housing Minister and a close adviser
to the president, recalls that paranoia ran high in San José that November, particularly after CIA chief William Casey flew down to San José
and Arias refused to see him in private. (Casey did not want his
presence in Costa Rica disclosed, so he flew back home in a huff.)

"British intelligence told us to be careful," Zumbado said in an
August 1988 interview. "The CIA was going wild and talking crazy.
The insinuation was that the CIA in Costa Rica might provoke a coup
or kill somebody—maybe the president."

Arias believed the Reagan administration had broken Costa Rican
law as well as the Boland Amendment. Had the Hasenfus plane not
gone down in Nicaragua, it is probable that Arias would have eventually blown the whistle on the illegal operation. But the unfolding
scandal gave him cover to openly and aggressively oppose Reagan
administration policy.

Only hours before Attorney General Edwin Meese's dramatic November 1986 disclosure in Washington that Iranian funds had been
transferred to the Contras, I met President Arias at his home in the
San José suburb of Sabanas. His house was modest, without even a
wooden fence separating the small front lawn from the busy street. In
his study, I asked why he opposed the Nicaraguan Contras when the
Reagan administration saw the "freedom fighters" as essential to Costa
Rica's security.

He responded with a question. "Why fight the Sandinistas where
they are strongest, in the military field, when they are weakest on the
political and diplomatic front?

"What has the Reagan administration achieved?" he asked rhetori-
cally. "The Sandinistas are using the Contras as an excuse to become
more totalitarian every day." Furthermore, he argued, "[The Contras]
don't have a chance militarily" because the Nicaraguan people
couldn't be expected to support a military force led by Enrique Ber-
mudez, the former Somoza National Guard colonel. Arias further
complained that the U.S.-backed war on Managua was hurting invest-

ment and tourism in his country, causing capital flight and filling Costa Rica with Nicaraguan refugees who taxed the government's social services.

A political scientist who graduated from the University of Essex in Great Britain, Arias was one of the most engaging and intelligent political figures I had ever met. What I liked most about him was his confidence in Costa Rica's democratic way of life, and his belief in the morality and strength of democratic law and institutions that appeared lacking in the Reagan White House. Arias spoke to me slowly, deliberately, like a teacher:

"Why don't you quote me on this: the Communist party in Costa Rica is smaller today than four years ago. Why is that? Because the people in Costa Rica have seen what has happened in Nicaragua. The best propaganda against communism in Costa Rica is to put [Costa Ricans] on a bus and send them to Managua."

Summing up his message, he said, "To keep Costa Rica at peace, we need good schools for all our children and good housing for all our families, not the military overthrow of the Sandinistas."

Before, Arias had been careful not to be caustic in his public criticism of the Reagan administration. But during a December 1986 visit to Washington, he dared to stoke the Iran-Contra fires at a "deep background" briefing with reporters and editors at the *Washington Post* in which he was not to be identified. A December 6 banner headline story in the *Post* based on the session with Arias stated: "Ambassador Lewis Tambs's efforts on behalf of the rebel resupply missions, the source [Arias] said, came while the administration was barred by Congress from assisting rebel military actions. Coupled with the disclosure that the senior U.S. military adviser in El Salvador closely monitored the air resupply network, Tambs's involvement indicates a significantly greater role by U.S. officials than has been acknowledged."

Tambs denied any knowledge of the resupply effort, but then resigned his post and returned to teaching at Arizona State University. Fernández was also asked to leave San José and forced to retire from the CIA. He was the only CIA employee to be indicted (in July 1988) on allegations relating to the scandal, for defying the Boland ban on arming the rebels, and lying to investigators in the cover-up.*

*Independent Iran-Contra Special Prosecutor Lawrence Walsh ended his attempt to prosecute Fernández in October 1990 when Attorney General Dick Thornburgh reaffirmed his refusal to release classified CIA documents for the case.

Fernández was accused of breaking U.S. and Costa Rican law, but he is still described by Contra leaders and active CIA personnel as having been a highly intelligent, effective agent and a committed family man. There are others more deserving of pity, but it should be noted that Fernández became the CIA's scapegoat as the agency squirmed out of trouble. From testimony before the Iran-Contra congressional committees, it became clear that Fernández was obeying the general instructions of CIA director William Casey, who died before facing what would have been major political and probable legal problems. A congressional investigation uncovered evidence that Clair George, the agency's deputy director for operations, and Alan Fiers, the chief of the CIA's Central American Task Force, were also well aware of Fernández's work in Costa Rica. George retired without disciplinary action. Fiers received a reprimand from CIA director William Webster but continued at his post.

Rid of Tambs and Fernández, and with the much-weakened Reagan administration now off his back, Arias cracked down on the Contra presence in Costa Rica throughout 1987 and 1988. The government closed Contra medical clinics, prohibited military leaders from living in the country, and beefed up Civil Guard patrols along the border.

At a regional summit of the five Central American presidents in February 1987, Arias unveiled his famed peace plan, which called for regional cease-fires, an end to outside aid for guerrilla forces, dialogues between governments and rebel groups, and democratization of all countries. The White House was outraged by the Arias plan because it had "no teeth" and would prohibit aid to the Contras by the United States, Honduras, and El Salvador. Worse still, his peace plan attracted the support of congressional Democrats who wished for an alternative Central America policy.

That June, while on the lecture circuit in Indiana, Arias was summoned to the White House. Believing he was going into a fifteen-minute photo opportunity with the president, Arias was surprised to find himself surrounded by Reagan, chief of staff Howard Baker, National Security Adviser Frank Carlucci, NSC aide José Solorzano, Abrams, Habib, and John Whitehead of the State Department. Reagan lectured Arias intensely for fifteen minutes. Arias listened and then went into his own half-hour lecture critiquing American policy in Central America. "You are alone on this policy," Arias told the American entourage. "Not even Margaret Thatcher supports the Contras."

Two months later, on August 7, 1987, Arias convinced his fellow

Central American presidents to sign his peace plan. It was a devastating defeat for the Reagan Contra policy. The Arias plan brought an uneasy cease-fire to Nicaragua and helped open political space in El Salvador and Guatemala.

Arias won the Nobel Peace Prize that fall, an award that gave the plan momentum and the kind of international support necessary to counteract Washington's opposition. To Reagan administration hardliners, what the Arias plan meant more than anything else was ammunition for congressional critics to cut off the Contras in February 1988 by a mere seven votes. Indeed, the Costa Rican's public call on Congress to stop military aid swayed several fence sitters on Capitol Hill and was the deciding factor in the cutoff.

Arias, more than any other leader, was responsible for ending the Contra war and bringing about the 1990 election that elected Violeta Chamorro president of Nicaragua.

The 1987 Tower Commission report and the Iran-Contra congressional hearings publicly revealed that the Reagan administration had operated a covert air strip for Contra resupply inside Costa Rica against the expressed will of that nation's president. Costa Ricans learned that not only had a CIA man and a U.S. ambassador tried to undercut Arias's regional peace efforts and violate the nation's sovereignty, but they also exposed their supposed ally to the wrath of the militarily stronger Sandinista government.

Costa Ricans took it all in stride. There were no mass demonstrations against Yankee imperialism, no general strikes, no terrorism. Costa Rican democracy is not a fragile flower, the Reagan administration could pull at its petals, but the flower would not wilt.

There have been a few domestic upheavals since the hard times of 1980–82, but none as potentially destabilizing as the U.S. policy had been. In June 1983, thousands of poor people in more than forty San José barrios set up barricades in what looked like an incipient insurrection against skyrocketing electricity rates mandated by an IMF-inspired austerity program. Consumers refused to pay their electricity bills, and the public utility began cutting off service in one block after another. But before the situation could get out of control, twenty-nine members of the Legislative Assembly took up the cause of the aggrieved consumers. Within weeks, the Monge government agreed to negotiate and reversed much of the rate hike.

In the mid-1980s, the Popular Vanguard party led a series of disastrous banana strikes on the Caribbean and Pacific coasts. Work stoppages and expensive contracts pushed Standard Fruit, United Fruit, and Del Monte to gradually move out of the banana industry, which represented 25 percent of the country's export earnings, in favor of producing the far less labor-intensive palm oil. United Fruit had moved out of Golfito, its company port, entirely by 1985, leaving more than 5,000 workers unemployed.

Such an economic dislocation in El Salvador or Guatemala might have produced a riot. But not in Costa Rica, where the workers blamed the radicals for their troubles. The Communist union in Golfito, for instance, went out of operation with United Fruit, because the members bitterly complained that the union had destroyed their jobs. Today, the government is attempting to rebuild Golfito by constructing a duty-free zone for shoppers from all over the region.

"We cooked in our own sauce and lost perspective," Jorge Conejo, a Communist labor organizer in Golfito, told me. He admitted that the disastrous strikes had moderated his views. "This is a very advanced democracy," he said. "We have important programs—the nationalized banking system, the nationalized electrical system, sweeping public education. We don't need to pick up arms and kill ourselves when we have programs like that."

Simply put, the radical left doesn't have to fight to make its presence felt. In late 1986, a development company went broke trying to build an industrial park outside the city of Cartago. Local activists of a splinter Communist group, Pueblo Unido (United People), convinced 15,000 landless and homeless people to invade the vacant property and create a rebel community named Santa Lucía. The government rejected the option of forcing the squatters off the lot to quash the radical challenge. Instead, the government negotiated with the squatters, allowed them to remain in their new community, and within months provided them with schools, water, and electricity.

When I walked through Santa Lucía's neat rows of freshly painted wooden houses in 1988, there was no sense of the conflict that founded the community. Children wearing sharp purple soccer uniforms rode bicycles on the paved streets. Women carrying parasols to protect themselves from the sun walked to and from the market in good spirits. I saw a government health worker visiting families, to examine children and pregnant women, as well as offer free medical advice and birth control.

One Pueblo Unido activist remained a member of the local community board, but most people I spoke to were warmly appreciative of what the government had done for them. Antonio Alvarez, a thirty-six-year-old bricklayer, for instance, complimented Pueblo Unido for its leadership during the land invasion, but he was quick to add that he was no Communist. "Oscar Arias and our deputies are giving us what we need," he told me while taking a break from laying a water pipe for a neighbor. "Our government helps us, it doesn't repress us."

Costa Ricans are passionate about politics, but they almost never let their differences get out of hand. In the heat of the 1989–90 presidential campaign, Jorge Luis Araya, a twenty-nine-year-old peasant horseman, bought a pack of cigarettes at a small general store owned by Bernardo Vueques, age fifty, on the outskirts of the Pacific port of Quepos. The two began talking about the campaign. Araya insisted that if Costa Ricans didn't kick President Arias's party out of power, a Communist takeover was only a matter of time. "Don't be ridiculous!" Vueques responded, raising his voice. "Your candidate can only mean trouble. He's as corrupt as a Nicaraguan!" Vueques walked away, but in the end, the two shook hands with grudging smiles. "After all, we are Ticos," Araya said, "we both want the same thing: democracy." Vueques agreed with a jolly laugh. "We like a good fight, but it ends at the ballot box." To make sure there were no hard feelings, Vueques offered his customer a free frosty beer.

6
Panama:
A Nation Without Heroes

Just before 1:00 A.M. on December 20, 1989, Gen. Manuel Antonio Noriega was carousing with a prostitute at La Siesta, a recreation club for top officers of the Panamanian Defense Forces (PDF). Cuban intelligence had informed Noriega that U.S. troops were on their way to overthrow him, but the dictator intended to enjoy the perquisites of his job even during his final hours in power. He waited until he heard the crackle of gunfire and the bursts of rockets, as U.S. Army Rangers overran the nearby Omar Torrijos International Airport, before he hiked up his pants and bid his companion a curt adiós.

Cut off from his men and command post, Noriega escaped in a Hyundai sedan. For the next four days, as his army collapsed and more than five hundred Panamanians were killed, Noriega acted like a convict on the run. Deciding that it would be hopeless to resist the invasion as a guerrilla in the jungles, he hid for a time at the house of a local arms dealer while he desperately sought asylum in the Nicaraguan and Cuban embassies. When Noriega realized he could not break through the cordon of American forces surrounding either, he gave himself up to the Catholic church.

It was a humbling end for a dictator who fancied himself Panama's modern-day Simón Bolívar, the nation-builder willing to confront the United States and dispose of American hegemony over the Panama Canal. But as it turned out, the vast majority of Panamanians jeered Noriega as soon as he was captured. Panamanians had become accustomed to Americans playing a leading role in their society and humiliating their leaders ever since President Theodore Roosevelt stole the province of Panama away from Colombia in 1903.

Panamanians celebrated President George Bush's invasion of their country as a "liberation," but their cheer betrayed an uncomfortable question: who will be the modern Panamanian heroes in their future history books? Not Noriega, of course. Not Gen. Omar Torrijos, founder of the corrupt military government that Noriega inherited and Panamanians would grow to despise.

Not even Guillermo Endara, the double-chinned lawyer who would never have become president had the United States not invaded his country. Proclaiming his government to the world from a fax machine on an American military base, Endara authorized a curfew that only an invading foreign army could enforce. No sooner did he demonstrate a modicum of independence by announcing he would deny extradition and force Noriega to stand trial for murder in Panama, than he thought better of it. He finally decided the U.S. judicial system could handle the legal tangles better than his own—a move that denied his country the purging it might have experienced by holding its own trial. Then, after scores of U.S. troops sacrificed life and limb to free his country, Endara made a spectacle of himself by going on a hunger strike as an appeal to the U.S. Congress to quickly send him economic aid.

The dilemma of Panama's chronic reliance on American leaders is more than an arcane academic question. As a symptom of Panama's long-standing identity crisis, it goes to the heart of why the United States had to invade Panama in the first place. It also explains why the United States will find that overthrowing Noriega was the easy part of its invasion. If a century of U.S. interventions in Panama is any guide, the one in December 1989 cannot guarantee the development of a reliable and democratic ally in the future. Bush's Panama action, no less than that of Teddy Roosevelt four generations earlier, will reinforce the dependency that keeps Panamanians from resolving their own problems.

"We don't have a history we can have a lot of pride in," conceded Arnulfo Escalona, a prominent politician. "We lived under Spanish domination until 1823. We were annexed by Colombia until 1903. And then we were made into a canal by the United States. We never had a chance to fight for a nation and create our own institutions and culture."

Such historical musings were not on the lips of the cheering Panamanians dancing with U.S. troops after they learned their hated dictator had finally departed the Vatican's nunciature for a comfortably distant courtroom in the United States. But all the goodwill could not conceal the fact that while it was the United States that overthrew Panama's dictatorship, it was also the United States that was instrumental in creating and perpetuating it.

Comparisons to Honduras's dependency are inviting. But because of its canal and strategic significance, Panama is even closer to being a colony of the United States. While Panamanians hate to admit it, Panama would probably not exist today if it hadn't been for the United States. Its independence was negotiated in New York and Washington. Its first flag—whose colors are red, white, and blue—was sewn by a Frenchwoman from silk bought at Macy's on Herald Square. Its currency is called the "balboa," but it is the same green dollar with George Washington's face on it.

More than any of its Central American neighbors, Panamanians have embraced American cultural and consumer values. Panama is the only country in the region where you can commonly find coffee to go (appropriately, in Styrofoam cups) and a wide assortment of American canned goods on the shelves of even the most modest supermarkets. Fords and Chevrolets still compete with Toyotas and Nissans, while in the rest of Latin America Japanese cars dominate. The degree to which Panamanians adapt to American customs can be seen as far as fifty miles from the Panama Canal, in the western provincial city of Chitre, where the local Dairy Queen has an intercom on its driveway for motorists to place orders.

There are rancid slums, but Panama City is also a city of shiny glass banks, shopping centers, and condominiums; its downtown looks like Miami without the beach. In 1988, the New York financial publication *Banker's Monthly* accurately commented that "the country more closely resembles California than it does Honduras."

In part, that is because more than 50,000 Americans live in and around Panama City (out of a total population of about 750,000), most of whom have some connection with either the American military or U.S. corporations that have $5 billion invested in the country. The old Canal Zone still feels American, with its manicured gardens and lawns, its Veterans of Foreign Wars and American Legion chapters, its bowling alleys and golf courses, and seven major U.S. military bases. More than 12,000 American servicemen are permanently based in the old zone, of whom about thirty marry Panamanians every month. Over the years, thousands of such American-Panamanian couples have remained on the isthmus and bred bicultural families.

An extraordinary number of Panamanians speak excellent English because of their constant contact with Americans and because thousands have attended American high schools and colleges in the old Canal Zone and in the United States. Noriega's last Finance Minister, Orville Goodin, for example, was educated at the City University of New York and speaks English better than Spanish. George Priestley, a prominent historian, was trained at Columbia University and is a professor at Queens College in New York. The noted Panamanian economist Nicolás Ardito Barletta received his Ph.D. at the University of Chicago, where he befriended George Shultz, who was teaching at the business school—a connection that would help him become president of Panama years later.

But intimacy does not always produce love. Noriega's anti-American rhetoric was fueled by the humiliation many Panamanians feel under their skins, a feeling that they share a mediocre history of subservience to Americans. "There is a love-hate relationship between Panamanians and North Americans that arose from the very outset of our independence," according to Panamanian newspaper publisher Roberto Eisenmann, Jr. "The only way to describe it is as a relationship similar to the love-hate relationship that develops between a teenage son and his overbearing father, where there is a rebellious attitude to make your own way. You know your father has been good to you, but you just want to get [out] from under that heavy wing." Unable to develop their own wings, Panamanians have developed little national identity, cultural cohesion, or shared history—a far cry from its western neighbor, Costa Rica. British travel writer Jan Morris described Panama nearly a decade before Noriega came to power as "a community of gamblers, jockeys, boxers and cockfighters, a place where characters habitually disappear to, or reemerge from, in old-fashioned thrillers."

. . .

Panama is less a country than the world's go-between, fixer, and transit route. It has been that way since Vasco Núñez de Balboa discovered the Pacific Ocean from Panamanian soil. The early Spanish colonists constructed the Camino Real, a stone path across Panama designed for mule trains to transport Incan golden treasures, Bolivian silver, and pearls across the isthmus. Thus the riches of the New World were loaded on galleons anchored at the Panamanian ports of Portobelo and Nombre de Dios, where they were shipped to mother Spain. Panama City became the third-richest city in Spanish America, while Portobelo's great seventeenth-century trade fairs attracted merchants from all over Latin America.

Panama is neither part of Central America nor part of South America.* Though once a province of Colombia, it is cut off from South America by the vast uncharted jungles and swampy rivers of the Darién Gap** and populated by a few thousand Chocó Indians. Divided from Costa Rica by the tough granite Talamanca mountains, it was never politically part of Central America. Such isolation from its immediate neighbors reinforced Panama's ties to the world at large.

Panamanians often refer to their recumbent S-shaped country of 2.4 million people as the Crossroads of the World and the Bridge Between the Seas, and to themselves as "Phoenicians." Also hemmed in by mountains, water, and warlike neighbors, the original Phoenicia, Panamanians note, likewise based its civilization on international maritime trade, not politics or ideology. For several centuries, the Phoenicians were pushed around by the stronger Assyrians and Greeks, but they were survivors who assimilated easily and never ceased doing business with their conquerors or the enemies of their conquerors.

Mutual dependency with foreigners is what makes Panama different from its Central American neighbors. Nicaragua, El Salvador, Honduras, and Costa Rica all look abroad for financial, political, and military assistance, but none of them is looked upon as vital by the world at large. Panama is, because of the Panama Canal—a fact that recent dictators have sought to exploit.

*Panama is the only country covered in this book that was not a member of the United Provinces of Central America, the nation that broke up soon after independence from Spain.
**Named after the Darien Company, a seventeenth-century Scottish company that attempted to seize territory from the Spanish crown.

. . .

"The canal will be strategically important," Theodore Roosevelt proclaimed. "We will use it against our enemies. Why else would we build it?" And true to his word, the United States used the canal as a vital asset in World Wars I and II, as well as in the Korean and Vietnam wars, for the shipment of troops and arms.

In war or peace, more than 12,000 ships from around the world sail through the fifty-one-mile-long Panama Canal every year, carrying 160 million tons of cargo, representing about 5 percent of the world's total seaborne trade. The canal is particularly vital to the economies of South America, connecting the Atlantic coast with the Orient, and the Pacific coast with Europe. Fifteen percent of all U.S. trade goes through the Panama Canal, and the oil pipeline that runs alongside it carries 600,000 barrels of Alaska crude every day to the U.S. eastern seaboard and beyond.

The canal is the foundation of many service industries that arise from world trade. More than 125 international banks have offices in Panama City, accounting for over $30 billion in assets and more than 10,000 jobs. There are probably more Xerox copiers and fax machines per block in Panama City than anywhere else in the Western Hemisphere. The hundred-acre duty-free zone in the port of Colón is the second-largest duty-free zone in the world (after Hong Kong's), bringing in wholesale automobiles from as far away as the Soviet Union as well as textiles and electronics goods from Japan, Taiwan, and South Korea and pharmaceuticals and fertilizers from the United States. Panamanian merchants import such goods in bulk, then assemble, process, repackage, and reship them to all major points of Latin America.

Panama's special geography and history make its people the most cosmopolitan in the region. Nearly 40 percent of all Panamanians have ancestors who were neither Spanish nor Indian, but who had come to the isthmus over the last 110 years to build or traverse the canal. (Most of the workers employed by the French and then the Americans came from Jamaica, Barbados, Saint Lucia, Guadeloupe, or China.) In Panama City, an Islamic mosque stands near a Bahai temple. Food stands sell tacos and barbecue ribs. Noriega practiced voodoo and Buddhism while one of the presidents who governed under him, Eric Delvalle, was a practicing Jew.

"Each ethnic group attempts to preserve its own culture," noted

Fernando Manfredo, then deputy administrator of the Panama Canal. "Along with the overwhelming presence of the United States in Panama over the years, that is the reason why our sense of nationhood is weak. I come to this conclusion from personal experience: my father is Italian, my mother is of Spanish descent, my sister-in-law of French descent, my wife was born in China, one of my daughters married a German, and another daughter just married a Cuban-American. Mine is a typical Panamanian family. That's what makes us different."

Panama's motley cultural heritage, commercialism, and undefined nationalism explains a lot about General Noriega. He worked simultaneously for the CIA, Cuban intelligence, and the Medellín Cartel. While Nicaraguan leaders compensated for their nation's history by siding with one foreign power or another, and while Honduran leaders always followed the lead of their American counterparts, Noriega sided with several foreign powers at once. In the words of one U.S. diplomat stationed in Panama City, Noriega was "a free-trade zone all by himself."

PANAMA'S AMBIVALENT NATIONALISM

Latin America's great liberator Simón Bolívar had big plans for Panama. He predicted the isthmus would someday become "the center of the universe, and chose Panama City to be the site of a grand hemispheric meeting to unite Latin America after independence from Spain was won. The summit, like Bolívar's dream, fell apart.

In less euphoric moments, Bolívar hoped that Panama's transit potential would motor the economy of the new nation of Gran Colombia, a federation that also included modern-day Colombia, Venezuela, and Ecuador. Bolívar's desire for a united Gran Colombia was also shortlived, as Ecuadorans and Venezuelans rose up in arms and easily won their own independence in the 1830s and 1840s. But Panama's merchant elite decided to hold fast to Colombia after Bolívar, from his deathbed, wrote a letter to the province's governor begging Panama not to secede. It was the beginning of a historical pattern: Panama felt it was more a part of something than something of its own.

Panama's ties with Colombia gradually loosened as its ties with the United States grew stronger. With Washington's acquisition of California in the Mexican-American War and the Gold Rush of the 1840s, a group of New York financiers built the Panama Railroad. Some 600,000 Americans crossed the isthmus between 1849 and 1870, bringing with them the greatest economic boom since the colonial Portobelo fair days.

The Americans established an overwhelming presence in the backwater Colombian province. The "Forty-niners" turned Panama City upside down, breathing energy into the sleepy port's commerce and nightlife. A couple of Americans founded Panama's first newspaper, the *Panama Star & Herald*—which exists to this day as *La Estrella de Panamá*—while waiting for a steamship to take them to California. Americans built an entire city, Aspinwall (now Colón), at the Caribbean terminus of the railroad, and populated the port with Jamaican rail-splitters.

Washington, which simultaneously took an interest in Nicaraguan affairs, also saw Panama's longterm canal potential. Under the 1846 Mallarino-Bidlack Treaty, Washington and Bogotá agreed to guarantee Colombian ownership of Panama in return for Colombia's reduction of tariffs on American transit and pledge to uphold free international passage on the isthmus. In alleged defense of the treaty, the United States Navy helped Colombian forces put down six relatively minor revolts between 1856 and 1902. Panama would become independent when Washington wanted it to be.

The last challenge to the United States on the isthmus came from France's Ferdinand de Lesseps, the renowned builder of the Suez Canal. De Lesseps established an engineering company in 1879 to construct a sea-level canal at an estimated cost of $214 million. De Lesseps's Compagnie Universelle du Canal Interocéanique de Panama paid the Colombian government $10 million for the canal concession, and in doing so infuriated Washington. President Rutherford B. Hayes claimed that De Lesseps's venture violated the intent of Mallarino-Bidlack, and dispatched the navy to cruise Panamanian waters as a sign of his displeasure. Hayes declared that the "policy of this country is a canal under American control. . . . An interoceanic canal [will be] virtually a part of the coastline of the United States."

Colombia disagreed with Hayes's interpretation of the treaty, called

Washington's bluff, and encouraged De Lesseps to dig. Hoping to allay Washington's fears, De Lesseps made a well-publicized effort to proclaim the neutrality of his future canal and find American investors for La Grande Tranchée.

The Hayes administration was the least of De Lesseps's problems. Disease, hard rains, solid rock mountains, mud, and the mighty Chagres River crossing the canal site strangled the French effort. The eighty-seven-year-old builder refused to accept the advice of many engineers that a sea-level canal, like the one built in the dry, flat Suez, was impractical in wet, mountainous Panama. De Lesseps's aides paid off French newspaper publishers to back his project in their editorials and news columns and otherwise spread false information to sell stock and bonds to an unsuspecting French public. Eventually, the truth overwhelmed De Lesseps's Panglossian confidence that somehow French know-how could conquer all obstacles. Within six years, De Lesseps's company was bankrupt, with barely half its task done. More tragic was the loss of human lives. Between 16,000 and 22,000 Caribbean blacks died from snakebite, sunstroke, beriberi, typhoid fever, and smallpox by the time De Lesseps gave up his project in 1889.

The canal failure humbled France, forcing the French to question basic values of their society. The virulent scandal unleashed intense popular skepticism and suspicion of the government and business community, as thousands of French families lost their life savings. The once-revered De Lesseps retired a broken, disgraced man—known to some as "the pallbearer of Panama."

For all the tragedy, France etched a permanent imprint on Panama. They brought sidewalk cafés and roulette to Panama, and some of their words crept into Panamanian Spanish. Their failure left the challenge of building an interoceanic canal to the Americans. After it took sixty-nine days for the battleship U.S.S. *Oregon* to sail from the Philippines around Cape Horn to Cuba during the Spanish-American War (a canal would have reduced the trip by 8,000 miles and forty days), Congress and the public pressed President William McKinley to move with speed to construct a canal.

All that was left was one important decision: was the canal site to be Panama or Nicaragua? Most of Congress supported the idea of building a canal across Lake Nicaragua and the San Juan River, a territory that was both flatter and less full of disease than Panama.

The fact that Panama is an independent country and has a canal today is due primarily to two men: President Theodore Roosevelt and

Philippe Bunau-Varilla, a French mining engineer and Washington lobbyist. A stern man with the appearance and demeanor of Napoleon Bonaparte, Bunau-Varilla was a former director of De Lesseps's canal company and diehard defender of the French canal dream. He carefully planned a strategy for convincing Washington to build the canal through Panama in the hope of selling the French Panama canal concession to the United States to recoup stockholder investments.

Bunau-Varilla's first challenge was to persuade Congress that Panama was a more practical option than Nicaragua. He was helped along by Nicaraguan dictator José Santos Zelaya, who proved to be a more demanding negotiator than his Colombian counterparts. Bunau-Varilla ultimately succeeded by distributing to every congressman a recent Nicaraguan one-peso postage stamp highlighting an erupting Momotombo volcano. Even though Momotombo was far from the proposed canal route, Congress came to fear the kind of volcano eruption that had devastated Martinique (and killed 40,000 people) only months before. The House followed the Senate's lead in June 1902 by a margin of only eight votes to favor the Panama option, a decision that, eventually, was worth $40 million for French investors— the most expensive real estate deal ever negotiated to that time.

Having pledged to abide by Capitol Hill's choice, Roosevelt pressed Bogotá. He agreed to pay Colombia $10 million in gold and annual rent of $250,000 for a canal grant on the isthmus. Crucial to the proposed treaty was an article that stipulated the United States would be granted sweeping administrative power over a three-mile zone on either side of the canal. The U.S. Senate overwhelmingly approved the Hay-Herrán Treaty, but the Colombian congress balked, rejecting it in August 1903.

Roosevelt expressed his outrage in a letter to Secretary of State John Hay: "I do not think that the Bogotá lot of jack rabbits should be allowed permanently to bar one of the future highways of civilization."

Bunau-Varilla realized that his only hope now was to help ignite a revolt in Panama. That September, the Frenchman offered to Dr. Manuel Amador Guerrero, the physician of the Panama Railroad and a Conservative party politician, that he would speak with President Roosevelt about enlisting military support for the independence movement. In return for his services, Bunau-Varilla requested that he be appointed Panama's official representative in Washington to draft the future canal treaty. Amador Guerrero agreed.

Bunau-Varilla fulfilled his part of the bargain by convincing President Roosevelt to join the conspiracy. The Panamanian revolt was timed to begin just as the U.S. warship *Nashville* set sail for Colón. Amador and his co-conspirators bribed Gen. Esteban Huertas, the commander of the hundred-man Colombian guard force in Panama, with $100,000 (the cash was provided by Bunau-Varilla) to win his loyalty, and the U.S. Navy blocked the approach of Colombian army reinforcements sent to quell the revolt.

Following their virtually bloodless victory (one old man died when hit by a stray cannon shot), Amador and his fellow liberationists sailed to the United States to enter negotiations with the Americans. But Bunau-Varilla had already gotten negotiations under way with Secretary of State Hay. In order to assure that the Senate would go along with the canal before the Panamanians made too many demands, Bunau-Varilla rewrote sections of the old Hay-Herrán Treaty to widen the Canal Zone from six to ten miles and to grant the United States "all the rights, power and authority" of a sovereign over the zone. Hay requested that the lease for the Canal Zone, representing about 5 percent of Panama's territory, be renewable once a century. Bunau-Varilla went a step further and penciled in the words "in perpetuity" instead. As far as the Frenchman was concerned, the Panama Canal Zone could be an American colony forever.

The 1903 treaty, which was negotiated without a word of Spanish spoken, was never signed by a Panamanian. Article II of the document gave the United States the right to intervene and occupy any lands *outside* the zone when it considered such property vital to the maintenance and defense of the waterway. Article VII granted the United States eminent domain in Panama City and Colón. Roosevelt would later remark, "I took Panama because Bunau-Varilla brought it to me on a silver platter."

Amador and fellow liberationist Federico Boyd were shocked when they met their freebooting agent at the Washington railroad station and were shown the document. Amador literally fainted when he read the document. Boyd slapped the Frenchman in the face. Bunau-Varilla responded with a threat: if the Panamanians didn't accept the treaty, the Americans would withdraw their protection of the new government from the angry Colombians, and then build the canal in Nicaragua. Panama's submissive founding fathers reluctantly went along with their French agent, who a week after he signed the canal treaty resigned his position.

Such a humbling birth would not serve Panama well, spiritually or politically. For generations, Panamanians would brand their founding fathers as agents of foreign powers, and believe the well-being and future of the nation was decided by events out of their control. "The way we were formed as a nation is a wound for us that bleeds to this day," commented Panamanian journalist Guillermo Sánchez Bourbón. "This humiliation is part of the Panamanian consciousness and soul." The motto of the Panama Canal Company only rubbed in the hurt: "The Land Divided—The World United."

Panama's humiliation opened the way for the United States to build its canal and become a world sea power. Learning from De Lesseps's mistakes, the Americans dammed the Chagres River to create the thirty-one-mile-long Lake Gatún, which became the heart of the canal, and built six giant locks on either side to rise and fall from the central upland down to either coast. In all, between 1904 and 1914, the United States spent more than $350 million and excavated 232 million cubic yards of dirt to build a project that in its day was as miraculous as the moon landing six decades later. Modern medical advances over malaria and yellow fever also helped the cause. (Still, 5,000 workers lost their lives.)

The engineering feat boosted the American national ego, reinforced Washington's commitment to police the Caribbean basin, and remade Panama. By importing 50,000 workers from around the Caribbean to build the canal, the United States overwhelmed Panama's turn-of-the-century population of 350,000. Suddenly, more than 10 percent of the isthmian population spoke foreign languages, and Panama City and Colón doubled in size. Americans took charge of the isthmus's security, health care, communications, sanitation, private banking, government finances, and even foreign policy.

William Howard Taft, Roosevelt's Secretary of War who supervised the building of the canal, called Panama an "opéra-bouffe republic." His comment reflected Washington's imperialistic glibness, though he wasn't far from wrong. Over Panama's first sixty-five years, thirty-eight presidents and dictators took and lost power, and much of the nation's turmoil centered on the inordinate role the United States played.

A crisis brewed within a year of the treaty-signing when Panamanians complained that Americans were collecting unfair tariffs on goods entering the Canal Zone. Many believed President Amador was too close to the Americans. The opposition Liberal party approached independence hero Gen. Esteban Huertas to over-throw Amador. Amador was no George Washington. When he heard he was about to be the victim of a coup, he locked himself in his house and called on the United States to save him. U.S. forces imprisoned General Huertas and disbanded the Panamanian army, replacing it with a new constabulary, the National Police,* which would be led for two decades by Americans. From 1904 until the canal treaties were renegotiated in the late 1970s, the U.S. armed forces took charge of Panama's defense, leaving police functions to the Panamanians. This heritage molded the National Guard in sev-eral negative ways. Guardsmen were paid less than professional sol-diers would have been, and they occupied a less prestigious place in Panamanian society. Consequently, social resentment within the mostly black force festered. At the same time, constant exposure to crime opened the door to institutionalized corruption.

Most stressful for the U.S.-Panamanian relationship was the Canal Zone itself. Many Panamanians resented the American "Zonians," who rarely hid their feelings of superiority over the natives while they thought it unnecessary to learn Spanish. Zonians had their own clubs, churches, schools, fire and police departments, and beautifully groomed tropical gardens. A dual wage classification system—Ameri-cans were paid in gold, Panamanians in silver—was a constant point of irritation and humiliation. As in the American South, there were "Whites Only" and "Blacks Only" bathrooms and water fountains in the zone until the 1950s.

At the same time, the Americans unintentionally taught the Panamanians to live by the sword. Inhabited by thousands of service-men, the zone was administered by a military governor, who was frequently more influential in Panamanian affairs than the U.S. ambas-sador. The zone also became the home of the Southern Command, headquarters of all U.S. military activities in Latin America. Panamani-ans were constantly exposed to U.S. military values, military uniforms, military organization, military technology, and military discipline.

With an American serving as commander of the National Police, local resistance to the American presence was left to civilians. Once canal construction was completed in 1914, Panamanians perceived the value of the waterway—and the tolls, duties, and taxes that the Ameri-

---

*The name of the National Police was changed to the National Guard in the early 1950s, a technicality that allowed for U.S. military aid.

cans accrued. Panamanian frustration occasionally flashed into violence, as in the case of a 1915 saloon brawl between Panamanians and American servicemen in Panama City's red-light district that left one American sailor dead and dozens injured.

In 1926, middle-class nationalists founded a political party named Communal Action with the aim of renegotiating the canal treaty. Communal Action's young leader, a Harvard-educated right-wing nationalist named Arnulfo Arias, would become a dominant figure in Panamanian politics until his death more than a half-century later. Arias held friendly meetings with Adolf Hitler and Benito Mussolini, then won election as president in 1940 by capitalizing on the feelings of "pure" Panamanians against Caribbean blacks, who still held most of the jobs in the Canal Zone. He called for the repatriation of blacks and Chinese.

As president, Arias moved swiftly on his nationalistic agenda. He removed English-language traffic signs, issued Panamanian paper money for the first and only time, and refused to cooperate with a U.S. plea to build scores of military bases and radar stations on the isthmus in preparation for World War II. Fearing that a Fascist was taking over the isthmus, the Franklin Roosevelt administration shelved its Good Neighbor sensibilities and condoned a National Police coup against President Arias while he was vacationing in Havana with his mistress. Roosevelt got his bases, and the American military placed 70,000 troops on the isthmus to defend the canal during the war.

Arias was reelected president in 1949, running again on a platform that charged the Americans with being overly influential in Panamanian society. In 1951, he was overthrown for a second time by the National Police, probably with American encouragement. (All told, Arias was overthrown or prevented from taking office as president a total of five times.)

Egypt's nationalization of the Suez Canal in 1956 shook Panama and ushered in an eight-year period of intense nationalism and anti-Americanism. In May 1958, university and high school students in Panama City marched on the Canal Zone and defied the law, planting seventy-two Panamanian flags on zone property. Fighting between Zonians and Panamanians followed, leaving nine people dead. One of the students who marched was a poor boy named Manuel Antonio Noriega.

In January 1964, after Zonian authorities decided not to fly either nation's flag on the grounds of Balboa High School, insensitive Zonian students hoisted the Stars and Stripes anyway. A crowd of several hundred angry Panamanian students invaded the zone and hoisted their own flag next to the American. Insulted, youthful Zonian chauvinists tore the Panamanian flag apart. Tens of thousands of Panamanians responded to the incident by marching down Fourth of July Avenue (since renamed the Avenue of the Martyrs), bordering the zone, then ransacked the U.S. Information Agency building, the corporate offices of several U.S. banks, Pan American Airlines and Braniff Airways, as well as the Firestone and Goodyear tire plants. Twenty Panamanians and four U.S. soldiers were killed in an exchange of heavy gunfire. The incident convinced the Johnson administration that a new canal treaty was required, otherwise the safety of the waterway would be jeopardized.

The 1964 riots also shook the National Guard, whose officers felt uncomfortable putting down students to defend American property. An increasing number began to question whether they might not have been on the wrong side of the barricades.

THE TORRIJOS LEGACY

The ever dogged Arnulfo Arias won the presidency a fourth time in 1968, promising to control the growing power and corruption of the National Guard. Arias took office, but he was only allowed to remain there for ten days. National Guardsmen led by Col. Omar Torrijos and Maj. Boris Martínez staged a coup to prevent an officer purge.

The National Guard governed without a plan or ideology for its first three years in power. First, the junta cracked down on the small Communist party and unions; then it moved to include those same leftist sectors in a military-led progressive coalition along with liberal professional technocrats.

It took Washington to give the junta some definition. In February 1969, New York Governor Nelson Rockefeller, who was representing President Richard Nixon on a tour through Latin America, met with Torrijos in the presidential suite at the Hotel Panama. According to top Torrijos aide Fernando Manfredo, who was present at the session, Rockefeller told the Panamanians, "You cannot put the country back in the hands of the politicians." Rockefeller had come to the conclusion that the United States would have to restructure the canal treaty or face a Castro-style revolution on the isthmus. Like a growing number of U.S. Latin America experts, Rockefeller believed that only a Panamanian military government independent of a popularly elected National Assembly could negotiate and ratify a new treaty that would also be acceptable to the American people and Congress. As a former Assistant Secretary of State for Inter-American Affairs with large investments in Latin America, Rockefeller had long looked with favor upon military governments in the region. He reported back to President Nixon that Latin militaries offered the best opportunity for order and social mobility for the poor in the region.

"Torrijos just listened to Rockefeller's advice," according to Manfredo, who went on to be Torrijos's Minister of Commerce and Industry. "Rockefeller may not have known it, but he convinced Torrijos to stay in power. Torrijos saw that he could move without the opposition of Washington." A month after the Rockefeller meeting, Torrijos exiled fellow junta leader Martínez and seized power for himself. Torrijos drove opposition political parties underground, closed independent newspapers and radio stations, and imprisoned as many as 1,600 political opponents in his first months in power.

Omar Torrijos was the mestizo son of rural teachers who began his career as a beat policeman driving a radio patrol car. He showed promise on the beat and won a scholarship to study at the El Salvador military academy and the U.S.-run counterinsurgency School of the Americas in the Canal Zone. He further advanced his career by demonstrating leadership during a campaign against a small guerrilla revolt in 1959. Chasing guerrillas and witnessing the 1964 riots persuaded Torrijos that Panama needed basic social change and a new canal treaty.

Unencumbered by any independent congress or a critical press, Torrijos governed as a populist caudillo. He decreed progressive labor laws, raised wages, and made it almost impossible for companies to fire their workers. His land reform, civic action, educational and health programs helped integrate the long-forgotten rural farmers into the canal-based national economy. At the same time, Torrijos soaked the rich with new taxes to build large urban housing projects for the poor.

Torrijos's favorite program was his sponsorship of nationalism. The Panamanian caudillo financed folkloric dance groups, introduced the study of pre-Hispanic Indian culture into the public school curriculum, and paid U.S. boxing promoters to sign up Panamanian boxers for bouts in New York City—anything to expand national pride. "Torrijos believed deeply that Panamanians needed heroes, even if he had to create them," Manfredo said.

Torrijos was charismatic, manly, and likable, but he was a man who, like his nation, ultimately lacked definition. "The United States was lucky to be dealing with Omar Torrijos," noted his drinking partner and biographer Graham Greene. "[He was] a patriot and an idealist who had no formal ideology." Torrijos applauded the Cuban and Chinese revolutions while he kept Panamanian Communists on a short leash. He publicly scolded the United States, but he remained quietly close to the Ford and Carter administrations. He was a man who could ingratiate Barry Goldwater while smoking a cigar given to him by Fidel Castro.

But Torrijos left his country with a checkered legacy. He expanded the National Guard from 5,000 men to 10,000 and uplifted its position in Panamanian politics. His ideal was to create an army that would serve as the society's progressive vanguard, but in so doing, he set the military above the law.

Under Torrijos, National Guard officers including Noriega set up trading companies that trafficked arms to both right-wing Cuban exiles and the Sandinistas. Torrijos lived modestly compared to most Latin American dictators, but criminal activity seemed to flourish around him. One of his business partners, Frank Marshall Jiménez, was a fugitive from Costa Rica who was reportedly involved in the smuggling of liquor on an extensive, international scale. One Torrijos brother, Hugo, was in charge of state gambling casinos and the national lottery, two institutions regularly skimmed for cash by corrupt National Guard officers. Another brother, Moisés Torrijos, the ambassador to Argentina and then to Spain, was indicted by a New York grand jury for drug trafficking in 1972, but the indictment remained sealed for six years— until the new Panama Canal treaty was signed and ratified. (His case was dismissed in 1980 for lack of evidence.) It was also Torrijos who established the nation's confidential banking laws, which made Panama City the favorite laundering center of Latin America's drug barons. The Carter administration always looked the other way, first to protect the treaty negotiations and later as a courtesy to Torrijos, a policy National Guard officers interpreted as acquiescence.

Torrijos will best be remembered for successfully negotiating the canal treaty with President Carter. This was a political task so difficult that Torrijos used to compare himself to a shoemaker attempting to satisfy a big-footed princess who asked for comfortable shoes that would look dainty to her subjects. On the one hand, Torrijos had to satisfy the nationalistic hunger of his people by acquiring sovereignty over the canal and Canal Zone; on the other, he (and Carter) had to reassure a suspicious American public and the U.S. Congress empowered to ratify the treaty.

(The canal struck a certain nationalistic cord in the American South and West. Former Governor Ronald Reagan nearly beat President Gerald Ford for the 1976 Republican nomination by promising to break off the canal negotiations. "We bought it," Reagan demanded. "It's ours, and we're going to keep it!")

After more than a decade of U.S.-Panamanian negotiations, Carter and Torrijos signed their treaty in Panama City on September 7, 1977, at the headquarters of the Organization of American States (OAS). The new treaty granted Panama higher rents and tolls, legal jurisdiction over the canal in 1980, and total sovereignty and operational control over the entire waterway on January 1, 2000. The Carter administration, however, managed to wring several major concessions out of Torrijos. The United States continued to have the right to operate military bases and control the waterway for better than twenty years, and Washington retained the ultimate right to intervene militarily in Panama in the event canal operations were threatened.

Still, chief Panamanian negotiator Rómulo Escobar Bethancourt expressed joy. "Getting control of the Canal Zone and the canal is one of Panama's oldest national desires," he said. "To generation after generation of Panamanians, the canal has symbolized the country's national patrimony—in the hands of foreigners. We developed a kind of national religion over the canal."

In its August 22, 1977, issue, Time magazine published a cover caricature illustration depicting a perturbed-looking Uncle Sam, clad in a red, white, and blue bathing outfit, warily preparing to step out of the canal as if it were an overheated bathtub. Inside, the cover story reflected American concerns over the controversial treaty by quoting historian David McCullough, who told Time that, by relinquishing the canal, "we are saying something profound about ourselves, that we have reached a turning point in our growth as a nation. . . . Have we become a people who are pulling in and withdrawing?" Carter lobbied, cajoled, horsetraded, and otherwise spent his administration's political capital to squeeze the treaty through the U.S. Senate—by a single vote.

Carter won more admiration in Latin America than in his own country for his effort.

Upon receiving news of the Senate ratification, Torrijos stripped off his pants and dove into the canal's waters head first. Then, getting down to more serious business, he fixed a Panamanian referendum to get the necessary two-thirds popular approval for the pact called for in his country's constitution. "There will be a vast political vacuum we will have to fill," predicted Torrijos. "We will no longer have the gringos to blame [for our problems]."

Former associates of Torrijos say he had believed by 1978 that it was finally time to build a democratic Panama. Torrijos hoped to institutionalize his social programs through a civilian government. With that in mind, he founded a reformist civilian political party called the Revolutionary Democratic party (PRD). His plan, say Nicolás Ardito Barletta and Fernando Manfredo, was to usher in true civilian rule with a presidential election scheduled for 1984 (the first since 1968). Nature or an assassination prevented him from completing his mission.

The Panamanian leader frequently flew in his private plane in bad weather, and his July 31, 1981, trip to his wooden hut hideaway in Coclecito was no different. In the midst of a storm, his plane crashed into a mountain. Ever since, there have been reports that peasants saw a bomb flash in the sky before the crash, and the National Guard took a suspiciously long twenty-four hours to announce the news. Noriega, the supreme conspirator in a nation of conspirators, emerged on top and renamed the military as the Panamanian Defense Forces (PDF).

MANUEL ANTONIO NORIEGA

Manuel Antonio Noriega, a man whose face is so horribly scarred from acne that he is popularly known as "Pineapple Face," is a profile of a twisted man who scratched his way through life without a moral concern. Like most children of the rancid Panama City barrio of Chorillo, Noriega was born poor and illegitimate. Abandoned by his father and orphaned at age five when his mother died of tuberculosis, Noriega lived in a single-room tenement apartment with an adoptive mother. As a teenager, he came to rely and revere his older half-brother, Luis Carlos Noriega, a Socialist-minded lawyer who was openly gay in a macho world. Manuel adopted Luis's ideas and friends as his own, and for the rest of his life he demonstrated an appreciation for painting, for things French, and for aesthetic sensibilities associated with the gay world.

The traditional way for the children of Chorillo to climb out of the ghetto is boxing. Noriega, however, was a quiet child who preferred to talk with his older brother's friends than play sports with his contemporaries. He also liked to read, and in 1952, he graduated close to the top of his class at the National Institute, a school with a long leftist activist tradition.

In his graduation yearbook, Noriega wrote that he wanted to become either president of Panama or a psychiatrist. But for a man of his economic class, such aspirations were impossible. Noriega found a way out of the ghetto—a military career—with the help of his brother. Serving in a minor post in the Panamanian embassy in Lima, Peru, Luis arranged a scholarship for Manuel to study at Peru's military academy.

Noriega was an operator even then. He made important connections among cadets from all over the hemisphere. He also caught the eye of the Defense Intelligence Agency (DIA) office in the U.S. embassy in Lima. The DIA noted Noriega's intelligence and popularity, as well as his need for money. For $20 a week, Noriega began to spy on fellow cadets, helping to assemble biographical files on his fellow students. The DIA was interested in knowing who among the cadets expressed leftist or rightist thinking, who showed leadership potential, who drank—anything that might be pertinent in figuring out the future military leaders of Latin America. Noriega proved to be a shrewd analyst of personality, and showed promise as a spy—such promise that the embassy intelligence staff continued paying him even after he was arrested for beating up a prostitute.

Noriega strengthened his ties to the United States when he returned to Panama in 1960; he was admitted into the School of the Americas, the military school run by the Southern Command in the Canal Zone. Here he took counterinsurgency courses from American instructors. In 1967, as a major, he studied counterintelligence and intelligence in the Canal Zone's Fort Gulick and psychological operations at Fort Bragg, North Carolina.

Noriega's big career break came the next year, when Colonels Torrijos and Martínez overthrew the young Arias government. Noriega had tied his career to Torrijos, who had taken an interest in him from their first meeting at a bar in Colón during Carnival in 1963. According to an account widely accepted in Panama, Noriega seized the opportunity to ask then Lieutenant Colonel Torrijos to intervene on his behalf for an officer's commission. Torrijos couldn't help Noriega immediately, but he took note of the young man's ambition and moxie. Within a couple of years, Torrijos became National Guard commander for Chiriquí province, and for his chief of intelligence, he chose Noriega. At that post, Noriega harassed and spied on union leaders organizing workers at banana plantations owned by the United Fruit Company. He passed on the information he gathered to Torrijos—and his other sponsor, the CIA, which put him on contract sometime in 1966 or 1967. Following the 1968 coup, Noriega succeeded Torrijos as Chiriquí province commander.

Torrijos's sponsorship of Noriega's career paid big dividends when officers attempted a countercoup in December 1969, while the military strongman was in Mexico attending the Caribbean Classic horse race. Before Torrijos departed Panama, his intelligence service had assured him that rumors of a conspiracy by certain CIA agents, businessmen, and National Guard officers to overthrow him had no substance. Torrijos was badly misinformed. Once he arrived in Mexico, three conservative colonels took control of National Guard units around Panama City and squeezed for power. They called the Panamanian ambassador to Mexico and ordered him to pass along a message to Torrijos: "Don't bother returning." With the rebels in control of the National Guard signal corp and telecommunications, Torrijos couldn't communicate with officers he hoped were still loyal to him.

Torrijos went into a rage, throwing furniture around his Mexico City hotel room. After he cooled down, he called Chiriquí commander Major Noriega. Torrijos said he was ready to fight his way back to Panama City. Noriega swore his support. Torrijos hired a private plane to fly to David, the capital of Chiriquí province, that night. The ever-resourceful Noriega positioned military trucks along the tarmac to light up the landing with their headlights. With the nine-hundred-man Chiriquí unit behind him, Torrijos easily regained power.

For his loyalty, Torrijos selected Noriega to be his new chief of intelligence, making him the second most powerful man in Panama. Noriega made himself indispensable to Torrijos by infiltrating leftist and rightist groups involved in the opposition movement against concessions Torrijos was known to be ready to make to negotiate a new canal treaty with Washington. At the same time, Noriega drew closer to the CIA while extending his contacts to the Cuban, Taiwanese, and Israeli intelligence services. He befriended a Mossad agent named Mike Harari, at the time the chief Israeli agent for Mexico and Central America, who would eventually replace brother Luis as Noriega's chief adviser.

Noriega abused his power to create a criminal network employing Panamanian embassies around the world to traffic heroin. He could do practically anything he wanted, as long as he kept Torrijos informed—a service Noriega provided better than anyone in Panama. Torrijos never forgot 1969.

Noriega kept complete files on all Panamanian officers and politicians, complete with the kind of personal grist that could be used for blackmail. His intelligence tentacles reached deep, even into Washington's own spy apparatus. While the CIA and DIA paid him to look out for their interests, Noriega turned around and bought eavesdropping tapes collected by the U.S. Army's Canal Zone–based 470th Military Intelligence Group from several U.S. Army sergeants he recruited. The reel-to-reel records, which contained information on leaders and opposition groups in Panama and the countries of Central and South America, must have been invaluable to Torrijos's activist foreign policy. Authorities at the National Security Agency, Washington's chief electronic spy agency, feared Noriega had also passed information from the pilfered tapes to Havana. But CIA director George Bush reportedly concealed the scandal, apparently to protect Gerald Ford against Ronald Reagan's challenge for the 1976 Republican nomination.

Some months later, within forty-eight hours of the Ford-Carter election, three bombs exploded in the Canal Zone. American intelligence agents discovered that Noriega's men in G-2 intelligence were responsible for the blasts, a sign of National Guard displeasure with American Zonians who filed a civil suit to block canal negotiations between the Ford and Torrijos governments. That December, Noriega flew to Washington, as he did from time to time. He probably expected a tongue lashing when he met with George Bush, who was still intelligence director. But, as U.S. Ambassador William Jordan described the session in his book *Panama Odyssey,* the meeting between the two intelligence chiefs was almost cordial:

Noriega dutifully denied any complicity of the Guard in setting off explosives, argued that Panama had nothing to gain by such actions, and insisted that the technology used was not part of the Guard's expertise. Bush listened courteously, never said what he really thought, and moved on to other matters. He was telling the Panamanian as subtly as he could: let's drop this subject—as long as it does not happen again.

Bush and other American officials rationalized that the intelligence chief could do them even more harm if they didn't pay him off. In any case, Noriega's antidemocratic authoritarian politics and anti-American feelings should not have been a surprise.

Noriega wrote an eighty-page manual in 1975 entitled "Psychological Operations: Fundamentals" as an educational guide for lower-echelon Panamanian agents. Reinforcing his arguments with obscure references to Genghis Khan, Aristotle, John Locke, René Descartes, Auguste Comte, Sigmund Freud, Carl Jung, Karl von Clausewitz, and Mao Tse-tung, Noriega depicted human nature and Panama's civic community as, above all else, formless and malleable. "Forgetting to think for himself, the mass-man grows accustomed to others thinking for him," Noriega wrote. "The masses have a great weakness: Their scarce or non-existent thinking power." His point of view was vaguely Marxist and pro-Soviet, as shown in the following passage:

> As General [Juan] Perón used to say: "The Northamericans don't make friends, they buy favors." They employ economic resources, while the Russians employ ideological resources, which acquire universal currency, even penetrating the United States, with its racial conflicts and its youth and student insurgency. In the recent Vietnam and Indochina wars, the Northamericans, despite all their military power, have been defeated by the Communists.

Over all those years, ample evidence had been gathered by American authorities that showed Noriega was detrimental to U.S. interests. John Ingersoll, Nixon's director of the Bureau of Narcotics and Dangerous Drugs, received a suggestion from one of his agents in 1971 that Noriega be assassinated for his coordination of heroin trade from Panamanian embassy consular offices. Ingersoll shelved the suggestion and took no action. Bush's CIA continued to pay the renegade intelligence officer $100,000 a year. The Carter administration's CIA director, Stansfield Turner, took Noriega off the payroll for a time, but the Pentagon and the State Department replaced the CIA as Noriega's protectors.

In 1978, agents of the U.S. Customs and the Bureau of Alcohol, Tobacco and Firearms discovered that Noriega was using a local Air Panama employee to purchase weapons in Miami gunshops and pawnshops for the Sandinista rebels in Nicaragua. The U.S. Attorney's office indicted five Panamanian associates of Noriega on gun-running charges, and were hot on the trail of the intelligence chief himself by late 1978. Dade County, Florida, and federal police agents were prepared to arrest Noriega in June 1979, when Noriega was scheduled to change planes at the Miami airport for a flight to Washington where he was to meet with Pentagon officials. Incredibly, U.S. military personnel based in Panama scotched the plan by warning Noriega of the trap. Noriega called off his trip for supposed health reasons.

The Noriega case was shut for good the following December when Torrijos decided to grant asylum to the Shah of Iran as a favor to Carter. By placing Noriega and Noriega-associate Carlos Wittgreen, one of the five Panamanians listed in the 1978 gun-smuggling indictment, in charge of the Shah's security, Torrijos guaranteed neither would be touched by Washington.

Assistant U.S. Attorney Jerome Sanford, an enthusiastic and dogged young prosecutor, would not give up despite pressure from his superiors in the Justice Department, particularly the FBI, to drop the investigation into Noriega. By January 1980, Sanford believed he had collected enough evidence to indict Noriega for the illegal export of $2 million in arms from Miami to Panama for transshipment to Nicaragua and El Salvador. His effort was blocked again by FBI intelligence, which, Sanford suspects, was a "conduit of what I would have to believe was the [Carter] White House."

A year later, after Reagan replaced Carter in the White House, Noriega was put back on the CIA payroll.

NORIEGA'S PANAMA

Air force pilot César Rodríguez and bagman-flyer Floyd Carleton, like most Panamanian men, enjoyed spending Father's Day with their families. But on that day in June 1980, then–intelligence chief Colonel Noriega was in a hurry for his two agents to make an urgent arms drop to the Salvadoran guerrillas of the Farabundo Martí National Liberation Front (FMLN). To speed their trip, the two pilots packed an extra fifty-five-gallon fuel tank in Rodríguez's Piper-Navajo Air Commander, enabling them to return to Panama that night without a refueling stop in Costa Rica.

On take-off, the Piper-Navajo groaned under the weight of the extra tank and the overloading of bullets and grenades. Unable to gain altitude fast enough, Rodríguez struck a guard fence at the end of the runway, tearing his plane's hydraulic fuel lines. Rodríguez recklessly chose not to abort the mission, and by the time he landed in the field of a Salvadoran farm, he had lost his brakes. Fortunately for Rodríguez, Carleton was flying right behind him in a Piper-Seneca. Rodríguez steered his landing at the branches of a recently fallen tree in the hope that he could cushion his impact and avert a fuel explosion. His maneuver worked, but he broke both his legs.

Carleton swooped down and landed to save his partner. With the left door and wing of the Air Commander's fuselage crushed into Rodríguez's broken body, Carleton smashed the windshield with the butt of his rifle and dragged his partner out head first.

Rodríguez and Carleton were Noriega's personal troubleshooters, as Carleton testified before a 1988 U.S. Senate committee hearing. One day they flew weapons, the next they flew laundered drug money. On their covert missions, their first order from Noriega was to destroy their aircraft if there was an accident. Noriega kept his extracurricular operations secret, even from his commander, General Torrijos, who in 1980 favored a political settlement to the Salvadoran conflict.

As Carleton dragged Rodríguez from the wreckage, the Panamanians heard two Salvadoran army helicopters coming their way in hot pursuit. Carleton was able to carry Rodríguez to his plane, but he had no extra time to torch the wreck. The two successfully took off and raced the slower helicopters out of Salvadoran air space. When they landed safely that evening in western Panama, Carleton telephoned their boss to report on the failed mission. Noriega immediately asked if they had left any evidence behind. Carleton lied, saying that he had destroyed the plane.

Within hours the news of the crash broke into international headlines. The tail registry of the wreck linked the aircraft to Panama. After an investigation, Torrijos upbraided Noriega and ordered an end to the supply flights. Some sources close to Torrijos suggest that he might have cashiered his intelligence chief, but Noriega's El Salvador activities were supported by other top National Guard officers who still wanted to cause trouble for the United States and promote leftist revolution.

Torrijos's order to end the arms trafficking lasted until his own fatal 1981 plane crash—a coincidence that has led several American and Panamanian analysts to suspect Noriega assassinated his commander. This was entirely possible. There was, after all, a motive. Within two months of Torrijos's death, Noriega had hosted two meetings in Panama City that assembled FMLN Comandante Joaquín Villalobos and other top members of the Salvadoran guerrilla directorate. Noriega and the Salvadorans agreed to establish two arms supply routes; one by water, across the Gulf of Fonseca; the another by land, from Nicaragua through Honduras into El Salvador—the so-called Ho Chi Minh Trail. To expedite the shipments, Noriega introduced the Salvadoran rebels to two ranking Honduran army colonels, Honduran army chief of intelligence Leonidas Torres Arias and armored division commander Hubert Boden, who were willing to usher the arms through their country for profit.

The arms deal, once finalized in Havana with Fidel Castro's backing, brought Noriega and his two Honduran co-conspirators several millions of dollars in profits, according to José Blandón, a key former Noriega aide. However, like the Father's Day airdrop, the dealings of the two Honduran colonels with the Salvadoran guerrillas leaked, creating a scandal within the Honduran officer corps. Before news broke out beyond Tegucigalpa, Noriega reported the activities of the two Honduran officers to the CIA, leaving out his own connection to them. Acting on Noriega's incomplete information, the CIA saw to it that the Honduran military ousted the corrupt officers. For such services, Noriega was considered a prized asset by intelligence director William Casey. Noriega had already been on the CIA payroll for two decades, and his help tracking Central American affairs in the early 1980s earned him a raise. By 1985, he was paid a retainer from the agency of $200,000—equivalent to the salary earned by the President of the United States.

Noriega's schemes for El Salvador were twisted beyond even the norms of the spy world. While he sponsored arms supply flights to feed the Salvadoran insurgency, he informed the Salvadoran army and the CIA of information he gathered on the FMLN and looked the other way when the United States flew secret spy missions over El Salvador and Nicaragua from Howard Air Force Base, located along the Canal. In 1985, Noriega helped settle a major crisis in El Salvador by serving as a mediator between President José Napoleón Duarte and the FMLN to negotiate the release of Duarte's kidnapped daughter Inés.

Noriega turned one of the Medellín Cartel's top money launderers over to U.S. law enforcement authorities, worked hard to stop marijuana cultivation in Panama, and won gushing congratulations from the U.S. Drug Enforcement Administration (DEA) for his efforts. Never mind that Noriega was also secretly passing the Colombian drug cartel information on DEA and U.S. Customs agents and their radio frequencies, and the schedules of coast guard and navy operations, as well as earning between $5 million and $10 million on good months from money laundering himself.

Noriega served anyone who would pay him. Nobody truly trusted him, but as strongman of Panama he had much to offer every power player in the Caribbean basin, from Communists to capitalists, from criminals to law enforcement agents. While the presence of the canal and the facilities of the Southern Command in Panama gave Noriega a large stack of chips in his dealings with Washington, the dictator always exploited the facilities of the Colón free zone to keep on the good side of the region's radical left.

The dictator permitted Cuba and Nicaragua to break the U.S. trade embargoes on their countries by importing and exporting with the United States through the free zone. Panamanian workers in the free zone repackaged Nicaraguan and Cuban shrimp or coffee and smuggled the contraband produce into the United States in packaging that claimed the contents were "Made in Panama." On the import side, the Cuban and Nicaraguan governments relied on the free zone to import American spare parts and luxury goods to satisfy the consumer tastes of their elites.

As a matter of course, Castro's intelligence agencies stole superior Western technology that came through the free zone to copy in Cuba's own factories and pass on to the Soviet Union. The free zone also periodically benefited the Colombian and Salvadoran guerrillas by serving as a way station for arms shipments originating in the European black market and Cuba. Such war matériel was usually stored in a free zone warehouse managed by the Explonsa explosives factory, a business owned by the Panamanian military.

Noriega also utilized the free zone as a means of greasing his military machine—the heart of his regime. Top officers remained loyal, most to the bitter end, because loyalty paid. Transit S.A., an international trade service company that earned $30 million annually, was owned by the PDF general staff and managed by Noriega business partner and 1989 presidential candidate Carlos Duque. Transit S.A. did nothing more than stamp cargo documentation on exports to Colombia for the 1 to 2 percent fee required by Panamanian law. Another "service" Transit S.A. performed was the repackaging of Colombian coffee in Panamanian sacks so as to get around the various coffee import quotas around the world. Under Noriega, all businesses were forced to pay off the PDF in order to construct and operate new stores and warehouses in the zone. One electronics merchant explained the process to me this way: "The government bureaucrats tell you to see one [PDF] officer. The officer breaks a few appointments, then sends you a second officer, who breaks more appointments. Finally you scream, 'How much?' They wore you down."

All the same, under Noriega's undisputed leadership, the PDF attracted $35 million in U.S. military aid (Torrijos barely got any) in order to expand its personnel from 10,000 to 17,000 men. But Noriega's open corruption robbed his military institution of its former nationalistic and populist appeal. Under Noriega, the Panama Defense Forces became nothing more than a criminal enterprise.

On paper, Noriega was a perfect ally for the Medellín Cartel. Not only was he a powerful military officer with intelligence links throughout the region, but he also had established a well-oiled arms smuggling operation during the Nicaraguan revolution that could be utilized for drugs.

The cartel probably began dealing with Noriega in 1982, when the intelligence chief served as a mediator between cartel boss Jorge Ochoa and the Colombian M-19 guerrillas who had abducted Ochoa's younger sister Marta Nieves. Noriega helped free her and gained the cartel's trust. That year alone, according to one report, Noriega arranged for the transport of four hundred kilos of cocaine through Panama, much of it flown by his own pilot, Floyd Carleton. Soon after Noriega took command of the PDF in 1983, he deepened his relationship with the cartel by condoning the opening of a major cocaine processing plant deep in the Darién jungle, for which he and top Panamanian officers were paid $5 million.

Panama would always be a sideshow next to the cartel's mushrooming operations in Colombia. But with Bogotá's brief crackdown following the May 1, 1984, murder of Attorney General Rodrigo Lara

Bonilla, the cartel needed a guardian angel outside Colombia. They found one in Noriega, who offered Ochoa and fellow drug kingpins Pablo Escobar and Jorge Vásquez bodyguards, secure offices, and safe houses in exchange for personal payments of at least $4 million. An estimated one hundred cartel personnel in all moved into Panama, for an arranged period of between one and seven months depending on the situation in Colombia.

But within weeks, according to Floyd Carleton's* 1988 testimony before a U.S. Senate subcommittee, Noriega began feeling pressure from U.S. law enforcement agencies concerned about cartel activities in Panama. Noriega panicked and ordered a raid on the Darién cocaine processing plant on May 29. Among twenty-three Colombians arrested at the Darién site was Lt. Col. Julián Melo, secretary general of Noriega's general staff.

The fugitive cartel bosses felt betrayed, and swore to get even. Israeli intelligence operative Mike Harari, who was growing increasingly close to Noriega, got wind of a cartel assassination plot and reported his discovery to the Panamanian dictator, who was at the time visiting Israel. Noriega delayed returning home; instead, he sent his aide José Blandón to Havana to meet with Castro and ask the Cuban leader to intervene with the cartel on his behalf.

Castro was new to the narcotics world, but he had recently worked out a mutually beneficial nonaggression arrangement between the cartel and the M-19 guerrillas. Castro agreed to help Noriega, whose help in supplying the guerrillas in El Salvador he deeply appreciated. The Panamanian strongman waited a week or so in London until Castro wangled a pledge from the cartel to rescind the assassination order—in exchange for repayment of their $5 million in bribes and the freeing of the twenty-three Colombians arrested at the plant. Though Castro had smoothed matters over, the cartel never relied on Noriega again. It took the U.S. government more time to learn.

Business as usual in Panama was sleazy. It corrupted the entire society. The poor youths of Colón and Panama City, who needed jobs desperately, lost whatever hope Torrijos had given them, little by little, with each year of Noriega's rule. More than ever they turned to crime.

*Carleton, Noriega's confessed chief liaison to the Medellín Cartel, is under protective custody in the United States.

On the Avenue of the Martyrs, the dividing line of the garbage-strewn Panama City slum of Chorillo and the Canal Zone, several unemployed teenage boys talked over their troubles with me while sipping Coca-Cola in a corner store late one May afternoon. "We have no hope here," said Guillermo Fernández, a skinny nineteen-year-old who had the annoying habit of shuffling his feet and swaying as he talked. "There are no jobs."

A twenty-one-year-old scruffy grunt of a man named Sammy, who wore a soiled white undershirt over a pair of patched blue jeans, leaned against a counter up next to me. It looked as if he was about to pick my pocket.

I asked him what he wanted. Sammy showed me a small plastic bag of cocaine, not bothering to hide it from the others. "It's white, very, very white," Sammy muttered urgently. I wasn't interested in his merchandise, but I invited Sammy to take a walk with me along the busy avenue, where the smell of bus diesel fuel hung heavy.

"Why do you sell drugs?" I asked him straight out.

"Noriega does it," Sammy said. "Why shouldn't I."

We passed under four giant murals proclaiming Noriega the "Comandante of Dignity." Sammy told me that the murals proved to him that "If you're clean, you don't make it in Panama."

THREE SOUR NOTES

The first time I visited Panama, during the 1984 presidential campaign, I attended a rally of mostly poor blacks in downtown Panama City in support of the Panamanian Defense Forces. About 4,000 people were in attendance to send a message to the opposition candidate, the four times–elected and four times–deposed eighty-two-year-old Arnulfo Arias, that his threats to rein in the military would be resisted. "You know why we love the Guardia?" a middle-age public employee named María García asked me. "Because our army is nothing like the armies of Guatemala or El Salvador. Our soldiers aren't killers—if they were, Panama would become like Central America. Our soldiers serve the people." María's words would have been music to Omar Torrijos's ears, but the symphony was about to end with three sour notes: a stolen election, a murder, and a coup.

With Panama's $3.6 billion debt (80 percent of the gross domestic product [GDP]) beginning to take its toll, Noriega chose thirty-nine-year-old economist Nicolás Ardito Barletta to be the presidential candidate of a coalition of centrist and leftist parties led by the official Revolutionary Democratic Party (PRD). As a former Torrijos Planning Minister and a vice president of the World Bank, Barletta was thought to be loyal to the military and the kind of technocrat that Panama needed to sustain good relations with Washington and the multilateral lending institutions. Barletta agreed to be the government's candidate on Noriega's verbal agreement that he would guarantee the independence of the civilian government.

Barletta was naive. As he negotiated with Noriega, the PDF, under the statutes of Law 20, took control of the railroads, the immigration department, the civil aeronautics administration, and the passport bureau—a vast network for corruption.

Barletta, now director of an economics think tank in Panama City, later recalled his October 1983 meetings with Noriega during which they discussed his candidacy. "Noriega told me, 'We need to fulfill the promise Torrijos made to the country [that Panama would become a democracy].' I asked him: 'Do you really mean it?' He said yes. I didn't realize the Defense Forces are as crooked as they are. I didn't know about the drug business."

The May 6 election between Barletta and Arias, by most accounts, was close. The eighty-three-year-old Arias probably won by between 10,000 and 40,000 out of 640,000 votes cast, but Noriega's election board delayed the vote count for a week and Barletta eked out an official victory by a mere 1,713 votes. All of Panama knew the truth. A week of antielection riots took at least one life and left dozens more seriously injured.

Washington didn't want to notice, largely because CIA director William Casey thought Noriega was a crucial asset in the region. Noriega reminded Washington how useful he could be by personally giving a $100,000 donation to the Contras' southern-front operation in July 1984, around the same time he secretly met with Casey and National Security Council (NSC) aide Oliver North in Panama City. Secretary of State George Shultz was perceived as having set aside his commitment to democracy and having gone along with Casey largely because he sympathized with Barletta on a personal level, dating back to their days together at the University of Chicago. Shultz attended Barletta's October 1984 inauguration with U.S. embassy–compiled evidence of election fraud tucked in his briefcase.

Considered an illegitimate and pathetic dependent by the military and by most civilian Panamanians, Barletta was no more effective as president than he was as a candidate. His austerity policies—he increased taxes and froze public wages in order to reach an agreement with the International Monetary Fund (IMF)—sparked both massive street demonstrations and discontent in the barracks. Barletta retreated on his tough economic policies within a matter of months, which only made him look weaker in the eyes of the public and military. But a far more serious challenge to Barletta's military-backed regime soon followed.

Dr. Hugo Spadafora, a restless former Torrijos vice minister of health and inveterate guerrilla who had fought in Nicaragua and Guinea-Bissau in the 1970s, openly threatened from his home in Costa Rica to form an armed rebel force in Panama. Spadafora had brought what he considered incontrovertible evidence of Noriega's involvement in cocaine trafficking to the DEA offices in Panama and Costa Rica.

On September 13, 1985, Spadafora crossed the Costa Rican border into Panama in a taxi, then boarded a bus for the city of David, where PDF intelligence believed he could stir trouble. A PDF intelligence officer trailing Spadafora got on the bus with him, and in the town of Concepción, he took Spadafora prisoner. The forty-six-year-old would-be liberator was found inside a mailbag beheaded and severely tortured, just across the Costa Rican border.

Spadafora's murder stunned Panama; in nearby El Salvador or Guatemala such a murder would have been unremarkable, but such political violence was almost unheard of here. The opposition newspaper *La Prensa* ran boldfaced headlines daily accusing Noriega of the crime, and the normally passive Roman Catholic church called for an investigation.

Barletta was shaken, but he decided to rise to the occasion and become a bona fide president. Following an emotional telephone conversation with Spadafora's father, he proposed appointing a commission to examine the evidence.

The mild-mannered Barletta never had a chance to beat the military, but he succeeded in forcing Noriega to publicly cover up the crime. Before flying to New York to speak to the U.N. General Assembly two weeks following the murder, Barletta made an adroit television appearance. Though he knew there was a possibility Noriega himself was involved in the murder, Barletta told the nation that he didn't think the military was involved in the crime. "We have no fear of the truth," he told the national audience. Noriega simmered.

The political drama unfolded with Barletta in New York City and Noriega vacationing at his chateau in southern France. Col. Roberto Díaz Herrera, a leftist cousin of Torrijo and second-in-command of the PDF, polled members of the high command to see if they wanted to move against Noriega in a coup to save the institution. When the officer corp wouldn't follow him, Díaz Herrera blamed the entire plot on the traveling president. In the meantime, Barletta called his two vice presidents and members of his cabinet and ordered that his appointment of a three-man commission to investigate the case be announced on public television.

Hours after returning to Panama from France, Noriega called Foreign Minister Jorge Abadía, who was traveling with Barletta, to tell him the president should return to Panama City that very evening, a day ahead of schedule. Abadía did as instructed.

Barletta and the presidential party departed Kennedy Airport at 2:00 A.M. and arrived sleepless and groggy in Panama City five hours later. Díaz Herrera called Barletta at the presidential hangar and advised him to come immediately to the Defense Forces Comandancia as soon as possible. "He spoke in a very friendly and respectful way," recalled Barletta. "He said, 'Nicky, everything is under control.' " Barletta, suspecting that Díaz Herrera was laying a trap for him, went home. The president probably should have gotten some sleep, but following a wild guess that the ever-ambitious Díaz Herrera had put Noriega under arrest, he called the comandancia and asked for the general. To Barletta's surprise, Noriega answered the telephone. "We would like to speak to you right away," Noriega told Barletta, who agreed to come as a sign that he still supported the military. Barletta arrived at Noriega's office at the comandancia at 10:00 A.M. He wouldn't leave for fourteen hours.

Noriega and Díaz Herrera were waiting in the general's luxurious office, graced with puffy sofas and fine Filipino rosewood furniture, as were Foreign Minister Abadía and three other top PDF commanders. Colonel Díaz Herrera did most of the talking, demanding that Barletta close the opposition daily La Prensa for inciting sedition. When the president refused, the colonel demanded he resign.

Barletta asked for some time to think about it, and he sat down at one of the desks on the far side of Noriega's office. It was just past noon when Barletta called his secretary. She told him that Assistant Secretary of State Elliott Abrams had called and left his phone number.

Barletta called Abrams and spoke under his breath, almost in code, to explain that he was in a desperate situation. "Hang tough," Abrams told Barletta. "We support you. Don't resign." Barletta responded under his breath, "That's exactly what I'm doing. So you do something about it!" Barletta later said it was his way of requesting a phone call from President Reagan, or at least Secretary of State Shultz or Secretary of Defense Caspar Weinberger, to Noriega not to overthrow him.

For the next ten hours, Barletta stalled for time. But no call came, not even from Ambassador Everett Briggs, who was himself flying back to Panama at the time. Abrams, who had only been on the job for a month, didn't realize the seriousness of the situation and apparently didn't consult with anyone higher in the government about what to do for Barletta.

As Noriega looked on, Díaz Herrera first obliquely tried to tempt Barletta with money, then threatened to harm his family unless he resigned. Barletta finally agreed to write up a document in which he "separated himself" from the office—a position short of resignation allowed in Panamanian law—for an indefinite period. He thought he could still return to office, if only the United States would lean on Noriega within the next few days.

U.S. Ambassador Briggs encouraged Barletta to do just that, and lobbied Washington to refuse to recognize Vice President Eric Delvalle, whose first act after the rubber-stamp legislature appointed him president was to dismiss the special commission appointed to investigate the Spadafora case. Briggs was considering what would be the best U.S. policy for Panama, but his boss, Elliott Abrams, had a broader agenda. According to Francis McNeil, the Deputy Assistant Secretary of State for Intelligence and Research, Abrams believed the administration could handle only one crisis in the region at a time; 1985 was Nicaragua's year. The U.S. Southern Command showed its lack of concern for Noriega's behavior by conducting joint military maneuvers with the PDF in Chiriquí province, a few miles from Spadafora's fresh grave.

NSC staffer Lt. Col. Oliver North met with General Noriega and his aide José Blandón on a luxury yacht docked off the grimy Panamanian port of Balboa in June 1985. This meeting, only three months before the Spadafora assassination, was perceived by Noriega as a green light to do what he wanted to protect his regime.

According to Blandón, North and Noriega discussed the military situation in Nicaragua for a while, during which time the American official expressed his hope that the Contras would soon revive their moribund southern front along the Nicaragua–Costa Rica border. "North said he wanted the United States to get more directly involved in the fight against Nicaragua," Blandón said; it was a remarkable disclosure considering Noriega was known to have close contacts with Havana and Managua.

Claiming he was speaking for William Casey, North asked if Noriega could do the American government two favors. The NSC aide requested that Noriega open Panamanian military facilities for the training of several hundred Contras and that the new civilian leaders of the United Nicaraguan Opposition (UNO) Contra coalition be received by the Panamanian government as a sign of political support. Noriega agreed to both requests on the spot, according to Blandón. In the next couple of months, at least 250 southern-front Contras trained in small-unit commando fighting and intelligence units under CIA auspices on two PDF bases.

President Barletta, still a figurehead months before his challenge over the Spadafora case, dutifully met publicly with three Contra directors at Panama City's Atlapa Convention Center that July. Barletta's imprimatur of legitimacy was deemed particularly important to the Contra leaders because Panama (along with Mexico, Venezuela, and Colombia) was a sponsor of the respected if ineffectual Contadora group attempting to mediate Central America's disputes.

At a second North-Noriega conversation witnessed by Blandón, this one in Noriega's office at Fort Amador only a month after Barletta's overthrow, the Panamanian general offered to sneak elite counterinsurgency units into Nicaragua to commit anti-Sandinista sabotage. North reminded Noriega of the negative international reaction to the CIA mining of the Nicaraguan harbor only the year before, but he said he would speak to his superiors about it.

Noriega and Blandón had one more matter they wished to discuss with North, who was alone except for an interpreter. The Panamanians wanted to know if North could relieve the pressure that was beginning to build in the U.S. Congress against their government. The constant attacks by Senator Jesse Helms were particularly annoying, and Panamanian officials believed the gadfly North Carolinian was hurting their chances for receiving the U.S. economic aid and multilateral lending they needed for economic recovery. Without mentioning his government's concern about the Spadafora killing or the coup overthrowing Barletta, North said he would see what he could do.

In the following months, the U.S. Agency for International Development (AID) boosted its annual assistance from $13 million to $75 million, easing the way for Panama's commercial creditors to refinance part of the nation's debt. In total, Washington helped Panama receive more than $200 million in loans and aid from the IMF, the World Bank, and private banks over the year following the Barletta removal.

It was during this period, from 1985 through early 1988, that the Reagan administration showed itself to be splintered, indecisive, and inept in responding to the developing Panama crisis. Unwilling to leave Noriega and Panama to their own fate, or to use force to overthrow the dictatorship, the Reagan administration settled on a compromise policy that increased tensions between the two governments without settling any of the issues.

In November 1985, as a follow-up to his talks with North, Noriega flew to Washington for an appointment with Casey. State Department officials figured the only sure way for Noriega to get the message was for him to hear it directly from the grim and stern CIA director. It was to be a heart-to-heart chat, intelligence chief to intelligence chief. But Casey had other ideas. He criticized Noriega for allowing the Cubans to use the Colón free zone to penetrate the U.S. market and acquire American technology, but he made no mention of Noriega's drug enterprise. He then followed up the conference by sending the dictator a personal intelligence briefing outlining his confidential position on the Contadora peace process. Casey's implicit message: the CIA would overlook drug offensives if Noriega would help with the Contra policy.

According to the congressional testimony of Francis McNeil, Casey's own memorandum on his meeting with Noriega "noted that Noriega had been nervous when he came . . . but departed reassured."

Washington's recent aggressive stance toward authoritarian regimes in Haiti, the Philippines, and, to a lesser extent, Chile, simply didn't apply to Panama. The State Department's 1986 political map of Latin America illustrated the Reagan administration's ambivalent policy; on it, democracies were colored green, dictatorships brown. Panama was illustrated in gray, for "not characterized."

Yet another minicrisis in U.S.-Panamanian relations occurred in February 1986, during Senate confirmation hearings for the newly designated U.S. ambassador to Panama, Arthur H. Davis. A blunt man by nature, Davis urged Panama to reopen the Spadafora case and move toward real civilian rule. He spoke of "rumors" he had heard that the PDF was involved in drug trafficking. The Panamanian opposition newspaper *La Prensa* reprinted Davis's remarks under banner head-lines, inciting the government to threaten that the new ambassador would be declared persona non grata. The State Department moved quickly to calm the storm by softening some of Davis's strongest remarks in an unusual editing of the original committee transcript. Panamanian Foreign Minister Abadía flew to Washington anyway to consult with Shultz and request an explanation "to satisfy our national dignity." Abadía, playing diplomatic brinkmanship, demanded a clari-fication of American policy more to his and Noriega's liking. After a thirty-minute meeting with his Panamanian counterpart, Shultz buck-led and released a statement denying that the United States "had any intention of interfering in any way in Panama's internal affairs."

Noriega's personal relationship with North and Casey was still not publicly known in 1986. But I could smell a story when my congressio-nal sources told me of the Davis hearings. What did American officials know about Noriega and rumors of his involvement with drugs? While the U.S. government criticized Nicaragua and Chile for narcotics trafficking or repression, had they nothing to say about Panama?

I interviewed Carleton Turner, President Reagan's personal assist-ant on narcotics matters, in the Executive Office Building a week after the Davis hearing. Turner was fighting a lonely battle against Noriega within the White House. He fumed that the U.S. government held evidence that Noriega was involved in international crime but would do nothing about it.

"The Guard controls everything that is necessary for a major drug trafficking organization to exist. The officers control the waters, inter-nal security, port facilities, and certain banks for laundering money," Turner said. "Noriega has had ties to drug traffickers since the early 1970s and the U.S. government has always known it. . . . We get free access to the canal so the Panama desk at the State Department is happy. The DEA is happy because the PDF throws them bones. And the Southern Command is happy because Noriega leaves the American military alone."

A U.S. military intelligence source stationed at the Southern Com-mand confirmed much of what Turner said. But as the White House antidrug official had predicted to me, just about everyone else in Washington protected Noriega. I couldn't believe my ears when I heard Brian Stickney, the chief Latin America intelligence officer at the DEA, say, "The Panamanian government has done a fairly credible job in dealing with the international narcotics community. . . . I'm not saying there isn't some corruption, but we don't have hard evidence." Sherman Hinson, the senior member of the three-person State Department Panama desk, told me relations between the two countries were "correct," and he complimented President Delvalle for dealing with the Panamanian economic mess far better than Barletta did. Hinson said he wasn't overly worried about the political situation in the country because "Panamanians are born with cash registers for hearts." Richard Wyrough, a second member on the desk, said that he had never seen any hard evidence that Noriega or the PDF was involved in drug trafficking. Besides, he warned, if the United States pushed Noriega out of the way, the leftist pro-Cuban Colonel Díaz Herrera would take over. "There's no reason to be uncordial," he said. I filed a story to the *Wall Street Journal* that a few White House and military officials were aware of Noriega's nefarious activities, which caused a ripple in Panama City when it was reprinted in the Panamanian newspaper *La Prensa.*

Noriega's good fortunes in Washington began to turn with the June 12 publication by the *New York Times* of an article by Seymour Hersh headlined "Panama Strongman Said to Trade in Drugs, Arms and Illicit Money." The investigative reporter took Noriega to task for a series of crimes, including money laundering, arms trafficking, stealing the 1984 election, and the Spadafora killing. Noriega assumed the revelations were a planned leak by the Reagan administration and a signal that Washington wanted him out. (Noriega hated Hersh for years after. When U.S. troops invaded Panama almost four years later, they found among Noriega's voodoo paraphernalia a tamale with Hersh's name wrapped inside. Voodoo experts said this was a "binding ritual" in which enemies were neutralized in flour goo.)

Feeling cornered in Washington, Noriega continued to play his Nicaragua card. He reportedly sent Roberto Corduvez, a Panamanian publicist and political ally, to contact North in August 1986 to propose that the Panamanian dictator order the entire Sandinista leadership assassinated in return for Reagan administration aid to improve Noriega's image and the lifting of a ban against U.S. military aid to Panama. Even if Noriega had "the assets" in Nicaragua to murder the comandantes, as he claimed he did, it is doubtful he really would have engaged in such an act of war against a neighbor with far greater military force. It was just Noriega's way of showing how far he would be willing to help the U.S. government.

In a follow-up meeting between North and Noriega that took place in London in September 1986, Noriega offered to take sabotage action against a list of strategic targets, from an oil refinery, to an airport, to dock facilities at Puerto Sandino.

How useful was Noriega to the Contra war? It is probable that Noriega promised to do much more in Nicaragua than he could or wanted to deliver. But there is evidence that Noriega did help to some degree. José Blandón testified under oath to Congress that Noriega deployed former Mossad agent Mike Harari to mount a war supply operation in 1985 and 1986 that ran guns from Eastern Europe through Contra bases sheltered in Panama under the auspices of the Southern Command. Some of Blandón's testimony is in dispute, but it has been confirmed that Noriega was responsible for a sabotage mission in March 1985 that blew up a military installation and hospital in Managua. Though no one was killed, it was the biggest military attack on Managua of the entire Contra war.

There is additional circumstantial evidence that Noriega knew much of the Reagan administration's illegal Contra resupply operation. Joe Fernández, the CIA station chief in San José who was a key operative in "the Enterprise," traveled frequently to Panama City to meet with Noriega. Furthermore, Noriega's personal lawyer wrote up the incorporation papers for Udall Research Corp., the dummy front company that owned the Santa Elena airfield from which Contra supply planes refueled in Costa Rica. Three other secret corporations set up by Iran-Contra operatives Albert Hakim and Richard Secord to hide money that was transferred from Iranian arms sales to the Contras—Lake Resources, Stanford Technology, and NRAF Inc.—were set up and based in Panama.

A report issued in 1990 by a Costa Rican government prosecutor linked Noriega (along with North, CIA asset John Hull, various drug traffickers, and Contra leaders) to the 1984 assassination attempt of mercurial Contra leader Edén Pastora. According to the Costa Rican report, which has been hotly denied by the Bush administration, the plot was an attempt to purge the Contra movement of Pastora.

Given how freely Noriega dispensed information to all parties, it is also possible, if not probable, that he passed on much of his knowledge of the Reagan administration's covert Contra operations to Managua. If such knowledge included flight patterns, it is conceivable that the Hasenfus plane was shot down with help from Noriega.

Whatever the truth, Noriega attracted administration protection against powerful enemies on Capitol Hill. As Noriega and North held their secret London talks, Senator Helms proposed an amendment to an intelligence bill in the Senate calling for a curtailment of aid to Panama until the Spadafora case was resolved. Helms was interested in making as much trouble as possible in his quixotic quest for the United States to regain control of the canal beyond the year 2000. Casey personally telephoned the North Carolina Republican to ask him to soften his attacks on the Latin dictator. Helms refused and curtly told the CIA director that the Reagan administration's Panama policy was a disgrace. Casey hung up in frustration.

The CIA continued to pay Noriega until at least June 1987, and as a sign of respect, if not affection, the agency even gave him a Christmas present that December—an expensive, stylized Peruvian beanbag game in the shape of a toad (Noriega's favorite animal and also the word in Panamanian Spanish for spy).

William Casey wasn't the only important official in the U.S. government who loyally continued to cooperate with Noriega. DEA director John Lawn continued to send the Panamanian general flattering letters through 1987 for interdicting traffickers (invariably those who didn't cooperate in his payoff schemes) and reforming banking laws to make money laundering marginally more difficult. In administration policy meetings, influential Deputy Assistant Secretary of Defense Nestór Sánchez, the CIA's top Central America man in the 1970s and an old friend of Noriega argued vigorously that the Panamanian dictator was Washington's best bet for ensuring the safety of the canal and continued operations of the Southern Command.

Meanwhile, officials within the DEA, the Justice Department, and the NSC discouraged the criminal investigations by the South Florida DEA office and Florida federal prosecutor Leon Kellner that eventually led to the indictment of Noriega on drug charges. During a visit to the Executive Office Building, Deputy National Security Adviser John Negroponte smugly asked Kellner, "Since when do district attorneys make foreign policy?" One reason for the reluctance to prosecute was a decision made by Noriega in late 1987 to push through the Panamanian congress a law that allowed American narcotics agents access to Panamanian bank accounts suspected of being used by money launderers. It was unclear how much access Noriega would allow, but the DEA and CIA still figured that any cooperation from their "asset" was better than none. It would take election year politics in 1988, not the facts on the ground, to finally unhinge Panama from the Reagan

administration's Nicaraguan tunnel vision and clarify Washington's
position on Noriega.

   While the Reagan administration discordantly fiddled, Panamanians tentatively began to light fires of opposition. Ironically, it was
Colonel Díaz Herrera, the PDF's leftist second-in-command, who
supplied the kindle and spark in June 1987 when he was abruptly
dismissed by Noriega. A bitter Díaz Herrera publicly confirmed reports
that Noriega was behind the Spadafora murder, the 1984 electoral
fraud, money laundering, drug trafficking, and even Torrijos's murder.
His charges made banner headlines in La Prensa and were the talk of
Panama. On June 8, six days after his removal from the military,
crowds gathered outside Díaz Herrera's Panama City home and opposition radio station KW Continente demanding an investigation into
this unlikely hero's disclosures. A brief riot broke out when special
PDF "Dobermen" antiriot police used birdshot, tear gas, and truncheons to break up the crowds. It was the first in a long series of
disturbances that over the next two years would periodically break out
in Panama and shake but never entirely disrupt the military government. Under Noriega's orders, President Delvalle declared a state of
emergency, suspended civil liberties and the constitution, and arrested
Díaz Herrera. (He was released soon afterwards.)
   The Panama City private sector, previously a pronounced enemy of
Díaz Herrera, jumped on his defection as a sign that Noriega's hold
over the military was weakening. Several business groups, including
such normally staid organizations as the Chamber of Industries and
Chamber of Commerce, founded a coalition called the National Civic
Crusade to promote nonviolent antigovernment action. The Civic
Crusade called for an indefinite general strike until Noriega resigned,
and managed to assemble 3,000 to 10,000 protesters in several antigovernment protests in upper-class neighborhoods and churches of Panama City. Unfortunately, they failed to make a major effort to organize
blacks and the rural poor. The Noriega regime easily put down the
rebellion by targeting opposition-owned businesses for attacks by newly
formed paramilitary militias.
   The general strike petered out after a few days, but it moved the
U.S. Senate to overwhelmingly pass a resolution calling for Noriega to
resign. In response, Panamanian government employees pelted the
U.S. embassy with rocks and splashed the building with red paint on

June 29 as PDF policemen looked on. Secretary of State Shultz was particularly offended by this expression of disrespect to the U.S. diplomatic corps, and he made sure all U.S. economic and military aid to Panama was suspended.

The Civic Crusade tried to keep the pressure up through July and August, sponsoring automobile caravans and several rallies that attracted more than 5,000 people. But as the businessmen upped the ante, so did Noriega's forces. The PDF tear-gassed an opposition mass at the elegant Santuario Nacional Church and detained or otherwise intimidated dozens of opposition leaders. Breaking up one peaceful demonstration on July 10, the PDF wounded or arrested more than seven hundred people. A month later, police closed the opposition press, fatally shot two opposition activists, and intimidated the entire country.

The leader who once thought of becoming a psychiatrist had become a master at psychological operations—and that is all that was needed to manipulate and subdue this essentially peaceful country. Noriega's repression was measured, just enough to terrorize the mostly middle-class opposition. And that wasn't much—a bomb scare at the factory of one opposition fund-raiser or a threat to a student leader's family was usually enough to quash trouble. Between June and September of 1987, the PDF contained the demonstrations by arresting and imprisoning up to 1,500 people (usually for up to three days), wounded about 500 people with birdshot (of whom 60 suffered serious eye damage), and killed 3. Unlike repression in neighboring El Salvador, Guatemala, and Nicaragua, this repression didn't have to be so bloody to be effective.

Panama's opposition was not manned by fired-up students, bitter unionists, or enraged peasants as it was elsewhere in Latin America, but by bankers and industrialists who demonstrated their feelings by joining protest caravans of Jeep Wagoneers and BMWs, in which they honked their horns and waved white handkerchiefs out their windows down fashionable Vía España or Calle 50. This may have been the first antigovernment movement to choose the white flag as its banner, or to call on its followers to withdraw their accounts from the Banco Nacional, the country's central bank, as a sign of rebellion.

The struggle was a complete mismatch: heavyset businessmen wearing white *guayaberas* up against the tough Dobermen police and their tear gas and birdshot. P. J. O'Rourke, the contemporary American humorist, observed in *Rolling Stone* magazine that at Civic Crusade demonstrations "protest signs are done with computer graphics, and slogans are displayed on word-processor printouts. In the better residential neighborhoods, the noon and 6:00 P.M. demos are marked by children, housewives, and kitchen help banging on pots and pans. At least one enterprising member of the opposition is selling a pot-banging cassette so dinner won't be late." It was hard to take the Panamanian opposition seriously in large part because most activists appeared to lack real courage and conviction. A majority of Panamanians believed that somehow, someway, the United States would come to their rescue.

When opposition newspaper publisher Roberto Eisenmann, Jr., told Ted Koppel on "Nightline" that a U.S. military invasion of Panama would not be helpful, Eisenmann was deluged with telephone calls for weeks from Panamanians telling him he had made a terrible mistake. The Civic Crusade had lost its momentum and appeal by early 1988.

But just as Noriega appeared to be winning on the home front, Panama began to emerge as a major political issue in the U.S. presidential campaign. Senator Robert Dole of Kansas, Governor Michael Dukakis of Massachusetts, and other candidates of both parties won strong applause with pledges to get tough on Panama to protect American children from drugs. It was a delicate issue for George Bush, who had been vice president and former head of the CIA at a time Noriega was on the payroll.

Bush had met with Noriega on a number of occasions over the years, although the vice president said he recalled only one brief session with the dictator. Bush was vulnerable to charges that he was soft on Noriega because he apparently scotched an investigation into the so-called singing sergeants of the army's 470th Military Intelligence Group who sold secrets to Noriega in 1976. Reports filtered out of Panama that Noriega told associates that he hoped Bush would win the election because he possessed compromising information on the vice president.

Therefore, domestic politics forced the Reagan administration to suspend Panama's sugar import quota and, more importantly, to allow the Florida federal prosecutor, Leon Kellner, to carry on his narcotics investigation into Noriega. On February 4, 1988, Miami and Tampa grand juries indicted Noriega and fifteen co-defendants, including PDF Capt. Luis del Cid, Noriega's money courier, and Medellín Cartel leaders Pablo Escobar and Gustavo Gaviria. According to the indictment, Noriega received payoffs totaling $4.6 million from the cartel to protect drug trafficking and to arrange for the transshipment of ether and other cocaine-related chemicals through the isthmus. The well-publicized indictments and the presidential campaign finally forced Noriega's backers in the Reagan administration underground, and moved Assistant Secretary of State Abrams into the foreground. Eager to get the Iran-Contra scandal behind him, Abrams picked up the Panama policy and ran with it.

The indictments deeply embarrassed President Delvalle, who was coming under increasing pressure from his family to cut his ties to Noriega. Delvalle traveled to Miami, ostensibly for medical attention, and secretly met with Abrams while he was there. The same assistant secretary who had bumbled on the phone with Barletta and failed to avert that coup was now strongly anti-Noriega. It is unclear whose idea it was, but when Delvalle returned to Panama he took the extraordinary measure of firing Noriega, thereby staging a constitutional crisis in late February. Delvalle's bold move was executed meekly. He taped his television address announcing the general's dismissal and rather than return to the presidential palace to make his stand, he slipped out of the station and went home. Then he went into hiding and exile in Miami. The National Assembly resolved that Delvalle's dismissal of Noriega had been illegal, forced Delvalle from office, and appointed Education Minister Manuel Solís Palma as the new president. Washington hoped the Delvalle action would spark a Philippines-like "people's power" reaction from the Panamanian people, but none developed, in part because Delvalle was too closely identified with Noriega.

The Reagan administration continued to recognize Delvalle as president and announced economic sanctions, including the escrowing of Washington's $6.5 million in monthly payments for use of the canal, the freezing of Panamanian government assets held in American banks, and the suspension of U.S. trade preferences on nearly $100 million worth of Panamanian exports. The sanctions were the strongest actions the State Department, Pentagon, and CIA could agree on, but they would fail to bring the dictator to his knees. The Joint Chiefs of Staff under its chairman, Adm. William Crowe, vetoed the idea of an invasion, except to save American lives.

Noriega's troubles appeared to peak on March 16, 1988, when a group of about fifty PDF officers led by police chief Leonidas Macías and intelligence chief Col. Bernardo Barrera staged a clumsy coup attempt in the military's main headquarters in Panama City. This attempt to seize power was clearly anticipated, leading to speculation that a CIA or Defense Intelligence Agency source had warned Noriega. There was brief gunplay, but Noriega escaped physical harm. For the next couple of days, the dictator appeared to be in trouble. Rioting broke out in the streets of the capital, public utility workers went on strike to cut off electricity, dockworkers shut down two ports, and the usually cautious Panamanian Catholic church called on Noriega and Solís Palma to resign. Assistant Secretary of State Abrams predicted publicly that Noriega would be out of power within weeks.

Noriega may have benefited from the coup attempt. Their loyalty tested, Noriega reshuffled his officer corps, giving his one hundred most trusted associates the top command posts and transferring or exiling suspected reformers. To further strengthen his position, Noriega launched the paramilitary Dignity Battalions as his personal shock troops. To train the battalions, consisting of joint units of common criminals, government employees, and off-duty PDF agents, Noriega recruited far-right-wing Argentine army Col. Mohamed Ali Seineldin.*

Noriega played for time by conducting a series of negotiations with middle-ranking State Department emissaries William Walker and Michael Kozak in 1988. Secretary of State Shultz believed Noriega could be convinced to give up power and leave Panama in exchange for dropping the indictments. Spain offered him asylum. But as the terms of the negotiations leaked, U.S. presidential politics, among other factors, complicated matters. Smarting from attacks by the Democratic presidential candidates and a particular campaign button that read "Bush-Noriega," Vice President Bush pushed against the State Department initiative in order to sustain the indictments. The differences between Reagan and Bush over Panama—the first to air publicly—led to open tensions at White House meetings that May. But Reagan, with the backing of Shultz and Abrams but against the advice of almost all his other top aides, stood his ground—all for naught.

As Bush worked on Reagan, top PDF officers worked on Noriega. Corrupt officers like chief of staff Col. Marcos A. Justines, chief of investigations Maj. Nivaldo Madriñan, and traffic police chief Luis Córdoba, argued that Noriega's forced removal would destroy their institution. The Medellín Cartel did its own lobbying. Apparently

---

*Later that year, the Argentine colonel would be implicated in a coup attempt against civilian President Raúl Alfonsín. The close ties between Noriega and Seineldin led to much speculation that the Panamanian dictator aided the Argentine military conspirators.

fearful that Noriega would squeal in Spain, a Colombian boss sent him a miniature mahogany coffin with his name engraved on it.

Once the negotiations broke down, the Reagan administration was left without a policy. At one interagency policy review session presided over by John Negroponte, Abrams suggested that the United States reinstall Delvalle as president on a U.S. military base guarded by American troops. Admiral Crowe's representative snuffed the proposal, arguing it would seriously complicate relations with other countries that hosted U.S. bases, like Greece, Turkey, Spain, and the Philippines.

At another interagency meeting, the CIA vetoed a suggestion by the State Department to replicate the Contra war by arming and financing a force of former Panamanian guardsmen to overthrow the regime. The CIA had its own idea—to enlist retired PDF Col. Eduardo Herrera, then living in Miami, to spark a coup. But the Senate Intelligence Committee vetoed that plan in July 1988 because Democratic members feared it could lead to Noriega's assassination, a violation of U.S. law. The pattern was classic: when it came to making policy in Panama, as in making policy in Nicaragua, Washington was so hopelessly divided it was unable to come up with a coherent course of action.

THE END AND THE BEGINNING

It was moments past midnight, the day before the May 7, 1989, presidential election. I had just arrived at my spartan room at the Aparthotel Las Vegas and had turned on the television set. A government station was broadcasting a tape of the campaign's closing rally.

Standing before a giant portrait of Omar Torrijos, the official presidential candidate Carlos Duque was speaking to 70,000 public employees who were forced or paid to attend. Duque, the manager of one of the PDF's corrupt operations in the Colón free zone, wore a wide-brimmed Panama hat and white *guayabera* shirt, and posed as a populist.

"Every one of your votes is a bullet in the heart of the Yankee empire," Duque screamed raspily. Banging his fist, he continued, "The Yankees hate our leader Manuel Antonio Noriega because he is the commander of dignity!" Duque referred to reports in the U.S. media that the new Bush administration had donated $10 million in covert campaign aid to the opposition election campaign and charged that Bush had a plan to destroy the Carter-Torrijos treaty.

Borrowing a phrase from the Nicaraguan Sandinistas and the Republicans of the Spanish Civil War, Duque bellowed, "No Pasarán! They Shall Not Pass! If the opposition wins, it will mean a step backwards, into the arms of the gringos! Never! Never! Never!"

Despite the best efforts of the government camera crews to find enthusiastic faces, it was clear that the reception to Duque was tepid. These were many of the same people who were at the campaign rally I attended in 1984, but the enthusiasm in the Torrijos revolution had long since been replaced by passivity and fatalism.

I turned the dial to another station, flipping for flashshots of the campaign just past. No opposition commercials were permitted on the air, but Duque's were broadcast in rapid succession. Noriega, the would-be psychologist, was at work. One spot showed Panamanian children, all wearing Carlos Duque T-shirts, playing and dancing arm-in-arm happily around Omar Torrijos's open-air tomb. Another depicted Ricardo Arias Calderón, Christian Democrat running on the opposition ticket for vice president, superimposed over film footage of Adolf Hitler speaking at a Nazi rally. Exhausted from my two flights that day, beginning in New York, I fell asleep with the set left on.

When I woke up later that morning, it took me a moment to figure out where I was. On the television was a documentary film produced by El Salvador's FMLN guerrillas. For a half hour, Salvadoran police brutalized workers, Christian Democratic politicians stole money, U.S. advisers showed the Salvadoran army how to kill more efficiently, and the rebels joyfully sabotaged the capitalist system. The documentary was rerun over and over that entire week. The subtle message: a vote for the opposition Guillermo Endara slate (which included Christian Democrats) would convert Panama into another El Salvador.

Noriega hoped to numb his people with the endless repetition of Orwellian lies and dilute their rage with fear. The public dialogue was poisoned, but Noriega's troubles with his old patron, the United States, gave the Panamanian people a new dose of spirit. They might not throw bombs, but they still could vote.

The next day an impressive 1.2 million Panamanians came out to cast their ballots. Few seemed to care that the CIA and other agencies were evidently giving some kind of aid to the opposition; they voted for Endara, an uncharismatic lawyer and former aide to Arnulfo Arias, by something like three to one.

On a voting line at a school in the town of Chorrera, Enrique Navarro, a forty-one-year-old truck driver, fiddled with the gold cross he was wearing around his neck. "If they steal the election, who knows? The people will lose all hope and then what?" he rambled nervously. "I'd rather the [American] marines invade than this dictatorship continue and we die of hunger." Navarro, like most Panamanians, blamed his economic troubles on Noriega rather than the U.S. economic sanctions. In the predominately black slum of San Miguelito, on the outskirts of Panama City, a thirty-seven-year-old high school history teacher who refused to identify himself to me found the name of his father, Gilbert Griffin, on a voting list even though he had been dead for nearly nine years. (Undoubtedly, Mr. Griffin voted for Carlos Duque as did all the dead people registered to vote that day.) "Something is obviously wrong," the teacher told me after he voted. "Panamanians have always been a passive, pacific people, but some countries remain pacific for years and then blow up. After the polls close today we don't know what will happen."

Noriega surrounded himself with sycophants who promised him he was still popular with the people, an anti-imperialist hero, the newest expression of Torrijismo. The people, most of Noriega's advisers told him, would support Duque over the opposition, and if he needed 20,000 to 40,000 votes to get over the top as in 1984, that was no problem. Noriega's latest handpicked president, Solís Palma, however, had his doubts. He argued that the U.S. covert intervention in the campaign handed the government the perfect excuse to call off the election until the political and economic situation improved. That would be far better, he argued, than stealing the election and handling the intense political fallout that would follow. But Noriega not only permitted the election to go on, he also welcomed former Presidents Jimmy Carter and Gerald Ford as election observers.

Noriega was wrong. Throughout election day, PDF officers and local pro-Noriega politicos reported back to their superiors that the government was losing by a large margin even though PDF officers and government employees were voting several times. The 1989 fraud was far worse than the one in 1984. Jimmy Carter, a man beloved by Panamanians more than any of their own leaders, said as much publicly in a devastating blow to Noriega.

The vote banditry was open for anyone to see. In Panama City, members of Noriega's Dignity Battalions (now totaling 10,000 men and women) torched ballot boxes, while other pro-government activists hauled boxes full of tens of thousands of votes away from voting stations with the open cooperation of the Panama Defense Forces. The repression was particularly crude in Colón. There, in five major voting centers, activists of the Democratic Revolutionary party and the allied Liberal party fired guns into the air and stole 21,000 out of 35,000 ballots. Opposition pollwatchers tried to protect the ballots, and at least five people were wounded and dozens more arrested in the rioting and gun battles that broke out.

The Panamanians showed themselves to be united, if not courageous, by voting overwhelmingly against Noriega's candidates. But they proved to be less resolute when it came to showing their feelings outside a voting booth. The day after the fraud, as Carlos Duque claimed victory, most Panamanians protested by banging pots and pans *inside* their homes. A mere three hundred people dared to gather in downtown Panama City at noon for a protest march on the Atlapa Convention Center, where the electoral commission cooked the vote tabulations. For better than an hour, the PDF allowed the small, unarmed crowd of protesters to march unimpeded. Noriega's apparent tolerance for the demonstration emboldened more Panamanians to join the protest as the afternoon wore on.

By the time the demonstration wound down Avenida Cuatro Sur, through the pleasant middle-class neighborhood of San Francisco, a barely respectable crowd of 4,000 people was chanting "Justicia, Justicia, Justicia!" and "Not One More Day!"

Three blocks before reaching the convention center, a fifteen-man squad of Centurions, Noriega's elite riot police, halted the crowd. Carrying shotguns, tear-gas grenades, and rubber hose whips and wearing helmets and shields, the Centurions formed a barricade on three sides of a city intersection, three blocks off Panama Bay. The leaderless crowd kept its calm and a safe distance from the police. I stood beside the Centurions, figuring if any trouble developed I would be better off standing behind those with the guns.

Suddenly, two station wagons driven by Noriega's thugs screeched through the crowd, dispersing the people in panic. Then the Centurions opened fire with birdshot—not on the vehicles but over the heads of and, in some cases, at the protesters. One Panamanian television cameraman was shot in the chest.

In the midst of the pandemonium, I dove for the ground and

crawled beside a wooden picket fence down a side street. One frightened woman ran over my right shoulder. With pellets whizzing over our heads, a dozen Panamanians and I made our way to cover by crawling behind a tin-roofed gray and white wooden house, where we crouched in a chicken coop below a shady mango tree.

As the only American in the group, I became the center of attention and the object of a spontaneous, heartfelt history lesson.

"I'm seventy-four years old and I have been a slave for twenty," said Fernando Fabrega, a pharmacist, referring to the two decades of uninterrupted military rule since a 1968 coup. Wearing a blue cotton tropical shirt and a gold watch, Fabrega looked nothing like a slave, but there was no doubt about his feelings for Noriega's Panamanian Defense Force. Impassioned by the repression of the moment, the old man lashed out at me. "Who put this government in power? I ask you," he said. I shook my head. "It was your government that put Torrijos and Noriega in power and it's your government that has got to get this gang out. This is not Panama's problem. This is the problem of the United States."

I pointed out that we were, after all, in Panama. "It sure looks like a Panamanian problem to me," I responded.

In more than a decade of covering conflicts in Nicaragua, El Salvador, and Guatemala, I had never heard such open demands for American intervention or seen people less ready to take responsibility for their own political affairs. Panamanians, demonstrating their psychological dependency on the United States, both held Washington responsible for their problems and depended on Washington to solve them.

Javier Martínez, a thirty-six-year-old unemployed former dry goods salesman, lectured me. "The American drug addicts are financing these military men, not us," he said. "Noriega doesn't leave because he's in debt to the cocaine dealers and to the CIA. It's up to the CIA to get rid of him." He added, "Super-equipped U.S. soldiers are stationed on bases less than three kilometers away from us right now. What's keeping them? How many Panamanians will have to die before your country puts an end to this?"

The Panamanians couldn't do the job themselves. The civic opposition effort climaxed three days after the election, when Endara and his vice presidential running mates, Guillermo Ford and Ricardo Arias Calderón, led a march down Avenida Central toward the presidential palace. Demonstrating rare courage, the three faced off—nose to nose—with a lineup of PDF riot police. Dignity Battalion paramilitaries suddenly arrived on the scene and attacked the demonstrators, swinging metal pipes, baseball bats, crowbars, and two-by-fours spiked with rusty nails and shooting an assortment of guns. Endara suffered a concussion when a Noriega ruffian hit him across the head with a pipe. Ford was beaten around the face and thoroughly soaked in the blood of his bodyguard, who was shot to death while lying on top of him. The image of the bloodied Ford fighting off the paramilitary appeared across the world, leaving the impression that Noriega was up against a popular uprising. But fear quickly replaced the people's glee for disrupting the regime. A general strike called later that week fizzled the first day.

Noriega froze the situation by nullifying the election, and settled on his customary strategy of mixing heightened repression with an array of delaying tactics. While the U.S. embassy repeatedly claimed that Noriega's end was near, Bush backed off for a time, and let the Organization of American States (OAS) pass a number of toothless anti-Noriega resolutions through the summer.

"Something has to give," a middle-ranking State Department official told me. "But don't ask me what."

Something almost did give on October 3, when the PDF, led by Maj. Moisés Giroldi Vega, captured and retained Noriega at his office in the comandancia for over four hours. Giroldi's plans, however, were half-baked. He could have killed Noriega on the spot, but instead Giroldi attempted to convince him to resign and retire with honor in Panama—that was his mistake. Noriega negotiated and stalled for time as he waited for reinforcements. Giroldi was counting on U.S. Southern Command forces to block pro-Noriega units from arriving at the comandancia over three major roads.

But the Americans never entirely trusted Giroldi, who had been loyal to Noriega for fifteen years, was a known torturer, and was crucial in putting down a coup only fifteen months earlier. Some U.S. officials suspected Giroldi was the Trojan horse in a Noriega trap. Compromising between doing nothing and taking decisive action, American forces were ordered to block two of the three roads. The coup fizzled as elite forces arrived to rescue their commander.

The failed coup was a terrible embarrassment for the Bush administration, which was seen as indecisive at the very time it was launching its war on drugs. Senator Helms called the Bush administration's foreign policymakers Keystone Kops. "We were half in, half out, and never in control," scolded an editorial in the October 30 issue of *The New Republic*. "Never mind Willie Horton. George Bush has let Manual Noriega out on furlough." Following two years of U.S. policy blunders, Bush was left with few policy choices.

Noriega used the failed October coup to overhaul the PDF, executing, imprisoning, and purging over one hundred officers and enlisted men. While he privately showed growing signs of paranoia (he reportedly slept in two or three different locations every night by December), to some Panamanians Noriega looked stronger than ever. Endara and other civilian opposition leaders despaired and pleaded with a visiting congressional delegation led by Republican Senator Robert Dole to push for an American invasion. Endara reportedly told Dole, "We are doomed if you don't save us."

The answer to Endara's prayers came just before Christmas, on Saturday night, December 16, when four U.S. Marines taking a joy ride around Panama City were stopped at a roadblock manned by Noriega's crack Machos de Monte (Machos of the Mountain) battalion. When the Panamanian troops cursed and threatened the Americans, Capt. Richard Haddad made history when he gunned the gas peddle. The Machos fired their weapons at the rear of the car, hitting Lt. Robert Paz in the back. Paz bled to death.

Among the witnesses to the shooting were a navy lieutenant and his wife, who had only minutes before finished a holiday dinner at a nearby restaurant. The Panamanian troops made a bad situation worse by gagging the couple and kicking the navy officer in the groin repeatedly while threatening to molest his wife. In and of themselves, the two related incidents might not have sparked an invasion. But they came within forty-eight hours of a declaration of a "state of war" against the United States by Panama's rubber-stamp Assembly along with Noriega's seizure of total dictatorial powers.

"This guy is not going to lay off. It will only get worse," President Bush told Vice President Dan Quayle and several senior members of the cabinet during a Sunday brunch at the White House the next day. Bush, who had felt he would eventually have to take direct military action ever since he was stung by bad publicity following the failed October coup, had already decided he had to move this time. Following the meal, Bush retired to one of the residence's more intimate offices with Defense Secretary Dick Cheney and Colin L. Powell, chairman of the Joint Chiefs of Staff. Sitting under Bush's favorite White House painting *The Peacemakers*, which depicts President

Lincoln consulting with his Civil War generals, the three reviewed the possible invasion strategies. Bush asked how he could apprehend Noriega and install Endara as president with the lowest cost in American lives. General Powell argued against Bush's suggestion of a surgical strike to kidnap Noriega because the risk of failure was too great. Discussing various options, the three kept returning to the benefits of an overwhelming invasion, which might not capture Noriega but would at least be sure to dislodge him from power. "Let's do it," Bush concluded. Within seventy-two hours, Bush launched the largest American military operation since Vietnam, and joined his hero Teddy Roosevelt in the Panamanian history books.

As military operations go, Operation Just Cause was a cakewalk. Copying the successful 1979 Soviet coup de main in Afghanistan, 7,000 American troops backed by elite navy, army, and marine forces overwhelmed the main PDF headquarters and prevented Noriega loyalist units in the countryside from entering the capital. The American arsenal of AC-130 Specter planes firing 7.62mm Gatling guns and 105mm howitzers, Stealth fighter-bombers dropping 2,000-pound bombs, and an assortment of helicopter gunships deploying hundreds of troops in dozens of positions at once, overwhelmed the PDF. It was a mismatch from day one, and the PDF quickly collapsed.

The Dignity Battalions, Noriega's private paramilitary force of criminals, lumpen losers, and radical toughs, took their rage out on the poor neighborhood of El Chorillo, where Noriega grew up. There was no strategic reason for their torching and sacking the wooden and concrete slums. Then they opened the gates of prisons around the city, freeing hundreds of common criminals. It was simply Noriega's revenge against his own people for choosing the Yankees over him.

For the first week of the invasion, looters made a shambles of the downtown business district and snipers made life difficult for American soldiers. But there was never any question where the Panamanian people stood. They sang songs for and danced with the American G.I.s, and waved American flags; the braver ones joined vigilante groups that attacked Dignity Battalion barricades with clubs, barbells, chains, and shotguns. In the poor Caledonia barrio, a traditional well of support for the PDF, graffiti appeared on the walls proclaiming: "Gringos amigos, Noriega malo." Civilians celebrating an end to military rule in the city of David stormed the local PDF headquarters. A poll taken three weeks after the invasion showed that over 90 percent of the Panamanians expressed appreciation for their invaders.

Panama once again tied its destiny to the United States. The country was bankrupt, but more than $1 billion in U.S. aid was on the way. Violent crime was on the rise, but the Southern Command promised that M.P.s would patrol the streets until Panama City was totally pacified. Meanwhile, American advisers would retrain and re-outfit a much reduced military force, renamed the the Panamanian Public Force.

The new Endara government cut a less than reassuring presence. First, it wavered on where Noriega should be tried. Then, it assured the Panamanian financial community that it would resist U.S. pressure to reform the banking laws to protect against future money laundering, only to reverse itself a week later. (By year's end, U.S. officials privately grumbled that Panama's banking system was as dirty as ever.) Cocaine trafficking continued to be a major business. The first commander of the Panamanian Public Force lost his job after only two weeks when he couldn't explain the presence of hundreds of thousands of dollars in a bank certificate of deposit. The second commander resigned a few months later, after which he was linked to rumored coup rumblings among certain active-duty and retired officers. More alarming still was the habit of Public Force officers to wield their old rubber truncheons—symbols of the old Noriega repression and thus banned by the new government—when their American advisers weren't looking.

Popular confidence in the new government lagged as a wave of murders and robberies made city streets far more dangerous than they had been before the invasion. Panamanians openly wondered whether their police were on their side or on the side of members of the Dignity Battalions, who were commonly blamed for the crime wave. Fear reached a high pitch in early March 1990, after a man driving a black Nissan sedan pulled up in front of a Panama City bar called My Place and lobbed a grenade inside. One American was killed, and thirty Americans and Panamanians were wounded. The terrorist, who shouted "Viva Noriega" before he drove off, was never apprehended. The nation froze once more when two small explosive devices were set off by unidentified terrorists outside the homes of the Housing Minister and the Comptroller General the same week in August.

On one score Endara proved to be resolute: he insisted that all glorifications of Gen. Omar Torrijos be removed from public property. The Torrijos International Airport was renamed. A giant mural depicting Torrijos on the National Assembly building was destroyed. School textbooks with Torrijos's face on their covers were taken out of circulation. Panamanians would lose their single modern hero, the man who told them it was time to make their own destiny.

EPILOGUE

In June 1990, Secretary of State James Baker traveled to Guatemala to attend the first Central American presidential summit in years that did not include Daniel Ortega. "Central America," Baker proclaimed at a press conference marking the end of his fifteen-hour visit, "is poised as never before to consolidate democracy, achieve lasting peace and disarmament, and create the conditions for growth and opportunity in which all of the peoples of this region, particularly the poor, can share."

Evidently, Baker saw nothing between the airport and his deluxe hotel to convince him otherwise. As far as the Bush administration was concerned, Violeta Chamorro's February 1990 election victory in Nicaragua ended the Central American crisis. Baker's fantasy of a blissful Central American democracy was preferable to Reagan's nightmare of Nicaraguan communism invading the Texas border, but it was fantasy nevertheless.

As Baker paid his short visit to Guatemala, Honduras was entering its most serious episode of labor unrest in over thirty-five years. For the next two months, more than 10,000 banana workers went on strike against Chiquita Brands, formerly United Fruit, demanding a 60 percent raise from their $246 monthly minimum. President Rafael Callejas managed to settle the strike in early August only by deploying army troops onto the plantations. Three people were wounded—including an undercover policeman—when a soldier fired his machine gun into an angry demonstration of workers. The union eventually settled for a modest raise, but not before it had bled the economy by $60 million and virtually destroyed President Callejas's austerity economic program.

Only three weeks after Baker's visit, Managua erupted in the most serious violence to hit Nicaragua's capital since the 1979 Sandinista insurrection against Anastasio Somoza. Armed Sandinista labor militants set up paving-stone barricades around the city as part of a ten-day July general strike to protest the Chamorro government's economic policies. Fighting between the militants and Chamorro stalwarts, several of whom identified themselves as former Contras, left about ten people dead and ninety more wounded. The antigovernment strike paralyzed several government ministries, closed the international airport and border crossings, and interrupted public transportation, mail service, banking, and electrical and telephone service. Former President Daniel Ortega urged calm, but he reiterated his postelection pledge that "we will govern from below."

At first the government refused to negotiate and declared the strike illegal, but Chamorro and her top advisers eventually decided they could not resist. They agreed to retreat from their economic program by suspending sales of the state textile and construction industries and planned cutbacks in government employees. The strike settlement buoyed the Sandinista party and further splintered Chamorro's governing coalition.

Nicaragua's future looked very much in doubt, even after Chamorro managed to convince the Contras to formally disarm in May in exchange for a territorial reserve. Humberto Ortega, who was supposed to remain the top commander of the Nicaraguan army for a few months, stubbornly held on to his post and incorporated much of Comandante Tomás Borge's police apparatus into the military. Meanwhile, former Contras clandestinely established the Brigades of National Salvation to fight the Sandinistas in case the army staged a coup against the Chamorro government. Sporadic fighting broke out around the countryside in September and October between former Contras and peasant cooperative militants in disputes over land.

El Salvador continued to bleed. Its civil war sputtered on into its eleventh year despite a U.N.-sponsored negotiation effort. The guerrillas said they had no choice but to fight on. To drop their arms and contest the government in elections, they said, would be equivalent to inviting their own death-squad murders. Several developments in 1990 reinforced their case: Roberto D'Aubuisson, the "President for Life" of the ruling Arena party, gained more influence every day; a judge dropped kidnapping charges against six military officers and right-wing activists; and President Alfredo Cristiani was unable to resolve the Jesuit murder case. For their part, the Salvadoran guerrillas went on a killing spree of Salvadoran officers and their families through the summer. The rebels demonstrated their lasting military power by launching a major offensive in seven of the country's fourteen provinces, hitting dozens of towns and army units in November and December. Signaling a new phase in the war, they downed two Salvadoran air force aircraft, an A-37 jet fighter-bomber and an AC-46 fixed-wing gunship, with advanced antiaircraft missiles never used in El Salvador before.

In Panama, retired Col. Eduardo Herrera, once the CIA's choice to lead a coup against Gen. Manuel Antonio Noriega, led a police rebellion against the Guillermo Endara government December 5. What made the apparent coup attempt less than one year after the United States invasion particularly distressing was that it took hundreds of American troops to crush it. It was that kind of dependency, ingrained during decades of intensive American involvement in the country, that contributed to the need for the 1989 invasion in the first place—by having helped make the Panamanian people reluctant to overthrow Noriega themselves.

Not surprisingly, the prospects for peaceful, democratic change looked poorest in Guatemala. In the closing months of his term as president, Vinicio Cerezo's much publicized partying and womanizing made him look all the more irrelevant as a lame duck. Cerezo's handpicked Christian Democratic candidate, former Foreign Minister Alfonso Cabrera Hidalgo, was repeatedly linked to heroin smugglers. Cabrera repeatedly denied the allegations, but he flew around the country for his presidential campaign in a helicopter borrowed from a businessman described by several diplomats and Guatemalan military officers as the country's most important narcotics dealer. Cabrera, in turn, looked like a saint compared to another major candidate, retired Gen. Efraín Ríos Montt, the dictator whose men slaughtered tens of thousands of Mayan Indians in the early 1980s. Ríos Montt would almost certainly have won the election had the Supreme Court not ruled during the final months of the campaign that his candidacy was unconstitutional on the grounds that he had once participated in a coup. With the retired general out of the race, his former chief of staff, Jorge Antonio Serrano, a right-wing Evangelical Christian, became the front-runner.

Whoever would eventually win the January election, the plight of the Mayas would surely remain grim. On December 2, 4,000 Indian villagers from Santiago Atitlán marched on a local army base to protest the recent abuses by four drunken soldiers. The demonstrators carried a white flag to manifest their peaceful intentions, but Guatemalan troops opened fire, killing thirteen and wounding seventeen more. Ten more Indians were reported missing.

The same ailments that fired Central America's most recent cycle of revolutionary violence—militarism, polarization, corruption, poverty, and dependency—exist today as virulently as ever. The next regional bloodletting might not come for five or ten years, maybe not for another generation, but it will surely come. Should the United States choose to intervene, it will probably only make a bad situation worse, again.

BIBLIOGRAPHIC NOTES

This book is the compilation of more than a decade of reporting in Central America. As such, most of the information that it contains comes from my travels and literally thousands of interviews. Many of the most revealing interviews, particularly with current and former American government officials, were conducted on background, meaning the sources could not be identified.

Needless to say, not every fact in this book comes from primary research. For contemporary information, I found the *New York Times,* the *Wall Street Journal,* the *Miami Herald,* the *Washington Post,* and the *Los Angeles Times* to be particularly useful. The *New York Review of Books, The New Republic, The Nation, Current History, NACLA, Time,* and *Newsweek* also published many useful articles on Central America during the last several years. Transcripts from public television documentaries also came in handy from time to time. In Central America, I found articles in a wide assortment of newspapers and magazines helpful, most notably *El Tiempo* in Honduras and *Barricada* and *La Prensa* in Nicaragua. *Estudios Centroamericanos,* a monthly magazine published by the Catholic University in El Salvador, was a gold mine for statistics. Many congressional reports and the endless flow of documents that arose out of the Iran-Contra affair were also central to my research. Reports by Amnesty International and Americas Watch were invaluable.

I relied on many books. I referred to several regional surveys, including: *Politics in Central America* by Thomas P. Anderson; *The Good Neighbor* by George Black; *Power in the Isthmus* by James Dunkerley; *Democracies and Tyrannies of the Caribbean* by William Krehm; *Inevitable Revolutions* by Walter LaFeber; *Confronting Revolution* by Morris Blachman, William LeoGrande, and Kenneth Sharpe; *The Central American Crisis Reader* edited by Robert Leiken and Barry Rubin; *War and Peace in Central America* by Francis McNeil; and *Central America* by Lee Van Woodward. A constant reference for the nineteenth century was John L. Stephens's classic two-volume *Incidents of Travel in Central America, Chiapas and Yucatán.* For inspiration, there was always *The Labyrinth of Solitude* by Octavio Paz.

Most of the military and government officials and others named in this book have denied involvement—either publicly or to me directly—in the unlawful or violent activities I have described. Roberto D'Aubuisson, for example, continues to maintain that he is innocent of any death squad activities. So, too, have Col. Lima, Gen. Ríos Montt, the Lucas García brothers, Joaquín Villalobos and Tomas Borge, among many others, denied involvement in the corruption or violence with which each has been associated in the press or official investigations.

GUATEMALA

For the Mayan and colonial period, I found several secondary sources useful, particularly *The Maya* by Michael Coe, *Ancient Maya Civilization* by Norman Hammond, *Conquest and Survival in Colonial Guatemala* by W. George Lovell, and *Spaniards and Indians in Southeastern Mesoamerica* edited by Murdo J. MacLeod and Robert Wasserstrom. The 1944 revolution and the CIA coup have been covered by *Guatemala* edited by Susanne Jonas and David Tobias, *Bitter Fruit* by Stephen Schlesinger and Stephen Kinzer, and *The CIA in Guatemala* by Richard Immerman. I found rich new documentation on this sad episode of the cold war in the declassified embassy and CIA reports at the Library of Congress and National Archives.

To supplement my own reporting on the modern period, I referred to *El Papel de la Mano de Obra Migratoria en el Desarrollo Económico de Guatemala* by El Instituto de Investigaciones Económicas y Sociales, *Garrison Guatemala* by George Black, *The American Connection,* Vol. 2, by Michael McClintock, *Guatemala: False Hope, False Freedom* by James Painter, and *Guatemala: Eternal Spring, Eternal Tyranny* by Jean-Marie Simon. A fall 1987 *Telos* article, "Permanent Counterinsurgency in Guatemala," by Ken Anderson and Jean-Marie Simon spurred much thought.

EL SALVADOR

For the early historical periods, *El Salvador: Landscape and Society* by David Browning was invaluable. I also referred to *Spanish Central America* by Murdo MacLeod and *El Salvador in Crisis* by Philip L. Russell. My leads for the section dealing with the beginnings of American involvement in the Salvadoran military came from documentation supplied by the National Security Archives. Other documents were available at the National Library and National Archives. *Función Política del Ejército Salvadoreño en el Presente Siglo* by Mariano Castro Morán, a book on the development of the Salvadoran army, was also a worthy reference.

For the modern period, I referred to several books, including two Grove Press anthologies on El Salvador, *El Salvador: The Face of Revolution* by Robert Armstrong and Janet Shenk, *Crossroads* by Cynthia Arnson, *Weakness and Deceit* by Raymond Bonner, *Scarcity and Survival in Central America* by William H. Durham, *Archbishop Romero* by Placido Erdozain, *Low-Intensity Warfare* by Michael T. Klare and Peter Kornbluh, *Revolution in El Salvador* by Tommie Sue Montgomery, and *El Salvador: Las Fuerzas Sociales En La Presente Coyuntura* by Segundo Montes.

NICARAGUA

Because of the Contra war, Nicaragua was the country that received the most attention in the press and among book authors. Therefore, I found myself taking a little from a greater variety of books and articles than any of the other countries.

For historical perspective, I used *Under the Big Stick* by Karl Bermann, *Nicaragua in Perspective* by Eduardo Crawley, *El Nicaragüense* by Pablo Antonio Cuadra, *Nicaragua's Mosquito Shore: The Years of British and American Presence* by Craig Dozier, *Intellectual Foundations of the Nicaraguan Revolution* by Donald C. Hodges, *The Sandino Affair* by Neill MacCaulay and *Guardians of the Dynasty* by Richard Millett, *Condemned to Repetition* by Robert A. Pastor, and *El Pequeño Ejército Loco* by Gregorio Selser.

For the modern period, I used *Nicaragua* by Shirley Christian, *Post-Revolutionary Nicaragua* by Forrest Colburn, *Memoirs of a Counter-Revolutionary* by Arturo Cruz, Jr., *With the Contras* by Christopher Dickey, *Sandinistas* by Dennis Gilbert, *FSLN: The Ideology of the Sandinistas and the Nicaraguan Revolution* by David Nolan, and *The Political Economy of Revolutionary Nicaragua* edited by Rose J. Spalding. Two distinctly different but helpful perspectives on American policy were presented in *Banana Diplomacy* by Roy Gutman and *Inside the National Security Council* by Constantine Menges. *Landslide* by Jane Mayer and Doyle McManus is also valuable for its insights into the Iran-Contra scandal.

HONDURAS

Precious little has been written about Honduras. More than any other chapter, my descriptions of history and culture came from interviews. The *Political Economy of Central America Since 1920* by Victor Bulmer-Thomas, *The Background of Capitalistic Underdevelopment: Honduras to 1913* (an unpublished doctoral thesis) by Charles Abbey Brand, and *Honduras* by Luis Marinas Otero were valuable exceptions to the otherwise sparse literature.

Much of my data for the modern period was gleaned from documents released during the Iran-Contra hearings, investigations, and trials. The Oliver North trial was particularly useful for the release of documents that proved how the Reagan administration was callously using Honduras to promote its war on Nicaragua. Also valuable was the transcript from the 1988 hearings before the Senate Subcommittee on Terrorism, Narcotics, and International Operations.

COSTA RICA

Because it is so peaceful, Costa Rica is frequently forgotten and rarely written about. There are, however, valuable exceptions. They include: *Democracy in Costa Rica* by Charles D. Ameringer; *The Costa Ricans* by Richard Biesanz, Karen Zubris Biesanz, and Mavis Hilunen Biesanz; *The Costa Rica Reader* edited by Marc Edelman and Joanne Kenen; *Costa Rica Before Coffee* by Lowell Gudmundson; *Costa Rica* by Carolyn Hall; *Nobel Costa Rica* by Seth Rolbein; *The Costa Rican Laboratory* by Sol Sanders; and *Quién Gobierna en Costa Rica?* by Oscar Arias Sánchez.

Again, the Iran-Contra scandal provided an enormous amount of data to document the Reagan administration's involvement in Costa Rican affairs. Such evidence was collaborated and enriched by interviews, mostly on background, with Costa Rican cabinet ministers.

PANAMA

My research for Panama came mostly from interviews with American diplomats and military and intelligence personnel and Panamanian journalists, academics, and officials. Several general histories of Panama were useful, particularly *The Panama Canal* by Walter LaFeber and *The Path Between the Seas* by David McCullough. *Panama Odyssey* by William Jorden helped me flesh out the Torrijos years.

Three books were particularly worthwhile for the Noriega years: *Our Man in Panama* by John Dinges, *Kings of Cocaine* by Guy Gugliotta and Jeff Leen, and *Divorcing the Dictator* by Frederick Kempe. Most useful of all were the 1988 report and testimonies produced by the Senate Subcommittee on Terrorism, Narcotics, and International Operations.

INDEX